40 Years of CORONATION ST.

DARAN LITTLE

GRANADA

Cider
Minerals
Baby Minerals
Fruit Juices
Baby Bubbly
Baby Mousseux
Whisky
Rum
Gin
Brandy
Gin & Vermouth
Gin & Lime etc.
Liqueurs
Port
Sherry
Vermouth

INTRODUCTION

> "There was life before *Coronation Street*, but it didn't add up to much."

Russell Harty

In the autumn of 1960 a young script-writer named Tony Warren sat at a typewriter and within twenty-four hours had produced the first episode of a new drama serial entitled *Florizel Street*. It featured the everyday lives of a series of ordinary folk – the superior landlady, the bitchy old dear, the retired solider, the angry young man and the good-time girl down the street. The programme underwent a name change and was broadcast on 9 December 1960. Nearly 5,000 episodes later *Coronation Street* is as popular as ever, leading the television ratings and basking in the knowledge that it is a national treasure. Ever evolving, it has captivated audiences for forty years.

Many books have been written about the success of the series and the private lives of its stars, but I have set out to produce something unique. As archivist of *Coronation Street* I have been able to watch every episode and here, for the first time, you can read and recall every storyline ever featured in the show. Year by year, this book chronicles major and minor events, linking themes and presenting a complete encyclopedia of *Street* history, which also gives a fascinating glimpse of the social history of Britain throughout the period. An index is included so the stories of specific characters can be followed throughout the forty years.

Coronation Street is probably the most important television series ever to be broadcast on British television. Its characters have become household names, its plot lines discussed in homes, offices and buses throughout the land. Thousands of creative writers, actors and technicians have worked on it over the years but the success of the show must lie at the feet of the man who started it all. Tony Warren was a genius who created a mould that television writers and producers have followed ever since. I wrote in my introduction to *The Coronation Street Story* that the British viewing public owed him a debt of gratitude. That still applies. If you are reading this with a glass in your hand, raise it to him.

Daran Little, January 2000

1960

Behind the Scenes

"There's some very peculiar people in this Street"

Ena Sharples

The story of how *Coronation Street* came into being has been told many times over the past forty years. The script writer Tony Warren was employed by Granada Television in Manchester to write scripts for a popular programme called *Biggles*. This was not a task he enjoyed and he begged producer Harry Elton to allow him to write something after his own heart. Elton gave him twenty-four hours to come up with a idea.

Tony spent the time updating a script called *Our Street*, which he had submitted to the BBC years before, and renamed it *Florizel Street*. Elton loved it. After a struggle (the executives hated the idea of a programme featuring ordinary people with commonplace troubles) Granada agreed to make sixteen episodes, and Tony worked with the casting department to fill the shoes of Elsie, Ena and Co. The first episode was transmitted live on 9 December 1960 as *Coronation Street*. The title change came about because Agnes the tea lady commented that 'Florizel' sounded like a disinfectant. The show was an instant hit.

Top Twenty

Pos	Character	No of eps	Total	Pos Prev Year
1	Elsie Tanner	7	7	-
2	Ena Sharples	7	7	-
3	Annie Walker	7	7	-
4	Linda Cheveski	7	7	-
5	Dennis Tanner	6	6	-
6	Christine Hardman	6	6	-
7	Martha Longhurst	6	6	-
8	Esther Hayes	6	6	-
9	Jack Walker	5	5	-
10	Harry Hewitt	5	5	-
11	Ivan Cheveski	5	5	-
12	Leonard Swindley	4	4	-
13	May Hardman	4	4	-
14	Frank Barlow	3	3	-
15	Florrie Lindley	3	3	-
16	Ida Barlow	3	3	-
17	Concepta Riley	3	3	-
18	Kenneth Barlow	3	3	-
19	Lucille Hewitt	3	3	-
20	David Barlow	2	2	-

Key Dates

1960

August 25	Granada decides to produce sixteen episodes of a new family drama *Florizel Street,* written by Tony Warren
December 5	Rehearsals start. Series renamed *Coronation Street*
December 9	First episode of *Coronation Street* transmitted live; the second episode recorded for transmission the following Monday. Elsie and Dennis Tanner, Annie Walker, Ena Sharples, Albert Tatlock, Kenneth Barlow and Florrie Lindley all appear
December 12	Jack Walker, Christine Hardman, Esther Hayes, Martha Longhurst and Harry Hewitt make first appearances
December 16	Minnie Caldwell and Leonard Swindley first appear
December 19	Lucille Hewitt first appears
December 23	Concepta Riley first appears
December 31	May Hardman dies – the first death

STORIES

1 A New Face

After thirty years of running the Corner Shop, Elsie Lappin sold up and retired to Knott End. Her place was taken by ex-barmaid Florrie Lindley, who soon got into trouble with the police for selling fire-lighters after 7.30 p.m. To her embarrassment the case went to court and she was fined a pound.

2 Elsie's Children

Linda Cheveski returned home to No.11 Coronation Street, to tell her mother Elsie Tanner that she had left her Polish husband Ivan. Elsie let her cry on her shoulder, then helped the couple to reconcile, and Linda told a delighted Ivan that she was pregnant. Elsie's son Dennis also caused her headaches when the police suspected him of burglary: he had twenty-five pounds in his pocket. Elsie believed Dennis was guilty until neighbour Harry Hewitt said he'd seen the lad win the money at the dogs.

3 Ungodly Behaviour

Mission of Glad Tidings caretaker Ena Sharples collapsed in her vestry after being caught drinking in the Rovers Return by her boss, Leonard Swindley. While Ena enjoyed a rest in hospital, giving daughter Vera Lomax the runaround, Swindley employed her friend Martha Longhurst at the Mission. When she found out, Ena discharged herself and threw Martha out.

4 Militant Barlow

English student Kenneth Barlow started a romance with Susan Cunningham from the posh side of town. He was embarrassed when she called at his home and met his working-class family. His father, Frank, was furious when Kenneth announced his intention to take part in a Ban the Bomb march. Kenneth ignored Frank's threats and carried his banner with pride – but his mother Ida feared he'd soon be homeless.

5 The First Death

Factory worker Christine Hardman was ashamed when her mother May spent a couple of weeks in a psychiatric hospital. When May returned home to No.13 complaining of headaches, Christine did not take her seriously and was horrified when May was found dead in the hall. She had had a brain tumour.

6 Runaway

Bus inspector Harry Hewitt worried when his eleven-year-old daughter Lucille ran away from the orphanage where she had lived since her mother's death. She demanded to spend Christmas with him but he felt he couldn't cope with her. Neighbour Esther Hayes stepped in to look after the girl until Harry managed to talk her into returning to the home.

CAST

Elsie Tanner	Patricia Phoenix
Dennis Tanner	Philip Lowrie
Linda Cheveski	Anne Cunningham
Ena Sharples	Violet Carson
Florrie Lindley	Betty Alberge
Frank Barlow	Frank Pemberton
Ida Barlow	Noel Dyson
Kenneth Barlow	William Roache
David Barlow	Alan Rothwell
Albert Tatlock	Jack Howarth
Annie Walker	Doris Speed
Elsie Lappin	Maudie Edwards
Susan Cunningham	Patricia Shakesby
Jack Walker	Arthur Leslie
Martha Longhurst	Lynne Carol
Christine Hardman	Christine Hargreaves
Harry Hewitt	Ivan Beavis
Esther Hayes	Daphne Oxenford
Ivan Cheveski	Ernst Walder
Minnie Caldwell	Margot Bryant
May Hardman	Joan Heath
Leonard Swindley	Arthur Lowe
Lucille Hewitt	Jennifer Moss
Vera Lomax	Ruth Holden
Concepta Riley	Doreen Keogh

1961

Behind the Scenes

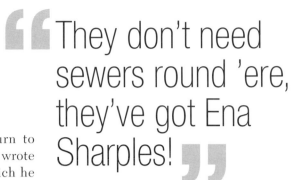

> "They don't need sewers round 'ere, they've got Ena Sharples!"
>
> **Elsie Tanner**

The success of *Coronation Street* took British television by surprise. The rounded vowels of the BBC actors and presenters had set the standard for those appearing on screen at the newly formed independent channel. Granada's franchise required the company to employ northern actors and writers and with the Street it fulfilled that obligation. Suddenly people with 'real' accents were on television screens across the land, and viewers in the south complained that they could only understand one word in ten. One journalist wrote that surely no one mended their bicycle in front of the living-room fire.

The original cast quickly signed long-term contracts to secure their immediate future, thrilled at the prospect of playing the same character for a significant period and not having to return to repertory theatre. Tony Warren wrote the first seven episodes, in which he defined the characters of the residents, and plotted the story-line for those that followed. Other writers, such as Jack Rosenthal, joined the team and began to build on Tony's foundations. The cast grew to fill the houses and the Rovers' bar. Harry Hewitt was given a friend, Len Fairclough, and timid Miss Nugent made her first entrance at the Mission of Glad Tidings.

The viewers greeted the programme with enthusiasm: they wrote fan letters and mobbed the new celebrities. Pat Phoenix became the forces' pin up, Alfred

Top Twenty

Pos	Character	No of eps	Total	Pos Prev Year
1	Elsie Tanner	84	91	1
2	Ena Sharples	84	91	1
3	Annie Walker	84	91	1
4	Jack Walker	83	88	9
5	Concepta Hewitt	76	79	17
6	Martha Longhurst	75	81	5
7	Minnie Caldwell	75	77	21
8	Harry Hewitt	74	79	10
9	Dennis Tanner	72	78	5
10	Albert Tatlock	70	71	24
11	Frank Barlow	60	63	11
12	Len Fairclough	59	59	-
13	Kenneth Barlow	57	60	18
14	Linda Cheveski	54	61	1
15	Florrie Lindley	54	57	14
16	Christine Hardman	50	56	5
17	Ivan Cheveski	46	51	9
18	Esther Hayes	38	44	5
19	Doreen Lostock	38	38	
20	Ida Barlow	37	40	14

Hitchcock posed for photographs in the Rovers, the *Sun* and the *Daily Mirror* both voted the show 'Best Television Programme' and when Violet Carson turned on the Blackpool illuminations mounted police had to be called to control the crowds. Noel Dyson, who had played Ida Barlow since the first episode, was appalled 'People used to come down to my cottage and lean over the gate. I felt like something in the zoo.' She was the first of the original cast to leave the show, but begged that heart trouble would not cause Ida's death. To her relief Ida met her end under the wheels of a double-decker bus.

The Street faced a change in scheduling when, in May 1961, it went fully networked – up to that point the Midlands hadn't received the show. The dates of transmission were changed from Friday and Monday to Monday and Wednesday, and the show was no longer broadcast live. Instead the episodes were recorded each Friday afternoon, but as if they were live – if mistakes were made they were not corrected – then transmitted the following week.

In September the show reached No.1 in the ratings and remained there for the rest of the year. In fact, in the last few months of 1961 there wasn't much competition: a strike by the actors' union, Equity, protesting against pay and conditions, meant that many famous faces couldn't appear on television. Granada were quick to ensure that the Street continued throughout the strike by agreeing with Equity that its fourteen main players could continue under long-term contracts. The fourteen were Pat Phoenix, Violet Carson, Doris Speed, Arthur Leslie, Betty Alberge, Philip Lowrie, William Roache, Frank Pemberton, Jack Howarth, Lynne Carol, Margot Bryant, Doreen Keogh, Ivan Beavis and Peter Adamson. Pat Phoenix, Violet Carson and Doris Speed emerged to become the nation's favourites

Key Dates

1961

January 27	Emily Nugent and Billy Walker first appear
February 2	Len Fairclough's first appearance
February 16	Alf Roberts's first appearance
March 3	*Coronation Street* fully networked, transmission changed from Friday and Monday to Monday and Wednesday
March 8	Joan Walker marries Gordon Davies
April 24	Jed Stone's first appearance
June 12	Paul Cheveski is born
August 7	Valerie Tatlock's first appearance
September 11	Ida Barlow is killed under the wheels of a bus
October 1	Concepta Riley marries Harry Hewitt

STORIES

1 The Return of Arnold Tanner

The last person Elsie Tanner expected to see on her doorstep was her estranged husband Arnold. After an absence of fifteen years he turned up to meet his children and ask Elsie for a divorce so that he could marry his girlfriend, Norah Dawson. At first Elsie refused but Arnold forced her hand by threatening to divorce her, citing her wartime romances. Ena Sharples failed to recognize Arnold, and when he called on Elsie she started to spread the word that Madam Tanner had a new boyfriend. Elsie was annoyed by the gossip and put a notice in the local paper threatening to take the perpertrators to court for slander if the talk continued. Her action led to a slanging match in the Rovers between her and Ena, and ten months later erupted into a full-scale battle in the Street.

Between Arnold's arrival and the Street fight, Elsie had enjoyed the company of three boyfriends – a sales representative, Walter Fletcher, a police detective, Arthur Dewhurst, and a naval officer, Bill Gregory. In Bill she felt she had found the man of her dreams – until she received an anonymous letter warning that her liaison with Bill was jeopardizing her divorce. Elsie told best friend Dot Greenhalgh that she wasn't going to allow anything to put at risk her future with Bill.

She accused Annie Walker of writing the letter – as the landlady had been heard criticizing the relationship – but when she swore innocence Elsie attacked Ena. The residents stood and watched as the pair traded insults and squared up to each other, but Ena ended the fight by pointing out that she wasn't afraid to stand by her principles and if she'd written the letter she'd have signed her name. The mystery was solved when Arnold apologized to Elsie, telling her that Norah had written the note for fear that Elsie's affair might hold up the divorce.

2 Christine's Plumber's Bill

Christine Hardman's first act after burying her mother, May, was to break with her flash boyfriend Malcolm Wilkinson: he had offered her no support over her mother's death. On discovering that May had dipped into her insurance money, Christine faced debts and struggled financially. She was amazed when a bill from a plumber's firm was paid by Joe Makinson, who had carried out the work. He explained that he hated to see such a pretty girl worrying over money and asked her for a date. Over the next few months Christine and Joe became an item and drifted into an engagement. Neighbours were pleased to see Christine smiling again but after a while she decided that Joe was dull, and that marriage to him would keep her rooted in a life she despised. He was heartbroken when she called off the engagement. When workmate Jean Stark fell out with her parents Christine took her in as a lodger, but she didn't stay long and Christine was left alone once more.

3 Annie and Jack's Children

Schoolteacher Joan Walkers' wedding was the first in the series when she married English teacher Gordon Davies. Joan was given away by her father, Jack. After the couple settled in Derby, Annie and Jack Walker were left with their son Billy, who hung around the area looking for something to do after completing his National Service.

He half-heartedly romanced factory girl Doreen Lostock, much to Annie's disapproval, and upset his parents by refusing to work with them in their pub, the Rovers Return. Instead Billy took a job at the Blue Bell garage in Chiswick, London. Before he moved south, he advised his old friend Dennis Tanner to follow his example before he rotted in the Street.

When the Walkers' resident barmaid, Concepta Riley, gave up her job to marry Harry Hewitt, they employed Doreen behind the bar. She soon grew restless and cockney Nona Willis moved into Concepta's old room. She wasn't easily accepted by the northerners, which she found hard, and eventually she gave notice, telling Jack she found the accents too difficult to understand.

4 Dennis Finds Employment

Keen to prove to everyone that his spell in prison was merely due to a lapse of character, Dennis Tanner took a job as front-of-house manager at the Orinocco club. He enjoyed mixing with the swinging crowd and startled Elsie by dating an exotic dancer, Eunice Bond, who used a boa constrictor in her act. Inspired, Dennis turned to singing, but when he was forced to stand in for the club's comic he didn't go down very well. Instead he decided to concentrate on theatrical management and left the Orinocco to work for Lenny Phillips' agency, under his stage name, Ricky Dennis.

When his friend from Borstal days, Jed Stone, invited him on a 'job', Dennis pleased Elsie by refusing and instead fixed Jed up with his old job at the Orinocco. Elsie's joy in Dennis's work prospects was short-lived when she returned home to find a chimp called Rupert in her kitchen sink – Dennis had been asked to look after him. Mother and son were horrified when the chimp disappeared and ran amok in the Rovers, breaking glasses.

5 The Street's Being Demolished!

Caretaker Ena Sharples had a troublesome few months, which started when the Street's residents were evacuated to her Mission during a gas leak. She refused to give them any 'luxuries', and turned out the lights at her convenience.

A month later, while at the Town Hall to complain about the length of time it took to boil a kettle on gas, she was alarmed to read a poster announcing the demolition of Coronation Street. She rushed back to the Rovers with the news, which caused uproar.

Albert Tatlock called an emergency residents' meeting where a plan of action was worked out. Frank Barlow, who had only just decided against buying his house for two hundred pounds as it was too expensive, decided to fight for his home and organized a petition. Esther Hayes

wrote to the Town Hall and an official was sent round to talk to the residents. He was adamant that there were no plans to demolish the Street. Ena explained what she'd seen and he produced the poster for all to see. It was Coronation *Terrace* that was to be pulled down. An embarrassed Ena was sent to Coventry by the residents, and Leonard Swindley sacked her for spreading rumours. Swindley's assistant Emily Nugent took over at the Mission and Ena moved in with her old friend Martha Longhurst.

Having Ena under her roof, moving her furniture around and generally running her life, was too much for Martha and she wrote to an agony aunt asking for help. Meanwhile, timid Miss Nugent begged Swindley to find another caretaker as she found the area far too rough and was suffering sleepless nights. When five applicants turned down the job Swindley had no option but to re-employ Ena, with a ten-shilling rise in salary. She didn't stay long: later in the year, Swindley sacked her again, this time after catching her drinking at the Rovers Return, which didn't seem fitting for the caretaker of a place of worship. Ena dumped herself on Minnie Caldwell, and Albert Tatlock took over at the Mission.

6 The Women in Kenneth's Life

The summer of 1961 saw Kenneth Barlow graduating from university with a 2:1 degree in Modern History and English. It also found him ending a romance that had shocked his family. After splitting with fellow student Susan Cunningham, Kenneth entered his first serious love affair with librarian Marian Lund. She worked at the university and was eleven years his senior, which had his mother, Ida, reaching for the smelling salts. However, his father, Frank, confided that he had once had an affair with an older woman.

While his parents were debating his brother's love life, David Barlow was spotted by a football scout and signed up to play with a second-division London team. He left his job at Ajax Engineering and headed south.

Kenneth's romantic dreams were shattered when his English lecturer, Mr Collinworth, explained that Marian was his girlfriend and that they were getting married. Disillusioned, Kenneth was glad to leave the university and applied for a teaching job at a public school in Surrey. He was offered the job but turned it down to stay at home when tragedy struck his family. Ida, out for the day to visit a friend,

was knocked down and killed by a bus. On hearing the news, her mother, Nancy Leathers, who had been living with the family since a heart-attack, collapsed and missed the funeral, as did David, who couldn't bring himself to attend.

Nancy was nursed by Valerie Tatlock, a nineteen-year-old hair-stylist, who was lodging with her uncle Albert at No.1. Valerie fell in love with Kenneth and slowly, with the approval of both Frank and Albert, they began a courtship. Kenneth allowed his father to believe he had not been successful in the Surrey job, which led Frank to tell him that he'd always been a disappointment and a failure. Instead Kenneth took the post of assistant personnel officer at Amalgamated Steel but resigned after a month as he couldn't bring himself to be hard on the workforce. He was taken on at Bessie Street School as an English teacher.

Nancy felt in the way at No.3 and moved into an old folks' bungalow, which sadly put an end to her companionable meetings with Albert. Valerie also left, moving north to Scotland when her father fell ill.

7 For the Love of Harry

Shopkeeper Florrie Lindley found herself attracted to Harry Hewitt at No.7 but was frustrated in her attempts to see him socially as she had a rival in the shape of blonde clippie Eileen Hughes. While the two women fussed over him Harry had eyes only for the Rovers' Irish barmaid, Concepta Riley. He made his intentions known at the bus depot's dance, but put romance on hold for a while when his sister moved in as housekeeper.

Alice Burgess was a bossy woman and did not approve of Harry's lifestyle, but as her presence in the house meant that his daughter Lucille could come home from the orphanage he kept quiet. However, Lucille hated her aunt and made her life a misery. After two months Alice packed her bags and left, prompting Harry to propose to Concepta during the Street's outing to Blackpool. The engagement period was brief but problematic: Concepta's parents objected to her marrying a non-Catholic Englishman, but after Harry agreed to let their children be brought up in her faith they gave their blessing. All the residents were invited to the October wedding, and after honeymooning on the Isle of Man Concepta moved into No.7 and set about mothering Lucille.

Concepta grew frustrated, however, when Harry started to take her for granted, and hated the way he expected them to sleep in the bed he had shared with his first wife. When she complained, Harry surprised her by buying new furniture but didn't have enough money for a new bed.

Concepta realized it was useless to expect her husband to see things from her point of view and decided instead to concentrate on his good points. But it was difficult to do that when he spent every evening drinking in the Rovers with his best friend, Len Fairclough.

8 A Bad Penny

Esther Hayes had lived at No.5 all her life. Since her mother's death in the fifties she had been alone and had forged a quiet life for herself. As a teetotaller she never frequented the Rovers but was happy to babysit Lucille or spend an evening chatting to Christine Hardman. Her life was turned upside down by the arrival of her wayward brother, Tom, fresh out of prison and looking for a cosy billet.

Tom was interested in fruit machines and tried to sell one to the Walkers. They refused so he attempted to get Esther to invest her savings in an idea he had concerning juke-boxes. She turned him down, and began to resent Tom's presence: he upset her routine and sponged off her. Her boss, Brian Foley, who had started to take her out to concerts and galleries, pointed out to Tom that he wasn't welcome, so Tom disappeared in the middle of the night. He didn't leave his sister a note but she was still relieved to see the back of him.

9 The Cheveskis of No.9

After reconciling with her husband, Ivan, Linda Cheveski continued to spend much of her free time visiting her mother, Elsie Tanner, at No.11. She hated living in Warrington and worked on Ivan to take a job in Weatherfield. She had her heart set on renting No.9, next door to her mother, but the landlord decided he wanted to sell the property. Linda made such a fuss that Ivan feared for the health of their unborn child and agreed to arrange a mortgage. The couple moved in just in time for the birth of their son, Paul, in June. When he heard he was a father, Ivan performed a traditional dance on the Rovers' bar using a salami as a prop. Under the circumstances, Annie Walker decided to ignore the incident.

Ivan took an evening job as potman at the pub to help pay the bills and Linda settled down to motherhood. Elsie was thrilled with her grandson but clashed with Linda over how he should be looked after. Linda resented the interference so much that she banned her mother from the christening, only relenting at the last minute. Christine Hardman, Dennis Tanner and Jack Walker were godparents and, to Elsie's annoyance, Ena Sharples gatecrashed the party afterwards.

For a few short months Elsie was happy to have her family around her, but low pay at the steel works caused Ivan to consider the future. After much thought and argument the Cheveskis decided it would be best for Paul if they left England and started a new life in Canada. When the news was broken to Elsie she washed her hands of the couple and refused to wish them well. It was only when the last of the baggage had been loaded on to the removal van that Elsie broke down and hugged her daughter before she left the country.

10 Open All Hours

Around the corner from the Rovers Return, a small parade of shops attracted the residents with their wares, and Sylvia Snape ran a café. She employed Doreen Lostock to serve Teddy Boys with frothy coffee, while her husband toured the area as a sales

representative. Doreen's friend, Sheila Birtles, contemplated leaving Elliston's raincoat factory to join her but the Snapes decided to move away. They sold the lease of the café to Italian immigrant Mario Bonarti, who opened a restaurant with his father, Leo, as chef. Ena Sharples vowed never to cross the threshold, referring to the food as Italian muck, but ironically she won a free meal in a raffle and didn't see the sense in depriving herself. Mario made a big play for Christine Hardman, but she found him too possessive.

Next door to the café, at No.16 Rosamund Street, Leonard Swindley's haberdashery was going through a lean time. He decided to merge with Emily Nugent's baby linen shop, causing his old retainer Miss Pemberton to resign, explaining that she couldn't share her counter with another woman. She also accused Swindley of leading her on for twenty-five years.

Emily was thrilled to spend her days in Swindley's company and gladly gave up her own independence to serve under him. Her father believed Swindley to be her suitor and she was horrified when the old man confronted Swindley and demanded to know his intentions. Swindley, concerned for Emily's feelings, assured James Nugent that he felt nothing but the utmost respect for her, but Emily was disappointed that he hadn't taken the opportunity to declare his feelings for her.

When business failed to pick up, Swindley introduced a credit scheme. While this scheme attracted customers, there was no money in the till to pay the bills and he faced bankruptcy.

CAST

Sheila Birtles	Eileen Mayers
Joe Makinson	Brian Rawlinson
Dot Greenhalgh	Joan Francis
Doreen Lostock	Angela Crow
Arnold Tanner	Frank Crawshaw
Norah Dawson	Avril Angers
Eileen Hughes	Prunella Scales
Len Fairclough	Peter Adamson
Emily Nugent	Eileen Derbyshire
Billy Walker	Kenneth Farrington
Malcolm Wilkinson	Anthony Booth
Joan Walker	June Barry
Gordon Davies	Calvin Malone
Alf Roberts	Bryan Mosley
Alice Burgess	Avis Bunnage
Sylvia Snape	Patricia Routledge
Walter Fletcher	Donald Morley
Arthur Dewhurst	Robin Wentworth
Marion Lund	Patricia Henegham
Jed Stone	Kenneth Cope
Jean Stark	Renny Rister
Tom Hayes	Dudley Foster
Nancy Leathers	Norah Hammond
Paul Cheveski	Victoria Elton
Mario Bonarti	Frank Coda
Leo Bonarti	Steve Plytas
Brian Foley	Denis Holmes
Valerie Tatlock	Anne Reid
Nona Willis	Barbara Ferris
Bill Gregory	Jack Watson

1962

Behind the Scenes

The Equity strike ended in time for the Street's first outside location sequence, filmed at Tatton Park and broadcast on Easter Monday. Before this all exterior scenes had been filmed inside the studios at Granada. With the end of the strike, old favourites such as Lucille Hewitt, Valerie Tatlock, Leonard Swindley and Emily Nugent all reappeared but others from 1961, such as Jean Stark, never appeared again. Another departure was Dennis Tanner, who left before the strike had ended when actor Philip Lowrie decided he no longer wanted to play him. The writers introduced a new young man, Jerry Booth, to work alongside Len Fairclough. Grahan Haberfield, a twenty-year-old Derbyshire lad, was delighted to be cast as Jerry – he regarded the programme as part-entertainment, part-documentary: 'Many highbrows have a sneaking regard for the serial. It appeals to the masses, because it pinpoints many facets and stresses of life in a small compact Northern community.'

The period of just fourteen cast members had highlighted areas where different characters were needed and after the strike had ended, some characters were given weightier story-lines. Although her character Christine Hardman remained in residence at No.11 throughout the strike, actress Christine Hargreaves had not appeared and by the time the strike ended she had returned to the theatre. She returned to the Street to film scenes of Christine's suicide bid then left for four months before signing a new contract. Another actress who took leave of absence, for a shorter period, was Pat Phoenix, who starred as a prostitute in the film *The L-Shaped Room* alongside Leslie Caron. To fill the gaps left by their absence, producer H.V. Kershaw built up the roles of Doreen Lostock and Sheila Birtles, two pre-strike factory girls. They were moved into the Corner Shop flat and were given stories in their own right. Another favourite with the viewers, Valerie Tatlock, was reintroduced and quickly married to Kenneth Barlow.

During June and July an investigation into the programme's appeal found that, unsurprisingly, the programme was most popular in the north: 91 per cent of available viewers watched it in the Granada area, 89 per cent in Tyne Tees. In the South the figures were strong too: 76 per cent watched in Southern and 69 per cent in Westward – south-west England.

The year's most contentious storyline was Ena Sharples's fight against the planned renaming of the Street: she announced her intention to write to Prince Philip for his support. This resulted in a House of Commons debate because the law stated that living members of the Royal Family could not be mentioned in stage plays or films. *Coronation Street* had broken the rules. The postmaster-general contacted Granada and insisted that all future references were dropped, but no action was taken against the company. However, after this other television programmes began to mention the Royals.

> "They've bin talkin' about me ever since I put me first pair o' nylons on."
>
> **Elsie Tanner**

Top Twenty

Pos	Character	No of eps	Total	Pos Prev Year
1	Annie Walker	95	186	1
2	Len Fairclough	95	154	12
3	Frank Barlow	94	157	11
4	Minnie Caldwell	94	171	6
5	Jack Walker	93	181	4
6	Concepta Hewitt	93	172	5
7	Albert Tatlock	92	163	10
8	Elsie Tanner	90	181	1
9	Harry Hewitt	90	169	8
10	Ena Sharples	89	180	1
11	Kenneth Barlow	88	148	13
12	Martha Longhurst	88	169	6
13	Florrie Lindley	85	142	14
14	Leonard Swindley	53	92	21
15	Doreen Lostock	51	89	19
16	Emily Nugent	50	81	23
17	Sheila Birtles	49	68	28
18	Lucille Hewitt	48	80	24
19	Valerie Tatlock Barlow	41	57	29
20	Jerry Booth	33	33	–

Key Dates

1962

June 20	Christine Hardman marries Colin Appleby
July 7	Minnie Caldwell's mother, Amy Carlton dies
July 23	Jerry Booth's first appearance
August 4	Valerie Tatlock marries Kenneth Barlow
August 6	Christopher Hewitt is born
October 12	Colin Appleby dies

STORIES

1 Trouble at the Rovers

It was not in Annie Walker's nature to give anyone the benefit of the doubt, and after finding four five-pound notes missing from the till she immediately accused Dennis Tanner of reverting to his thieving ways. However, her belief that he had been alone in the bar was dismissed by Ena Sharples, who testified that she had been sitting in the Snug all the time, with a clear view of the till, and he hadn't been near it. One by one Annie turned on her regulars, accusing each of robbing her and prompting Elsie Tanner to organize a picket of the pub. Ironically, it was Dennis who broke the picket as he needed to use the phone and the Walkers had the only one on the Street.

Jack Walker was horrified to see his pub empty of customers while the Flying Horse benefited. He tried to resolve the situation by planting twenty pounds of his own money in the till and then discovering it. At this point Annie broke down and confessed that two days before she had found the missing notes jammed at the back of the till. Jack took matters into his own hands and apologized to all the regulars for Annie's behaviour. Slowly they returned, although by mutual consensus they waited a week before telling Ena, Minnie and Martha that the boycott had been lifted. Thus everyone enjoyed seven days of peaceful drinking.

2 A Day at the Races

When Concepta Hewitt ordered husband Harry to get rid of his two whippets – 'nasty, smelly creatures they are' – he swapped them for a greyhound named Lucky Lolita. Harry planned to use the dog as a racing machine and fed her up with steak and port. Behind Concepta's back he spent the week's housekeeping on entering Lucky in a local race, and made a handsome profit when she romped home first. News of Lucky's winning form caused the residents to catch gambling fever: they raided cocoa tins and hunted under mattresses for stake money. Dennis Tanner even went so far as to steal his mother's holiday fund. Len Fairclough laid on a coach to a race meeting at White City and the residents watched in mounting tension as Lucky won her second race. Luckily for Dennis he was able to return Elsie's money with a hefty profit. Unfortunately Lucky's winning streak was short-lived. When Dennis persuaded Elsie to reinvest her savings, she lost the lot when the dog limped home last.

3 Survival of the Fittest

Kenneth Barlow spent a busy two weeks tapping away at his typewriter and was paid twenty-five guineas for an article in a left-wing magazine, *Survival*. The article criticized the working class and was picked up by the local paper, which printed edited highlights. The residents were enraged, and Len Fairclough was furious at what he saw as a betrayal by Kenneth of his neighbours and family: 'He might be a walkin', flamin' dictionary, be he 'asn't the guts of a louse.' When Frank Barlow heard Len insult his son in public he laid into him with his fists. Kenneth realized he couldn't hide behind his principles and needed to confront his critics. However, his attempt to put across his views to Len earned him a black eye when Len brawled with him in the Rovers. The article caused a stir beyond the Street as well: sightseers turned up to view the 'lazy-minded, politically ignorant' residents and the *Banner* newspaper offered Kenneth 180 guineas for three articles on 'life in a typical northern town'. Although tempted by the money, he turned it down

and instead started work on a novel about three lads growing up together in a back-street. Ironically, the original article shamed the Street's landlord Edward Wormold into making repairs on all his properties, although Len maintained that was just a coincidence.

4 Ena Bed Hops

Three months as caretaker of the Mission of Glad Tidings was more than enough for Albert Tatlock and he handed in his resignation, along with the suggestion that Ena Sharples be reinstated. The committee agreed and Ena moved her belongings back into her old home. Minnie Caldwell's mother, Amy, celebrated her departure by getting out of bed for the first time in six years.

Just weeks after moving back, Ena found herself tucked into a hospital bed after she had a mild stroke and was knocked unconscious as she fell. A night lying on the old Mission floor added hypostatic pneumonia to her problems and it was a week before she could recognize any of her visitors. Her friends Minnie and Martha smuggled in a bottle of stout, concealed in the middle of a bouquet of flowers, but Ena revealed that her bedside cabinet was full

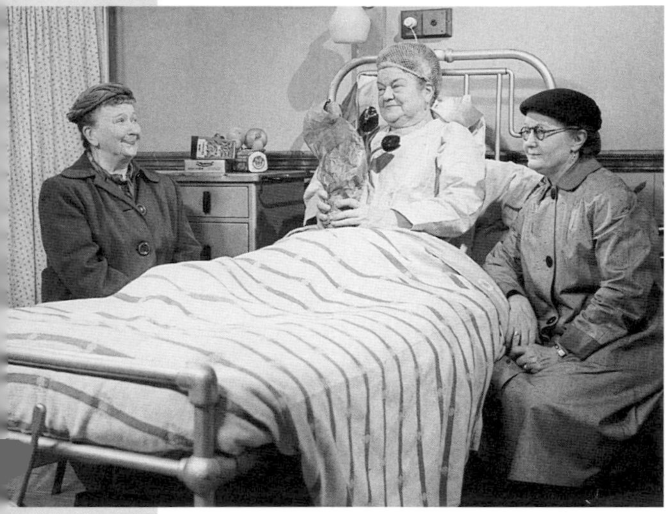

of her favourite tipple: the patients were allowed a bottle a day on the NHS, but the rest of the ward were teetotal. The big surprise for Ena was when Elsie Tanner was so concerned over her welfare that she posed as her daughter in order to visit her.

Ena returned home in an ambulance and took an instant dislike to the welcome home present Minnie had bought her – a mynah bird named Archie. The bird had spent too long in Minnie and Martha's company and repeated 'Ena won't like it,' day and night. Ena refused to give him house room so Martha took him in.

5 Two Lonely Hearts

The gossips set to work eagerly when it was discovered that widower Frank Barlow had started sharing his evenings with Florrie Lindley. They took to frequenting the tea rooms and dances suitable for a middle-aged couple. Frank sought and received Kenneth's blessing on the liaison, and spoilt Florrie on her fortieth birthday, buying her a blouse and treating her to a show in Manchester. The relationship rolled along for four months until Florrie grew frustrated with the way Frank failed to show any recognition of her feelings. He was more than happy for them just to remain friends,

saying he only sought companionship, but she was looking for more. By mutual consent their dates ebbed away.

6 A New Baby

When she discovered she was pregnant at the age of thirty-four, Concepta Hewitt's initial joy was overshadowed by hearing that the neighbours felt she was too old to see the pregnancy through to delivery. Harry did his best to reassure his wife that all would be fine, and tried hard to show how useful he could be about the house when he put his mind to it. He even went so far as to sell Lucky to buy a family saloon car – the first private vehicle in the Street. Concepta gave up her job behind the bar of the Rovers and on 6 August Christopher was born.

The entire Street doted on the new baby, with the exception of Harry's twelve-year-old daughter Lucille, who resented all the attention he was given. She complained that he cried all the time, robbing her of sleep and concentration when doing homework, and threatened to run away from home. She did disappear, for an evening, and was found sheltering from rain under the viaduct by Ena Sharples, who persuaded her to return home and advised Concepta to remember she had two children to care for.

To mark their first wedding anniversary the Hewitts threw a party, but the celebrations turned sour with the news that Christopher and his pram had been

snatched from outside Leonard Swindley's shop. The police were notified and the residents turned out to search while Concepta was sedated. When Christopher failed to turn up after twelve hours the police set up mobile headquarters in the Street and Detective Sergeant Sowman gave orders for the canal to be dragged. He spent hours talking to Lucille, whom he suspected of harming the baby, but she pleaded with Harry to believe that Christopher had been safe in his pram when she'd left him outside the shop.

The strain was too much for Concepta, who had a breakdown and was found wandering the local streets, screaming her son's name.

Three days later Elsie Tanner returned from her holiday in Blackpool to find the Street in uproar. She bumped into Joan Akers, a young woman who had been at school with her daughter Linda, and visited her in her tiny bedsit where she was surprised to see a baby. Recognizing the child as Christopher, Elsie called the police, Joan was arrested and mother and baby were reunited. Concepta refused to forgive Joan, even after hearing that the girl's own child had died.

7 Len's New Venture

For the first time in years Elsie Tanner found herself alone at No.11. Dennis had left to seek his fortune in London after a concert he'd organized at the Mission Hall went disastrously wrong: he sold three times too many tickets, then was forced to house two frisky seals in Annie Walker's bath and four exotic dancers in her bed. Needless to say, Annie was not amused when she discovered them.

Without Dennis the house seemed quiet, and Elsie spent more time than ever in the Rovers, much of her gin and tonic bought for her by old schoolfriend Len Fairclough. When Len's downtrodden wife

Nellie packed her bags and left with their son Stanley, the gossips decided that she'd had enough of Len's carryings-on with Madam Tanner. But Elsie didn't worry about the gossips: instead she started to cook and clean for Len. To return the favour Len skived off work to rip out the old range in Elsie's living room and put in a modern fireplace. However, Martha Longhurst thought it disgusting that Elsie and Len should spend so much time together and reported him to his bosses at Birtwistles Construction. Len was given his cards.

When Concepta reprimanded Len for hurting Nellie by installing Elsie in her home he told her that he viewed women as comfort zones, herself included. In response Harry thumped him, accusing him of insulting his wife, while Elsie announced in the Rovers that she was not Len's lover. She stopped looking after Len, and Nellie came home.

Len leased an empty yard at the back of his Mawdsley Street house and started his own building firm, taking on Jerry Booth from Viaduct Street as an apprentice.

8 The Finsbury Beauty Queen

Reading in the Sunday papers that her son was to marry a well-known beauty queen did not put Annie Walker in a good mood. She refused to talk to the press when they telephoned, assuring herself that the article had to be false – after all, if Billy was engaged she would have been the first to know. However, when Billy visited, with the blonde and glamorous Philippa Scopes in tow, Annie was forced to reassess the situation. She took an instant dislike to the girl and complained to husband Jack that she was too common to marry a Walker. Billy borrowed Harry's car to take Philippa for a spin in the Cheshire countryside, but when the front axle broke they were forced to spend the night in the car.

Philippa's stay at the Rovers turned the local men into stuttering wrecks while young Lucille Hewitt hero-worshipped her and begged her for makeup tips. The end for Billy and Philippa came when she discovered a rival beauty queen had landed a part in a film. Unhappy with the idea of giving up her glamorous life for Billy, she finished with him and returned to London. Annie was glad to see the back of the blonde, but saddened when Billy also headed south.

9 Renaming The Street

Postman Frank Barlow was the first with the news that as there were eight Coronation Streets in the area the council had decided to rename seven to avoid confusion. The residents were indignant when it was announced that their street would be known as Florida Street. Ena Sharples took up her pen to write, as she thought, to the top man in the country: the Duke of Edinburgh. Although she never had a reply from him, she received a visit from a Matilda Grimshaw, a cantankerous old biddy from a nearby Coronation Street where the residents had been told that their address would change to Florida Street. Matilda flew at Ena in the Rovers, accusing her of interfering with officialdom. However, the redoubtable Ena sent her scampering home with a flea in her ear while the delighted residents applauded their own cantankerous old biddy.

10 The Tragedies of Christine Hardman

Nothing much had happened to Christine Hardman since her mother's death. No men showed an interest, her days were spent operating a noisy machine at Elliston's raincoat factory and her evenings either in the Rovers or stuck at home mending and cleaning. For a while her workmates had thought her subdued until one day she climbed silently out of the factory window and up on to the roof, to look down at the Street seven floors below. The police were called but they failed to talk her down. Eventually it was her old schoolfriend Kenneth Barlow who succeeded, making her see that her death wouldn't help her mother or anyone else. She allowed him to lead her back to the ground and gave in to the attention of concerned neighbours. Fellow machinist Sheila Birtles tried to bring her out of her depression by taking her bowling and it was there that she met up with an old boyfriend, Colin Appleby.

Colin was a representative for a pharmaceutical company, passing through his native Weatherfield. He told Christine he was due in London at the end of the week, and by the time he stepped on the train to go south Christine was his wife. She grabbed her chance to escape and took only a small suitcase with her, leaving the rest of her things to rot. The residents wished her well but no one gave the marriage more than six months. It actually lasted four, but not because it broke up: Colin was killed in a car crash and it was as a widow that

Christine returned to the Street. Elsie Tanner took her in as a lodger at No.11 and found her a job working alongside her at Miami Modes department store, in the Slightly Better Dress Department. In trying to run away all Christine had achieved was to move next door.

11 A Tale of Two Lodgers – One Furry, One Scouse

All her life Esther Hayes had lived at No.5 Coronation Street. One by one the rest of her family had either died or moved away and she was alone. At last she decided that she deserved a less antiquated environment and put down a deposit on a new flat in Moor Lane, all mod cons and an inside toilet. To mark her departure her friends on the Street gave her a print of old Weatherfield.

Her house didn't stay empty for long. When Minnie Caldwell's mother died at the age of ninety-two she decided she didn't want to remain in the Jubilee Terrace house they'd shared in their widowhood. She took the tenancy of No.5 and moved in with her cat Bobby. To help with the rent, which she always had trouble in finding, Minnie took the first in a long line of lodgers when she found Jed Stone sitting on his suitcase in the Street.

Jed had left his native Liverpool after the local police grew too interested in him and hoped to put behind him his spells in Walton prison. He was a wheeler-dealer, always on the lookout for a quick buck, and used Minnie's front parlour as a warehouse for the goods he acquired then sold on at the market. Although Ena Sharples saw him as the Devil's disciple, sent to tempt her old friend with goods on hire purchase, Minnie regarded Jed as the son she'd never had and was thrilled when he started to call her Ma.

12 The Barm Cake Girls Move In

In 1962 Doreen Lostock's life was buzzing. First she was employed as sales assistant at the chain store Gamma Garments that had opened up on Rosamund Street after owner Nick Papagopolous had taken over Swindley's Emporium. Leonard Swindley and the faithful Miss Nugent were still employed there and Doreen became their junior. Away from work her private life also

picked up when she persuaded Florrie Lindley to let the bedsit above her shop to her and her schoolfriend Sheila Birtles. Sheila's parents were moving to Rawtenstall and she was thrilled with the chance to live away from their stifling influence. The first thing the girls did after moving in was to set up their record-player and do the Twist. Downstairs in the shop Florrie wondered if she had made a mistake.

13 A Murderer in Their Midst

Jerry Booth had a surprise when his uncle, Sam Leach, turned up from Newcastle looking for work. Jack Walker took him on as potman at the Rovers and provided him

with a small bedroom, but Jerry puzzled as to why his uncle had left his auntie Maureen. However, Sam fitted easily into life on the Street: he was mild-mannered and one of life's gentlemen. A regular Good Samaritan, in fact – Leonard Swindley was so impressed with his good turns that he decided to write a piece on him for the *Mission Gazette* until the police came looking for Sam. While the residents speculated on the chances of Sam having murdered his wife, the object of the gossip packed his bags and left the Rovers.

He sought refuge at the Mission and told Ena Sharples that the police wanted him for deserting Maureen, not killing her. On Ena's advice he went to the police station then returned to Newcastle. Ena had promised not to tell anyone about the desertion, so when the residents discovered she'd taken him to the police and asked why, she remained silent. They sent her to Coventry, accusing her of shopping Sam to the coppers. Only Minnie Caldwell stood by Ena, refusing to believe she'd help the police, and when Sam wrote to the Walkers explaining the situation and sending thanks to Ena the others were forced to apologize.

14 Wedding Bells for Kenneth

Valerie Tatlock returned from spending nearly a year in Scotland with her sick father and had only been back for two days when Kenneth Barlow proposed to her. Absence had definitely made his heart fonder, and he intended to make sure she didn't leave him again. However, while Kenneth sold his scooter to finance the wedding reception, Valerie began to fear that he was marrying her because he needed mothering and not because he loved her. On a visit to Ida Barlow's grave, though, Kenneth assured her that he really did love her and he longed for her to be his wife. They married at St Mary's in August. Albert Tatlock gave the bride away, Lucille Hewitt was bridesmaid and the best man was a friend of Kenneth's from university – brother David had football commitments.

After honeymooning in London the newlyweds moved into No.9, which Kenneth had bought for five hundred and fifty pounds. Neighbours Elsie Tanner and Concepta Hewitt were relieved to have the house occupied again – empty, it had become the meeting-place of a gang of teenagers. Valerie closed down her hair-salon on Rosamund Street and transferred

the business to her new front parlour, while Kenneth considered giving up teaching to become a full-time writer. He sent off his completed novel to a publisher but when it was rejected he decided for the time being to continue writing as a hobby.

15 The Navy Drops Anchor

Bill Gregory, Elsie Tanner's sailor, returned from the sea to her waiting arms. No sooner had they picked up from where they had left off than Ena Sharples's sharp eyes saw him writing a letter to a Mrs P. Gregory. She confronted Bill's friend Len Fairclough and forced him to confirm that Bill had a wife. She ignored Len's advice to keep Elsie in the dark – 'I won't see anyone on this

street made a fool of' – and went straight round to No.11 to drop the bombshell.

Elsie was angered by Ena's interference, upset by Len's keeping quiet but, most of all, disgusted with herself for not seeing the warning signs. She confronted Bill, who tried to explain that he and Phyllis had lived apart for years and he considered himself single. But Phyllis herself appeared on the scene, having travelled from Scotland to seek a reconciliation with him. Elsie warned Bill that she couldn't make up his mind for him; he had to choose between her and his wife. Bill waited for a sign from Elsie to show him that if he divorced Phyllis she would let him move in with her. When none came he agreed to try again with his wife, and together they left the Street.

16 Silver Anniversary

In October Jack and Annie Walker celebrated twenty-five years of wedded bliss by throwing a party for all the regulars at the Rovers. However, tempers were frayed when the couple returned from their summer holiday in Babbacombe. They had gone with friends but Annie had spent most of the two weeks in the company of a Mr Forsythe-Jones, a retired civil servant who had charmed her with his love of the arts. On their return to the Street Annie lost no oportunity to compare him with her husband, and Jack always seemed to come off worst. By the time their anniversary came round the Walkers were a far from harmonious pair. On the day Annie annoyed Jack by preparing food for the party while he struggled single-handedly with the bar. The guests all had a whale of a time with mountains to eat and free drink but the 'happy' couple retired to bed early, worn out.

17 Hot-tempered Len

Len Fairclough had always carried a torch for Elsie Tanner and, with Bill Gregory off the scene, he harboured hopes that they could be more than friends. He tried to overlook the fact that he had a wife at home but, as Elsie kept pointing out, this was a major problem. However, bookie Dave Smith had no wife, and when he cast admiring glances in Elsie's direction she agreed to a couple of steak dinners and a ride in his Jag. Len took an instant dislike to the flash Cockney and made snide comments about him when Dave took Elsie

for a drink in the Rovers. Dave warned Len to back off,whereupon the builder let rip with a punch that sent him flying across the Rovers' bar. Dave bundled Elsie out of the pub and the next morning phoned his solicitor. Len was arrested, charged with assault, and bound over to keep the peace. Elsie washed her hands of Len, as did Nellie, his wife. She stormed out of the house with their son Stanley and her bags, telling Len that she was sick of being treated like a drudge and was going to live in Nottingham with the insurance man, Harry Bailey.

18 Lollipop Albert

Pensioner Albert Tatlock took on the job of lollipop man outside Bessie Street School and soon grew concerned for one of the pupils, Susan Schofield, who was often covered with bruises. He befriended her

and questioned her about her home life. Eventually she broke down and admitted that her father was violent. Albert visited the girl's home where he found that her mother was as frightened of Jim Schofield as Susan. When he heard that Albert had been interfering, Jim threatened him, but the old man was more than a match for him. Backed up by the men of the Street, he warned Schofield that if he ever saw another mark on Susan the police would be brought in immediately.

19 Leonard Swindley, Man of the People

The news that draper Leonard Swindley was entering local politics was greeted with amusement by the majority of his customers. Even faithful Miss Nugent couldn't bring herself to give him her full support, believing he was too selfish to put anyone's interests before his own. Swindley stood for the Progressive Property Owners Party and counted upon the support of the local small traders rather than individual residents. Minnie Caldwell happily allowed him to set up his headquarters in her parlour and thrived on all the activity. However, Ena Sharples was delighted when the Mission boiler exploded during his election talk to the residents.

On polling day Swindley struggled to keep a smile on his face when he received 405 votes to the Labour candidate's 1,642. He bounced back by taking on the task of producing the Mission Hall Players in a play, *Lady Lawson Loses*, a Victorian melodrama, starring Emily Nugent as a romantic, cunning jewel thief. Annie Walker tried to steal the show as the Duchess of Bannock while Kenneth Barlow looked dashing as the lead. It took two stiff brandies to get Emily through the performance, and even then she passed out during the curtain call. Elsie Tanner's daughter Linda Cheveski, over from Canada with husband Ivan for Christmas, said that the sight of Emily kissing Kenneth had made the long sea journey well worth it.

Lady Lawson Loses

Emily Nugent and Leonard Swindley formed the Mission Hall Players to perform a melodrama written by unknown playwright Edgar Nugent (no relative to Emily). The cast was as follows:

Gilda Montefiore, a thief...Emily Nugent
Gerald, Duke of Bannock, a hero...Kenneth Barlow
The Duchess of Bannock, a society lady...Annie Walker
Lady Priscilla Dauntsey, an heiress...Christine Appleby
The Hon. Reggie Fitzgerald, an officer...Harry Hewitt
The Duke of Selina, a guest...Frank Barlow
Manders, the faithful butler...Albert Tatlock
Lady Rhona Philbeach, a family friend...Minnie Caldwell
Mrs Savage, a neighbour...Concepta Hewitt
Nellie, a maid...Florrie Lindley

Ena Sharples accompanied on the piano, Jed Stone prompted, hair was by Valerie Barlow

CAST

Matilda Grimshaw	Marion Dawson
Jerry Booth	Graham Haberfield
Colin Appleby	Lawrence James
Phyllis Gregory	Mary Quinn
Sam Leach	Frank Atkinson
Dave Smith	Reginald Marsh
Joan Akers	Anna Cropper
Arthur Forsythe Jones	Ian Colin
Susan Schofield	Ann Mitton
Jim Schofield	Richard Butler
Harry Bailey	Ray Mort
Philippa Scopes	Jacqueline Jones

1963

Behind the Scenes

The Street's producer, Margaret Morris, was forced to bow to public opinion when news leaked to the press that Sheila Birtles was to be seen to commit suicide. Granada bosses panicked at the stream of outrage, and actress Eileen Mayers returned to work to record the scenes again, just minutes before the programme was transmitted. The new scenes saw Sheila swallowing just a couple of tablets, rather than a bottleful and then gassing herself. The story continued with Sheila's rescue, and having thought her character was to be killed off, Miss Mayers lived to act another day, although she was annoyed that the well-crafted scene was never screened: 'It was a bit flat to suddenly feel after all that work it wasn't even shown.'

Actor Christopher Sandford joined the cast as singer Walter Potts and found himself a pop star when his song in the show 'Not Too Little, Not Too Much' reached No.17 in the charts. Granada's publicity department took photographs of him with the Beatles, and while he worked crowds of teenage girls laid siege to the studios.

Top Twenty

Pos	Character	No of eps	Total	Pos Prev Year
1	Elsie Tanner	101	282	8
2	Minnie Caldwell	93	264	3
3	Valerie Barlow	92	149	19
4	Ena Sharples	92	272	8
5	Albert Tatlock	91	254	7
6	Annie Walker	90	276	1
7	Harry Hewitt	90	259	8
8	Concepta Hewitt	90	262	5
9	Len Fairclough	90	244	1
10	Martha Longhurst	89	258	11
11	Jack Walker	87	268	5
12	Kenneth Barlow	85	233	11
13	Florrie Lindley	85	227	13
14	Frank Barlow	83	240	3
15	Jerry Booth	79	112	20
16	Emily Nugent	75	156	16
17	Lucille Hewitt	60	140	18
18	Doreen Lostock	60	149	15
19	Dennis Tanner	58	154	23
20	Leonard Swindley	57	149	14

"I'll say this about David Barlow. He did get himself away from this place an' not just talk about it like most of 'em do."

Ena Sharples

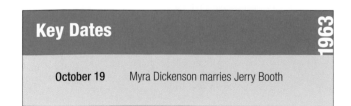

Key Dates 1963

October 19	Myra Dickenson marries Jerry Booth

STORIES

1 The Merry Widow

Widow Christine Appleby caused ripples in the Street by dating Frank Barlow, the father of her schoolfriend Kenneth, who was furious when Frank announced his engagement to Christine and accused her of taking his father for a fool. To give the couple some peace, busybodies Ena Sharples and Elsie Tanner joined forces and spread rumours that Christine had

dropped Frank for a younger man. Unfortunately they forgot to warn Frank of what they were doing and he was heartbroken when he heard the gossip. Then Christine actually started to go out with old flame Joe Makinson. Frank's workmate Alf Roberts found out about their friendship and attacked Joe in the Street. Christine dropped him and set the date with Frank for 4 May. Then she felt claustrophobic. She left her lodgings at No.11 to move in with friend Esther Hayes and told Frank the wedding was off as she didn't love him. She threw herself into her work, was made supervisor at Miami Modes and lorded it over Elsie, criticizing her work and manner. When Elsie complained to the management, Christine was transferred and left Weatherfield.

2 Wheels and Deals

Jed Stone employed Sheila Birtles as his assistant at the market to sell his blackmarket wares but sacked her when her parents thought he wanted to marry her. When Ena had a week's holiday, Jed took on her caretaking role at the mission. Supervisor Leonard Swindley was certain the week would end in disaster and was proved right when the over-sixties bingo session turned into a wild night with impromptu dancing. The neighbours complained of noise and the police were called out. Shortly afterwards Jed did a moonlight flit to Liverpool in Harry Hewitt's old car, which he was buying in instalments and on which he still owed twenty pounds.

3 Gamma Madness

The staff at Gamma Garments had an eventful year. As profits were down Leonard Swindley was told to sack his assistant Emily Nugent. Emily put on a brave face but Swindley threatened to leave with her and saved her job. Their boss, Mr Papagopolous, gave them six weeks to improve sales. The residents rallied and takings rose – so much so that Swindley was promoted to head office. The victory was short-lived: Emily and assistant Doreen Lostock stood by while a couple of conmen walked off with their entire stock, having told them they were transferring everything to another branch. When the police were called the ladies refused to give descriptions of the men as they had been so

charming and good-looking.

Neil Crossley arrived to take over as manager and horrified Emily by dipping into the petty cash. However, Doreen's flatmate, Sheila Birtles, fell for the worldly Crossley and started to date him, two-timing her long-standing boyfriend Jerry Booth. Along with the neighbours, Jerry sensed that Crossley was no good and, finding him with Sheila, challenged him to a fight. He knocked Crossley unconscious

and Sheila finished with him, swearing love to Neil. But what had started as an amusing diversion for Crossley had become a problem and he dropped her. Then, when she became hysterical, he hit her. Emily, appalled, reported him to Papagopolous for stealing the petty cash, and Crossley was sacked. He left the area, but Sheila still pined for him. She decided she couldn't live without him and attempted suicide in the flat, but was rescued by Dennis Tanner. Ashamed and upset, she left the Street to live with her parents in Rawtenstall. A few weeks later Doreen joined the Women's Royal Army Corps and left determined to see the world.

4 The Prodigal Returns

When her landlord announced a rent increase, Elsie Tanner refused to pay. The bailiffs were called in but she barricaded herself inside No.11 and prepared for a

long siege. Unfortunately this was cut short by the return from London of her son Dennis, who casually let the bailiffs into the house. Elsie was forced to pay the arrears in order to hang on to her furniture.

Dennis had been followed north by besotted Cockney Mavis Fox. Elsie thought she was a nice girl and was amused to discover that Dennis had sold himself to her as a wealthy mill-owner who only came to the Street to visit his old gran. She was less amused to find herself introduced as Gran's faithful nurse and Elsie forced Dennis to come clean. Disenchanted, Mavis left town. It was only after she'd gone that Dennis told Elsie that Mavis's mother owned a chain of hotels.

Dennis had returned home to manage the northern office of the Lenny Phillips theatrical agency and immediately started his quest to find the next Helen Shapiro. His big discovery was window-cleaner Walter Potts, and he set about turning him into singing sensation Brett Falcon. When Walter's landlady threw him out for practising in his room, Dennis lodged him at No.11.

Lenny Phillips's partner, Laurie Fraser, arrived from London and was an instant hit with Elsie, who fell for his flash way. He approved of Walter and encouraged him to cut a record 'Not Too Little, Not Too Much'. Dennis looked forward to a glamorous life as Walter's agent until he was sacked by Laurie for incompetence: Dennis had failed to sign Walter to an exclusive contract.

5 Frank Does It Himself

Frank Barlow recovered from Christine Appleby's betrayal by resigning from the Post Office and opening a DIY shop on Victoria Street. It was a success but Frank had trouble with the tenant in the flat above the shop, Ethel Tyson, who refused to pay an increase in rent. He threatened her with eviction so she asked her brother George Pickup to help. He tried to lean on Frank, threatening him with violence, and when Frank still refused to lower the rent George

and his son Jim started a fire in the shop. Luckily Frank managed to extinguish it and Ethel realized she might have died if the fire had spread. She was aghast and left, still owing rent.

6 Ena – Poor Pensioner or Battleaxe?

Despite landing the job of cleaner at the Rovers Return, Martha Longhurst was always first in the queue to collect her pension. Sometimes she collected Ena's and Minnie's too, and it was on such a day that she lost Ena's pension book. It was returned two days later by schoolboy Michael Butterworth, who claimed to have found it. When Ena found that a week's money had been drawn she called the police, ignoring pleas from teacher Kenneth Barlow. Michael appeared at the juvenile court and was put on probation.

Months later Ena broke down on finding her vestry ransacked, with all her belongings slashed and broken. Suspicion for the crime fell on Len Fairclough, who had been angered over her decision not to hold a children's party at the Mission. When the police discovered Michael was the culprit, though, his name was cleared.

7 Back-street Blues

It was an unhealthy life in Coronation Street: the houses were damp and the shadow from Elliston's factory cut off the sunlight. Christopher Hewitt developed a chesty cough. Concepta, who had been brought up in the country with plenty of fresh air, suggested to husband Harry that they move to Ireland. Her garage-owning father had decided to retire and they could take over. Harry was willing to try and gave up his job on the buses, but his daughter Lucille was horrified at the thought of leaving her home town and dug in her heels. Harry saw her point, but when he sided with her Concepta swore she'd go without them. Eventually she agreed to stand by him, despite her misgivings. Harry took a job driving coaches and found himself taking charge of the Rovers' darts outing to New Brighton. Pensioner Albert Tatlock got drunk on the trip and ended up being fined ten pounds in court for assaulting a policeman.

8 Len Dates Elsie

Len Fairclough's prejudices came to light when he argued with black bus conductor Johnny Alexander. Len swore he'd paid his fare and lodged a complaint against Johnny, who lost his job. The residents were disgusted with Len when he admitted later that he hadn't paid, and Johnny was offered his job back. However, he refused to work for the company again.

With his divorce going through, Len's thoughts turned to romance and he started dating Elsie Tanner, taking her to the Federation of Master Builders' dance. She enjoyed his company but upset him by refusing to marry him: she felt they would end up hating each other.

Len's apprentice, Jerry Booth, had better luck in the marriage stakes. In August he met typist Myra Dickenson, who immediately set her cap at him then stunned him, a fortnight later, by starting to plan their wedding. Her enthusiasm carried him away and in October he exchanged vows with her at St Paul's Church. After a brief honeymoon the couple moved into No.13, Jerry having taken on a five hundred-and-twenty-five pound mortgage.

9 Annie's Dark Secret

While researching for a school topic 'Thirty Years Ago', Lucille Hewitt read through press cuttings kept by Ena Sharples and unearthed an article about a local Lady Godiva. Annie Walker was shocked that Ena had kept the story of her exploits in the 1933 Co-op Pageant of the Ages and accused her of planning blackmail. But if she had wanted all this kept quiet she should never have accused Ena, who immediately told the residents all about it. When Dennis Tanner threw a surprise *This Is Your Life* in the Mission, Annie found that she was the subject and was even more appalled to be reunited with Alf Nuttall, who had led the horse on which she had ridden. Another guest that evening was daughter Joan, who panicked Annie by announcing that her two-year marriage was over. Jack Walker told Joan to stop complaining and sent her back home to her husband.

CAST

Johnny Alexander	Thomas Baptisto
Mavis Fox	Maureen Davis
Michael Butterworth	Roy Holder
Neil Crossley	Geoffrey Matthews
Walter Potts	Christopher Sandford
Myra Dickenson	Susan Jameson
George Dickenson	Stan Jay
Ethel Tyson	Susan Field
George Pickup	Bunny May
Laurie Fraser	Stanley Meadows

1964

Behind the Scenes

In 1964 the cast of *Coronation Street* suffered a devastating blow, dealt by the new twenty-nine-year-old producer, Tim Aspinall. He decided that the cast needed a shake-up. Since the programme started, the stories had centred around the same core characters, and the actors were stunned to be told that ten of them were to be culled. The press brought the news to the programme's 2.6 million viewers, and the cast started to fight back. Violet Carson threatened to resign when she heard Lynne Carol's character Martha Longhurst was to be killed off, but Granada boss Cecil Bernstein talked her round. He also stepped in to save Jennifer Moss, and her character Lucille Hewitt: the programme needed a teenager, he said. Lucille's parents, played by Ivan Beavis and Doreen Keogh, were not so fortunate, and Frank Pemberton, who played Frank Barlow, was fired too. He couldn't find acting work afterwards and had a stroke while in a dole queue.

Aspinall's reign was brief but he left a legacy in the shape of Stan and Hilda Ogden, whom he originally conceived as 'real sluts – Dad is a long-distance lorry driver and Mum is the kind of woman who spends the kids' dinner money in the pub'. Jean Alexander nearly turned down the role of Hilda as she had been offered a twelve-week series at the BBC: 'Bernard [Youens] and I both signed for three months and we didn't know how long we'd be staying. We'd never heard of each other before we met for the first audition but we hit it off immediately. For ever afterwards we knew each other's lines. It was an amazing sort of rapport.'

Top Twenty

Pos	Character	No of eps	Total	Pos Prev Year
1	Jack Walker	90	358	11
2	Annie Walker	90	366	6
3	Len Fairclough	90	334	6
4	Elsie Tanner	88	370	1
5	Ena Sharples	86	358	3
6	Valerie Barlow	81	230	3
7	Kenneth Barlow	78	311	12
8	Minnie Caldwell	76	340	2
9	Dennis Tanner	75	229	19
10	Albert Tatlock	72	229	5
11	Emily Nugent	70	226	16
12	Lucille Hewitt	60	200	17
13	Florrie Lindley	58	285	12
14	Irma Ogden	56	56	–
15	Concepta Hewitt	49	311	6
16	Charlie Moffitt	46	46	–
17	Harry Hewitt	45	304	6
18	Stan Ogden	45	45	–
19	Hilda Ogden	39	39	–
20	Leonard Swindley	38	187	20

Key Dates

1964

January 27	Irma Ogden's first appearance and Susan Schofield dies
May 13	Martha Longhurst dies
May 21	Frank Barlow leaves
June 29	Stan Ogden's first appearance
July 8	Hilda Ogden's first appearance
August 26	Harry and Concepta Hewitt leave
October 18	Nellie Fairclough dies
November 27	Rita Littlewood's first appearance

> "Annie Walker'd attend her own funeral if God let 'er."
>
> **Albert Tatlock**

Aspinall was replaced by H.V. Kershaw, the original story editor on the programme who had served as producer in 1961. He brought stability with him. He decided to keep Ken and Val Barlow and Albert Tatlock, but told Betty Alberge that her character, Florrie Lindley, would leave in the new year. A newcomer this year was Barbara Mullaney, playing Rita Littlewood, a character who wouldn't appear again until 1972.

STORIES

1 Kenneth's Principles

Without consulting his wife Valerie, Kenneth Barlow moved his colleague Dave Robbins into No.9 as lodger. Valerie resented the intrusion and didn't rest until she'd managed to get rid of him: she installed him in the flat over Frank Barlow's DIY shop. Ken and Dave both petitioned for a children's crossing across busy Rosamund Street but no one was interested until young Susan Schofield was knocked down and killed by a lorry.

While Ken threw himself into the politics of the situation, Valerie comforted grief-stricken Dave and began to wonder if she'd married the right teacher. Ken appeared on television to debate the situation with a local councillor, but his performance was poor and as a result he was denied promotion at work. He wallowed in self-pity and Valerie packed her bags: he didn't want a wife, just a housekeeper, she decided. She turned up at Dave's flat but was humiliated to find that he didn't want her.

Ken brought her home and took a new job, as head of English at Granston Tech. His principles got another airing when butcher William Piggott offered him a hundred-pound bribe to ensure his son passed an exam. Ken publicly returned the money and called in the police. Meanwhile, Valerie mused that the money might have been handy as she was pregnant with twins.

2 Dennis and Elsie go Clubbing

Stung by his mother Elsie's remark that he was afraid of hard work, Dennis Tanner took a labouring job at Amalgamated Steel to prove that he wasn't. He hated the job and was relieved when Elsie talked her boyfriend Laurie Fraser, with whom Dennis used to work, into employing him at

his new venture, the Viaduct Sporting Club. It was situated in the basement of the raincoat factory and lay preacher Leonard Swindley strongly opposed its presence. He had a nervous breakdown over conflicting interests when his boss ordered him to sell curtains to Laurie for the club.

Laurie employed Elsie there as a croupier, to operate the roulette wheel, but she resigned on the opening night when she discovered that one of her customers was Laurie's wife Rosemary. She finished with Laurie because he had lied to her over his marital status, and in revenge Laurie sacked Dennis. Dennis's discovery, Walter Potts, had better luck. His single hit the charts, made him a lot of money, and he went off on a European tour. As a thank-you present he gave Elsie the funds to have a bathroom installed at No.11.

3 Bye-bye Booths

Newlyweds Jerry and Myra Booth found their marriage falling apart due to her overspending on hire purchase. Jerry had handed over the running of their finances to Myra, and was furious to discover she was behind with the mortgage and in debt to the neighbours. On top of this, when she discovered she was pregnant she gave up her job at Gamma Garments. The

electricity was cut off and the bailiffs called in. Eventually the couple were so much in debt that their only option was to sell the house and move in with her father George, who paid off what they owed.

4 A Tin of Peaches Too Far

The locals muttered about folk having grand ideas when shopkeeper Florrie Lindley redesigned the Corner Shop and opened a sub-post office, employing Irma Ogden as her assistant on five pounds a week. Florrie was a private person with few friends among her customers. She seldom ventured into the Rovers and felt uncomfortable talking to people without the security of her shop counter to keep them at a safe distance. Eventually she had a nervous breakdown and ended up throwing a tin of peaches through the shop window because no one loved her. The residents felt certain she'd sell up and retire but instead she surprised everyone by falling for Irish Tickler Murphy, who lodged with Minnie Caldwell at No.5. Tickler enjoyed having a shopkeeper for a girlfriend but grew alarmed when she spoke of marriage, and fled the country.

5 The Trio Becomes a Duo

Martha Longhurst made a last pathetic attempt to clutch romance when wealthy Ted Ashley returned to his native Weatherfield after fifty years in Australia. She threw herself at him and followed him on a trip to London, hoping he'd propose to her. In her absence, Minnie Caldwell took over her job cleaning the Viaduct Sporting Club and took a tumble on a badly built staircase. Ena Sharples fought for Minnie's rights and won her fifty pounds compensation from builder Len Fairclough.

After Ted had refused to have anything to do with her Martha returned from London and cheered herself up with the thought of her first foreign holiday: she was going to Spain with her family to help look after her grandchildren.Unfortunately she never even saw the airport: she suffered a fatal heart-attack in the Rovers' Snug. Her death took place in the middle of Frank Barlow's leaving party. He had won five thousand pounds on the Premium Bonds and had bought a detached house in leafy Bramhall. He annoyed his erstwhile neighbours by declaring that the Street was fit only for slum clearance.

6 Emily Pops the Question

On his return to Weatherfield after his breakdown, Leonard Swindley settled back into his old routine and was stunned when timid Emily Nugent took advantage of the Leap Year to propose to him. At first he turned her down but then had a change of heart and bought her a twenty-five-pound engagement ring. The wedding was planned, with Lucille Hewitt as bridesmaid, Len Fairclough as best man and Jack Walker standing in for Emily's absent father. At the last minute Emily realized she was making a mistake and left Swindley standing at the altar, but he understood when she told him he didn't love her and never would, and that a marriage without love was a travesty. Far from ruining their relationship the incident strengthened it, and at the end of the year they co-produced *Cinderella*, with Lucille in the title role.

7 New Jobs for the Tanners

Dennis Tanner decided to follow his creative urges and enrolled in a hairdressing academy. Valerie Barlow gave him experience at her salon but his only achievement was accidentally to dye

Lucille Hewitt's hair blonde. To pay for his studies, Elsie took an evening job as a life model at the School of Design, where art teacher David Graham became infatuated with her. They had a brief fling but Elsie grew alarmed by his intense passion and decided she was making a fool of herself with a man young enough to be her son. However, when she attempted to end the affair, David produced a gun and threatened to kill her. Thankfully Dennis arrived and managed to overpower him. Elsie was quick to give up the job.

When Len Fairclough heard that his ex-wife Nellie had died, he toyed with the idea of providing a home for his son Stanley. He proposed to Elsie, who, to prove to him that this was a bad idea, demanded a trial

marriage. With Minnie Caldwell keeping a strict eye on their night-time activities, the set-up lasted less than a weekend, with Len finally admitting that Elsie was too much of a handful to be his wife.

8 The Ogdens Arrive

In June No.13 was sold to lorry driver Stan Ogden, who bought it to prove to his daughter Irma that he wanted to provide for his family. His wife Hilda replaced Martha Longhurst as cleaner at the Rovers and Irma became the pub's barmaid. Fourteen-year-old Trevor Ogden got them both the sack when Annie Walker discovered they had helped him to use her cellar as a storeroom for a load of blackmarket onions. However, Annie had to re-employ the Ogdens when faced with the prospect of cleaning the pub herself.

Stan had had a variety of jobs – as lorry driver, chauffeur, all-in wrestler, waste-paper collector – and was always willing to give his neighbours the benefit of his muscles. When digging Albert Tatlock's back yard, he unearthed an unexploded bomb and the whole street had to be evacuated until it was made safe. While they made themselves comfortable in the Mission hall basement Trevor raided their homes and absconded to London with the pickings.

9 Leave It To Charlie

Minnie Caldwell was delighted to take in her new lodger, Viaduct Sporting Club comic Charlie Moffitt. He moved into her back bedroom with his greyhound Little Titch and stored his pigeons in the yard. He soon fell out with his female neighbours after arranging a party for the local men with a group of female exotic dancers. Val Barlow was disgusted when her husband Ken admitted to spending the evening talking to the lovely Pip Mistral, although he omitted to tell her he'd pleaded with the blonde to take him to bed. In an attempt to make amends, Ken paid Charlie to decorate No.9 for Val.

While he was up in the loft, Charlie wandered into No.11's loft space, fell over

and made a hole in Elsie Tanner's bedroom ceiling. The incident was hushed up, though, because Elsie was away and Dennis had allowed exotic dancer Rita Littlewood to use her bed for the night.

10 Some Teenage Angst and a Cheque Stub

Lucille Hewitt's year was disrupted when her parents decided to go to live in Ireland. Concepta had nagged at Harry until he finally agreed to take on her father's garage business. The decision was made to leave Lucille behind until she'd finished her schooling and she moved tearfully into the Rovers as the Walkers' ward. She missed her father and became rebellious, playing truant from school to work at Mason's record shop, but Annie Walker took her in hand and tutored her in being a young lady. She was pleased with the result but amazed when Lucille beat her at the Viaduct Sporting Club's talent show, winning first prize for singing 'My Guy'.

Annie's husband Jack found himself in trouble with the police for serving after hours when, as a joke, Stan Ogden had stopped the bar clock. This paled into insignificance, however, when he discovered Annie had left him. After finding their bank account overdrawn by sixty-three pounds Annie had found cheque stubs made out to a Mrs Nicholls and suspected Jack of infidelity. She returned when Ena Sharples tracked her down and explained that Jack was paying their unemployed son Billy's rent.

Christmas Pantomime

The Mission Hall Players performed *Cinderella* for local children on Christmas Eve. The show was staged by Leonard Swindley with the following cast:

Cinderella......Lucille Hewitt
The Prince.......Elsie Tanner
Buttons.......Dennis Tanner
The Fairy......Annie Walker
Ugly Sisters.......Irma Ogden & Charlie Moffitt
Dandini......Emily Nugent
The Baron......Albert Tatlock
Broker's Man.......Len Fairclough

Minnie Caldwell prompted, and teas were served by Ena Sharples, Hilda Ogden and Florrie Lindley

CAST

Dave Robbins	Jon Rollason
Irma Ogden	Sandra Gough
Ted Ashley	Gerald Wells
Rosemary Fraser	Clare Owen
Charlie Moffitt	Gordon Rollings
William Piggott	George A. Cooper
Pip Mistral	Elaine Stevens
Stan Ogden	Bernard Youens
Hilda Ogden	Jean Alexander
Trevor Ogden	Jonathan Collins
David Graham	Roger Adamson
Tickler Murphy	Patrick McAlinney
Rita Littlewood	Barbara Mullaney

1965

Behind the Scenes

Betty Alberge bade farewell to the series after four years of playing Florrie Lindley, and, in the story, the shop was sold to Lionel Petty. The actor playing him, Edward Evans, was a famous face on television: he had starred in the first British 'soap' as the father in *The Larkins*.

When *Coronation Street* was sold to Australia it found a whole new audience and became an instant success. The five-hundredth episode was broadcast this year, featuring a classic confrontation between Elsie Tanner and Len Fairclough after he discovered she had been to a pub to pick up a man: 'You're nothing but paint and mush, Elsie Tanner!'

Key Dates 1965

April 15	Susan and Peter Barlow born
June 2	Florrie Lindley leaves
September 15	Robert Maxwell dies
September 29	Five-hundred episode transmitted
October 21	Violet Carson is awarded the OBE
December 18	Irma Ogden marries David Barlow

> "One does get rather tired of this dreary landscape. This desert of bricks and cobbled streets. Blackened chimneys piercing the sultry sky like jagged teeth."
>
> **Annie Walker**

Top Twenty

Pos	Character	No of eps	Total	Pos Prev Year
1	Len Fairclough	97	431	1
2	Stan Ogden	90	135	17
3	Jack Walker	89	447	1
4	Annie Walker	89	455	1
5	Elsie Tanner	87	457	4
6	Irma Ogden Barlow	81	137	14
7	Hilda Ogden	80	119	19
8	Minnie Caldwell	72	412	8
9	Kenneth Barlow	69	380	7
10	Albert Tatlock	67	393	10
11	Valerie Barlow	67	297	6
12	Lucille Hewitt	64	264	12
13	Dennis Tanner	63	292	9
14	Emily Nugent	63	289	11
15	David Barlow	62	94	32
16	Charlie Moffitt	60	106	16
17	Ena Sharples	56	414	5
18	Jerry Booth	48	193	23
19	Lionel Petty	41	41	–
20	Sandra Petty	33	33	–

STORIES

1 Ena Globe Trots

Ena Sharples started the year with a stroke of good fortune when she discovered a member of the Mission congregation had died and left her property – No.11 Coronation Street. Elsie was thunderstruck to discover Ena was her new landlady and promptly demanded house repairs. The Mission circuit decided it couldn't maintain both of its Mission Halls and Ena was warned she might lose her home if her Mission was closed. She decided to live at No.11 herself and gave Elsie notice to quit. Elsie refused to leave and the pair fought in the Street: Ena smashed Elsie's window with her handbag. The fight upset both parties – they were too old for public battling. When the Mission was saved Ena sold the house to local landlord Edward Wormold.

Soon afterwards she received a surprise visit from her brother's son, Tom Schofield, from America. He persuaded Auntie Ena to get a passport and fly to Boston to spend a three-month holiday with the brother she hadn't seen for fifty years. In her absence the Mission employed hypochondriac Clara Midgeley as caretaker.

2 Jerry Returns

Len Fairclough advertised for a housekeeper in the hope that he would land a young blonde. Instead he ended up with

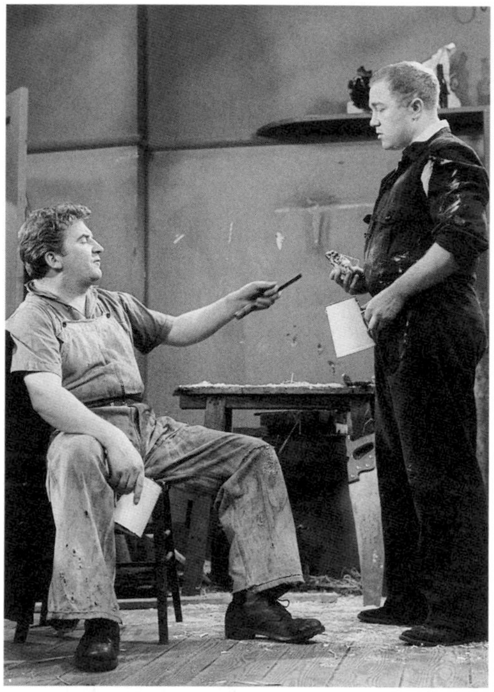

his ex-apprentice Jerry Booth, who returned to the area following the break-up of his marriage. Jerry lodged at the Corner Shop flat before moving in with Len in Mawdsley Street. William Piggott offered Len a contract to convert an old house in Blackburn into flats, but Len turned it down. Jerry took it on and he quickly discovered what Len had suspected: that Piggott was only interested in a cheap cowboy job. He returned, disillusioned, to Weatherfield. Len took him on again and made him a partner in the firm.

3 Charlie Goes On With the Show

Charlie Moffitt decided to quit showbusiness, borrowed fifty pounds from Ena Sharples and bought into an insurance round. All was well until he lost a cigarette packet stuffed with twenty-five pounds. While he searched for it, Hilda Ogden gleefully set about spending some money she'd found. She was distraught to learn that it was Charlie's money and returned the goods she'd bought to give the money back. However, she was too late: fearing the sack, Charlie had run away leaving his landlady Minnie Caldwell beside herself with worry. A month later he was found working as a comic in a working-men's club and was persuaded to return to No.5.

Along with Stan Ogden, Charlie brewed beer and stored it in Minnie's front room, telling her it was a tonic. In need of a pick-me-up, she and Emily Nugent opened a few bottles and were soon drunk. Charlie and Stan never got to taste the brew themselves as the remaining bottles exploded. In the autumn Charlie decided to tread the boards again and left for a season in panto.

4 Florrie's Past Catches Up With Her

Shopkeeper Florrie Lindley had allowed her customers to think her a widow so they were stunned to discover she was merely separated from her husband. Norman Lindley was an engineer who worked overseas. He returned to England to seek a divorce but while he was in Manchester he

took a fancy to Elsie Tanner. Believing the Lindley marriage to be over, Elsie went out with him, but when Florrie confessed she still had feelings for Norman Elsie dropped him. The Lindleys decided to give their marriage one last chance, and Florrie sold the shop to ex-Sergeant Major Lionel Petty. She and Norman started afresh in Canada.

5 Swindley Bids Farewell

Emily Nugent bought a 1959 Morris Minor, which she named Annie, and started to take driving lessons. Leonard Swindley took her out on a local trip but they were stopped by the police after driving the wrong way down a one-way street. To make matters worse, Swindley's licence had expired and the pair found themselves before the magistrate. Emily was fined five pounds but the bench accused Swindley of setting a bad example as a lay preacher. Shortly afterwards he was transferred to another branch of Gamma

Garments and bade farewell to Emily and Rosamund Street. Emily became manageress of the shop, and employed Elsie Tanner and Lionel Petty's daughter, Sandra, as assistants. Emily was full of ideas for improving trade and held a fashion show at the Mission. The event was a near disaster: all the outfits had to be altered to fit the models and Emily was up all night with her needle and thread.

6 Lucille Grows Up

Sixteen-year-old Lucille Hewitt entered the world of dating when the girls' school she

attended joined with a boys' school to put on a production of *Way of the World*. Lucille fell for juvenile lead Roger Wain, the son of a bank manager. Delighted, Annie Walker invited him for high tea but was unprepared when he announced he was a vegetarian. Lucille was influenced by Roger into giving up meat, but reverted to her carnivorous ways after he ended the romance. She left school with O Levels in Science, English, French and Geography. When father Harry turned up to take her to live in Ireland, she refused to go with him. Instead, she decided to remain at the Rovers and took a job at Marshall's Mill, working in the laboratories. She was devastated when her old home, No.7, collapsed when a faulty front beam gave way. Edward Wormold, the landlord, decided to demolish the house rather than rebuild it, and the council placed a bench in the space it had occupied.

7 Ken Becomes a Father

Kenneth Barlow was delighted when his wife Valerie gave birth on 15 April. The babies

were named Susan Ida and Peter, with Emily Nugent standing as godmother and Ken's brother David as godfather, and Valerie had the front parlour at No.9 converted from a hair salon into a play room.

Worn out with looking after the babies, she decided to exercise her mind by taking evening classes in sociology. She soon gave that up, though: she couldn't trust Ken with the children. On the first night she was out he went to the pub, leaving the twins alone, and when Val returned the house was full of smoke – a piece of coal had fallen from the open fire.

8 Everyone Loves Dennis

Dennis Tanner completed his hair-stylist's course only to find that his diploma was useless: the course was not recognized by the authorities. However, he was taken on as a trainee at Gerrard's exclusive salon. When a couple of socialites invited him to a day at the races, he thought he was moving up in the world. It was a humiliating experience: the Cheshire Set patronized him and mocked his working-class manners and ideals.

Lionel Petty's daughter, Sandra, fell for Dennis in a big way and trailed him for months like a lovesick puppy. Eventually she grew annoyed by the way he treated her as a sister rather than a lover and struck out on her own: she took a flat and left the Street. Lionel struggled on at the shop single-handed until, sacked from the salon, Dennis stepped in to help him.

9 Old and Unwanted

Albert Tatlock was upset when his treasured coin collection was stolen by a young vandal. Thankfully, the thief was more interested in the case than its contents and the coins were returned after they had been dumped. An old friend, Ted Bates, moved into No.1 with Albert in an attempt to escape the old folks' home his daughter had sent him to. Albert fought to keep Ted with him but the daughter brought in the authorities: she said her father didn't know his own mind, or what was good for him and, defeated, Ted left No.1.

10 Annie Socializes

Landlord Jack Walker despaired when he learned that Annie had decided to become big in the licensed trade. She had set her heart on becoming chair of the Licensed Victuallers' Association (Weatherfield, Ladies' Section) and wooed big cheese Nellie Harvey. Annie demanded that Jack be on his best behaviour during Nellie's visit to the pub but was stunned to discover they were old friends, having been dancing partners in the past. Nellie confided that she had always thought Annie stuck-up but had decided now that if Jack was her husband she must be all right. She pledged her support, Annie was duly elected and opened the champagne in celebration.

Jack wasn't celebrating when a customer, Frank Turner, started to blackmail him after discovering underage Lucille Hewitt managing the bar in his absence. Turner demanded money for his silence and the strain caused Jack to collapse. When the regulars discovered what was going on they decided to teach

Turner a lesson. He was beaten up in the back alley and the residents congratulated Stan Ogden on his handiwork, only to discover that mild-mannered Jerry Booth had done the deed.

11 Elsie Gets Desperate

Elsie Tanner left Miami Modes, worked briefly at Gamma Garments then went to manage the Rosamund Street launderette, the Laundryer. However, she soon tired of working on her feet and despaired of ever finding a knight in shining armour. Instead of looking for love in the Rovers, though, Elsie went upmarket and visited a Cheshire pub, the Fox and Hound. She attracted the attention of solicitor Robert Maxwell, and

agreed to let him drive her home. On the way they pulled into a lay-by and he told her how unhappy his wife made him. After they drove off Robert suffered a fatal heart-attack and the car crashed. Elsie panicked and fled the scene. She turned to Len Fairclough for help but he was sickened at the thought of her prostituting herself.

After finding her gloves in the car, the police tracked Elsie down and she was forced to give evidence at the coroner's court, where Maxwell's wife, Moira, attacked her, accusing her of luring her husband away. Elsie kept quiet about his views on his wife. In an attempt to cheer herself up she had a phone installed at No.11, and enjoyed a good flirt with the engineer, Jim Mount.

12 David Returns To His Roots

Kenneth Barlow's younger brother David returned to Weatherfield after being suspended from professional football, suspected of taking a bribe. After he was cleared, he was furious when Ken admitted that he thought his brother had been guilty. The young men brawled in the Rovers, and David knocked Ken out.

After starting a romance with Irma Ogden from No.11, David decided to stay in the area and sought lodgings at No.1 with Albert Tatlock. Having given up his London job, he became player coach with a local team, managed by Sid Lambert, and started writing a football column for the local paper. During the Street's outing to the Blue John mines in Derbyshire, he bought a ring and proposed to Irma on the coach home. Thrilled, she accepted, and the couple planned a church wedding.

Irma's parents, Stan and Hilda, were pleased for their daughter but Ken begged David not to marry an Ogden – the family was too common, he said. When the prospect of the wedding became too much the couple decided to elope to a local register office. Their secret was spoilt when a taxi driver leaked their plans. Hilda was upset that Irma wouldn't let her attend the wedding but contented herself with gatecrashing the reception, along with the other residents. The newlyweds moved into a new flat on Sandy Lane and looked forward to a rosy future. That came to an abrupt end when David injured his knee during a charity football match and the doctor told him he'd never be able to play again.

CAST

Edward Wormold	Robert Dorning
Norman Lindley	Glyn Owen
Roger Wain	Frazer Hines
Lionel Petty	Edward Evans
Sandra Petty	Heather Moore
Sid Lambert	Graham Rigby
Tom Schofield	Tom Halliday
Clara Midgeley	Betty Hardy
Ted Bates	William Wymar
Nellie Harvey	Mollie Sugden
Frank Turner	Tom Watson
Bob Maxwell	Donald Hewlett
Moira Maxwell	Ann Castle
Jim Mount	Barry Keagan

1966

Behind the Scenes

The new producer, Peter Eckersley, decided to introduce different situations and characters. Eckersley incorporated research findings that showed that religious congregations were dying off into scripts by having a community centre open in the Mission. He also reopened the factory across the cobbles, employing among others, machinist Bet Lynch. The stories featured more violence, and issues such as an illegitimate baby and attempted rape infiltrated the programme, which was among the top ten TV shows for the year, with a peak of 9 million viewers during the summer. However, the audience didn't seem to be as keen on the new-look Street as the writing team. When Eckersley moved on, H.V. Kershaw took back the reins and the writers were told to concentrate on the popular original characters.

Kershaw took Patricia Phoenix, Arthur Leslie and Doris Speed on a two-week tour of Australia, where the programme was now even more successful than it was in the UK. The tour started with dinner at 10 Downing Street with the Prime Minister, Harold Wilson, and his wife, Mary. While posing for photographs on the doorstep James Callaghan, Chancellor of the Exchequer, declared that Pat was 'the sexiest thing on television'. In Australia 50,000 people mobbed the Street stars in Adelaide.

By the end of the year, though, confidential reports were flying around Granada concerning the end of *Coronation Street* and the structure of a couple of spin-offs, one centring around the Walkers, the other around Len and Elsie. The omens weren't good: residents had been evicted from their homes in Archie Street, the Salford street featured in the opening titles of the show, as the council announced its demolition. With the future of its most popular characters in question it looked as if the Street would close within the next year.

Top Twenty

Pos	Character	No of eps	Total	Pos Prev Year
1	Len Fairclough	85	516	1
2	Elsie Tanner	83	540	5
3	Jack Walker	81	528	3
4	Jerry Booth	80	273	18
5	Annie Walker	77	532	3
6	Hilda Ogden	76	195	7
7	Ena Sharples	74	488	17
8	Kenneth Barlow	70	450	9
9	Irma Barlow	69	206	6
10	Dennis Tanner	69	361	13
11	David Barlow	66	160	15
12	Minnie Caldwell	66	478	8
13	Lucille Hewitt	65	329	12
14	Valerie Barlow	64	361	10
15	Stan Ogden	63	198	2
16	Albert Tatlock	60	453	10
17	Jed Stone	56	108	–
18	Sheila Birtles	42	154	–
19	Ruth Winter	22	22	–
20	Jim Mount	18	18	–

Key Dates 1966

February 21	Ray Langton's first appearance
May 23	Bet Lynch's first appearance

"Elsie Tanner's a loud-mouthed, pig-'eaded, painted tramp, wi' a bustful o' brassiere an' nowt on top. An' with the right man on 'er arm, she'd turn into the best wife a lad could wish for."

Ena Sharples

STORIES

1 The Irish Challenge

Elsie Tanner's taste in men was always shaky, and she never seemed to learn her lesson: she couldn't help falling for a hairy chest and pair of strong arms. Jim Mount was a rough-and-ready Irishman who moved in as lodger at No.13, paying the Ogdens four pounds a week in rent. He took Elsie out but enjoyed playing the field.

When the Walkers went on holiday the brewery installed Brenda Riley as manageress. Jim was overjoyed as she was an old girlfriend, but she refused to rush into his arms and instead went out with Len Fairclough. Len wasn't happy with the offhand way Jim treated Elsie and fought with him when he said Elsie was only a back-street tart. Elsie finished the relationship, but Jim wasn't bothered. He skipped town with Brenda after the Walkers returned home to discover she'd turned the pub into a speakeasy, with dancing on the bar and a billiard table in the Public.

2 Ken Plays Around

While Valerie Barlow existed on little sleep and wandered around with her infant twins, her husband Ken's head was turned by a glamorous reporter called Jackie Marsh, whom he had met when she was interviewing his brother David about his football career. Ken fell for her and started to meet her behind Valerie's back. After Elsie Tanner saw the couple kissing she warned Ken not to throw away his family, but Ken told her to keep out of his affairs and made plans to spend the weekend with Jackie, telling Val he would be attending a National Union of Teachers' conference. However, when Val carefully packed him a lunch for the journey Ken realized he couldn't betray her any more. He ended the affair, relieved that he'd managed to keep it secret.

A couple of months later, though, Val and he had a row and she revealed she'd known all about Jackie. She took the twins and left him, to spend time with her parents in Scotland. When she returned, a month later, it was to tell him she'd forgiven him. He tried to make amends by being more attentive and bought a Mini so that they could have outings.

3 Barlow Provisions

Lionel Petty had never fitted into the Street so in January he decided to sell the Corner Shop and go into business with his brother in Wales. Dave Smith showed an interest in buying the shop and converting it into a betting office, but Ena Sharples swore to oppose the venture. In the end Dave backed out of the deal as Lionel was asking too much money for the shop. Meanwhile, unemployed since his knee injury, footballer David Barlow faced a bleak future. His club offered him three hundred pounds' compensation and he sank into a

deep depression, seeking solace in alcohol. His bride of a month, Irma, refused to hang around while he wallowed in pity and moved back to her parents' house. When David apologized she gave him an ultimatum – either he bought the Corner Shop or they were finished. Irma had worked at the shop since 1964 and felt certain she could run it herself. David agreed and paid one thousand seven hundred and fifty pounds for the premises and two hundred pounds for the stock. Lionel left for Wales and the Barlows moved in. Their first task was to close the sub-post office.

For a short time everyone was happy. Then Irma started to feel trapped behind the counter with penny-pinching David. She decided she wanted some excitement and took a job as a plastic welder at the PVC factory that had just opened up at Elliston's across the Street. David was aghast when Irma introduced him to his new shop assistant – her mother, Hilda. Working away from David gave Irma the independence she needed, although she was useless at her new job. She also demanded nights out with sister-in-law Valerie. One evening, at the cinema, they were chatted up by two lads, Ron Jenkins and Brian Thomas. Irma encouraged them, calling herself Avril and Val Gail. The lark backfired, though, when Ron stole Irma's compact and refused to return it unless they had a date. The only way Irma could get rid of him was to introduce him to her husband then face the music.

4 Hilda Meddles in Stan's Affairs

Stan Ogden couldn't believe his luck when his numbers came up on the pools. He celebrated a seventy-five-thousand-pound win by buying drinks all round at the Rovers, but the bubble was soon to burst when Hilda confessed to filling in the winning numbers on the coupon as they were read out on the radio. Irma had to act fast to stop Stan killing her mother.

Shortly afterwards Stan bought an ice-cream round and started selling his wares around town. He crossed swords with established ice-cream baroness Rose Bonnetti, who used her sons as spies to

ensure she kept one street ahead of him. Stan was unable to sell any ice-cream and his stock melted. Feeling sorry for him, Rose took him on as her assistant, but Hilda didn't like the idea of Stan working for a woman and reported him to the authorities for trading without a licence. Stan was sacked and took a job as a milkman, getting revenge on Hilda by forcing her to wake at four o'clock every morning to cook his breakfast before his round. He enjoyed the work as he was finished by late morning and was able to spend the rest of the day in the Rovers. Unfortunately by Christmas he had been made redundant. Before that, though, the summer of 1966 found the Ogdens taking a rare holiday as they joined David and Irma in a week's caravanning. The holiday was a disaster: the caravan was crowded and they were evicted from a farm after letting a herd of cows escape from a field.

5 The Bad Penny Returns

Minnie Caldwell took to her bed, unable to buy coal to keep warm as she owed the debt collector seventeen pounds. She had no hope of repaying the debt and the interest kept rising each week. Salvation came in the shape of Jed Stone, who returned to lodge with her again. He realized debt collector Nuttall was running a scam and conned him into buying a load of reject socks for twenty pounds, which he gave to Minnie.

Jed's return coincided with Dennis Tanner entering a period of depression and reassessment of his life. The pair decided to go into partnership. First they tried to sell second-hand waxworks, then opened a bargain boutique in the arch under the viaduct. When that business failed they turned to song writing, with Ena Sharples putting their lyrics to music. Disillusioned Dennis took a job selling novelties but he wasn't a natural salesman and was soon sacked. Then he and Jed opened auction rooms under the viaduct but had to close as they had no planning permission. Finally they decided to board dogs in kennels but both got into a state when they lost a valuable dog owned by local villain Arthur Johnson. By now Dennis had decided he had had enough and took a job as entertainments manager at a holiday camp in Carlisle.

Jed stayed on in the Street until September when, during Minnie's birthday party, he was arrested for handling stolen blankets. Minnie was devastated when he was sent to prison for nine months. Jed

insisted that Minnie auction his belongings to pay herself the rent he owed her. The residents rallied round and gave her over the odds for Jed's junk, leaving her with twelve pounds ten shillings. Annie Walker bought a cameo brooch for a pittance, which turned out afterwards to be worth fifteen pounds. Ena Sharples insisted she gave Minnie the true value, but Annie compromised and gave her four pounds.

6 Emily's Big Sacrifice

Emily Nugent was thrilled when a holiday friend invited her to look after his souvenir shop in Majorca. She resigned from Gamma Garments and looked forward to a new life on the island but on the eve of her departure her sister contacted her to say that their father had had a stroke. Emily refused to give up her plans, insisting that as she had kept house for him in the past it was the turn of one of her siblings to nurse him. However, they were all married and threatened to put him into a home so Emily was forced to move to Harrogate to look after him, although she allowed the residents to believe she'd gone to Spain.

7 Jerry Under Investigation

Len Fairclough and Jerry Booth started their partnership with a contract at Newton & Ridley, building store rooms. It was a big job so they took on ex-Borstal boy Ray Langton to help with the plumbing. Len enjoyed working at the brewery and made the most of it, drinking and playing cards with the storemen. While he was thus entertained, Jerry took a tumble off some scaffolding and was rushed to hospital. When it came to light that Len had used sub-standard scaffolding the contract was terminated. Soon after his recovery, Jerry was thrilled to hear that his old girlfriend Sheila Birtles had returned to the area. She moved into lodgings at No.11, converting Elsie Tanner's front room into a bed-sit, and took a job at the PVC factory. She and Jerry started to date and she introduced him to her baby son, Danny, who was looked after by foster-parents. She revealed Neil Crossley was the father and that she had had the baby in secret. Jerry swore he didn't mind and said he wanted to marry her – but he was still married to Myra. When he asked for a divorce, Myra's father became suspicious of his motives and hired a private detective, Harry Bishop, to snoop. Elsie Tanner found out about Bishop and posed as an informant for him, taking twenty-five pounds a time off him for false information.

However, despite Jerry's efforts to get a divorce, he was destined never to have Sheila. Returning home on a train one day, she bumped into Neil Crossley and realized she still loved him. Jerry was heartbroken when she told him she was leaving to marry Neil and for Danny to have a father. The night Sheila left for her new life in Sheffield, Jerry went out to a club where hostess Margot fleeced him of his money then dumped him in the gutter.

8 Bad-boy Ray and Handy Bet

Lucille Hewitt fell for plumber Ray Langton in a big way. She was attracted by his manly ways and that he appeared years

older than he was. Ray took advantage of their nights together baby-sitting to steal money from the Barlows and from the Rovers' till. When Lucille objected he threatened to break her arm if she told. Then he pressurized her to have sex with him. Eventually she broke down and told Len Fairclough what was going on. He saw Ray out of town and advised Lucille to be more selective in future.

To Annie Walker's horror, Lucille gave up her secure job at the mill to work at the PVC factory on thirteen pounds a week. Lucille was a quick worker – on the machines and in her personal life: within days she'd started to date storeman Kenny Pickup. The PVC machine room was run by foreman John Benjamin, who worked the girls hard while he did little but fondle his favourite, Bet Lynch. When Lucille's fast work showed the other girls up, Bet ordered her to slow down and thumped her in the eye. Len was upset to see Lucille's shiner, and threatened Benjamin with retribution if he didn't sort his girls out.

9 Young At Heart

Clara Midgeley announced to Minnie Caldwell that she had fallen in love with cheeky Albert Tatlock from No.1. Albert remained unaware of Clara's feelings and agreed to holiday with her in Cleveleys. While they were away together she popped the question but he hastily returned home, telling disappointed Clara that he was too set in his ways to marry again.

Minnie, too, became an object of desire when Elsie Tanner's chimney-sweep father-in-law, Wally Tanner, moved into No.11 and set about wooing her. Elsie hated Wally hanging around her house, scrounging off her, and dumped him in the local sweet shop run by her ex-husband Arnold, who begged her to take care of his father, but she refused.

Minnie was disappointed that Wally had moved on but she had worse things to worry about after she collapsed in the Snug with head pains. The doctor told her she'd been doing too much and that she should rest more. Her friend Ena Sharples was baffled as she couldn't work out what Minnie had been doing 'too much' of.

10 The Lady Unmasked

While she was cleaning out the Rovers' cellar Annie Walker uncovered an oil painting of an aristocratic lady. As she examined the painting a mask fell out from behind the frame. Annie called in local historians and convinced herself that the painting was of a titled lady of the eighteenth century, who had lodged at an inn on the site of the Rovers while her lover visited her in disguise. She decided to change the name of the pub to the Masked Lady but was distracted by something far more important: the Federation of Women's Associations sent a Mrs Arkinstall to ask her to stand as their candidate in the local elections. Delighted, Annie agreed, much to Jack's horror, and pictured herself heading local government. She was furious to discover that Len Fairclough would oppose her and the residents were forced to take sides. While Annie concentrated on issues such as better street-lighting, Len

called for the demolition of Coronation Street and the terraces near it. The voting ended in a draw, as did the re-count. A coin was tossed and Len was duly elected councillor. Annie retired with a migraine.

After the election David and Irma Barlow suffered as voters went down with a mysterious stomach bug after eating pies, bought from the shop, at the election party. A health inspector called and the Barlows were cleared of suspicion, but none of the residents believed the official report and trade fell off for a while.

The Barlow marriage nearly fell off as well when a young Cockney called Merle Baker turned up announcing that David had asked her to marry him. Irma was bemused and David swore he'd never heard of Merle. When they met up Merle did not recognize him, and Annie was horrified when she identified as David Barlow the lad in a photograph on Annie's sideboard – her son Billy. She telephoned Billy, who admitted to her that he'd given a false name and promised marriage to lure Merle into bed. Annie was disgusted with him and Jack paid off Merle.

11 Elsie's Troubled Family

Dennis Tanner returned from Carlisle ninety-four pounds in debt. Elsie had left the Laundryer to become supervisor at Miami Modes but even though she was earning more she was in no position to help Dennis, who started to panic when he heard that a couple of heavies had followed him. Elsie realized he was in danger and begged wealthy Dave Smith to help. He agreed to pay up, but on the condition that Elsie slept with him. Dennis refused to let his mother prostitute herself and faced the heavies. Elsie tried to protect him with the poker and Jack Walker, ashamed that none of the other menfolk wanted to get involved, waded in. The two thugs weren't happy about beating up a lad, a woman and an old man but followed their orders until they were stopped by Len Fairclough, who flung the money at them. In return, he ordered Dennis to start work as a labourer at his building firm.

Elsie's daughter, Linda Cheveski, also returned, with her son Paul. She announced that her marriage to Ivan was over: in Canada she'd fallen for a Mountie called Mike. Ivan followed, took a job in Birmingham, and begged for a reconciliation. Linda refused and waited for Mike to send for her.

While trying to help her daughter sort out her life, Elsie endured weeks of obscene telephone calls, which wore her down until she had a breakdown. The police were called in and discovered that Hilda Ogden had made a call. Elsie tore into her and Hilda admitted to having made just one call; she had decided to jump on the band-wagon and call Elsie all the names she could down the line. The mystery caller was eventually uncovered as Moira Maxwell, the wife of the solicitor who had died giving Elsie a lift home from a country pub. Moira blamed Elsie for her husband's death and finally attacked her with a knife. Luckily Len was on hand, once again, to rescue her.

But in her darkest hour, Elsie turned on Len. When six-year-old Paul disappeared on the way home from school, the residents turned out to search for him and he was

eventually found on the canal bank: he had been pulled from the water by an unknown rescuer. He was rushed to hospital with pneumonia and doctors gave him only a 30 per cent chance of survival. Elsie and Linda spent two days and nights by his bedside. Elsie was sickened to discover that Len had voted against a council plan to fence off the canal and flew at him. Paul's father Ivan had the same idea: he attacked Len with a plank and only stopped when Linda arrived with the news that Paul had pulled through. The incident brought the Cheveskis back together and they left for a new life in Birmingham together.

12 Ena's Nightmare Year

Ena Sharples was saddened when her daughter Vera Lomax announced that she had left her husband and was in debt. Ena gave her her savings and was left without any money. The next week she was caught shoplifting a tin of salmon at the Summit Supermarket. She swore it was an oversight but was arrested and appeared in court. Her uncooperative attitude annoyed the magistrate, who fined her two pounds and lectured her on abusing her position as Mission caretaker. Worse was to come: Ena was put under the supervision of Ruth Winter, who moved into the Mission and set about turning it into a community centre. Ena was aghast at the idea of OAP whist drives, table tennis sessions and toddler groups, and promptly moved out of her vestry once again. She briefly took a job as live-in housekeeper to Len Fairclough in Mawdsley Street. The council offered her a flat in a high-rise block, but the thought of living on the sixteenth floor was too much for her: she was forced to eat humble pie and return to the vestry.

Ruth threw herself into setting up activities for the community and started dating Len Fairclough. She organized a quiz, which Ena won, and encouraged Ken Barlow to start a film society. The only film he ever showed was pornographic: it had been sent by mistake. The residents didn't seem to want the centre, but Ruth persisted, throwing a party for the local teenagers. During the evening a couple of lads lured Lucille Hewitt into the vestry and attempted to rape her. Ena came to her aid but the lads produced a knife and threatened to 'carve her up'. Luckily Ruth appeared and disarmed them with her martial arts. Shortly afterwards the centre closed through lack of support. Ruth finished with Len, then flew to Rome to marry her boyfriend who worked as a movie stuntman.

Ena's Christmas was the worst she'd ever lived through. Vera returned with nowhere to live so Ena took her in. She complained of head pains, which Ena thought were invented until the doctor told her Vera had a tumour and only days to live. Ena agreed not to tell Vera how serious her condition was but Vera guessed when her mother started to be nice to her.

FANCY DRESS PARTY

Held at the Mission of Glad Tidings, on Boxing Day.

Dennis Tanner	Batman
Albert Tatlock	Father Christmas
Ken Barlow	Laurence of Arabia
Val Barlow	Nell Gwyn
Lucille Hewitt	chimney sweep
Minnie Caldwell	Old Mother Riley
Elsie Tanner	Spanish dancer
Irma Barlow	flapper
David Barlow	old-time butcher
Len Fairclough	Batman
Jerry Booth	Robin
Annie Walker	Queen Elizabeth I

CAST

Jackie Marsh	Pamela Craig
Ray Langton	Neville Buswell
Brenda Riley	Eileen Kennally
Arthur Johnson	Peter Vaughan
Ruth Winter	Colette O'Neil
Wally Tanner	George Betton
Bet Lynch	Julie Goodyear
Rose Bonnetti	Lila Kaye
John Benjamin	David Burke
Kenny Pickup	Warren Clarke
Mrs Arkinstall	Lally Bowers
Harry Bishop	Derek Smith
Merle Baker	Dilys Watling
Paul Cheveski	Marcus Saville
Ron Jenkins	Ben Kingsley
Brian Thomas	Michael Blackham

1967

Behind the Scenes

> “Flippin’ street we live in! You only ’ave to ’ave a bath an’ everyone knows if you get your toe stuck in the tap!”
>
> **David Barlow**

Writer Jack Rosenthal became the Street’s new producer and steered the programme through its most ambitious storyline to date: Elsie Tanner’s wedding. The press gave a running commentary on the preparations for the big day and the *TV Times* produced a special edition souvenir to mark the occasion; 9.45 million viewers tuned in to see the exchange of vows, making it the most watched television programme of the year. Writing in the *Sunday Times*, Ruth Hall expressed the opinion that the Street was too well crafted: ‘The trouble is that the characters are only too real. They are small, narrow and boring. They shout endlessly about trivia and mean nauseatingly well under their harsh exteriors. Now that the first impact on romantic southern intellectuals of documentary drama about the industrial north has worn off, such characters no longer command intellectual interest.’

A casualty of the wedding was actor Ivan Beavis, whose character Harry Hewitt was killed off. The groom also suffered. Canadian actor Paul Maxwell brought Elsie’s wartime sweetheart Steve Tanner to life (he was given the same name because Elsie Tanner was so popular that no one wanted to change hers). Paul was a Hollywood actor whose voice had been famous as that of Steve Zodiac in *Fireball XL5*, but the viewers had always hoped Elsie would marry Len Fairclough and were hostile towards his charcter, Steve. After marrying the couple another new producer, Richard Everitt, decided to send them to America, the idea being that Elsie would soon return alone.

Great plans were afoot to alter the face of the programme, starting with the building of an exterior set. Up to this point all scenes set in the Street itself had been recorded in one of Granada’s studios, along with the interiors. Filming a train crashing off the viaduct pushed this practice to the limits. In November a piece of railway yard was hired from British Rail for ten guineas and plans were drawn up to build façades of the houses. New writers were employed and told to spice up the Street, with stories about sex (Len and Elsie), pregnancy (Emily), drugs (Lucille) and homosexuality (Jerry). However, when it came to scripting, all of these themes were dropped for fear of upsetting the viewers. Instead, new characters were planned who could play more issue-led stories, including plans for the programme’s first black family.

Key Dates 1967

January 11	Vera Lomax dies
May 3	Steve Tanner first appears
May 11	A train crashes off the viaduct, Sonia Peters is killed
September 4	Elsie Tanner marries Steve Tanner Harry Hewitt is killed

Top Twenty

Pos	Character	No of eps	Total	Pos Prev Year
1	Annie Walker	89	621	5
2	Jack Walker	88	616	3
3	Elsie Tanner	85	625	2
4	Len Fairclough	83	599	1
5	Ena Sharples	81	569	7
6	Irma Barlow	72	278	9
7	Jerry Booth	72	345	4
8	Albert Tatlock	69	522	16
9	Stan Ogden	68	266	15
10	Valerie Barlow	67	428	14
11	David Barlow	67	227	11
12	Dennis Tanner	67	428	9
13	Lucille Hewitt	67	396	13
14	Kenneth Barlow	62	512	8
15	Hilda Ogden	62	257	6
16	Minnie Caldwell	61	539	11
17	Emily Nugent	60	359	26
18	Steve Tanner	57	57	–
19	Dot Greenhalgh	17	59	–
20	Dave Smith	14	24	–

STORIES

1 Ena's Tragic Year

1967 started badly for Ena Sharples as she watched her daughter Vera die of a brain tumour. To the last Vera insisted that her mother did not love her. She was buried at North Cross cemetery in the same grave as her father, Alfred. A few short months later it looked as if Ena would be joining her when a goods train crashed off the viaduct at the end of the Street. Rescuers pulled PC Jimmy Conway from the wreckage of his car but his girlfriend, Sonia Peters, was declared dead, and apparently the lifeless body of Mrs Sharples was found near her. David Barlow crawled under the debris to reach her and she was rushed to hospital, miraculously with only cuts and bruises.

Visiting Vera and Alfred's grave later in the year, Ena was surprised to find fresh flowers on it. When her bank balance rose by a hundred pounds she turned detective to find out who her mystery benefactor was. She traced the flowers to a Henry Foster in St Anne's and confronted him. He confessed that in the 1930s he'd taken a job that should have gone to Alfred. Since then he'd made his fortune and felt guilty. Ena refused any more of his conscience money, and told him that Alfred had died of starvation during the Depression.

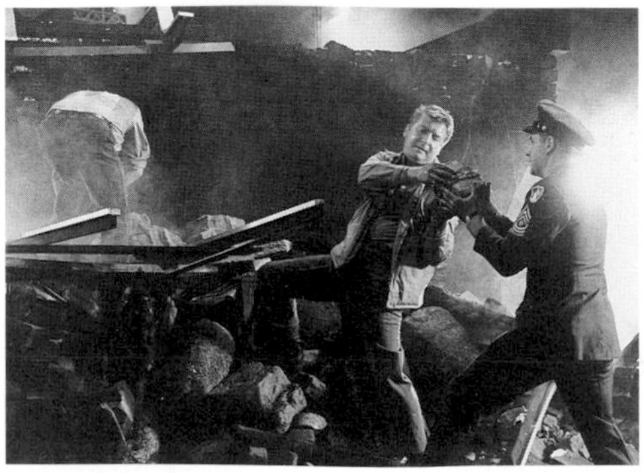

2 The Undynamic Duo

After nursing her father back to health Emily Nugent returned to Weatherfield. She rented the Corner Shop flat and revamped Gamma Garments into a modern boutique. Her return coincided with a change in Dennis Tanner's fortunes. He had resigned from Len Fairclough's building firm after accidentally setting fire to Len's kitchen while decorating it. Against her better judgement, Emily took on Dennis as the Gamma Man and lured Lucille Hewitt into accepting a post as her assistant by offering eight pounds a week and commission of sixpence in the pound. Lucille and Dennis threw themselves into their new swinging jobs but felt that Emily put off the younger generation with her outdated image. They convinced her to buy a whole new wardrobe, and to prove that she looked fab, Lucille asked her friend Brian Thomas to chat Emily up. The only problem was that Brian fell in love with Emily, who was embarrassed by his attentions. He decided to propose but Emily distracted him by introducing him to her young friend Audrey Hargreaves.

When business grew bad credit sales were blamed, so Emily made Dennis the shop's debt collector. He had an awful time chasing money and was threatened by burly Bert Tate when he tried to get him to pay for a jacket. Dennis won Bert's respect by standing up to him, and Bert ended up agreeing to take on the debt-collecting role.

3 Work-shy Oggie

Stan Ogden enjoyed living an idle life on his dole money, but when he refused to take a mill job his dole was stopped. Hilda threatened to throw him out so Stan took a

job shifting coal, then replaced Dennis Tanner as labourer at Len Fairclough's yard. On his first day he injured his back and spent the rest of the week in hospital.

Stan was delighted when he beat the local men at darts and won a cup-final ticket. On discovering it was worth ten pounds he sold it, without telling Hilda, unaware that she had managed to get hold of a ticket for herself. When she told Stan they'd be able to have a good day out together in London he panicked and burned her ticket, allowing her to think she had lost it. To carry off the charade, Stan left the house at five a.m. and spent the day on a park bench, listening to the match on a radio. A week later Hilda discovered the truth and made him paint the house as a penance.

4 The Truth Game

Annie Walker and husband Jack sat down with a cup of tea and tested each other with the *Gazette's* Truth Game. They ended up at each other's throats when Jack had to list his wife's faults. He eventually grew tired of

Annie's nagging about it and left home, supported by the Rovers' customers who all felt he should have left years before. He stayed with Albert Tatlock at No.1 but Annie, unaware of this, suspected him of lodging with Elsie Tanner and confronted her on her doorstep. Jack was amused at being thought one of Elsie's men and decided to have some fun. He let himself into No.11 via the back door and startled both Annie and Elsie by leaving through the front. The Walkers were only reconciled after Jack admitted he had often thought of leaving Annie but hadn't done so because he loved her.

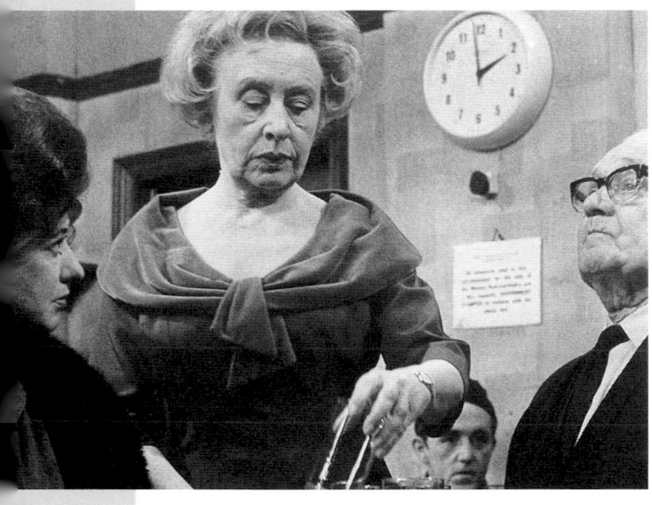

The Walkers' ward, Lucille Hewitt, celebrated her eighteenth birthday in May and became annoyed when Annie continued to open her mail. She hit back by sending off for hundreds of circulars in Annie's name but her revenge missed its mark: Annie won a weekend in Paris with a French film star for being the millionth customer at Cutie Beauty Cosmetics. Annie loved every minute of the break and on her return attempted to bring some Gallic colour to the Rovers, until Jack stopped her.

When Lucille announced she was going to attend a football match Annie decided to accompany her to see pitch hysteria and hooliganism for herself. After the match Annie was taunted by a couple of fans and, in an attempt to make a citizen's arrest, threw a football rattle through a shop window. She was arrested – but the Rovers' regulars were disappointed when the police released her with a caution.

5 Albert and Minnie Come a Cropper

When Minnie Caldwell's insurance policy matured she became seventy-two pounds richer. A couple of conmen, Eastham and Wade, saw her with the money and, posing as roofing inspectors, demanded that she make repairs to her chimney. Minnie worried herself sick until Eastham offered to carry out the repairs for her. Then, when he was alone at No.5, he stole the money. Minnie was devastated. Ena Sharples promised that God would avenge her, and the residents raised five pounds in a whip round.

It was while he was placing a bet for Minnie with bookmaker Dave Smith that Albert Tatlock found himself in the middle of a fight. Two thugs, Phil and Eric, were terrorizing the cashiers and when Albert attempted to stop them he was knocked unconscious. The residents were shocked by his injuries and backed Ena in her battle to have the betting shop closed down. She started a petition to have Dave's licence revoked, but Dave persuaded her to drop her action by 'sorting out' the thugs and paying Albert twenty-five pounds in compensation.

6 Barlow Brothers' Despairing Wives

Ken Barlow was incensed when the council refused permission for students to hold an anti-Vietnam meeting at the Town Hall. It took place regardless, and Ken joined in. The police were called and Ken was charged with taking part in a banned demo. He refused to pay a fine and instead opted to spend seven days in prison. Both his wife Val and brother David were horrified by his decision and, reminding that him he had responsibilities to his family, urged him to ignore his principles for once. He refused and PC Conway led him away to Strangeways, leaving Val to face the loneliest week of her life.

The local rate-payers' association admired Ken's fortitude and decided to ask him to stand for the council. Unfortunately they contacted the wrong Barlow. David was pleased to be asked but his wife Irma was horrified at the thought of being married to a councillor because it sounded dull and threatened to leave home if he stood. Instead, David took an evening job managing the Weatherfield Hotspurs, a female football team. Irma was alarmed to discover how attractive its captain, Beryl Thom, was, and joined the team to keep an eye on David. During her first game she strained a ligament, which ended her short football career.

Irma and Val swapped jobs for a day to prove that the other had an easier life. Irma allowed the twins to run riot, calling it self-expression, and said there was nothing to being a mother. Just a few months later she announced her own pregnancy but tragically miscarried in the fourth month. She felt she would never be able to have children so she and David signed up to become foster-parents. At Christmas they took in eleven-year-old Jill Morris while her mother went to hospital. The experience was good for Irma and she decided she was ready to try for another baby.

7 Elsie and Dot Go Yanking

Elsie Tanner was deceived by a stranger, Percy Bridge, after he introduced himself as the man who had rescued her grandson Paul from the canal. Elsie showed her gratitude by taking him to bed, before Dave Smith produced Paul's school cap to prove

that he was the rescuer. Len Fairclough saw off Bridge and Elsie started an affair with Dave. They went on holiday together, which upset Len who still carried a torch for her. Elsie didn't like to see him jealous so she ended her relationship with Dave. She didn't stay single for long, though, as the American army and air force returned to Burtonwood after a twenty-two-year absence. Elsie's friend Dot Greenhalgh was delighted to find her wartime lover Gregg Flint in town, and his young friend, Gary Strauss, fell for Elsie and dated her, even though he was twenty years her junior.

Elsie's heart leapt when she learnt that her own wartime sweetheart, Steve Tanner, was at the base and longing to see her. At first she was reluctant to meet him, fearing she was no longer the young girl he had loved, but Dot and Gregg threw the pair together and the Tanners rekindled their love as Len and Dave snarled in the sidelines.

A month later, when Steve was assaulted in his car outside Dave Smith's shop, Dave was the natural suspect. Nothing could be proved, though, so Gregg and Steve decided Len was the guilty party and attacked him. Elsie stopped them from knocking him unconscious by telling them that Dot's husband Walt had attacked Steve, thinking he was Gregg.

8 The Swedish Connection

Dennis Tanner followed his mother's example by celebrating the summer of love. He fell for au pair Inga Olsen and gave her English lessons. When she was summoned home to Sweden he resigned from Gamma Garments and took a barman's job on a ferry running between Immingham and Gothenburg, which enabled him to see Inga once a week. A couple of months later he returned, but instead of Inga he brought with him her sister Karen and announced to an amused Elsie that he loved her more than her sister. Karen moved into the front parlour at No.11, and Dennis wrote to the Swedish consulate, in the name of Steve Tanner, saying that he was employing Karen to look after his children. When officials called, Dennis borrowed the Barlow twins and paid Lucille Hewitt to pose as his wife. However, the officials saw through the charade and Karen was sent to work in Putney.

To earn a crust, Dennis took a series of jobs – sandwich-boardman, ice-cream seller, cleaner and taxi driver. After Elsie left to get married he also turned No.11 into a boarding-house, taking in a six-piece girls' pipe band and then a family of acrobats. The mother of the group, Mrs Cook, took advantage of Dennis's easy-going nature and dominated the household. Dennis feared she'd never leave but the formidable woman packed the family's bags when she discovered that one of her sons had a heavy crush on Val Barlow. Dennis's final lodger was his grandfather Wally who used the house as a social club for OAPs and depressed everyone by talking about his imminent death. It was not long before Dennis was at the end of his tether and sent the old man back to Dennis's father, Arnold.

9 A Limited Company

While employed as bookkeeper at the building firm, Emily Nugent discovered the accounts were three hundred pounds out. Jerry Booth was furious when Len Fairclough confessed to investing the money in a property deal which he had then lost out on. To make sure it didn't happen again Jerry insisted that he and Len became a limited company with equal shares.

The firm suffered another blow when Len's estranged son, Stanley, arrived on a visit and started a fire in the yard only to be trapped by the flames. Len tried to rescue him but was overcome by smoke. A passer-by dragged them both to safety. Afterwards Len recovered in hospital and Stanley returned to Nottingham.

Minnie Caldwell felt sorry for lonely Jerry and tried her hand at matchmaking, pairing him off with librarian Sally Frost. Sally fell for Jerry but had a complication in the shape of a boyfriend. Jerry had no wish to upset the apple cart and backed out of the relationship, leaving Sally believing that her boyfriend had seen him off.

10 Elsie's Fairytale Wedding

Gregg Flint thought Elsie was too common to marry his pal Steve Tanner, but Steve refused to listen and bought her a diamond engagement ring. Whilst Elsie planned a big white wedding her neighbour Hilda Ogden became jealous of her good fortune and had a nervous breakdown. She disappeared in her slippers, and husband Stan was asked to identify the body of a woman found in the canal. To his relief Hilda was found safe wandering in Liverpool still in her slippers.

The Ogdens were both invited to the Tanner wedding, as were all of the other residents. The ceremony, attended by the Cheveskis and the Hewitts from Ireland, took place in a Methodist chapel in Warrington. Dennis gave the bride away, and at the reception afterwards Annie Walker got drunk and flirted outrageously with the American servicemen. On the way to the reception Len Fairclough's van broke down. Harry Hewitt tried to mend it but the jack gave way – and he was crushed to

death beneath it. His widow Concepta and daughter Lucille were devastated.

The Tanners honeymooned in Lisbon then settled into a smart apartment in Altrincham. Elsie felt out of place in the huge flat and found herself befriending her neighbour's charwoman who, she felt, was more on her level. Steve's mother Emmeline paid a visit and declared Elsie a social disappointment. Soon the couple had started to argue over the way Elsie insisted on maintaining her links with Coronation Street and cracks appeared in the marriage. Hoping for a fresh start, on Christmas Day the newlyweds flew out to a new life in America.

11 Emily Searches For a Man

Emily Nugent shocked her neighbours by joining a marriage bureau. Her first date,

on her birthday, was with farmer Frank Starkie. She viewed his seventy-acre holding in Clitheroe but was forced to finish with him when she discovered she was frightened of his dairy herd. Her next introduction was to hotelier Douglas Preston. His sister Amy saw Emily as grasping and worried she would take Douglas away from her. Emily gave Douglas the confidence to stand up for himself and stop Amy running his life, but she ended the relationship anyway: she made Douglas see that all he'd ever wanted was to escape Amy, not find a wife.

12 A Hostile Street

Ena Sharples entered the Street in the council's Best Kept Street competition. The other residents weren't interested until they heard of the hundred-pound prize money. Annie Walker attempted to take charge and ordered Hilda Ogden to scrub all the brickwork by hand. When they embarked on tidying up No.3, which was empty, the residents discovered a family of squatters living there. Betty Lawson had been made homeless after her husband's death and had broken in to provide shelter for her two young sons. Val Barlow felt sorry for her and gave the family money and food, but Ken, looking after his father's property, demanded their eviction. During the judging of the competition, the authorities descended and forcibly evicted the family, dragging the children off to a home.

To Ena's fury Inkerman Street won the competition but her mind was soon occupied by the news that the Mission of Glad Tidings, her home for thirty years, was to be demolished.

CAST

PC Jimmy Conway	Colin Edwynn
Henry Foster	Norman Shelley
Audrey Hargreaves	Polly James
Bert Tate	Oliver MacGreevy
Harry Eastham	Ken Jones
Johnny Wade	Noel Davis
Phil Ferguson	Geoffrey Hughes
Eric Briggs	Leslie Southwick
Beryl Thom	Anna Summerfield
Jill Morris	Linda Cook
Mrs Cook	Jesse Evans
Percy Bridges	Jack Smethurst
Gregg Flint	Bill Nagy
Gary Strauss	Callen Angelo
Steve Tanner	Paul Maxwell
Walt Greenhalgh	Derek Benfield
Inga Olsen	Gabrielle Drake
Karen Olsen	Jennie Woodford
Stanley Fairclough	Ronald Cunliffe
Sally Frost	Morag Hood
Emmeline Tanner	Stella Bonheur
Frank Starkie	Mark Hignett
Douglas Preston	John Baddeley
Amy Preston	Katherine Parr
Betty Lawson	Eve Pearce

1968

Behind the Scenes

> I'm just a thing now; a thing you've got. And all you're interested in is keeping it polished. And if anything happened to me you wouldn't lift a finger to help me. Because you don't love me. You love yourself!
>
> **Val Barlow to husband Ken**

In January the frontage of Coronation Street houses was erected in Manchester at the junction of Water Street and Grape Street – behind Granada Television and now the entrance to the Granada Studios Tour. The actors were not keen on traipsing to and from the studio so usage of the new lot was kept to a minimum.

The modernisation of the show started with the shooting of a new titles sequence, while the stories were planned to be controversial and aimed at a young audience. Teenage actors Nigel Humphries and Gillian McCann were introduced, but the prospective black family never made it to the screen, and instead of the show being flooded with fresh faces and new storylines, all that happened was that the new, younger actors were soon involved by 'old' storylines. Humphries and McCann played young lovers Dickie and Audrey who eloped when she was just sixteen. When they moved into the Street they were meant to challenge established values but the writers shied away from using them in such a way and their stories became staid.

Neville Buswell was reintroduced as Ray Langton after his popular début in 1966, and an opportunity arrived to introduce a new family at the Corner Shop. Originally a pregnant Emily Nugent was to take the helm with her blind Hungarian lover, but after viewers showed an interest in gamekeeper George Greenwood, played by Arthur Pentelow, it was suggested that he should be the new shopkeeper. Eventually a new family was introduced in the shape of the Cleggs, alcoholic Les, herbalist Maggie and studious Gordon. West End actress Irene Sutcliffe, cast as Maggie, was an instant hit with the viewers as she started a six-year stint behind the counter. Twenty-two-year-old Liverpudlian Bill Kenwright was cast as her son, Gordon, and the Street's first male pin-up.

The Mission and the warehouse were demolished to make way for seven modern maisonettes, which were meant to bring a cosmopolitan feel to the show, with a chorus of new faces to occupy them. When it came down to it, though, the Barlows and Ena occupied two, and only one other was given a new resident, Effie Spicer. The remaining four stayed empty as the casting budget had dried up, a situation that didn't change for the three years of the maisonettes' existence.

Key Dates 1968

April 1	Maggie Clegg first appears
May 29	Dennis Tanner marries Jenny Sutton
July 15	Dickie Flemming marries Audrey Bright
September 28	Steve Tanner is murdered

Top Twenty

Pos	Character	No of eps	Total	Pos Prev Year
1	Annie Walker	92	713	1
2	Len Fairclough	87	686	4
3	Jack Walker	84	700	2
4	Kenneth Barlow	77	589	14
5	Valerie Barlow	71	499	10
6	Elsie Tanner	69	694	3
7	Minnie Caldwell	68	607	16
8	Hilda Ogden	64	321	14
9	Stan Ogden	62	328	9
10	Ena Sharples	58	627	5
11	Emily Nugent	58	417	17
12	Maggie Clegg	58	58	–
13	Lucille Hewitt	57	453	10
14	Ray Langton	53	67	–
15	Gordon Clegg	51	51	–
16	Albert Tatlock	44	566	8
17	Dickie Flemming	37	37	–
18	Audrey Flemming	37	37	–
19	Dennis Tanner	34	462	10
20	Jerry Booth	34	379	6

STORIES

1 Homeless Ena

The demolition ball swung in Coronation Street to set in motion the council's redevelopment plans. Ena Sharples wept as the Mission of Glad Tidings was wiped off the map and the residents turned on Councillor Len Fairclough, calling him Judas. Minnie Caldwell took in her old friend Ena at No.5 but they soon fell out, and Ena moved to St Anne's to stay with Henry Foster. With Ena gone Minnie grew lonely and advertised in the Corner Shop for a male companion. She was persuaded by concerned neighbours to take down the card and instead started running a catalogue.

Ena was eventually rehoused in a ground-floor maisonette built on the site of the old Mission. She soon ran foul of the council by holding prayer meetings and annoying neighbour Valerie Barlow with her harmonium playing. When officials threatened to evict Ena she and Val came to an understanding whereby she could play between nine thirty and eleven thirty a.m., and between six and eight p.m. Minnie was a regular attender at the prayer meetings. She was very upset when her beloved cat Bobby went missing. Then Stan Ogden rescued a cat from the viaduct but it wasn't Bobby. However, on Ena's advice Minnie took in the stray and called it Sunny Jim.

2 Devil Worshippers at No.11

Lucille Hewitt persuaded Dennis Tanner to throw a New Year party at No.11. The guests turned out to be a group of hippies who, after the party, refused to leave and turned the house into a commune. Having fallen for the leader, Robert Croft, Lucille moved in with the group. Her guardian, Annie Walker, was horrified and notified the landlord that devil-worshippers had kidnapped her ward. Edward Wormold was quick to act, and as Dennis was behind with the rent, gave him notice to quit. Dennis called Annie an 'interfering old cow' and decided to move on with the hippies, but was stopped by the arrival of Jenny Sutton who appeared looking for her sister Monica, a member of the commune. Dennis found Jenny a job at the hotel where he was working as a waiter. When she was groped by bar steward Maurice Rowe, Dennis stood up for her and realized he loved her. When Jenny returned to her native London Dennis followed.

Later the couple returned to the Street and discovered Dennis's mother was in residence. Elise refused to let them share a bed, and Dennis responded to this by calling her a hypocrite: she'd slept where and with whom she'd liked. Jenny found lodgings with Minnie Caldwell and struggled to maintain the peace with disapproving Elsie, while Dennis took a job as sales representative with Crowning Glory, a company that traded in hairdressing sundries. He bought Jenny a zircon engagement ring, borrowing the money from a lender at 48 per cent interest. The couple were married in a register office, with Dennis's sister Linda and grandfather Wally in attendance. Elsie paid off Dennis' debts, and when he was promoted to Bristol the couple started a new life.

3 The End of the Fairytale

Following the collapse of her marriage to Steve, Elsie Tanner had returned to

England in March. She told Len Fairclough that as soon as they had reached the States her husband had ignored her and she had felt completely out of place in his world. Now she took a job at MacAverty's department store, in the food hall, and started driving lessons in a white Jag bought for her, then stolen, by her nephew and lodger Gary Bailey. Stan Ogden gave her an extra lesson but the car ran out of petrol on the moors. When the couple returned home at 7.30 a.m. Stan's wife Hilda accused Elsie of being after her husband. Elsie laughed in her face and told her she'd never be that desperate. When Gary left, Elsie took in Ray Langton as a lodger. She admitted to fancying him but was upset when he made a crude pass at her. When she called for help, Len beat him up for her.

4 Business is Good for Len

There were celebrations in the Mawdsley Street building firm when Len and Jerry won a contract to work on the new maisonettes being built on Coronation Street. Jerry hoped it would be the start of something big and re-employed Ray Langton as plumber. Len, however, liked things as they were and had no plans to expand. Edged out by Ray, Stan Ogden resigned from the firm and was taken on as general labourer on the site. He didn't last long in his new part: he dropped a partition from the second floor level, narrowly missing workmen below, and was then sacked. Len felt sorry for him and took him on again, which caused the other workmen to down their tools in protest. Hilda was unhappy to hear her Stan described by them as a 'useless liability', but Len came up with a solution: Stan would work on small jobs away from the site.

All this time Jerry's mind wasn't on his work: his estranged wife Myra had turned up, looking for a reconciliation, just days before their divorce became absolute. Jerry refused to take her back but she called Jack Walker as a witness to say that he had seen her in Jerry's room, in her nightie, first thing one morning. This was true, but Jack told Jerry he was willing to commit perjury to help him out. In the end Jerry told the court that he had refused to go to bed with Myra despite her attempt at seduction. In May he decided he had had enough of Weatherfield and left for pastures new.

In order to expand the business premises, Len knocked down his Mawdsley Street house and moved into No.9 Coronation Street, having bought it from Ken Barlow for a thousand pounds. Ray Langton became his lodger.

5 Emily's First Love

The demolition of the old factory and the Mission Hall caused quite a bit of excitement. This was mainly due to the arrival of demolition expert Miklos Zadic. He was a Hungarian who had escaped during the 1956 uprising and now sought intellectual stimulation. Emily Nugent supplied it, but not before he'd become a hero by rescuing the Barlow twins from death as they cowered inside the factory during demolition. Then he was cast as villain: Albert Tatlock accused Miklos of stealing his precious coin collection, until a casual site worker was unmasked as the thief. Emily surprised the neighbours by revealing her sensual side when she embarked on a relationshop with Miklos.

They talked of Communism and danced barefoot to folk music, but he grew frustrated when she refused to have sex, holding out for marriage. When he was transferred to Newcastle Emily realized she had little time left to show her love, and they went away together on holiday to Scotland. On her return Emily confided to Val Barlow that she had no regrets.

Emily moved into lodgings at the Rovers Return and found herself helping out occasionally behind the bar. When Mr Papagopolous went bankrupt she lost her position at Gamma and took a job at the local import-export company where she soon realized her bosses were on the fiddle. She informed the police then resigned, and started helping out in the nursery at St Mary's Church. To raise money for the church she directed a production of *Aladdin*, and pressed the residents to appear in it. In another good turn Emily took in Dolores, the donkey belonging to rag-and-bone man Tommy Deakin. She stabled Dolores in the Rovers' yard believing Tommy to be in hospital. She wasn't pleased to discover that he was really holidaying in Majorca.

6 The Barlow Brothers Move On

As he stood behind the counter of the Corner Shop every day David Barlow felt his life was in a rut. Behind his wife Irma's back he started to play football again and was thrilled to discover that his old knee injury had healed. A team in Australia offered him a contract but Irma refused to consider leaving England and slapped his face when he put it to her. However, her mother, Hilda, was much taken with the idea of a fresh start, but then Stan put his foot down and refused to leave Weatherfield. Slowly Irma was won over; she was pregnant, and the idea of living in a hot country with plenty of opportunities was too tempting to pass up.

David had trouble selling the shop as prospective buyers were put off by all the redevelopment in the area. He gave an interview to the *Gazette* about the move, hoping a potential buyer might read it. Eventually someone came forward and Hilda bade a tearful farewell to the Barlows as they headed for Sydney, where their eight-pound son Darren was born in November.

David's brother, Ken, was also on the move. He had sold No.9 and moved across the cobbles to a nice new two-storeyed maisonette. Val was delighted with her new home but her tranquillity was shattered when an escaped prisoner, Frank Riley, broke in while Ken was out, directing a production of *The Country Wife* at college. A terrified Val was held hostage by Riley. She managed to raise the alarm by banging on the water pipe to Ena in the flat below. The police were summoned and burst in to overpower Riley, who urged Val to confirm that he hadn't touched her. She did so but Ken refused to believe she hadn't been raped and was tormented about how he, a pacifist, should react in such a situation.

After this, the Barlows settled into a life of domesticity. Val took a job as assistant at the Corner Shop, while Ken took up playing the trumpet.

7 Embarrassment for Annie

The Walkers rang the changes in the Rovers when they removed the old beer pumps from the bar and replaced them with nozzles. Annie also had the pub decorated in Silver Buckingham wallpaper, although the brewery refused to pay. She had to dip into her own purse again after students kidnapped her for rag week. They demanded a five-pound ransom but the regulars only came up with a penny and that was from her husband Jack.

Annie's feelings were further bruised after she was asked to attend a meeting of the Lady Crusaders and deliver a speech on 'Fifty Years of Women's Suffrage'. Annie spent days preparing for it, and was humiliated on arrival at the event to discover they had thought she was social commentator Alice Walker.

8 Hilda Blossoms

One day, when out walking the Barlow twins in the park, Hilda Ogden befriended park-keeper George Greenwood and was thrilled when he flirted with her. She became a regular visitor to George's shed where she sat drinking tea and admiring his

budgie, Winston. Then George's wife, Agnes, found Hilda's scarf in the shed. Far from being upset she was delighted. She tracked Stan down, told him of Hilda and George's liaisons and explained that George was always at it, there was nothing to worry about. She urged Stan not to confront Hilda, telling him that a guilty spouse is an attentive one. Stan discovered this to be true as Hilda ran round after him and fed him his favourite foods. It was only when Hilda found out that Agnes had visited Stan that she ended her stolen moments with George: she feared Stan was being unfaithful.

9 A New Family, An Old Secret

In April Barlow's Provisions was bought by Les and Maggie Clegg. They were natives of Weatherfield and looked upon the purchase of the shop as a fresh start. Their seventeen-year-old son, Gordon, was a studious lad, and the customers took an interest in the range of herbal remedies stored by Maggie. But behind the convivial

mask the family presented to the customers lurked the reason why they had moved from one address to another: Les was a violent alcoholic. He had promised Maggie he would give up the drink but shortly after moving into the shop he came home drunk and smashed the window. Maggie remonstrated with him and was slapped across the face. Incensed, Gordon struck out at his father and knocked him unconscious. Les recovered in hospital but that was the end of the Clegg marriage. He sought psychiatric help while she filed for divorce.

Gordon fell in love with Lucille Hewitt but she had eyes only for Ray Langton. Her problem was Ray's girlfriend, Shirley Walton. Ray told the girls to fight it out between them, and Lucille saw off Shirley but then decided Ray wasn't worth it and annoyed him by going out with gentleman Gordon. On Gordon's eighteenth birthday Ray dared him to prove his manhood by getting drunk in the Rovers. Maggie was disgusted and scolded Annie Walker for serving her boy alcohol. After this, Lucille decided that Gordon was a mummy's boy and went out with American GI Gary Strauss. This prompted Gordon into action: he won Lucille's heart by fighting Gary for her then proposing to her. To both Maggie's and Annie's horror, the pair announced their engagement and eloped to Gretna Green. They returned unwed as their train had been delayed, but their gesture forced their parents to take their intentions seriously. Gordon sat his exams on mercantile law, while Maggie started a relationship with Len Fairclough.

10 Class Wars

Ena Sharples settled into her new maisonette at No.6 and took an instant dislike to her neighbour at No.4, a retired woman called Effie Spicer. Effie offended Ena with her airs and graces and by hanging out her washing on the Lord's Day. She was the widow of a well-known sports writer but had fallen on hard times. She also turned out to be an old girlfriend of Jack Walker's, and Annie could not conceal her discomfort at 'Jonty's pleasure in finding his old dancing partner living in the Street. Ena didn't help by announcing gleefully that she'd caught the pair dancing to an old record. Effie was no threat to Annie – she was pleased to have found a friend in her new environment – but Annie warned her off and Ena continued to be unpleasant: she had resented Effie's middle-class status. After putting up with the hostility for a couple of months, Effie told Ena she'd won and that she would leave her flat. Ena was surprised to discover that the other woman had been so affected by her attitude and was immediately repentant: she held out an olive branch in inviting Effie to join her in the Snug.

Effie lost the last of her savings when she had to pay off a dead relative's debts; her television was repossessed and she was forced to beg Maggie Clegg for credit. Ena was helping out at the shop, found the slate book and upset Effie by giving her advice on how to eke out her pension.

11 Young Love

Eighteen-year-old Dickie Flemming was an engineering apprentice with an old head on young shoulders. While his friends hung around the cinema and pubs, Dickie saved his money, and when he had five hundred pounds in the bank he started to look for a house to buy. He took an interest in No.9 but couldn't afford the amount Ken Barlow was asking. Instead Ken offered him his father's house, No.3, which had been empty since 1964 and was going for four hundred pounds. Dickie bought it and used the rest of his savings to furnish it. Then he eloped to Gretna Green with his sixteen-year-old girlfriend Audrey Bright and, as man and wife, they moved into No.3. A week after getting married Audrey left school and took a job as a petrol pump attendant to become their main breadwinner. Dickie befriended Ray Langton, who caused the couple to have their first row when he suggested that Audrey enter a beauty competition. Dickie didn't like the idea but Audrey went ahead and won fifty pounds and the title Miss Petrol Pump 1968.

12 Trench-foot Albert

Albert Tatlock was an old soldier, a Great War veteran, and interested in anything relating to the war. Ken Barlow bought him a book on the battle of Lys, which Albert read then announced that the author had got his facts all wrong. Ken offered to put the record straight by writing Albert's account of the battle for the *Gazette* and invited all Albert's old comrades to reminisce with him.

It soon became apparent that Albert didn't know what he was talking about: he'd missed the battle after getting lost on patrol. Nevertheless he had seen plenty of other action and was pleasantly surprised to receive a visit from his old Sergeant, Harry Dunscombe. Harry told the residents that Albert had saved his life in the trenches and in gratitude he offered Albert a job as resident curator of the Fusiliers Museum in Bury. Albert happily accepted and left the Street, with Effie Spicer living at No.1 where the rent was cheaper than it had been at her maisonette.

Later in the year Albert returned for a holiday and invited himself to stay with the Flemmings at No.3. Audrey tried in vain to get rid of him, eventually succeeding after taking Ena Sharples's advice and inviting his old flame Alice Pickens to call. One sight of amorous Alice was enough to send Albert running back to Bury.

13 Cleanliness Next to Godliness

Stan Ogden left the building yard after buying a window-cleaning round from I-Spy Dwyer for forty-five pounds. Straight away he found the new job too demanding and persuaded Hilda to help him by suggesting that the bored housewives bothered him. While Hilda worked away on the windows Stan found a housewife he didn't mind being bothered by: Clara Regan at No.19 Inkerman Street. After a couple of weeks Hilda collapsed through overwork, so Stan cleaned at the Rovers for her until she had recovered.

Jill Morris arrived in the Street looking for David and Irma Barlow who had looked after her when her mother was in hospital, not knowing they were now in Australia. Hilda took the girl in and hid her from Stan, fearing that he'd object to her presence. However, Stan was delighted to have Jill in the house and was as sad as Hilda when she returned home. December found the Ogdens celebrating their twenty-fifth wedding anniversary: they threw a party in the Rovers and Stan presented his delighted wife with a fun fur.

14 Who Killed Steve Tanner?

The Americans returned once more to Burtonwood, and Gregg Flint visited Elsie Tanner to plead with her to talk to her estranged husband Steve. Elsie decided to tell him she wanted a divorce, but on her way in a taxi to see him she heard over the car radio that Len Fairclough had also ordered a cab to go to see Steve. Elsie told her driver to turn back to Weatherfield, and the next day the police called to say that Steve had been found dead at the bottom of a flight of stairs. Elsie panicked and gave Val Barlow as an alibi, saying they'd spent the evening talking. Val covered for her but the police saw through

the pretence and warned Elsie that she was in serious trouble. Elsie felt certain that Len had killed Steve, and he was arrested and questioned. He told the police that he had fallen out with Steve over his treatment of Elsie, had gone to hit him but had struck the wall instead. They insisted he take part in an identity parade but when he was not picked out by the witness Len was released. However, the police told him that he and Elsie remained the prime suspects.

Dot Greenhalgh was furious when her boyfriend Gregg was forced to give an alibi and revealed he'd been out with another woman. Steve's colleagues Gary Strauss and Joe Donnelli were also questioned and gave each other alibis. The police discovered Steve owed bookie Dave Smith a thousand pounds and he, too, was questioned, but eventually the coroner's court returned an open verdict on the death.

Dave bought the Gamma Garments premises on Rosamund Street and opened a florist called the Pink Posy Bowl. He employed Elsie as manageress, made Lucille Hewitt her assistant, then took Elsie away for a holiday in Wakefield.

Upset that Elsie could abandon him so soon after the investigation, Len disappeared with the petty cash from the building firm. Ray Langton struggled on with the work but lost some important contracts. When Len returned three weeks later, he offered Ray a partnership, which Ray turned down.

Len had been followed home by landlady Marj Griffin, with whom he had had a fling while staying at her pub. Her husband Basil came after her and dumped her belongings, including Marlon, her pet monkey, on Len. Marj declared her love for Len, who immediately felt trapped. Hoping to scare her off, on Ray's advice he proposed marriage – and was aghast when she accepted.

Aladdin

The residents put on a performance of *Aladdin* to raise money for St Mary's Church. It was produced and directed by Emily Nugent

Aladdin.................................Lucille Hewitt
Princess Balroubadour...............Audrey Flemming
Wishee Washee........................Hilda Ogden
Genie............................Albert Tatlock
Emperor Ming..........................Reverend James
Empress................................Annie Walker
Widow Twanky.......................Stan Ogden
Abanazer...............................Len Fairclough
Slave Girls...........Elsie Tanner,
Maggie Clegg, Marj Griffin

CAST

Robert Croft	Martin Shaw
Monica Sutton	Angela Pleasance
Jenny Sutton Tanner	Mitzi Rogers
Maurice Rowe	Philip Anthony
Gary Bailey	Warren Clarke
Miklos Zadic	Paul Stassino
Reverend James	Eric Dobson
Tommy Deakin	Paddy Joyce
Frank Riley	Sean Caffrey
George Greenwood	Arthur Pentelow
Agnes Greenwood	Kathleen Helm
Maggie Clegg	Irene Sutcliffe
Les Clegg	John Sharp
Gordon Clegg	Bill Kenwright
Shirley Walton	Stephanie Turner
Effie Spicer	Ann Dyson
Dickie Flemming	Nigel Humphries
Audrey Bright Flemming	Gillian McCann
Harry Dunscombe	Henry Longhurst
Alice Pickens	Doris Hare
I-Spy Dwyer	Roy Barraclough
Joe Donnelli	Shane Rimmer
Marj Griffin	Marjie Lawrence
Basil Griffin	David Daker

1969

Behind the Scenes

The nature of British television changed dramatically in 1969 with the arrival of colour. The Street's producer, H.V. Kershaw, had started planning their most ambitious storyline to date months before the change came to the Street in November: the whole cast were to spend a weekend on location, filming the Street's outing to the Lake District when the magnificent scenery would be shown off in its autumnal blaze of colour. However, when it came to it, the cameras used on the programme couldn't cope with the new colour stock and the trip was filmed in black and white. It ended with a coach crash, and the next episode, when the residents were in hospital wards, was the first to be transmitted in colour. It was all a bit of an anticlimax, and this first colour episode now looks rather strange: it contains some black and white inserts.

Now that Elsie Tanner was free of her American marriage, the decision was taken to marry her to Len Fairclough and knock their neighbouring homes (Nos.9 and 11) into one. However, the actors felt that marriage would ruin their characters' unique relationship and Kershaw introduced another element into the equation. He gave Elsie a new man, Alan Howard. Geordie actor Alan Browning was cast in the role, fresh from his role as the heart-throb in BBC's *The Newcomers.*

Another newcomer was Betty Driver. During the 1940s she had been a big band star and had three starring film roles under her belt. She had retired and was running a pub in Derbyshire when Kershaw tracked her down and suggested that if she was pulling pints they might as well be in the Rovers.

Top Twenty

Pos	Character	No of eps	Total	Pos Prev Year
1	Elsie Tanner	89	783	6
2	Hilda Ogden	89	410	8
3	Emily Nugent	85	502	10
4	Jack Walker	81	781	3
5	Annie Walker	81	794	1
6	Ena Sharples	81	708	10
7	Stan Ogden	77	405	9
8	Ray Langton	77	144	14
9	Len Fairclough	76	762	2
10	Valerie Barlow	72	571	5
11	Ken Barlow	62	651	4
12	Minnie Caldwell	62	651	7
13	Maggie Clegg	62	120	10
14	Audrey Flemming	60	97	17
15	Dickie Flemming	57	94	17
16	Betty Turpin	57	57	–
17	Albert Tatlock	50	616	16
18	Lucille Hewitt	43	496	13
19	Cyril Turpin	43	43	–
20	Dave Smith	32	73	27

> "You know what your trouble is, Stan? You're lax – lax from the neck up and relax from the neck down."
>
> **Hilda Ogden**

Key Dates
1969

June 2	Betty Turpin's first appearance
November 24	First colour episode transmitted
December 1	Alan Howard's first appearance

STORIES

1 Ray's Kid Sister, a Crooked Bookie and an Unpaid Debt

Ray Langton managed to free landlord Len Fairclough from his unwanted engagement by passing off two local lads as Len's sons. Marj Griffin refused to become a mother to them and quickly returned to her husband. Len was grateful for Ray's intervention and gladly allowed his younger sister Janice to stay at No.9. Janice was on the run from her probation officer and upset Ray by making a play for Len. She then used her friendship with Len as a cover for her affair with Borstal boy Bob Neale, and together they stole Dave Smith's Jag from its parking place in the Street. Ray found the car and returned it, which made Dave suspect he had stolen it in the first place. He demanded the return of five hundred and fifty pounds in cash that had been in the car, and Len threatened to sack Ray if he

didn't give back the money. Ray caught Janice sharing the cash with Bob and took it from them, then threw her out of No.9. As Len and Dave suspected him of stealing the money anyway, he decided to run off with it but Ena Sharples stopped him and talked him into returning it to Dave.

Dave enjoyed throwing his weight around the Street and when Minnie Caldwell fell into debt through gambling with him he demanded repayment of the ten pounds she owed. Dave's girlfriend Elsie Tanner asked him to go easy on her so he agreed to wipe the slate clean until Ena badmouthed him in the Street and he changed his mind. However, Ena guessed correctly that the five hundred and fify pounds came from a tax dodge and confronted him with this, whereupon he offered her hush money and agreed to forget about the ten pounds. Meanwhile, fearful Minnie disappeared, leaving a note begging someone to take care of her cat. Ena and Dave joined forces in organizing the residents to search for her but Ena broke down, fearing her friend would kill herself. After two days Minnie was located in hospital where she'd been taken after living rough. To please Elsie, Dave made a fuss of Minnie and put a limit on her gambling.

2 Bigoted Annie Walker

The Walkers were delighted to receive a visit from their son Billy, who brought his girlfriend Jasmine Choong to stay. Annie was charming to Jasmine until she discovered that Billy was planning to propose to her. There was no way Annie was having a Chinese daughter-in-law so she staged a breakdown: she collapsed behind the Rovers' bar and took to her bed. Then she told Billy she was dying and begged him to find a more suitable wife. The Rovers' paying guest, Emily Nugent, saw through Annie's play-acting and told Jasmine that the landlady was an old fraud. However, Jasmine refused Billy's marriage proposal and left after telling Annie that she had nothing to fear: there was no way her family would allow her to marry into a bigot's family. Billy was furious with his mother, accused her of wrecking his happiness and vowed never to set foot in the Rovers again. Annie blamed Emily for her son's reaction and threw her out of the pub. Elsie Tanner took pity on her and moved her into her back room, but realized she'd made a mistake when Emily started to moralize about Elsie's relationship with Dave Smith. Both Annie and Emily were relieved to make the peace and Emily returned to the Rovers.

Annie annoyed the customers by entering a brewery competition to find the perfect landlady. In an attempt to win customer approval she started cooking hot-pot and installed a telephone in the bar for their convenience. Jack was astounded when Annie won the competition but enraged her by refusing the prize of a holiday in Majorca, saying that he couldn't fly. In anger Annie invited Ena Sharples to accompany her and was horrified when she accepted. After a week Ena returned alone and told Emily that Annie had spent the whole time in the company of brewery representative Douglas Cresswell. Annie had given Ena a letter for Jack but Ena refused to hand it over, fearing that Annie had written of her infidelity. Two weeks later an irate Annie returned, wondering why Jack hadn't contacted her. She revealed that Cresswell had offered the Walkers the chance to run a pub in Spain. Ena and Emily were mortified to discover they had stood in the way of the Walkers' future, but the couple were denied the pub anyway because of Jack's age.

3 Stan's Busy Year

Restless Stan Ogden embarked on a year of get-rich-quick schemes that all went wrong. First he entered the world of antiques and bought Albert Tatlock's sideboard for five pounds, only to discover it couldn't be removed from the house as it had been built *in situ*. Then he set Hilda up as a clairvoyant and rushed around drumming up trade by ensuring that her predictions came true. After he received a bill from the Inland Revenue relating to his window-cleaning business he took a job as barman at the Rovers, but spent all his wages on beer. To avoid the tax he made the business over to Hilda and was horrified when she sold it – and his services – to Ray Langton. After that he became a street photographer with Marlon the monkey as a prop but gave that up when the animal bit Dave Smith. When his bike was run over by a steam-roller Stan took up junk sculpture and was offered a solo exhibition, but all his 'works of art' were taken away by the binmen. Finally, his daughter Irma Barlow, home on a visit from Australia, told him she despised him for sponging off Hilda and not making an honest living.

4 Trouble for Maggie

Gordon Clegg caused upset in the Street when he jilted fiancée Lucille Hewitt while she was trying on her wedding dress. He decided he was too young to marry and left for London, where he found work as an accountant. Lucille was devastated by his departure and, on the rebound, made a pass at Dave Smith after starting work at his betting shop. Dave made her see that she was just trying to hurt Gordon and turned down her advances. Annie Walker was furious that anyone could break an engagement with her ward but Gordon's mother Maggie was delighted. The only upset for her was that Gordon was no longer around. However, his room was taken by Maggie's older sister, Betty Turpin, who moved into the shop with her husband, Cyril, a police sergeant.

Betty took a job as barmaid at the Rovers, and showed off her skills as a champion darts player. Annie took an instant dislike to her and sacked her for incompatibility. However, as Jack had employed her, Betty refused to leave and Annie was forced to accept her presence behind the bar.

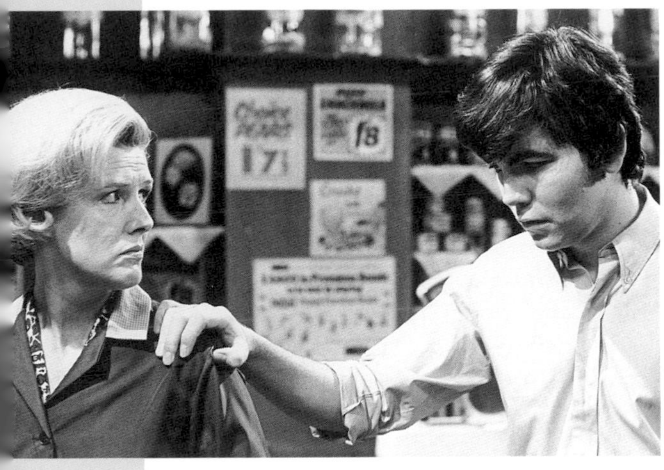

Betty had a domineering personality and sister Maggie soon tired of having her under her feet. To give herself a break she stayed at No.9 while Len Fairclough was working away from home. Ena Sharples found her in the house in her nightwear and started a rumour that she'd been sleeping with Len. Len invited Maggie to move in with him but she refused as she was still legally married. Ena tried to use her knowledge of Maggie and Len's relationship to blackmail him into voting against a plan to build on the site of an old cemetery where her grandfather was buried, but Len turned the tables on her by announcing in the Rovers that his and Maggie's relationship was platonic.

5 Dickie Runs With the Devil

Audrey Flemming celebrated her eighteenth birthday at No.3 with the knowledge that she had run up a two-hundred-pound bill on hire purchase. Dickie decided that it was unmanly to be financially dependent on his wife so gave up his apprenticeship at a local engineering company to work as an engineer at an amusement arcade. Local thug Eddie Goulden threatened Dickie with violence unless he rigged the machines to pay out for him, and Dickie didn't know how to react. In the event he was sacked for being an easy touch. He took a labouring job at a building site until the residents convinced him that it would be better to carry on with his apprenticeship.

While Dickie was struggling, his friend Ray Langton left Fairclough's and started up his own building firm. He moved into No.3 as lodger and took on Audrey as his secretary. Dave Smith became a sleeping partner in the business by investing two thousand pounds and Ray started to land good contracts. His old flame Lucille Hewitt grew jealous of his relationship with Audrey and spread rumours that they were having an affair, which led Dickie to throw him out of the house.

It was only once he'd left the Flemmings' that Ray decided he had strong feelings for Audrey and set about wooing her. During the Street's outing to Windermere he took her to a secluded spot and she allowed him to kiss her. Dickie found them together, threw a punch at Ray, and ended up in a brawl with him. On the way home the coach crashed and Ray was flung through the windscreen. In hospital he was diagnosed as having transversemyelitis and was warned he might never walk again. As a result Dickie took pity on him and moved him back into No.3, where Audrey devoted her time to nursing him.

When Dave cancelled his partnership Len took Ray back at his yard.

6 The Executive Family

Ken Barlow swallowed his socialist principles and sold his car to pay for his wife Valerie to have a private operation on her knee. While she was in hospital he invited her mother, Edith Tatlock, to stay so that she could look after him and the twins. Edith took the opportunity to suggest that Coronation Street wasn't really in keeping with Ken's position as a professional man. She ignored Val's protests and took them round a show house on a new estate. Ken was taken with the idea but Val refused to leave her roots. Then Edith and Val had a major falling out after Edith lost the twins during an outing to Belle Vue amusement park. Five hours later they turned up safe and sound but Val accused Edith of incompetence and told her to go home.

Val had a further shock when Dave Robbins, the man for whom she'd once left Ken, visited them. Ken was keen to rebuild his friendship with Dave but Val didn't trust him. Her suspicions were proved right when he helped a homeless family to break into one of the maisonettes and squat there. Val called the police and insisted they were evicted.

7 Bridegroom Albert

Effie Spicer decided to brighten up No.1 by decorating it but was furious when her landlord, Albert Tatlock, put her rent up, saying she now had more pleasant surroundings. She refused to play his games and left the Street to live with her niece, giving the house keys to Alice Pickens who moved in with her mynah bird Kitchener. There was outrage in the Street when Albert refused to let Alice stay and dumped her belongings on the pavement. Minnie Caldwell took her in, and the residents boycotted a trip to Albert's museum to reinforce their disapproval of him. Later, Alice arranged a visit to the museum, which so startled Albert that he fell and broke his arm. He was forced to give up his job and go home to recover. After the doctor threatened to have him put in a home, Alice moved in to nurse him, and Albert soon realized that having Alice around to cook and look after him was a blessing. He proposed to her and Alice eagerly accepted.

Albert's daughter, Beattie Pearson, and Alice's son, Douglas, were quick to arrive in the Street to find out their parents' motives, each suspicious that the other was after their inheritance. Albert and Alice put them straight by pointing out that neither of them had any money. With their children's blessing the couple prepared for their wedding. The Barlows agreed to be best man and matron-of-honour, and Albert got drunk on his stag night. He ended up clinging to a lamp-post singing 'If I Ruled The World'. However, although both bride and groom turned up at the church in time, the vicar had a puncture and was late. Alice took this as a divine sign and called off the wedding. She went on honeymoon to Morecambe alone.

To take his mind off his disappointment, Albert agreed to train the Rovers' football team in their match against the Flying Horse. On the eve of the match he attempted to kidnap the Flying Horse's mascot, Tommy Deakin's donkey Dolores. His plan was scuppered, though, when Dolores trod on star striker Stan Ogden's foot. The Rovers team – Len, Cyril, Betty, Dickie, Audrey, Stan and Hilda – eventually

won the match even though Hilda scored an own goal.

8 Militant Ena

When the local pensioners' clubhouse was threatened with demolition, Ena Sharples rallied the troops and organized a sit-in at the council offices. She was carried away by the police and cautioned, but the protestors won and the hut was reprieved.

Minnie Caldwell had been a key figure in Ena's over-sixties gang, acting as look-out at the sit-in. She became confused about her cat's name and, on Ena's advice, changed it from Sunny Jim to Bobby. She herself caused even more concern when she was knocked out during the Street's outing to Windermere. Ena prayed by her bedside non-stop for thirty-six hours before her old friend came round.

Ena gave up her maisonette when she became resident caretaker at Ernest Bishop's camera shop. She'd been friends with Ernest's mother, Carrie, and met him at Carrie's funeral. Emily Nugent was also there and, after meeting Ernest, agreed to work at his shop on the condition that he allowed Ena to move into the flat above it.

Ena enjoyed having premises to look after again, but realized her ability to judge character had dulled after she disturbed an intruder in the middle of the night. His name was Cliff Stone and he told Ena he was just trying to retrieve some money he'd left under a floorboard when he had worked at the shop. Ena gave him the benefit of the doubt – until she discovered the petty cash was missing. The police eventually caught up with Stone after he robbed a post office.

9 A New Start for Emily

Emily's friendship with the Reverend Mr James came to an end when she realized it wasn't going anywhere. He had grown disillusioned with the lack of community spirit in the area and she was forced to agree with him when the church was vandalized and the residents only turned out to help put it straight when she offered to pay them.

She started work at Ernest Bishop's camera shop and was flattered by the attention of Douglas Pickens. He showered her with gifts and made a pass at her, having been told her name was Elsie Tanner and that she had a racy reputation. Once the mistake had been sorted out Douglas left to rejoin the navy and Emily was left to ponder what might have been.

As well as working at the camera shop, Emily continued to help out behind the Rovers' bar. At the end of the year she was indignant to discover that Annie Walker suspected her of stealing a valuable brooch, lent by her friend Mrs Hepplewhite. When Annie accused Betty Turpin and Hilda Ogden of the theft they downed tools and walked out. Then, Emily revealed that the brooch hadn't been stolen: its owner had taken it back in Annie's absence. To make up to Betty and Hilda, Annie bought them each a pair of tights.

10 Elsie's Strange Affairs

Dave Smith was startled when his estranged wife Lilian arrived in town and announced that she was divorcing him and citing Elsie Tanner as co-respondent. He panicked when he discovered he might lose a third of his income in a divorce case and decided to fight it, dragging Elsie's name through the courts. Lilian paid Hilda Ogden to spy on the couple but eventually settled for a larger allowance from Dave. She introduced Dave to her crooked boyfriend, Leo Slater, and Elsie joined them all for a pleasant, civilized evening together.

Now that she had her inheritance from Steve Tanner, Elsie had money to burn. When she heard that Len Fairclough had asked to borrow money from Jack Walker, she gave Jack three hundred pounds to pass on to him. Len confided to Elsie that he intended to use the money to settle down as he had a new girlfriend. He introduced her to Town Hall clerk Janet Reid, who blurted out to Elsie that she didn't love Len and felt trapped by him. When Janet refused to marry him, Len accused Elsie of warning her off and slapped her face. Elsie disappeared, leaving Jack to give Len a good talking-to during which he told Len that the money he had given him was Elsie's.

Len tracked Elsie down to Sheffield where she was staying with her friend Sheila Crossley. He sold his van to repay her and brought her home, but she told him she couldn't forgive him for hitting her and that their friendship was over.

After a row over her time-keeping, Elsie walked out of the Pink Posy Bowl and was grateful when her old friend Dot Greenhalgh found her a job at Miami Modes. Leaving work one night with Dot's bag, Elsie was searched by Security. The bag was found to contain stolen dresses and Elsie was arrested. Frightened of going to jail, Dot begged Elsie not to involve her. Elsie maintained her innocence and the case was dismissed in court through lack of evidence. Both Elsie and Dot were sacked from Miami and Elsie told Dot she never wanted to see her again.

Having finished with Dave, Len and Dot, Elsie was at an all-time low when her niece and nephew, Sandra and Bernard Butler, arrived to cheer her up. Despite her objections, they moved into No.11 and took jobs in Alan Howard's newly opened hair-salon. Alan was a friend of Len's and had bought the Posy Bowl to transform it into a modern salon. He employed Valerie Barlow as head stylist and Elsie as manageress. While the other local women swooned over Alan, Elsie announced she wasn't impressed by his money and looks.

Coach Crash

Emily Nugent's Street outing to the Lakes ended in disaster when the brakes failed on the coach, which ploughed off the road and hit a tree. The coach driver died but luckily the passengers only sustained injuries:

Jack Walker Facial and head cuts; broken sternum
Annie Walker Shock and fractured jaw
Ena Sharples Forehead injury
Elsie Tanner Fractured wrist
Stan Ogden Broken ribs and elbow; sprained ankle
Hilda Ogden Bruised eye
Minnie Caldwell Dislocated wrist; loss of blood
Maggie Clegg Pelvic fracture and head injury
Betty Turpin Forehead injury
Cyril Turpin Cut and bruised face and head
Audrey Flemming Sprained ankle; cuts and bruises
Dickie Flemming Dislocated shoulder; knee injury
Albert Tatlock Broken arm
Ray Langton Spinal injury
Ken Barlow Dislocated shoulder; sprained wrist
Val Barlow Concussion
Emily Nugent Cuts and bruises

Talent Concert

Emily Nugent rallied the residents for an evening of fun and frivolity on Christmas Eve, throwing a concert in the Rovers Select:

Master of Ceremonies.........**Cyril Turpin**
Singing 'Drink To Me Only'...........**Emily Nugent and Ernest Bishop**
Reciting 'The Owl and the Pussycat'.......... **Minnie Caldwell**
Playing the Trumpet............**Ken Barlow**
As Hylda Baker and Cynthia............**Irma Barlow and Bernard Butler**
Reciting 'The Girl I Kissed On The Stairs'.......... **Albert Tatlock**
Singing 'Cockles And Mussels'........**Emily Nugent and Ena Sharples**

CAST

Janice Langton	Paula Wilcox
Bob Neale	Bob Keller
Jasmine Choong	Lucille Soong
Douglas Cresswell	William Fox
Betty Turpin	Betty Driver
Cyril Turpin	William Moore
Eddie Goulden	Bill McCabe
Edith Tatlock	Clare Kelly
Beattie Pearson	Gabrielle Daye
Douglas Pickens	John Collin
Ernest Bishop	Stephen Hancock
Cliff Stone	Douglas Livingstone
Lilian Smith	Rhoda Lewis
Leo Slater	Donald Morley
Janet Reid	Judith Barker
Sandra Butler	Patrica Fuller
Bernard Butler	Gorden Kaye
Alan Howard	Alan Browning

1970

Behind the Scenes

Celebrations for the thousandth episode of *Coronation Street* dominated the year, and the *TV Times* produced a special souvenir magazine to mark the event. June Howson took over as producer, after running the popular Granada drama *Family at War*. Her first task was to tell the actors playing the Butlers and the Flemmings that their contracts were not to be renewed. It wasn't all doom, though, as she insisted upon the return of Bet Lynch. Julie Goodyear had appeared in *Family At War* and impressed June with her talent. On discovering that Julie had played Bet in 1966, June placed her behind the Rovers' bar, where she was to remain for twenty-five years.

Patricia Phoenix wasn't happy with the idea of Elsie Tanner taking a third husband but was won round when she was told she could choose the actor. As Peter Falk wasn't available she opted for Alan Browning, and he was hastily brought in to the show for a quick register-office ceremony. However, the writers had to suddenly bankrupt him to keep the couple in No.11 rather than moving away, as had happened in 1967 when Elsie had married affluent Steve.

The programme's popularity was increasing abroad: it was now being shown in New Zealand, where it was the most watched television programme, Australia, Canada, Singapore, Gibraltar, Hong Kong, northern Nigeria and Holland, and was the world's most popular television programme.

The strain of appearing twice a week for ten years was showing in some of the longest-serving cast members. Executive producer H.V. Kershaw managed to persuade Pat Phoenix, Doris Speed and Violet Carson to stay in the show but failed to talk Anne Reid out of her decision to bid farewell to Valerie Barlow. Anne told them that her mind was made up and that, once gone, she would never return. The news was a blow to the production team, and June Howson says, 'I really did not want her to go. The Street goes on but it was one of the things I thought was a mistake. But she was determined.' The writers decided to save Ken Barlow, which meant Val had to die. Although the scenes were written at this point they were not recorded until the early days of 1971.

Top Twenty

Pos	Character	No of eps	Total	Pos Prev Year
1	Ena Sharples	70	778	4
2	Ray Langton	70	214	7
3	Annie Walker	69	863	4
4	Elsie Tanner Howard	67	850	1
5	Betty Turpin	65	122	15
6	Valerie Barlow	63	634	10
7	Len Fairclough	63	825	9
8	Hilda Ogden	63	473	1
9	Maggie Clegg	59	179	11
10	Irma Barlow	57	361	31
11	Ken Barlow	54	705	11
12	Emily Nugent	53	555	3
13	Stan Ogden	53	458	7
14	Alan Howard	53	63	28
15	Albert Tatlock	51	667	17
16	Minnie Caldwell	50	701	11
17	Bet Lynch	49	58	–
18	Lucille Hewitt	43	539	18
19	Billy Walker	35	85	30
20	Sandra Butler	35	49	25

> Elsie's a sparrow in a dirty street. She wouldn't survive in an aviary with birds of paradise. She tried it once and they nearly pecked her to death.
>
> **Len Fairclough**

The biggest blow to the cast, writers, producers and fans was the sudden death of Arthur Leslie, everyone's favourite landlord. His death, from a heart-attack, at the age of sixty-eight, shattered the close group of actors. Doris Speed issued a statement saying, 'The qualities of sweetness and kindness which came over in Jack Walker came in fact from Arthur Leslie.' Three thousand fans lined the streets in Lytham to pay their respects as the funeral cortège passed. The Archdeacon of Lancaster conducted the ceremony and summed up the character of Jack Walker: 'The man with the bowler hat and the overcoat on, going down the Street to someone in trouble, and the simple, kindly, "I thought you might like to talk, it sometimes helps to get it off your chest," was the character of a good man who wants to do good things.'

Key Dates 1970

April 8	David Barlow dies in Australia
April 9	Darren Barlow dies in Australia
June 30	Arthur Leslie dies while holidaying in Wales. He appeared in 807 episodes as Jack Walker
July 8	Jack Walker dies in Derby
July 22	Elsie Tanner marries Alan Howard.
August 24	1,000th episode transmitted
December 12	Joe Donnelli kills himself

STORIES

1 Len's Troubled Love-life and Emily's Dilemma

Len Fairclough started the year by growing a moustache and turning his thoughts to romance. Maggie Clegg made certain he knew she was available after she had started divorce proceedings against her estranged husband Les. However, Len favoured young Flying Horse barmaid Anita Reynolds, and proposed to her. She accepted, but he changed his mind when he discovered that he was the same age as her father. He suggested they settle for a long engagement but she broke with him, determined to be a married woman.

Emily Nugent, as Len's bookkeeper, found herself in a dilemma when local businessman Willie Piggott threatened to cancel the lease on her new boyfriend Ernest Bishop's camera shop unless she spied on Len for him. Piggott was interested in a tender Len was putting in for a student-hostel contract. Against all her principles, Emily went through Len's files

and gave Piggott the information he wanted. Piggott promptly put in his own tender at a lower rate and renewed Ernest's lease. Emily was stunned when the contract finally went to another local firm, Roscoe & Pitts, after Len, guessing what was going on, tipped them off and sold them materials they needed to take the job on.

2 Audrey Causes Waves

Ray Langton stunned the residents, and himself, by stepping out of his wheelchair to play darts. The doctors told him he would gradually regain the use of his legs and he started to make plans for the future, going into partnership with Len Fairclough. Elsie Tanner's niece, Sandra Butler, fell for Ray and proposed to him. He accepted, but said he would not marry until he could walk again. Then he employed his old flame Audrey Flemming as his secretary, which upset Sandra, who realized that Audrey still had a crush on him.

After spending a month at a special clinic, Ray regained the full use of his legs and thrilled Sandra by booking St Mary's for 23 May. Audrey was also pleased to see him up and about and kissed him, telling him she'd always loved him. Maggie Clegg was embarrassed to see the kiss and urged Audrey not to be unfaithful to Dickie, but Audrey refused to listen to her. She decided that Dickie was boring and that Ray was everything she wanted. Ray was flattered by the attention and admitted to Audrey that he loved her. His ex-girlfriend Lucille Hewitt found out about the affair and ran to Dickie with the news. Dickie refused to let Audrey make a fool of him again and packed his bags. As he left the Street he told Sandra what had been going on behind their backs. Sandra was devastated and her angry brother Bernard took Ray by surprise in the Rovers and thumped him, whereupon Audrey threw herself at Ray and was furious when he said he didn't want her any more. She left the Street to move in with her mother in Preston.

With Audrey out of the way, Ray looked forward to marrying Sandra but she told him there was no way she could trust him again and broke the engagement. A few weeks later she, too, left the Street.

3 Elsie's Third Husband

The Street gossips had plenty with which to occupy themselves when Elsie Tanner and her boss Alan Howard decided to remain good friends rather than embark on a romance. Ena Sharples and Annie Walker exchanged wry looks and speculated on

how long that state of affairs would last. Alan led a fast life, but Elsie didn't understand just how strong her feelings were for him until she heard he had been involved in a crash while driving his racing car. Luckily, he walked away from the wreckage, but then found his feelings for Elsie tested by the arrival of her old flame Bill Gregory. Bill had sought out Elsie to tell her his wife was dead and that he was buying a wine bar in Portugal. He pleaded with her to join him in the venture as his wife. Elsie was tempted but Bill left alone when Alan told her he didn't want her to go. However, any romantic ideas she might have had flew out of the window when Alan told her he was buying a house in Bramhall and wanted her to live with him, but not as his wife. Elsie felt that if he wasn't prepared to marry her he couldn't love her so she turned him down. Regretfully, Alan sold the hair-salon to Dave Smith and returned to his native Newcastle. Elsie continued to work at the salon as manageress – but had gone off men.

Months later, when Alan returned, he found her bitter and depressed, and was shocked by the way she'd let herself go. He startled her by proposing to her and, after initially rejecting him, she agreed. He didn't give her the chance to change her mind and married her a week later, by special licence. The residents threw a surprise reception for the couple before they flew to Paris on honeymoon. Soon after their return the bubble burst for Elsie when Alan confessed to being insolvent, and owing over five thousand pounds. She was forced to take a job selling door-to-door for Charm Cosmetics, while Alan found employment as a mechanic at the Canal Street garage.

A month into the marriage, Elsie was stunned when Alan's teenage son, Mark, turned up on the doorstep – she hadn't known he existed. While Alan made the lad welcome, Elsie encouraged Lucille Hewitt to date him. Lucille reported back that Mark was disturbed and dangerous. When he overheard Elsie flirting with Len Fairclough, Mark told his father that the pair were having an affair. Elsie ordered Mark out of the house and was annoyed that, although he went, Alan sided with him.

4 An Unhappy Return

Tragic news from Australia put the Street in mourning: a car crash had resulted in the deaths of David Barlow and his baby son Darren. Dave Smith lent the Ogdens six hundred pounds so that Hilda could fly out to comfort her bereft daughter Irma, but Ken shocked the residents by refusing to attend his brother's funeral. He said it would be a waste of money.

When Hilda returned, she brought Irma back with her and when Irma confessed that the accident had been her fault, Ken was furious and took her to task.

Well-wishers sent enough money to the Ogdens for them to pay back Dave, but instead Stan gave him the deeds to No.13 and used the cash to buy Irma a partnership in the Corner Shop.

Irma moved into the flat above the shop with her old friend Bet Lynch and started to rebuild her life. She caused a storm by going out with Dave, but dropped him when she discovered her parents only approved of him because he held the deeds to their home. When bumbling Bernard Butler made a play for her she told him she wasn't interested so he packed his bags and returned home to Saddleworth.

Everyone thought Irma had recovered from her loss, but she was still grieving privately for her son and kidnapped a local baby, Anthony Lock, from outside a post office. She convinced herself Anthony was Darren but Bet returned the baby to his mother then revealed to Irma that she had a son of her own, who had been adopted when she was just sixteen, at which Irma broke down.

5 Devious Stan and Desperate Hilda

Stan Ogden gave up window-cleaning to take a job as nightwatchman at Holmes' bakery. He enjoyed his new position as he

could spend the days drinking and his nights at a local strip-club rather than working as no one was around to check up on him. When Hilda found out, she was so furious that she reported him to his bosses.

After he discovered that Ena Sharples wrote songs, Stan stole some of her tunes and, passing himself off as a songwriter, sold them to club entertainer Mickey Malone. The songs went down well and Stan was commissioned to write more. However, when Ena chanced to hear Malone singing one of her compositions, 'Dreaming Time', she realized what had happened. In revenge she gave Stan another song which, when Malone played it, turned out to be 'Onward Christian Soldiers'.

Eager to earn a few extra bob, Stan allowed Tommy Deakin to lodge his greyhound, Duke, at No.13. Hilda took a fancy to the dog and, thinking him too thin, fed him up – only to discover she'd ruined his racing potential. She went on to ruin the Corner Shop too when she took over the business to give Irma and Maggie a holiday. All went well until it came to ordering stock: unsure about regular suppliers, she placed a large order with a firm dealing in exotic goods. No one wanted to buy the fancy fayre so she was forced to hold a sale. When Irma returned she found the business twenty pounds down.

6 All Change at the Rovers

The news that Jack Walker had died of a heart-attack while visiting his daughter in Derby saddened the residents. They rallied round Annie and urged her not to retire but to take on the Rovers' licence herself. She did so, but only after her son, Billy, agreed to move up from London to live at the pub. However, he refused to become a landlord and instead bought the Canal Street garage to continue working as a mechanic. He upset Annie by going out with the common Irma Barlow and when Annie attempted to see her off the pair hatched a plan: they let Annie think that Irma was pregnant with Billy's baby.

Although Emily Nugent had helped out behind the bar for a number of years now, she decided to stop when her associates on the Mission circuit disapproved. Betty Turpin continued to work at the pub although she had had an unnerving experience when one of the customers, Keith Lucas, had stalked her.

Lucas was fresh out of prison and wanted revenge on Cyril Turpin, the policeman who had arrested him three years before. Betty tried to ignore Lucas but when he trapped her in her own home she broke down. Cyril found out and attacked Lucas, continuing to hit him when he was unconscious. Cyril told his superiors that he had lost control and resigned from the force, taking an office job as a clerk.

7 Ena's Blind Date

Minnie Caldwell found herself an object of desire when wealthy Handel Gartside returned to his native Weatherfield after an absence of thirty-three years. He met up with Minnie in the Rovers and admitted he had always had a crush on her. Ena Sharples was put out when the couple started spending time together and Minnie became worried that Ena would try to split them up. She asked Handel to find a date for her friend. As a result, ex-professional boxer George Mulliner joined the trio at a fancy tea-room. Ena didn't take to him and annoyed Minnie by flirting with Handel. Minnie was disappointed when Handel assured her that his intentions towards her were honourable, but she stood up for him when Albert Tatlock presented him with a white feather, having discovered he had

been a conscientious objector during the First World War.

Meanwhile, Ena had started to spend time with another male – twelve-year-old Tony Parsons. She discovered him playing the harmonium in the Victoria Street Mission, realized he had talent and marched him off to the local college of music where she talked the principal into giving him a scholarship.

8 Bet Arrives

Bet Lynch started drinking in the Rovers again, after an absence of four years. She moved into the flat above the Corner Shop with Irma Barlow and took over as manageress of the Laundryer on Rosamund Street. Around the time of her arrival, two

ex-jailbirds turned up looking for their mate Ray Langton. Frank Bradley and Jud Johnson swore they were reformed characters and talked Ray into giving them work. Against his better judgement, he employed them to build a display cabinet for Ernest Bishop's shop. While there, the men stole an expensive camera and threatened to blame Ray unless he helped them pull off a robbery. Ray managed to return the camera and was grateful when Ken Barlow frightened off Frank and Jud by posing as a policeman.

Bet wasn't bothered by Frank's past: she threw herself at him and embarked on a passionate affair with him.

When Billy Walker caught Frank using his garage as a cover to rig stolen cars, he threatened to bring in the police but Bet persuaded him to drop the matter by promising to keep Frank on the straight and narrow. At nineteen, Frank was nearly half Bet's age and she worried that he might leave her so she tried to steer him towards a permanent relationship but he felt hemmed in and left town, leaving her heartbroken. She moved into a bedsit of her own, at 44 Victoria Street, and took a new job – as barmaid at the Rovers Return.

9 Lucille's Good Causes

Annie Walker was pleased when her ward, Lucille Hewitt, announced her intention to work with the less fortunate. She became a helper at the Salvation Army and was assigned a difficult pensioner, Arthur Noblett, to look after. Arthur resented Lucille's interference and kept her locked out of his house for days before finally letting her in to clean it. She offered to have his old radio repaired and took it to Billy Walker who succeeded in wrecking it. Lucille offered Arthur a television in its place but he was adamant that he wanted his radio and threatened to report Lucille for incompetence. Ena Sharples eventually sorted him out by giving him her old radio, and Lucille resigned from the Salvation Army.

Then she turned her attention to a group of gypsies who were camped on a slum clearance site. Ray Langton and his friends were hostile towards them and wanted them moved on but Lucille befriended them and helped them with a sick child. Reuben Ward and the Smith family headed up the camp and were grateful for her help, but when Ray suspected Reuben of stealing scrap from his yard, he arranged for his mates to attack the camp. Lucille was caught up in the fight that ensued. The police were called and

moved the gypsies on, which so enraged Lucille that she threw a brick through a police car windscreen. She was arrested and spent a night in the cells before being released with a caution.

10 Domestic Problems for the Barlows

When Alan Howard decided to sell his hair-salon on Rosamund Street, his chief stylist, Valerie Barlow, thought her ship had come in. Alan agreed that she could buy it but he needed four hundred pounds down on the deal. Val's husband Ken asked Dave Smith for a loan but when he refused Ken cashed

CAST

Anita Reynolds	Elizabeth Sladen
Mickey Malone	Bill Maynard
Keith Lucas	David Webb
Frank Bradley	Tommy Boyle
Jud Johnson	Neil Kennedy
Handel Gartside	Harry Markham
George Mulliner	Fred Crossley
Tony Parsons	David Hill
Mrs Parsons	June Brown
Arthur Noblett	Jack Woolgar
John Smith	Shane Connaughton
Ellen Smith	Maggie Steed
Reuben Ward	James Donnelly
Mark Howard	Nicholas Jones
Joe Donnelli	Shane Rimmer
Jean Mosley	Lois Dane

in the family's insurance policies to raise the money. In the meantime, alerted to the sale of the salon, Dave approached Alan and bought it from him. Ken fumed when Dave thanked him for tipping him off. Valerie resigned herself to never being a boss but was satisfied when Dave gave her a pay-rise, with commission.

The Barlows' domestic arrangements were upset when the local women went on strike after the men supported the idea of a rowdy football bus calling in the Street. Annie Walker organized a petition, which all the women signed. Valerie told the women to withdraw all services for the men but in retaliation Ken organized the men into a male commune. Eventually the women won their case when they sent in their secret weapon, Elsie Tanner, to use her sexual charms to weaken the male reserve.

There was drama in the Barlow household when little Susan suffered stomach pains. The doctor felt nothing was wrong but Susan was rushed to hospital with acute appendicitis and had to undergo emergency surgery. Thankfully she pulled through and Ken celebrated by buying a second-hand Mini to take the family out for trips.

Valerie wasn't happy, though, when he took a sabbatical in New York to study education techniques. In his absence she persuaded Ray to give her driving lessons. She was terrible behind the wheel but enjoyed his company. The neighbours started to gossip about their relationship, and Emily Nugent went as far as to write to Ken and warn him about the situation. When Ken phoned to confront her, Valerie was furious and assured him everything was above board.

11 The Return of the Yanks

Female hearts beat faster towards the end of the year when the Americans returned once again to Weatherfield. First to arrive was Joe Donnelli. He moved into No.5 as Minnie Caldwell's lodger, telling her that he had been demobbed. Shortly afterwards Gregg Flint and Gary Strauss were in Weatherfield to look for him: he had deserted. While he was in town, Gregg took Maggie Clegg out while Bet Lynch threw herself at Gary. Joe also enjoyed some feminine company when he became Irma Barlow's lover.

Gary and Gregg grew anxious when they heard reports that Joe had put a German woman in hospital. Then an ex-girlfriend, Jean Mosley, tracked Joe down and demanded compensation for the bruises he had inflicted on her. At this point Irma tried to back out of the relationship but he turned on her with a pair of scissors and told her he had killed Steve Tanner two years previously. He admitted that he'd owed Steve money through gambling, and when Steve had demanded repayment Joe had broken his neck. Irma was terrified that she would be his next victim but managed to call for help when he held her captive in her flat. Gary and Gregg took control and freed Irma, but Joe took sanctuary at Minnie's, holding her at gunpoint. The police and the army cordoned off the Street while Ena Sharples prayed for the safety of her oldest friend. Stan Ogden heard that Joe was frightening Irma and confronted him at Minnie's, unaware that he had a gun. Joe's response was to release Minnie and force Stan to sing carols at gunpoint. Stan obliged, but half-way through 'Silent Night' Joe turned the gun on himself and blew his brains out.

1971

Behind the Scenes

Anne Reid's departure, amid the flames of her gutted home, stunned viewers who had looked upon Valerie Barlow as a friend. They had felt an affinity with her as they watched her struggle to look after the twins and pander to Ken's ego. Her departure was the most publicized and mourned since that of Lynne Carol's Martha Longhurst in 1964. The writers toyed with the idea of having Ken emigrate, unable to live in the same Street any more, but they decided to keep him on to follow the struggles of a man bringing up young children on his own.

Another departure, towards the end of the year, was Sandra Gough, whose personal problems had affected her work as Irma Barlow. A storyline involving Irma's affair with Alan Howard had to be hastily rewritten when Sandra suddenly left the country. Janet Reid was brought back to woo Alan and gave viewers a fantastic showdown with Elsie.

The writers took advantage of Valerie Barlow's death to demolish the maisonettes, which had never really fitted into the fabric of the show. There had been seven flats in the complex but only three had ever been inhabited and in 1971 only the Barlows lived in them. They were replaced by a community centre and warehouse, returning the programme to its roots of meeting place and sweatshop. New faces included Lynne Perrie as Ivy Tilsley (originally credited as Tyldesley), fresh from her acclaimed performance in the film *Kes*, and Thelma Barlow as Mavis Riley. Originally Mavis was to have appeared in only one episode but she was such a hit with the writers and viewers that in 1972 she was given another episode before becoming a full-time member of the cast in 1973.

> "Life turns out to be just a bloody cheat, and I can't even whimper."
>
> **Ken Barlow**

Key Dates

1971

January 21	Valerie Barlow electrocutes herself
February 8	Last black and white episode transmitted
June 14	Ivy Tilsley's first appearance
August 14	Mavis Riley's first appearance

Top Twenty

Pos	Character	No of eps	Total	Pos Prev Year
1	Stan Ogden	77	535	12
2	Annie Walker	76	939	3
3	Len Fairclough	75	900	6
4	Elsie Howard	74	924	4
5	Hilda Ogden	69	542	6
6	Betty Turpin	68	190	5
7	Ray Langton	67	281	1
8	Bet Lynch	67	125	17
9	Ken Barlow	63	768	11
10	Emily Nugent	62	617	12
11	Maggie Clegg	62	241	9
12	Lucille Hewitt	60	599	18
13	Alan Howard	58	121	-
14	Minnie Caldwell	56	757	16
15	Irma Barlow	55	416	10
16	Ena Sharples	53	831	1
17	Albert Tatlock	52	719	15
18	Alf Roberts	42	88	-
19	Billy Walker	40	125	19
20	Ernie Bishop	30	54	33

STORIES

1 Housekeepers Wanted

Ray Langton and Len Fairclough advertised for a housekeeper and were forced to choose between a sensible woman who was a good cook, and a curvaceous blonde, who was hopeless about the house. As far as the men were concerned there was no contest and bubbly Gina Fletcher was employed. Ray and Len ignored the fact that she was useless but were furious to discover she was entertaining her boyfriend in No.9 while they were at work. Gina was sacked but Hilda Ogden found employment when she fussed over Albert Tatlock, believing him to be wealthy. He allowed her to cook and clean for him for a week before revealing he was penniless.

2 The Howards' Hard Times

When Elsie Howard refused to fire a sales representative who had suffered a breakdown she found herself dumped by Charm Cosmetics. Alan was annoyed as he needed Elsie's salary to help pay off his debts.

The couple decided to have some fun when, with Billy Walker and Irma Barlow, they borrowed the mayoral Rolls-Royce which was at the Canal Street garage for servicing. They drove out to the Brookside Motel, which Annie Walker had been asked to open on behalf of the brewery, and were mistaken for the mayoral party. As Annie had been putting on a pretence herself she couldn't rat on them for merely doing the same so the Howards enjoyed pretending to be the Mayor and Mayoress. This joy-ride was the only fun the Howards had in 1971.

Elsie celebrated too soon when she landed the job of checking supervisor at the new warehouse, built on the site of the maisonettes. When she refused to give Hilda Ogden a job, Hilda told her bosses about Elsie's 1969 appearance in court on a shoplifting charge. As a result, Elsie was suspended from work, and Hilda was snubbed by the residents. Maggie Clegg and Annie Walker called on personnel manager Dennis Maxwell and pleaded Elsie's case so successfully that she was reinstated.

Elsie's checkers, Ivy Tilsley and Edna Gee, suspected her and Dennis Maxwell of being more than work colleagues and spread rumours that reached Alan's ears. However, Dennis's interest in Elsie did not extend to her body: he thought she was an experienced thief and asked her to join him in stealing from the company. She refused, and was relieved when he was moved to the Solihull branch.

Alan took over the management of the Canal Sreet garage from Billy, with 15 per cent of the profits as his salary. He was amused when Elsie suspected him of infidelity with a woman interested in buying a car, but less so when she uncovered his real romance with shop assistant Janet Reid. Elsie discovered that the pair had spent a night together in a

Leeds hotel, confronted Janet and saw her out of town. Weeks later Elsie was offered promotion in Solihull but Alan refused to let her take the job, fearing that Maxwell was behind the move. The Howards' marriage was rolling down a slippery slope and on New Year's Eve Alan walked out on Elsie.

3 The Courting of Annie Walker

Annie Walker found herself facing prosecution when officials discovered the gin she was serving had been watered down. The pub emptied of customers and the staff were given a week's notice. Annie feared losing her licence but Len Fairclough saved the day when he overheard drayman Arthur Burrows boasting that he'd watered the gin because Billy Walker had stopped him fiddling the Rovers books. Len took Burrows to the police and the case against Annie was dropped.

Butcher Harold Dewhurst started to court Annie and persuaded her to join him on a cruise around the Mediterranean. Billy encouraged her to go, saying Jack wouldn't want her to mourn him for ever, but once on the ship Annie and Harold both fell for other people and parted as friends.

Then Annie turned matchmaker, hoping to marry Billy off to her friend Lorna Shawcross. Billy was keen and bought her a brooch but Lorna revealed she had a fiancée in Zambia and ended their friendship. Billy was upset by the break, moved south and bought a garage in Chiswick.

At the end of the year Annie attended a ball held to raise funds for the lifeboats. Although she found the comic Bernard Manning's jokes distasteful, she was charmed by Lieutenant Commander Gerald Prince and spent the evening dancing with him.

4 A Death in the Family

The Barlows began the New Year with the promise of a fresh start when Ken was offered a teaching job in Jamaica. To Albert Tatlock's distress he accepted it and the family prepared to emigrate. With Albert looking after the twins for the night, Ken waited for Valerie at their farewell party in the Rovers while she got ready. Although she knew the plug on her hairdryer was faulty, she plugged it in anyway and received a fatal electric shock. As she fell dying to the floor, she knocked an electric fire into a packing case and within minutes the maisonette was ablaze. Fire teams rushed to the scene, and Ken had to be held back when Val's body was removed from their gutted home.

After the funeral he moved into a hotel, and attracted the interest of receptionist Yvonne Chappell, but he soon left to move back to the Street where he rented No.3 from Audrey Flemming and settled in with the twins. Betty Turpin applied to become the children's nanny but Ken refused to employ her, thinking she'd smother them with too much affection. Instead he took on Margaret Lacey. She was a strict disciplinarian and Ken gave her a free hand with them. The residents worried as the children became moody and naughty, and Lucille Hewitt revealed that she remembered Margaret from when they both lived at the orphanage. She told Ken that Margaret was a sadist, but he refused to sack her. Instead Margaret resigned,

upset by the attention. Then Ken took on Bet Lynch to look after the children but Val's mother Edith moved into the house and, thinking Bet too tarty, got rid of her.

One of Ken's colleagues, Olive Rowe, took a fancy to him and threw herself at him but he wasn't interested. Instead he got drunk and made a fool of himself over nightclub hostess Candy Brown. She carried him home to No.3, upsetting Edith who announced he wasn't fit to be a parent. She decided to seek custody of the children and eventually Ken agreed that it would be best for them to move to Glasgow with Edith and her husband as his own life was so unstable.

Alone at No.3, he started a band with old friend Dave Robbins. He annoyed Albert next door with the loud music and was reported to the police by Albert's daughter Beattie Pearson. The police sent a constable to investigate the complaint but he turned out to be a keen guitar player and joined the set-up. Ken was indignant when the others decided he wasn't any good and formed their own group without him. When Yvonne Chappell re-entered Ken's life they started to go out together. Eventually he proposed to her but she turned him down, saying that while she'd love to marry him she knew that in his eyes she would only ever be a replacement for Val. They parted company and Ken decided to start afresh, leaving Granston Technical College and taking a job teaching English at Bessie Street School.

5 Ena Back in Charge

When the maisonettes were demolished, councillors Alf Roberts and Len Fairclough announced the news that a community centre and a warehouse would be built on the site. The residents opposed the idea of the warehouse, fearing it would turn the peaceful residential area into a busy industrial one. Emily Nugent and Lucille Hewitt led the protest and organized a sit-in on the building site. Emily was assaulted by builders, and in the local press Lucille was accused of riot. Eventually the protestors were defeated, and the warehouse, owned by the Mark Brittain Mail Order Company, was opened.

Ena kept quiet over the protest, hoping to be made caretaker of the community centre when it opened. She was interviewed for the post but lost out to Hetty Thorpe. So desperate was she for the job that she invited Hetty to tea and told her stories of vandals and rough neighbours. Hetty declined the job and Ena was duly appointed. She was thrilled to move into the caretaker's flat, which was on the site of the old Mission vestry. The centre was opened in memory of a dead councillor, Thomas Walsh, and was to be used by and for the good of the community. In the elections for the committee, Ernest Bishop lost the chairmanship post by one vote, although Emily and Alf were both elected to serve. Emily, shamefaced because of her protest, also accepted a job as clerk at the warehouse.

The first community event at the Centre was a flower show, where Albert Tatlock won the challenge cup for his blooms. Local business people judged the contest and Annie Walker was furious when a cartoon of her at the event was printed in the local paper. She gave Ernest a piece of her mind because he had drawn it, and accused him of being malicious. However her view changed when a friend asked for the original.

6 Ernest's Offence Against Morality

Ernest Bishop faced a dilemma when the Mission committee told him that if he wanted to remain a lay preacher he would have to marry. He decided that Emily Nugent was the woman for him and was delighted when she accepted his proposal. He bought a diamond engagement ring and panicked when he lost it in the Rovers. Thankfully it was found – in one of Stan Ogden's turn-ups – in time for the engagement party at the community centre. Emily's friend from the warehouse, Mavis Riley, became bitter at Emily's success in finding a husband while she was still on the shelf, and Ernest's sister, Edie Burgess, was furious when he cut the allowance he paid her each week. She tried to see Emily off but Ernest stood up to her and got rid of her instead.

Emily wasn't happy when Willie Piggott contracted Ernest to travel around the world taking photographs for his new travel agency business. She was upset that he would be photographing glamorous models, but Piggott reassured her, saying that the reason he had picked Ernest was because he had high moral standards, so Emily resigned from the warehouse to run the studio in Ernest's absence. Later, she was mortified to hear that he had been arrested in Santa Eulalia, charged with offending against public morality by taking photographs of topless models on a beach.

7 Unlucky Stan

Ray Langton decided to have some fun at Stan Ogden's expense after discovering that he had slept all night in a van when he should have been working as bakery nightwatchman. With Stan in the back Ray drove the van away and left it on wasteland where it was found by the police. Stan lost his job and attacked Ray, trapping him in the ladies' toilet at the Rovers. Ray sprained his wrist while escaping out of the window, but made peace with Stan by employing him at the building yard. Stan demanded more money and formed his own union, Stan Ogden District Union (SODU for short). He called in union representative Charlie Dickinson to fight his case against Len Fairclough and Ray and celebrated when Charlie persuaded them to pay him a pound over the union rate. Stan was thrilled until he discovered that Len and Ray had been paying him two pounds over the rate.

Stan and Hilda decided to move up in the world and bought a colour television set. However, as they didn't keep up with the payments it was repossessed. To cheer Hilda up, Stan constructed a serving hatch between the living room and the front parlour. Unfortunately he used designs for a works canteen and the hatch dominated the wall. Then the Ogdens celebrated a five-hundred-pound win on the Premium Bonds and Hilda planned to sell up and move but, against his principles, Stan used the money to repay Dave Smith what he owed him for Irma's share of the shop, receiving back the deeds to No.13. With the money they had left the Ogdens went on a spending spree and bought a cocktail bar for their house. Hilda threw a party, which was doomed to failure when Stan drank the alcohol beforehand and refilled the bottles with water. She was further embarrassed when he entered the centre flower show with an orchid he had stolen from the park. The judge turned out to be Hilda's old beau, George Greenwood, and she wished she'd gone off with him rather than staying with useless Stan.

8 The Return of the Bad Penny

After being mugged for the betting shop's takings while on her way to the bank Lucille Hewitt ended up in hospital with concussion. The residents were horrified by the assault and were furious when, blaming Lucille, Dave Smith sacked her. Bet Lynch was pleased when her ex-boyfriend Frank Bradley looked her up, but Lucille recognized his voice and told her that Frank had been one of her attackers. Frank asked Bet to keep quiet about his involvement in the attack, promising to show her a good time, but Bet felt guilty that Lucille had suffered so much and told Dave. Dave settled the matter by calling on Frank with a couple of heavies, and told Bet afterwards that Frank was no longer so pretty.

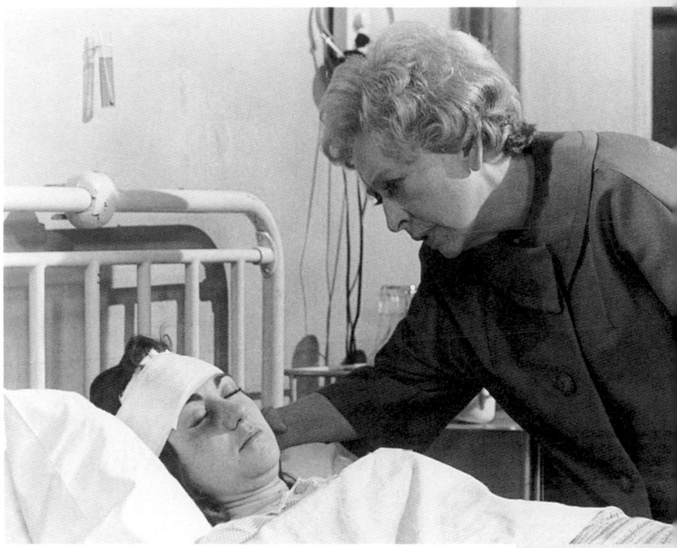

Lucille enjoyed being unemployed but her dole was stopped when she kept turning jobs down. Annie Walker threatened to make her move out if she didn't find a job so she went to work as a go-go dancer at the Aquarius pub, telling Annie she was working as a receptionist at the YWCA. However, she was spotted there by Annie's friend Nellie Harvey, who delighted in luring Annie to see the spectacle for herself. Outraged, Annie demanded that Lucille resign but she secured her job by writing a letter to the brewery, owners of the Aquarius, saying how much Annie disapproved. When Annie went away overnight Lucille and Bet entertained the regulars at the Rovers by go-going on the bar.

9 The Return of the Good Samaritan

Unemployed Jerry Booth returned to the Street after a three-year absence and was taken on at once by Len Fairclough and Ray Langton, who sacked Stan Ogden in his favour. Jerry refused to take Stan's job until they had assured him that Stan was useless and that they had planned to sack him anyway. Stan's friend Jim Stocker got at Jerry in the Rovers, accusing him of sucking

up to Len, and earning himself a thumping from Jerry in the process. Jerry was arrested for assault and went to court, where he received a twelve-month conditional discharge.

10 Maggie's Upset

Maggie Clegg was pleased when Alf Roberts started to show an interest in her but her enjoyment of their friendship was spoilt by her sister, Betty Turpin, who warned her not to get close to Alf as he was a married man. Her son, Gordon, now in London, also caused concern when he became engaged to Jennifer Swann, a snooty career girl. When Jennifer visited Maggie, she looked down her nose at the shop and the Street, and when she told Maggie that after the marriage she wouldn't be welcome in Gordon's life any more, Maggie broke down. Jennifer got her comeuppance when Ray Langton revealed her cultured manner to be fake: she had grown up in the same street as he had. Maggie was relieved when Gordon broke off the engagement.

11 Football Crazy

Irma Barlow found life behind the Corner Shop counter very boring and amused herself by pretending to be French. Ray Langton was so taken by this that he took her on a date to a club to impress a businessman who had a real French girlfriend. Ray hoped to go into partnership with Mel Ryan, selling saunas, but they fell out over Mel's bad workmanship and the dinner ended in a fight. The evening left Ray with a bill for damages from the club owner.

Romance entered Irma's life in the shape of county footballer and local personality Eddie Duncan. Irma demanded nights on the town but, as a result, Eddie's form suffered. Club chairman Dave Smith threatened to sack him if he didn't give Irma up, but before he could decide what to do Irma left town, telling Maggie she was going to start afresh in Wales.

Eddie wasn't alone for long as Bet Lynch jumped into Irma's shoes and his bed. Eddie's performance improved and he was promoted to play for Torquay. He invited Bet to leave with him but she realized that his true love was football, that she'd only ever be a poor second, and allowed him to go alone.

CAST

Gina Fletcher	Deirdre Costello
Yvonne Chappell	Alex Marshall
Arthur Burrows	Kenneth Jones
Harold Dewhurst	Stuart Saunders
Margaret Lacey	Josie Kidd
Olive Rowe	Anne Kristen
Candy Brown	Gwendolyn Watts
Dennis Maxwell	William Lucas
Hetty Thorpe	Marjorie Withers
Mel Ryan	Gareth Thomas
Ivy Tilsley	Lynne Perrie
Edna Gee	Mavis Rogerson
Lorna Shawcross	Luan Peters
Charlie Dickinson	Bill Owen
Mavis Riley	Thelma Barlow
Edie Burgess	Elizabeth Kelly
Jim Stoker	John F Landry
Jennifer Swann	Carolyn Lyster
Eddie Duncan	Del Henney
Bernard Manning	Himself
Lt Comm Prince	David Davies

1972

Behind the Scenes

At the beginning of the year Eric Prytherch replaced Brian Armstrong as producer and instructed the writing team to counterbalance the age of the Street's characters. After twelve years the longest-serving characters were past middle age and he thought the programme would benefit from an influx of younger women. Diana Davies was a northen actress, who had become a regular face on *Family At War*. When that series finished Prytherch snapped her up and cast her as shop assistant Norma Ford. She was followed by eighteen-year-old Anne Kirkbride, who had trained at Oldham Repertory Theatre. Like Diana she had been spotted in

Top Twenty

Pos	Character	No of eps	Total	Pos Prev Year
1	Len Fairclough	81	981	3
2	Elsie Howard	78	1002	4
3	Ray Langton	77	358	7
4	Billy Walker	76	201	19
5	Maggie Clegg	74	315	10
6	Jerry Booth	73	488	22
7	Annie Walker	70	1009	2
8	Alan Howard	70	191	13
9	Hilda Ogden	68	610	5
10	Emily Nugent Bishop	66	683	10
11	Betty Turpin	64	254	6
12	Ken Barlow	62	830	9
13	Bet Lynch	61	186	7
14	Stan Ogden	59	594	1
15	Ernie Bishop	59	113	2
16	Norma Ford	58	58	–
17	Lucille Hewitt	56	655	12
18	Ena Sharples	56	887	16
19	Minnie Caldwell	56	813	14
20	Alf Roberts	54	142	18

"They named a trifle after me at one Labour Club I played."

Rita Littlewood

a Granada programme, *Another Sunday and Sweet FA*, and given an episode as dolly-bird Deirdre Hunt. She proved an instant hit, and over the next year her part was built up as a possible love interest for Ray Langton.

1972 saw the return of Barbara Mullaney (in 1977 she married and changed her name to Knox) as Rita Littlewood. Barbara had recently retired from showbusiness after many years spent as a stooge to famous comedians. At first when she was asked to appear in two episodes as the mother of a schoolboy she refused, but her daughter talked her into taking the job as a final engagement. The writers were impressed by her performance and, realizing she'd appeared in an episode in 1964, gave her the same first name, Rita, and wrote her into more episodes. It was felt that she could fill the gap of 'sexy redhead' left vacant following Elsie Tanner's marriage to Alan Howard. The original description of Rita, written by Susan Pleat, spells this out: 'In mid-thirties. Very attractive in a blowsy way. A sentimental, good-time lady. Irresponsible, with muddled values, but in no way hard.'

In December life imitated art when Patricia Phoenix married Alan Browning, who played her screen husband. They had fallen in love soon after their alter egos married, but Pat waited until Alan's divorce came through before proposing to him. The bride wore purple velvet and was given away by executive producer H.V. Kershaw, the wedding march was composed by Stephen Hancock (Ernest Bishop) and writer Adele Rose was a bridesmaid, along with Irene Sutcliffe (Maggie Clegg). The happy couple spent their wedding night opening a bingo hall in Warrington.

Key Dates

1972

April 3	Emily Nugent marries Ernest Bishop
May 29	Norma Ford's first appearance
June 26	Alec Gilroy's first appearance
September 18	Phyllis Roberts dies of cancer
November 20	Deirdre Hunt's first appearance
December 23	Patricia Phoenix and Alan Browning marry at Etherow Methodist Chapel, Broadbottom in Cheshire

STORIES

1 The Rovers Return

Billy Walker found himself back in Weatherfield following the collapse of his Chiswick garage business. Annie was pleased to have him home and offered to pay his debts with the insurance money from Jack's death but he refused to let her. Instead he sold the Canal Street garage to Alan Howard and started to work full-time at the Rovers. The brewery were keen to keep him on and offered him the tenancy of the Rovers. When Annie found out, she called him Judas and refused to stand down in his favour. Billy turned down the tenancy and assured Annie that her position was safe so she left the running of the business to her son and started to socialize more with fellow landlady Nellie Harvey. They both competed for the attention of Licensed Victuallers' Association national president Ethne Willoughby when she visited the north, but Annie won her friendship by giving her a ticket to visit the famous Preston Guild.

Later, Annie suffered the humiliation of having her stomach pumped when it was feared she had taken too many sleeping tablets. Determined to put on a brave face, she thanked her customers for their concern and swore she felt ten years younger.

Annie and her ward Lucille Hewitt were delighted to receive a visit from Lucille's stepmother, Concepta, who told them of her plans to marry a younger man. Lucille took an instant dislike to Sean Regan and accused Concepta of using the business her father had built up as a snare to catch herself a husband. However, Concepta managed to convince Lucille that she genuinely loved Sean, but was unaware that he had taken a fancy to Bet Lynch and kissed her during his engagement party. Lucille decided to keep Concepta in ignorance and she returned to Ireland, happy to have her stepdaughter's blessing.

2 Business Booms for Alan

The Howards spent the New Year living apart but Elsie's attempts to milk Len for sympathy failed when he refused to comfort her or take her side. Without the familiar shoulder to cry on, Elsie cut short the estrangement and the couple were reconciled. Alan bought the Canal Street garage from Billy Walker, borrowing the money from his first wife, Laura. Elsie wasn't happy with the idea of being beholden to her, and she refused to allow Laura to write off the loan, much to Alan's annoyance.

Elsie's workmate Ivy Tilsley dumped herself on the Howards after finding her husband entertaining another woman. Ivy enjoyed herself at No.11 and started a liaison with storeman George Harrop. Elsie was reprimanded when work was disrupted while Ivy fought Edna Gee, who had spread rumours that Ivy fancied Alan, and was relieved when Ivy returned home. A more welcome visitor was eleven-year-old Paul Cheveski who came to stay with his granny Elsie. He exhausted her, though, and he attempted to poison Minnie Caldwell's cat, Bobby. Elsie was glad to see him go home

to Birmingham but Alan enjoyed seeing her maternal side.

When an old endowment policy matured, and Elsie found herself £296 better off, Alan insisted she spent the money on whatever she wanted, but regretted this when she had the bathroom painted black and a pink suite installed.

The garage business did well for Alan and he entered into a partnership with Jimmy Frazer, selling used cars. Elsie thought Jimmy was a bad influence on her husband and was annoyed when he introduced Alan to dolly-bird Deirdre Hunt, who promptly threw herself at him.

3 Emily Finally Marries

When Ernest Bishop was released from his Spanish jail he returned to Weatherfield sporting a beard. Delighted, Emily Nugent

pressed forward with their wedding plans, but was faced with a dilemma on what to do with her bedridden auntie May. She didn't want the old woman to live with her after the marriage, but hated to think of her alone. Ernest solved the problem by moving her into a nursing home. He sold his huge Victorian house, which Emily found too peaceful, and talked Audrey Flemming into selling No.3 to him. Ken Barlow, who had been renting the house,

graciously moved into the back room of No.1. Emily asked Ernest to shave off his beard for the wedding, and waited patiently with bridesmaids Bet Lynch and Lucille Hewitt while the groom suffered last minute nerves and had to be driven round and round Mawdsley Street Chapel several times before steeling himself for the ceremony. Esther Hayes returned to the Street for the wedding, and Emily's friend Mavis Riley enjoyed dancing with Jerry Booth at the reception. After honeymooning in Edale the Bishops settled into married bliss.

4 Enter Rita

Ken Barlow started a new job, teaching English at Bessie Street School, under headmaster Wilfred Perkins. Perkins wasn't keen on Ken's teaching techniques and warned him to take a firmer hand with the pupils. When twelve-year-old Terry Bates was continually late Ken kept him in after school, then discovered his mother used him to look after his younger sister. Rita Bates objected to Ken's interference but made it clear that she was attracted to him

and flirted with him at a PTA meeting. Perkins disapproved of Mrs Bates and ordered Ken to keep clear of her.

Rita moved on to Councillor Len Fairclough and went out with him because he was on the housing committee and her home was due to be demolished. Len was annoyed when she introduced him to her husband Harry but agreed to help them find accommodation. When she learnt they would have to provide a marriage certificate, Rita had to admit that she wasn't Harry's wife. Harry accused Rita of fancying Len, beat her up and threw her out. Len was appalled by her bruises, hit Harry and told him to stay away from her in future. Later, Rita revealed she was a night-club singer and her real name was Rita Littlewood. Len went to see her sing at the Victoria Street club, run by her agent Alec Gilroy, and told her he wanted a relationship with her.

5 Maggie's Situation Vacant

After Irma Barlow's sudden departure, Maggie Clegg struggled to cope alone at the shop. She was grateful when Lucille Hewitt stepped in to help her but her new assistant was determined not to stay long and Maggie was stunned when she forged references to get a job at the warehouse. Then, suddenly, Maggie found herself in the middle of two hostile business bids. Cyril Turpin decided it was time Betty stopped working at the Rovers and offered to buy Irma's share of the business for her. Maggie confided to Alf Roberts that the idea of working with her domineering sister terrified her, and Alf tried to warn Cyril off. Cyril took exception to this and they nearly came to blows but Alf backed out of the argument – and Maggie's life – when his wife Phyllis suddenly died of cancer.

Annie Walker also put in a bid for Irma's share of the shop on Lucille's behalf, even though the girl didn't want it. Eventually, fed up with the wrangling,

Maggie took out a bank loan and bought Irma's share herself.

Norma Ford moved in as Maggie's resident assistant and quickly proved her worth. However, she was a young woman with a secret and was forced to confess that her father, Jacko, was a jailbird. When Jacko was released from Strangeways, Maggie offered him a room and had him taken on as potman in the Rovers. Betty didn't trust him because he'd been in prison, so Billy Walker set a trap to prove his honesty: he put three pound notes under the telephone to see if Jacko would be tempted. This annoyed Jacko, who resigned and left the area.

Meddling Norma upset Maggie when, thinking Maggie was lonely, she placed an ad in a lonely-hearts column to find the perfect man for her. Despite herself Maggie agreed to meet up with one of the responses and found herself falling in love with draughtsman Ron Cooke. They went out a few times until he admitted to being an alcoholic and she dropped him.

Norma's love life was just as unsuccessful: she fell for Ken Barlow and paid him to teach her English literature. Jerry Booth fell for her and joined the classes but gave up when he realized he was playing gooseberry. Norma felt foolish when, after throwing herself at him, Ken read her a poem to show her he wasn't interested in her.

6 Domestic Problems at No.9

Ray Langton annoyed Jerry Booth by treating No.9 like a hotel and letting Jerry do all the work. Jerry felt undervalued and refused to cook for the household until Ray and Len Fairclough agreed to pay him housekeeping money each week. They wanted to keep the rebellious Jerry in the kitchen, and were amused to discover that he was building a boat in his spare time. Their amusement soon turned into interest, and they muscled in on the construction. Jerry named the craft *Shangri-La* and took lessons from the Sea Cadets on how to sail. Sadly the boat's maiden voyage ended in disaster when it capsized under Stan Ogden's weight.

Ray's love life was just as disastrous as Jerry's sailing exploits. He fell for Vicki Bright, who had arrived to look after the sale of No.3 for her cousin Audrey Flemming, and proposed to her even though she was pregnant with another man's baby. She was tempted to marry him but feared he wouldn't love the baby and turned him down. Just weeks later Ray bounced back after seeing attractive Sue Silcock driving around in her sports car. Sue was amused by Ray's attention and looked upon him as a bit of rough. However, Ray

reminded her father Tommy of himself and he encouraged her to marry him. Sue was annoyed that Tommy and Ray got on so well and dumped Ray, telling him to go out with her father instead.

7 Appearing Nightly at the Capricorn – the Weatherfield Nightingale

Dave Smith sold his Rosamund Street betting shop to Londoner Benny Lewis, who set about leaving his mark on the town. He employed Lucille Hewitt and Rita Littlewood, and commissioned Ray Langton and Len Fairclough to transform the shop's flat into a luxury penthouse with state-of-the-art fittings. Then he fell for Rita and proposed to her, showering her with expensive presents. Rita accepted his proposal then dumped him when Len made it clear he was still interested in her. She left the betting-shop to become hostess and resident singer at the club Benny opened with Jimmy Frazer, the Capricorn. Alan Howard spent a great deal of time there and Elsie warned Rita off when she suspected the pair of being lovers. Rita was quick to reassure her that fondness for women wasn't Alan's weakness: alcohol was.

Weatherfield was changing and was now integrated into Greater Manchester. The Mayor, Harold Chapman, and Alderman Rogers were told to elect Chapman's successor, who would be the borough's last mayor. The councillors decided the race was between Alf Roberts and Len Fairclough but the latter's hopes of prestige were damaged on opening night at the Capricorn when Rita, his chosen mayoress, ended up in a fight with another woman. When Len told her she was too common for his image, Rita poured her drink over his head.

Benny's luxury pad attracted the interest of local crooks when Ray attempted to show off by letting barmaid Sharon Duffy believe he owned it. When she found out he was lying she agreed to help Frannie Slater do the place over, and stole the key from Ray. After Jacko Ford returned to the area Frannie set up an elaborate plot. He stole five thousand pounds from the flat and framed Jacko to take the blame. Detective Inspector Patterson jumped on Jacko as the culprit and arrested him. While Jacko waited in remand at Risley, Norma Ford and Ken Barlow set about clearing his name.

8 Hilda the Work-Horse

By the autumn of 1972 Hilda Ogden had five jobs: cleaning at the Rovers, the betting shop, Benny Lewis's flat and the Capricorn, as well as washing dishes at the club. Stan was delighted to see the money flowing in: he decided to retire and let Hilda be the breadwinner. She was outraged and promptly gave up the Capricorn jobs. Earlier in the year, Stan had decided to treat Hilda by taking her to Paris for her birthday. However, they spent so much time drinking duty-free that they missed the flight and returned to the Street having to pretend that they had been away.

Stan returned to work, driving long-distance lorries, but ended up in hospital after a crash while transporting bananas. Hilda's brother, Archie Crabtree, moved into No.13 to keep her company, and promised to build her a porch outside the house. Hilda was delighted with the construction but Ray Langton dismantled it one night after discovering that they should have had planning permission.

On his recovery, Stan gave up lorry-driving for good and resumed his window round, but trouble arose when the huge Henshaw brothers accused him of operating on their patch. Eager not to upset them, Stan accepted another street from them as a swap, only to arrive with his ladders just as it was demolished.

Stan was used to looking into windows but was aghast when he was accused of being the local peeping Tom: a man had disturbed the Street's womenfolk so the residents formed a vigilante group and caught Stan lurking in a back alley. They

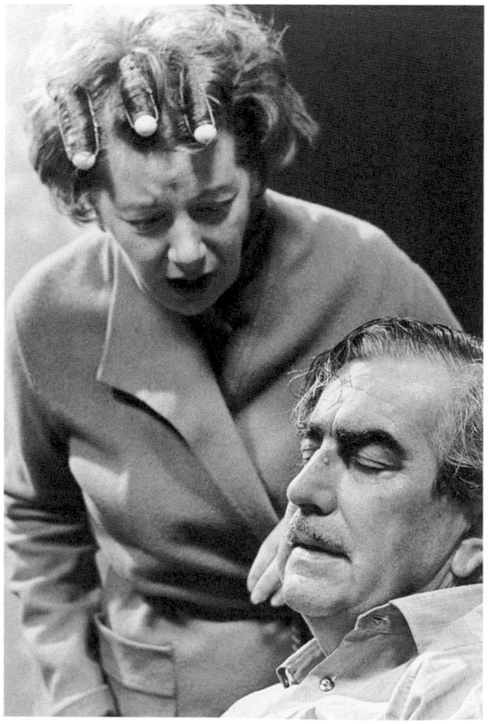

turned on him and he broke down. Hilda spat on the Rovers' floor as a demonstration of her hatred of them. Days later, another man was arrested and, shame-faced, the residents apologized to Stan.

9 Troubled Times for Ena

Ena Sharples nearly lost her job at the community centre after forgetting to lock away the new colour television. As a result it was stolen and the committee decided to appoint an assistant caretaker to help her. Albert Tatlock was given the job, much to independent Ena's frustration. Albert arranged a trip from the centre so that the residents could enjoy the spectacular event the Preston Guild, held only every twenty-five years.While there, Ena was startled when she was called over the Tannoy and told to return home immediately. Her grandson, Colin Lomax, had called on a visit with his wife Karen and baby son Jason. The baby had been snatched from outside the Rovers and the police had been called. Ena tried to comfort a distraught Karen as the canal was dragged and the police followed up a report from a local woman who admitted to killing Jason. The woman was a hoaxer and the baby was found by Emily Bishop and Betty Turpin as they searched wasteland. Ena led the residents in prayers of thankfulness. The police had no idea who had stolen the baby but months later Emily was startled when a stranger, Christine Peters, turned up asking after him.

10 Plenty of Muck

Rag-and-bone men Tommy Deakin and Dirty Dick brought the residents some fun when they held a competition to decide who was the rightful owner of Dolores the donkey. They stood at either end of the Street and called her, but she refused to move. The men rented space under the viaduct and housed Dolores in a makeshift stable. Tommy decided to get one up on Dick by giving him the donkey then starting a rumour that he was planning to sell her to the slaughterhouse for thirty pounds. Tender-hearted Minnie Caldwell immediately started up the Save Dolores campaign and raised the money which she gave to the bewildered Dick. When Tommy's lie was uncovered the residents insisted Dick kept the money and buy a stove with it to keep Dolores warm in winter.

The 1940s Show

Ernest Bishop put together a spectacular show to entertain the residents on Christmas Day in the Rovers Select. The show was set around the theme of the 1940s and involved:

Billy Walker as the Master of Ceremonies

Albert Tatlock reciting a monologue as Rob Witon

Ernest Bishop and Alf Roberts as the Western Brothers

Ray Langton and Jerry Booth as Flanagan and Allen singing 'Underneath The Arches'

Rita Littlewood as Marlene Dietrich singing 'Lily Marlene'

Norma Ford, Bet Lynch and Betty Turpin as the Andrews Sisters, singing 'Apple Blossom Time'

Annie Walker as Britannia, singing 'There'll Always Be An England'

Emily Bishop as Carmen Miranda

CAST

Wilfred Perkins	Wensley Pithey
Terry Bates	Steve Barratt
Harry Bates	William Simons
Laura Howard	Stella Tanner
Paul Cheveski	Nigel Greaves
Vicki Bright	Clare Sutcliffe
George Harrop	John Malcolm
Archie Crabtree	John Stratton
Norma Ford	Diana Davies
Jacko Ford	Robert Keegan
Harold Chapman	Frank Crompton
Sue Silcock	Angela Scoular
Tommy Silcock	Ivor Roberts
Alec Gilroy	Roy Barraclough
Fred Henshaw	Brian Glover
Benny Lewis	Jeremy Young
Det Insp Patterson	Tony Steedman
Ethne Willoughby	Barbara Lott
Ron Cooke	Eric Lander
Colin Lomax	Alec Sabin
Karen Lomax	Rosalind Elliott
Jason Lomax	Samantha Ferguson
Dirty Dick	Talfryn Thomas
Sharon Duffy	Susan Littler
Franny Slater	Michael Angelis
Sean Regan	Tony Doyle
Jimmy Frazer	John Barrie
Alderman Rogers	Robert Dorning
Deirdre Hunt	Anne Kirkbride
Christine Peters	Frances Tomalty

1973

Behind the Scenes

Coronation Street reached a crisis this year when its viewing figures slumped to an all-time low. The most-watched episode was Hilda Ogden's birthday party in February, winning 8.3 million viewers. Immediately after it was transmitted over a million more viewers tuned in to watch *Bless This House* star Diana Coupland on *This Is Your Life*. Viewers worried for the future of the characters as Ena Sharples collapsed, Annie Walker contemplated retirement and Elsie Howard suddenly left town.

In reality Violet Carson's health was troubling her and she was written out for most of the year, Doris Speed rested for two months and Patricia Phoenix decided that thirteen years was too long to stay in one job. With her husband, Alan Browning, she told H.V. Kershaw that she wanted to leave and concentrate on her stage career. On screen Elsie went with a whimper, purely because she had already been written out for a thirteen-week period so that Pat could tour with a stage play, *Subway in the Sky*. It was during this absence that she decided not to return, so Elsie was denied a dramatic exit. However, Pat was still hedging her bets: she told reporters, 'I should be happy to think that some time in the future – maybe years from now – I may return.'

After two years of widowhood Ken Barlow's love-life was spiced up when the writers threw him into the arms of a succession of women. Joanna Lumley appeared in nine episodes as middle-class Elaine Perkins, but there was no question of her staying longer as the decision had been taken to marry Ken off to super-bitch Janet Reid, who had already jilted Len Fairclough and had attempted to break up the Howard marriage. Actress Judith Barker knew the marriage would never last and struggled with the public's reaction to the character: 'She was used as a device, in the Ken relationship, and people were encouraged to hate her. I used to go about being terribly nice and pleasant to everybody in the hope that people would like her more.'

Top Twenty

Pos	Character	No of eps	Total	Pos Prev Year
1	Betty Turpin	81	335	11
2	Len Fairclough	80	1061	1
3	Bet Lynch	77	263	13
4	Ray Langton	76	434	3
5	Jerry Booth	71	559	6
6	Rita Littlewood	70	123	21
7	Annie Walker	69	1078	7
8	Ken Barlow	69	899	12
9	Hilda Ogden	68	678	9
10	Elsie Howard	65	1067	2
11	Stan Ogden	64	658	14
12	Lucille Hewitt	63	718	17
13	Norma Ford	62	120	16
14	Alf Roberts	61	203	20
15	Albert Tatlock	60	829	22
16	Alan Howard	60	251	7
17	Emily Bishop	59	742	10
18	Minnie Caldwell	59	872	17
19	Maggie Clegg	59	374	5
20	Ernie Bishop	56	169	14

> "Elsie Tanner's heart is where a fella's wallet is – and the bigger the wallet, the more heart she's got."
>
> **Hilda Ogden**

Key Dates

1973

September 24	Tricia Hopkins first appears
October 8	Patricia Pheonix leaves the programme after thirteen years to concentrate on stage acting
October 29	Ken Barlow marries Janet Reid

STORIES

1 Angst for the Bishops

Do-gooders Ernest and Emily Bishop faced a dilemma after discovering that local woman Christine Peters had kidnapped baby Jason Lomax the previous year. Christine's sister, Jean Cooper, begged Emily not to bring in the police, saying that Christine had been mentally unstable after the death of her own child. Emily was all for turning a blind eye, but Ernest insisted the police were informed and brought in Detective Inspector Patterson. When Christine was arrested, Jean slapped Emily's face.

Patterson had a busy week: just days after Christine's arrest he got a lead on the break-in at Benny Lewis' flat and finally caught up with Frannie Slater. Jacko Ford was released from custody, much to Norma's delight, but rather than settle with her in the Street he left for a job in Oakhill as resident handyman to a gentleman of independent means.

Meanwhile, business was bad for the Bishops so Ernest decided to employ a roving photographer to drum up trade. Emily was keen to take on the job herself and became jealous when Ernest employed Rita Littlewood. Rita assured Emily that her relationship with Ernest was strictly professional, but to prove her own worth, Emily took on an assignment to photograph a troupe of strippers. Not only did she win Ernest and Rita's respect, she also made a lot of new friends.

2 Rita Sells Her First Paper

Rita Littlewood's relationship with Len Fairclough continued to be an on-off affair. She tried to make him jealous by going out with Ray Langton and employing randy Johnny Mann as her theatrical manager, but Len knew that Ray wasn't a threat and annoyed her by hitting it off with Johnny. She continued to sing at the Capricorn but the club slipped downhill and Len was alarmed to discover that its new owner was using it as a cover to show pornographic movies. He insisted that Rita resign, and she was grateful for his concern. She was astounded when the son of her common-law husband Terry turned up and begged her to take him in, saying that he had been placed in care and had run away from home. She announced her decision to adopt him but Ken Barlow warned her not to get involved: she faced a six-month jail sentence if she was found harbouring him. Reluctantly she allowed the authorities to take him away.

Biddulph's was a dirty newsagent's on Rosamund Street with a lending library and café at the back. Len surprised Rita by buying it and making her manageress. Ray was annoyed – he'd considered buying the shop himself and had offered his girlfriend,

Deirdre Hunt, the job of running it. Rita was delighted with the shop and the flat that went with it, but refused to employ Deirdre, saying she wanted to find her own assistant. Jerry Booth talked his friend Mavis Riley into applying and she was taken on, despite having a fit of hiccups during her interview.

As part of the Manchester Festival, Weatherfield took a twin town – Charleville in France. To celebrate, Len, along with the other councillors, spent a two-week holiday there. Rita was furious to discover that he could have taken her along if he'd wanted to, and in revenge told him he was not welcome in her flat.

3 Love Blossoms for Ray, Jerry and Len

With Len Fairclough's girlfriend, Rita, installed in the Kabin with Jerry Booth's girlfriend, Mavis, as her assistant, Ray Langton decided to claim some of the action for his piece of skirt, Deirdre, and installed her as secretary in the Yard. Len wasn't happy with the idea but Deirdre proved her worth by bringing order to the business and, making it more efficient. Despite all her efforts, though, the firm suffered a blow with the introduction of VAT, and especially when Len and Ray received a demand for VAT payable on a job for which they hadn't been paid. When Weatherfield Plastics went bust, Len and Ray were outraged to discover they still had to pay the VAT. They went to court, prepared to go to prison if necessary, and were infuriated when Jerry paid off the debt, ending the court case. He explained that he had no desire to see the business go under, but his bosses were so annoyed that they refused to work with him and disappeared.

Jerry refused to abandon the firm and soldiered on with Deirdre. Mavis became

jealous of their working relationship: as she explained to Rita, Jerry's head might so easily be turned by a dominating personality like Deirdre's.

When Len and Ray finally returned they found the business thriving and agreed to make Jerry a partner. Outside work, Jerry continued to be romantically interested in Mavis and encouraged her to take part in a sponsored swim. She agreed, once the judges allowed her to wear a swimsuit instead of a bikini, and collapsed after eighteen lengths.

4 The Howards Leave the Street

The Howards' marriage cracked open as Elsie watched Alan drink more and more. The matter came to a head when he nearly burned the house down while he was drunk. He refused to accept that he was an alcoholic but Elsie sobered him up by threatening to walk out on him. He agreed to have counselling and started to sort out his life, dissolving his partnership with Jimmy Frazer and going on the wagon. The couple took in a 'surrogate daughter' shortly after Lucille Hewitt decided to leave the Rovers to branch out on her own. At first she took a bedsit, paying rent to landlord George Scully. It was a dump and Lucille felt trapped in it until Alan stepped in and helped her escape Scully's clutches. She moved into the spare room at No.11, much to Annie Walker's dismay. Elsie enjoyed having a youngster in the house but wasn't happy when Lucille's friends started muscling in – they found Alan attractive. After a night out of town, Elsie returned home to find Deirdre Hunt asleep in her bed. Alan was amazed as he had no idea Deirdre had stayed the night.

When it came to the crunch Elsie decided she couldn't trust Alan. Her son had started to serve a three-year jail sentence for his involvement in a double-glazing fraud and Elsie was too ashamed to tell Alan that she had to visit Dennis in a London prison and told him instead that she was seeing a friend in Scarborough. Upset after her reunion with Dennis, Elsie left her handbag on a park bench and, on her way back to fetch it, was knocked down by a black cab. She was rushed to hospital with a fractured skull and severe concussion and lay, unidentified, for two weeks. Alan finally tracked her down and brought her home, promising that no one knew about Dennis.

Hilda Ogden gossiped relentlessly over what had kept Elsie in London, which eventually culminated in a fight in the Rovers between Stan and Alan. Elsie couldn't handle the gossip, and when the chance of promotion came she grabbed it.

The new job was in Newcastle, and

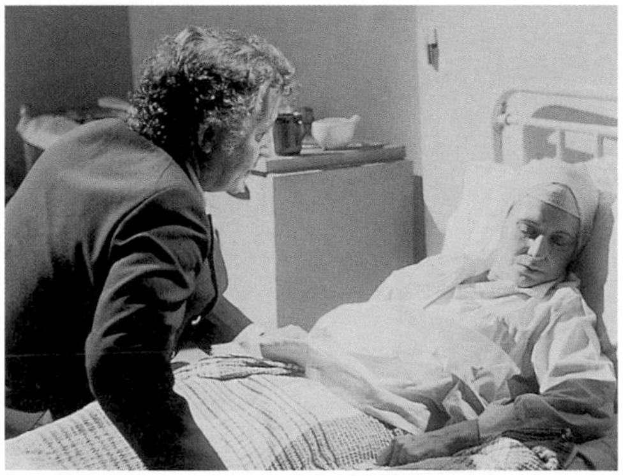

Alan was pleased too: it meant he could return to his roots. Leaving Lucille alone at No.11 the Howards left for Newcastle. A few weeks later Alan returned to tidy up their affairs and, as one last gesture of goodwill to the community, agreed to put on a firework display on Guy Fawkes' night. The fun went terribly wrong when a firework exploded by schoolboy Mark Hillkirk, who had to have a skin graft on his leg. Alan blamed himself and returned to Elsie with a heavy heart.

5 The Highs and Lows of Being an Ogden

1973 was a mixed bag for the Ogdens. It started with public humiliation when the residents discovered that Clara Regan at No.19 Inkerman Street was having her social security cut because the authorities had discovered she was cohabitating with a man. Hilda knew that Clara had offered Stan comfort in the past and jumped to the same conclusion as her neighbours. Stan swore he was innocent but was put out when Hilda discovered Clara had indeed moved a man in but that he was definitely not Stan.

Stan put his foot in it again when he insisted that Hilda was fifty when she celebrated her birthday. She produced her birth certificate to prove she was forty-nine and demanded a commemorative album and a party to make up for the insult. After studying an etiquette book, she decided on a Barbara Cartland style bash and donned a blonde wig and fake eyelashes to greet her guests in the 'drawing room'.

While Hilda enjoyed herself tangoing with bookie's clerk Ted Loftus, Stan got steadily drunk. Later, finding her bedroom door locked and hearing Edna Gee inside, Hilda stopped the party, fearing that Stan was frolicking. Once again Stan swore his innocence, and the next day Billy Walker produced Edna's knickers to prove he'd been the one locked in her clutches.

When Hilda went away to visit her brother, Stan failed to look after himself and a concerned Elsie Howard called in the health inspector after seeing a mouse in the kitchen. Hilda returned in time to find her home being fumigated. She was distraught and Stan felt helpless. In an attempt to cheer herself up, Hilda started ballroom-dancing lessons with Ted, and was miffed when Stan failed to appear in the least jealous.

After nine years of wondering what had happened to their son, Trevor, Hilda talked Stan into making contact with him. With Irma now living away she feared they would never have any family around them. Trevor was tracked down to Chesterfield and was horrified when his parents sprang a surprise visit. They were delighted to discover they had a grandson, Damian, but heartbroken when Trevor's wife, Polly, confessed he'd told her they were dead.

6 Alf's Troubled Private and Public Lives

Weatherfield Council decided to honour Alf Roberts by making him the borough's last mayor. Alf was proud and, to show there were no hard feelings, appointed as deputy his opponent Len Fairclough. Maggie Clegg was pleased to be asked to be Alf's mayoress but declined the post, saying she would hate him to get the wrong idea and think her feelings for him were more than friendship. Alf was upset by her rebuff and allowed Annie Walker the thrill of being mayoress, a position she was born to. The gloss nearly went out of the position when, giving Bet Lynch a lift home from the Rovers, he reversed into a private drive and knocked into the householder. The old lady was unhurt but her son Norman Leach decided to make the most of the situation and threatened to go to the papers unless Alf paid him two hundred pounds. Fearful of the bad publicity, Alf gave Leach a cheque but Bet, guessing that he had form, made him return it by threatening to go to the police. A furious Leach vowed vengeance on Bet.

A few months later Bet celebrated a win of seventy-five pounds on the pools.

She had entered a syndicate with Ray Langton, Stan Ogden and Alan Howard, and soon afterwards twenty-three points come up on their coupon. After receiving her share of the pay-out Bet was savagely mugged in the back alley. Her handbag was stolen, she was beaten and left for dead. Stan found her in a pool of blood and she was rushed to hospital. The police suspected a local man and were intrigued to find her handbag with the money still inside. Fingerprints found on the bag matched Leach's, and he was arrested but denied everything. In order to help Bet, Alf decided to tell the police about the blackmail attempt but first called at the Town Hall to resign his mayoral office. He was stopped in the nick of time by the news that Leach had confessed to the mugging and was sentenced to seven years in prison.

Alf continued to be attracted to Maggie and was put out when she received a visit from Mike Ritchie, an American with whom she had been romantically involved in the past. He was jealous of Maggie's obvious delight at being with Mike and tried to warn him off her – with good reason, as it turned out. Although he was genuinely attracted to Maggie, Mike had a lover in America; when she wrote to say that she was prepared to marry him, he caught the next flight back to Wichita. Maggie was upset by his departure and accused Alf of driving away the man she loved.

7 Romeo Ken

Ken Barlow had a busy year in the romance stakes. He fell head over heels in love with Elaine Perkins, the sophisticated daughter of his headmaster. She introduced him to her friends at the cricket club and thought he lived in a 'sweet little house'. However, while she was fond of him she was not prepared to tie herself down. When he proposed, she let him down as kindly as she

could, but he was annoyed when she revealed she'd also been seeing a Liberal politician. Seeking solace, he reached out to Norma Ford, knowing that she was obsessed with him. She couldn't believe her luck, and dared to dream of becoming the next Mrs Barlow, but Ken was only using her and when a better offer turned up he dropped her. The better offer came in the shape of Rita Littlewood, who was momentarily between boyfriends, and they spent a couple of nights together at her flat. When Norma found out she told Ken he didn't deserve either her or the children he seemed to have forgotten about.

The thought of the twins caused Ken to reassess his life and he decided that, rather

than satisfying his own desires, he should be looking for a wife who could be their mother. Janet Reid was working as a secretary at the Town Hall and Ken had heard enough of her as Len Fairclough's and Alan Howard's lover to know that she was another lonely soul seeking love. The pair started a relationship, and eventually married in Keswick. He took her to meet the twins and was annoyed when Edith Tatlock refused to give him her blessing. When Peter took against his new stepmother Ken decided to let the children stay in Scotland until he and Janet were more settled.

Albert Tatlock was another family member who didn't think Janet a suitable replacement for Valerie, but he forced himself to keep quiet as the couple were sharing his home. Norma couldn't cope with the idea of Ken being married and left the Street in tears.

Janet was an ambitious woman and, having secured a husband, demanded a large detached house. Ken went along with the idea as Janet made it clear that she wouldn't entertain having the twins to live with them until they had a new house. She set her heart on a property named Manderleigh, but when the purchase fell through she vented her anger on Ken, calling him spineless and useless.

8 Ena's Past Returns to Haunt Her

Minnie Caldwell had a terrible shock when, looking through Ena's belongings, she found a letter written in 1919 from her husband Armistead, declaring his love for Ena. Minnie confronted her old friend with the letter and was mortified when Ena revealed that Armistead had begged her to marry him until she had made him see that he was better suited to Minnie. Ena informed Minnie smugly that if it hadn't been for her she would never have been Mrs Caldwell.

When Ena's older brother, Thomas, died in America, his son Tom returned to Weatherfield, after an absence of eight years, to introduce his wife, Faye-Marie, to Auntie Ena. Faye-Marie was delighted with the quaint Street but alarmed Ena by

making a play for Ken Barlow. Tom confessed that theirs was an open marriage but assured Ena that Faye-Marie would do no more than 'experience' Ken, who was flattered by the attention. Later he organized an outing to Woburn Abbey, where a delighted Minnie bought a tea-towel from the Duke of Bedford.

Ken caused problems for Albert Tatlock when he bought a new cooker for No.1. Jerry Booth installed it and only days later was stricken with panic when Minnie found Albert unconscious in the kitchen: he had been gassed by an ill-fitted pipe. The Street was evacuated and Albert was rushed to hospital where he was placed in an oxygen tent. His daughter, Beattie Pearson, arrived on the scene and demanded compensation from Jerry.

Jerry was genuinely upset at the thought of Albert dying and when the old man came round he ordered his daughter to stop fleecing the younger man. Shortly afterwards, Jerry joined Albert in his bid to walk the Pennine Way after Albert's friend Herbert James boasted he had walked all 270 miles of it. Albert and Jerry's venture ended after a few miles and Albert lost the desire to try again when Herbert died of a heart-attack.

Albert and Ena both won a fortnight's holiday in Wales in a raffle but Ena's trip was cut short when she suffered a mild heart-attack. She returned home but kept quiet about her health problems until she suffered another attack and collapsed in the Snug. She refused to take things more slowly and vowed that she wanted to die in Coronation Street.

No matter how fond they were of Ena, committee members Emily and Ernest Bishop couldn't turn a blind eye when Ena disappeared with the centre keys and a children's party had to be cancelled. They told Ena she would have to leave her job and gave her a month's notice. Ena walked out immediately, then told everyone that the Bishops had thrown her out on to the street. Minnie offered her a bed but Ena moved to St Anne's. After her departure

Albert realized how lonely life was becoming and proposed to Minnie. After weighing up her options, she accepted.

9 New Faces at the Rovers

Preparing for her role as mayoress of Weatherfield took over Annie Walker's life to the extent that she handed over the running of the Rovers Return to her son Billy. To help with any future public speaking, she hired elocution teacher Sybil Cudlipp, much to the delight of the regulars. Sybil only lasted one lesson because Annie decided she knew more than her teacher. Then she mistook retiring mayoress Ethel Bostock for an applicant after a cleaning job. Ethel wasn't in the least put out, and Alf told Annie that if she could emulate Ethel's common touch he would be delighted.

The thrill of the Mayoral Instalment was ruined for Annie when Billy confessed he had been gambling with the pub's takings and owed two hundred pounds. She was forced to pay the debt and felt betrayed when he left for London. Eventually she decided she had no desire to run the pub alone and planned her retirement. The brewery installed Glyn Thomas as manager, and allowed him a free hand in updating the place. He installed a one-armed bandit and started entertainment in the Select, contracting organist Renee Delafonte as a regular attraction.

The residents were appalled by the changes to their local and, on learning that Annie was planning to call time for good, they petitioned the brewery to stop her. She was flattered by their support, agreed to stay on and Glyn left for a new pub in Runcorn. Shortly afterwards, Annie showed those same customers that she wasn't going to stand any nonsense from them: when she discovered under-age Tricia Hopkins drinking in the pub she laid into her mother Vera, accusing her of neglect.

The Drag Show

When the local men took on and beat the ladies in a bowls match, they demanded their opponents paid a forfeit and entertained them with a drag show in the Rovers Select. The women rose to the occasion.

Emily Bishop was Mistress of Ceremonies
Norma Ford was Ken Dodd
Bet Lynch and Betty Turpin performed a Laurel and Hardy routine
Rita Littlewood dressed as Danny La Rue and sang

CAST

Jean Cooper	Margaret Shevlin
George Scully	Alan Gerrard
Johnny Mann	Charles Pemberton
Norman Leach	Freddie Lees
Mike Ritchie	Murray Kash
Ted Loftus	Ted Morris
Sybil Cudlipp	Helen Cherry
Herbert James	Llewellyn Rees
Ethel Bostock	Pearl Hackney
Faye Marie Schofield	Jane Casson
Duke of Bedford	Himself
Glyn Thomas	Alan David
Renee Delafonte	Wendy Marshall
Elaine Perkins	Joanna Lumley
Trica Hopkins	Kathy Jones
Vera Hopkins	Kathy Staff
Peter Barlow	Linus Roache
Mark Hillkirk	Mark Adshead
Trevor Ogden	Don Hawkins
Polly Ogden	Mary Tamm

1974

Behind the Scenes

Writing for *TV Life* magazine, Street writer and former producer Les Duxbury commented on the importance of the show's format – characters trapped in a tiny community – and quoted G.K. Chesterton: 'He who lives in a small community lives in a much larger world. He knows much more of the fierce varieties and compromising divergencies of men. The reason is obvious. In a large community we can choose our companions. In a small community our companions are chosen for us.'

This was particularly true of the Street in 1974. New producer Susi Hush was determined to tackle controversial storylines and drag the programme up to date. In the first months post-Phoenix, viewers had deserted the show and flocked to *Crossroads*, where Noelle Gordon was ruling the roost. Deprived of Elsie, they seemed to need another strong female lead to relate to. On top of this Violet Carson suffered a stroke and had to hang up her hairnet. She appeared in only thirteen episodes in the year.

The character of Deirdre Hunt was built up, giving her a home – 20 Victoria Street – and a mother, Blanche. Susi had to choose between two actresses for the role of Blanche Hunt, Patricia Cutts and Maggie Jones. She felt that Maggie's face was too familiar as she had starred in the Granada series *Sam* so the job was given to Patricia but after completing only two episodes she committed suicide. For the first time in the Street's history, another actress took over the role of an adult character. The writers had plotted stories for Blanche, and Maggie Jones quickly stepped into Miss Cutts's shoes.

After six years of serving behind the Corner Shop counter Irene Sutcliffe decided to say goodbye to Maggie Clegg. She had always been based in London and found her departure from Weatherfield easier than most before her; fewer people recognized her and theatre offers came in. Her departing storyline – in which she married an old flame – was tarnished by the sudden sacking of Jennifer Moss, who had played Lucille Hewitt since the fourth episode. She had developed a drinking problem, and while actors in the 1990s might have been helped through such a period, she was offered no such support. Another sour note was struck for Miss Sutcliffe when Susi Hush decided to make Gordon Clegg Betty Turpin's illegitimate son. The foundation of Maggie's character was thus ripped apart and Irene felt hurt by the story.

The Corner Shop – that cornerstone of the Street – was handed over to a new family, the Welsh Hopkinses. Fierce matriarch Granny Hopkins was intended to fill the gap left by Violet Carson but she never won any sympathy from viewers, who saw her as a mean old woman with no warmth. Her daughter-in-law, Vera, had more potential but the actress playing her, Kathy Staff, had to be written out just after starting work as she had a previous commitment on a new series called *Last of the Summer Wine*. The family had been created as a vehicle for Granada starlet Kathy Jones, so she was given a best friend, Gail Potter, to be silly with.

Top Twenty

Pos	Character	No of eps	Total	Pos Prev Year
1	Betty Turpin	87	422	1
2	Len Fairclough	81	1142	2
3	Bet Lynch	79	342	3
4	Rita Littlewood	73	196	6
5	Ray Langton	72	506	4
6	Annie Walker	71	1149	7
7	Jerry Booth	70	629	5
8	Deirdre Hunt	69	104	23
9	Billy Walker	68	299	24
10	Ken Barlow	68	967	7
11	Ernie Bishop	67	236	20
12	Emily Bishop	65	807	17
13	Stan Ogden	61	719	11
14	Alf Roberts	59	262	14
15	Hilda Ogden	56	734	9
16	Mavis Riley	53	89	22
17	Minnie Caldwell	53	925	17
18	Albert Tatlock	52	881	15
19	Maggie Clegg	42	416	17
20	Idris Hopkins	38	38	-

> "I never fitted in in this Street because I never wanted to. I despised round 'ere. The littleness of it, the dinginess, the acceptance that this was all there ever was or ever would be. Streets like this suck you down to their level in time."
>
> **Janet Barlow**

Key Dates 1974

February 25	Cyril Turpin dies
July 1	Jennifer Moss leaves the programme after appearing in 749 episodes as Lucille Hewitt
July 10	Maggie Clegg marries Ron Cooke
July 12	Gail Potter's first appearance
August 19	Vera Duckworth's first appearance
December 23	Eddie Yeats' first appearance

STORIES

1 A New Face

With Ena Sharples no longer working at the community centre, the council held interviews to find a replacement. The Ogdens applied for the job but lost out to Gertie Robson, who moved in with her nephew, Gary Turner. Gary was a talented footballer but longed for a career as a chef. His father, Eric, was appalled by the idea and persuaded a team interested in him to pay Gertie to talk him round. Gertie turned down the money and urged her nephew to follow his heart. She soon found the work too much and decided to give up the centre to become Annie Walker's housekeeper. However, before she could move in Freda Barry, the landlady at the Flying Horse, poached her, which infuriated Annie.

2 The Residents Turn On Len

Needing an assistant, Rita Littlewood employed a sixteen-year-old lad, Chris Cullen, but sacked him after just one day when he made a pass at her. Lucille Hewitt took over from him and found herself carrying the business when Rita became preoccupied with a redevelopment scheme. Douglas Wormold was touring the area looking for property to buy. Len Fairclough and Alf Roberts were both told of the council's plan to demolish Coronation Street and build a high-rise block. Ignorant of this, Maggie Clegg had plans drawn up to enlarge her shop and was grateful when Len put her wise to what was going on, although upset that her friend Alf hadn't had the guts to tell her. Wormold offered

Len five thousand pounds for the Kabin, but Rita reminded him that the shop was in her name and that she wasn't selling. Len felt that the profit he would make on selling No.9 and the yard wasn't enough and

insisted that Rita sold up. She retaliated by going public on the development news, which caused an outcry in the Street. The Bishops set up an action group but Len refused to have anything to do with it, so

Emily Bishop threw a brick through his window. In the end the plan was outvoted by the councillors, including Len – who was startled when Rita told him she'd have nothing to do with him if he voted for the development. He took the opportunity to propose to her, and she accepted happily. However, the engagement was short-lived as he wouldn't commit himself to a wedding date.

Wormold's assistant, Jimmy Graham, continued to pressure Rita to sell. When she refused he invited her out for a meal. Before long, the pair were lovers and planning a future together away from Weatherfield. Once again, Rita's joy turned to despair: after running into his wife and children, Douglas passed Rita off as a client. Rita saw that he only looked upon her as a bit on the side and ended the affair, wondering why no man ever wanted to marry her.

3 Annie Walker – Temptress of the Street

Nellie Harvey's downtrodden husband Arthur stunned Annie Walker by turning up on her doorstep and declaring his love for her. He had left Nellie and decided he could no longer hide his desire for Annie. The revelation that she was an object of lust confused Annie and she did all she could to put Arthur off. However, she became embroiled up to her neck when Nellie called and found Arthur behind the bar wearing Billy's pyjamas – Annie had allowed him to sleep off a hangover. Nellie jumped to the wrong conclusion and announced her intention to divorce him, citing Annie as co-respondent. Fearing a scandal, Annie persuaded Arthur to return home and acted as a marriage guidance counsellor to reconcile the couple.

Annie's ward, Lucille Hewitt, found herself in a similar situation after moving in with mechanic Danny Burrows. When she discovered he was married he swore he had been separated for eighteen months. She was satisfied with that, until his wife Sandra turned up with their baby and explained that Danny had abandoned her. Lucille gave her five pounds and packed her bags and moved back in with Annie at the Rovers, but her stay was short and she left the area in July to live with the Regans in Ireland.

4 Deirdre's Caught In the Middle

Billy Walker returned to the Rovers once more and bought the Canal Street garage from Alan Howard. He brought with him a stack of money he'd cheated out of a customer, Stuart Draper, selling him a four-hundred-pound car for a thousand. Draper tracked him down and demanded compensation, but when Billy refused he drove the car into the Rovers' doors. Both Billy and Draper were arrested but released when the police agreed that Draper had been happy enough with the car in the first place.

Ray Langton and Deirdre Hunt had been seeing each other for months and he seemed to be taking her for granted. Deirdre was flattered when Billy took an interest in her and agreed to go out with him, much to the interest of her mother Blanche, who admitted to fancying him herself.

Ray, meanwhile, had problems of his own when Alison Wright, a girl he'd met at a party, turned up with her baby son Jonathan. As Ray took her in, the local gossips jumped to the conclusion that the baby must be his. In reality her rich boyfriend, Harvey Shaw, had dumped her after she became pregnant and Ray had felt sorry for her. Jonathan's cries got to Len and he tracked Harvey down and reconciled the family. With Alison gone, Ray realized with alarm that Deirdre and Billy had grown closer. He became jealous and started to victimize her at work, until Blanche attacked him in the Rovers. Once Billy and Deirdrie decided to marry, Billy's mother Annie was alarmed at the prospect of her precious son marrying a harlot like Deirdre but he threatened to leave home if she interfered.

Across the Street, at the warehouse, storeman Fred Bolton was pleased when his teenage son Tony was taken on in the packing department. Then Tony discovered a stash of leather jackets and stole them, keeping them in his van which he stored in Billy's garage. When the police investigated the theft Tony put them on to Billy and the jackets were found in his possession. He was arrested and charged with receiving stolen goods. Ken Barlow secured his release after he made Fred see that Tony needed teaching a lesson before his thieving got out of hand. The Boltons were arrested and Billy was freed without an apology.

5 Stan's Lodgers

When Hilda Ogden sunk into a deep depression Stan grew concerned over her state of mind. The doctor told her to take a holiday but with no savings this didn't seem to be a possibility until Stan stumbled over a job vacancy. Hilda was taken on as cleaner on the *Monte Umber*, cruising around the Caribbean. She joined the seamen's union and set off happily, leaving Stan with enough housekeeping to last the six weeks she would be away. A drinking spree saw off the money in two days and Stan was forced to take in lodgers to buy food. His guests were rag-and-bone men Tommy Deakin and Michael Ryan, who lodged Dolores the donkey in the backyard. Stan was delighted when the pair took him for a day at the races in a chauffeur-driven Rolls-Royce but on the way home, after he had taken the wheel, the police stopped the party. Stan's breathalyser test was positive. Tommy and Michael moved out but left Dolores in residence, so Maggie Clegg reported Stan to the health inspector. Hilda returned home to find Dolores being removed by the authorities and Stan summonsed to appear in court. She used the money she had earned to pay for a top solicitor for Stan and the couple celebrated when he was fined just fifty pounds. Then they received the solicitor's bill for £143.

Hoping to break their run of bad luck, the Ogdens decided to sell their home and become caretakers at the community centre. Once again their hopes were dashed when the council refused to employ them due to their record with the Environmental Health. Never down for long, Stan bought a tandem so that he could provide a cheap holiday for Hilda. They decided on a trip to Derbyshire but the journey to the station was so strenuous that they left the tandem with a porter. He brought it back to Coronation Street and gave it to Ray Langton, who tried to trick the Ogdens by painting the blue bike white. Stan, however, baffled him by stealing it back and repainting it.

6 A Broken Engagement

Minnie Caldwell startled Albert Tatlock by demanding an Easter wedding. There was a great deal of dispute over where they should live afterwards and Minnie found that Albert irritated her. Then she did some research and discovered that once they were married they would be financially worse off, so she broke off the engagement. He was pleased and said he had been having second thoughts as well.

Alf Roberts had trouble finding a permanent caretaker for the centre and pressed Albert into taking on more responsibility. Albert wasn't keen but went along with the idea until football hooligans roughed him up and broke his glasses.

Christmas brought the return of Ena Sharples, who found Minnie expecting a visit from Jed Stone, straight from prison. However, Jed's parole was cancelled and his cell-mate Eddie Yeats arrived in his place and wowed the pensioners by cooking their Christmas lunch. Eddie took an instant fancy to Bet Lynch and talked her into a date. On the day, there was a power-cut. Eddie had been warned of it by the friend who caused it so that he could rob a local supermarket. Eddie bought up all the candles in the Corner Shop, then sold them at a profit in the Rovers. His scam backfired because Bet refused to go out as it was so much fun in the candle-lit pub.

7 The Barlow Breakup

Janet Barlow wasn't impressed when Ken suggested renting No.11 from the Howards while they looked around for a larger house. She agreed to the move when he promised to buy her the house of her dreams, but had decided she did not want to have his children living with them and investigated boarding schools. Ken was furious when he discovered Janet's plans, then hurt when the twins told him they didn't want to live with him anyway: their lives were now in Scotland.

The mail-order warehouse situated across the street from the terrace had caused problems for local residents due to the increase in traffic moving to and fro. Ken complained to the company's boss, Sir Julius Berlin, and impressed him so much that he was offered the position of northern executive administrative assistant. He didn't tell Janet about this and allowed her to end their short marriage. She told him she no longer loved him or had faith in him. The day after she walked out he took the job. His first day at the warehouse was a disaster as he was told to reprimand a worker, Gaynor Burton, for being late . . . because she'd spent the night with him after a party at the Rovers. Ken was quick to tell Gaynor their relationship could only be professional.

He found himself caught in the middle when the workers threatened to strike over the management's decision to keep the union out of the firm. Ken's socialist beliefs meant that he was in sympahty with the workforce but Sir Julius made it clear where his loyalties had to lie. When Ken discovered that packer Peggy Barton was the main antagonist, he worked with her to find a solution to the problem. He persuaded Sir Julius to accept the union on the condition that Peggy would resign and that Ivy Tilsley, who was less militant, would be made shop steward. Everyone was happy until the company announced that all women over sixty would have to retire. Ivy and her co-worker Vera Duckworth called in Peggy, who had taken a job directly with the union, but there was nothing Peggy could do as the union supported the lowering of the retirement age and she found herself being accused by Ivy of siding with her boyfriend, Ken. Ken solved the problem by retiring the workers but saying they could consider themselves 'on call' and might be needed to help out with rush orders.

8 Unhappy Emily

Ernest Bishop started up the Rovers Amateur Dramatic Association (RADA) and tried to interest the residents in

performing a radical new play called *Sand*. Emily was aghast when she discovered the plot was pornographic and stood out against the idea. She persuaded the players to tackle a more conventional project and work began on *The Importance of Being Earnest*. Her hopes of playing Lady Bracknell were dashed when Ernest gave the plumb role to Annie Walker but she ended up taking over the production when the cast grew tired of Ernest's tantrums. The play was performed at the Community Centre with the following cast:

Algernon	Ken Barlow
Jack	Jerry Booth
Cecily	Bet Lynch
Gwendolyn	Deirdre Hunt
Lady Bracknell	Annie Walker
Lane	Len Fairclough
Miss Prism	Emily Bishop
Canon Chasuble	Ernest Bishop
Masters	Billy Walker

The experience alerted the Bishops to problems in their marriage and caused Ernie to seek help from a marriage guidance counsellor. To give themselves a shared interest the couple registered as foster-parents and were united during the short time they looked after Lucy and Vernon Foyle. They planned a family Christmas with the children and were upset when this was cut short by the arrival of their father, fresh from hospital.

9 Bet's Big Adventure

In the spring a young soldier, Martin Downes, appeared in the Street looking for the mother who had given him up for adoption when he was just six weeks old. He realized Bet Lynch was the woman he

was seeking but was horrified by her tarty clothes and flirtatious manner, and left the area without talking to her.

After Len Fairclough insinuated that women knew nothing about football, Bet roped in her friends and entered the Find the Ball competition in the local paper. They were amazed when they won the first prize – a holiday for two in the Bahamas. Bet managed to change the prize to a holiday for eight in Majorca, and the party set off for a week of sun, sea and passion. Bet shared a room with Deirdre, Emily with Annie, Rita with Mavis, and Betty with Hilda. During the holiday, Bet fell for property tycoon Martin Barratt, decided to stay on and let the plane return home without her. Then she discovered that Martin had moved on to his next conquest and didn't want anything to do with her. She had to rough it for two weeks before she found someone willing to lend her the air fare home.

10 Betty's Secret

Cyril Turpin's sudden death of a heart attack at the age of fifty-four left his widow Betty alone and confused. She was found wandering the streets looking for him and had to be sedated. Her sister Maggie Clegg arranged the funeral and prepared to bury Cyril without Betty. However, at the last minute Betty gathered herself together and attended the ceremony. Maggie grew fearful that Betty would become too dependent on her and was thrilled when Ron Cooke returned with the announcement that he hadn't had a drink for two years. He had taken a job in Zaïre and proposed to her, then asked her to join him in Africa.

Alf Roberts took the news badly and accused Maggie of leading him on. He also proposed to her but Maggie knew she could never love him and went ahead with her wedding plans. Alf tried to ruin the wedding by telling Gordon about Ron's alcoholic past but Gordon merely announced that if Ron was good enough for his mother he was good enough for him. Gordon proudly gave Maggie away when she married Ron at St Mary's. Among the guests was Norma Ford, who stunned her old ex-neighbours by arriving with her sixty-year-old sugar daddy.

With Maggie gone, Gordon looked for someone to buy the shop. In the short term he agreed to rent it to the Hopkins family. Granny Hopkins took over the running of the business while her son Idris worked nights at a local factory. Idris' wife, Vera, was put upon by Granny and left the shop to nurse her terminally ill mother. Her daughter, Tricia, took a job as Ken Barlow's secretary at the warehouse, where she became friendly with teenager Gail Potter. Gail encouraged Tricia in her obsession with Ray Langton and took a Polaroid of the two kissing. When Granny found the picture she laid into a tearful Tricia, keeping her locked in her room while Idris saw off Ray. After her mother's death, Vera returned to find Granny bending over backwards to please her: she wanted the money Vera had inherited to buy the shop. Vera agreed to put up a deposit but was wary of becoming Granny's business partner.

Then while clearing out Maggie's furniture, Granny found Gordon's birth certificate and discovered that his mother was not Maggie but Betty. She told Betty she knew the truth and promised that her secret was safe. Worried, Betty summoned Maggie who agreed with her that Gordon should not be told the truth.

11 Mavis and Jerry – Never to Be

When Mavis Riley's parents moved to Grange-over-Sands she left the area, and her job at the Kabin. She had been prepared to stay if Jerry Booth had declared feelings for her, but instead he confessed he was still married. Two months later Mavis returned and was taken on as an assistant at the Corner Shop. When Jerry started divorce proceedings, Mavis looked forward to getting closer to him but this was spoilt by the arrival of Sheila Crossley, who stayed with the Bishops for a week and threw a party for her old friends. During the gathering, Ray Langton spiked Jerry's drinks with vodka and Mavis was upset when he stood on a table to declare his love for Sheila, his old girlfriend.

During the women's holiday in Majorca, Mavis had fallen head over heels with a Spanish electrician named Pedro. Back in Weatherfield, Bet Lynch decided to play a joke on her by getting her new neighbour, Carlos, to ring her pretending to be Pedro and arrange a meeting. Jerry was upset by Mavis's excitement at the prospect of seeing Pedro again, and even more so when she met Carlos, discovered the truth, but was taken with him anyway.

CAST

Arthur Harvey	Henry Moxon
Christopher Cullen	Peter Duncan
Douglas Wormold	Michael Elphick
Stuart Draper	George Innes
Gertie Robson	Connie Merigold
Danny Burrows	Ian Liston
Sir Julius Berlin	Leonard Sachs
Gary Turner	Michael Duggan
Eric Turner	Clifford Cox
Michael Ryan	Jim Bartley
Alison Wright	Rosalind Ayres
Jonathan Wright	Samuel Taylor
Harvey Shaw	John Oxley
Martin Downes	Louis Selwyn
Idris Hopkins	Richard Davies
Granny Hopkins	Jesse Evans
Freda Barry	Joy Stewart
Gail Potter	Helen Worth
Jimmy Graham	Colin George
Gaynor Burton	Maureen Sutcliffe
Vera Duckworth	Elizabeth Dawn
Blanche Hunt	Patricia Cutts and Maggie Jones
Peggy Burton	Lois Daine
Fred Bolton	Donald Morley
Tony Bolton	Terence Macarthy
Martin Barrett	Stephen Yardley
Pedro	Tim Horand
Carlos	Malcolm Hebden
Vernon Foyle	Paul Bligdeon
Lucy Foyle	Andrea Bligdeon
Eddie Yeats	Geoffrey Hughes

1975

Behind the Scenes

The Street celebrated its fifteenth year with a spectacular storyline involving the burning down of the mail-order warehouse and the death of popular Edna Gee. Fire crews and paramedics worked with the production crew to create the blaze, making it the most ambitious disaster the Street had ever seen.

Mavis Rogerson, the actress who had portrayed blowsy Edna for five years, was unhappy with the decision to kill off her character but the story line demanded that a husband was created for her. Fred Gee became one of the most popular charcters of the late seventies.

Ken Farrington shocked Susi Hush by announcing his intention to leave the show and scripts had to be quickly rewritten so that Deirdre married Ray rather than Billy. The turnabout took the viewers by surprise and made Anne Kirkbride question her character's motives: 'There were no hearts and flowers involved and it was all very much matter-of-fact really. But it worked.'

The cast were in mourning in October, following the sudden death of Graham Haberfield. He was a much-loved work colleague who died of a heart-attack at the age of thirty-four. He had appeared in two episodes of the Street that hadn't been transmitted and Granada offered to edit him out but his widow, Valerie, asked for the scenes to remain intact as a tribute to him. As well as his thirteen years as Jerry Booth, and work on other shows such as *The Dustbinmen*, Graham left a lasting legacy on the original Street transmission tapes: standing in the studios waiting for the start of each show he would call out, 'Goodbye, real world,' which made the rest of the cast laugh away their anxieties.

Although each episode featured more scenes filmed on location than ever before – mainly involving characters talking on the Street itself – most scenes continued to be set in interiors and were recorded in the studio. Editing was kept to a minimum and the scenes were recorded in story order, one after another without a break. If anything went wrong the actors were encouraged to carry on regardless.

> "I've always wanted to be stormy, passionate and tempestuous. But you can't be. Not when you're born with a tidy mind."
>
> **Emily Bishop**

Key Dates — 1975

January 29	Lynne Johnson is murdered
July 7	Ray Langton marries Deirdre Hunt
September 29	Fred Gee's first appearance
October 1	Edna Gee killed in the warehouse fire
October 17	Graham Haberfield dies of heart failure, aged thirty-four, after appearing in 684 episodes as Jerry Booth
November 10	Jerry Booth dies

Top Twenty

Pos	Character	No of eps	Total	Pos Prev Year
1	Ray Langton	87	593	5
2	Len Fairclough	86	1228	2
3	Bet Lynch	86	428	3
4	Betty Turpin	84	506	1
5	Rita Littlewood	75	271	4
6	Hilda Ogden	74	808	15
7	Deirdre Langton	73	177	8
8	Annie Walker	70	1219	6
9	Ken Barlow	68	1035	9
10	Ernie Bishop	66	302	11
11	Alf Roberts	65	327	14
12	Blanche Hunt	61	73	29
13	Tricia Hopkins	60	92	22
14	Minnie Caldwell	58	983	16
15	Stan Ogden	58	777	13
16	Jerry Booth	55	684	7
17	Mavis Riley	54	143	16
18	Emily Bishop	53	860	12
19	Albert Tatlock	51	932	18
20	Ena Sharples	41	995	27

STORIES

1 Eddie Joins the Ogdens

Eddie Yeats finally got to grips with Bet Lynch in her bedsit but their passion was interrupted by the arrival of police, who marched Eddie away for overstaying his parole. Three months later he returned and moved back into lodgings at Minnie Caldwell's, announcing that he was now on the straight and narrow.

The Ogdens had a scare when Stan fell off his window-cleaning ladder and collapsed in the Street, suffering from otitis media, which disturbed his balance. He looked forward to a long rest but was refused dole as he hadn't paid his stamp for six months. Hilda was forced to take on the round and made a success of it, assisted by Eddie. When the doctor told Stan he was well enough to return to work he opted not to tell Hilda. She was furious when, a fortnight later and worn out, she visited the doctor and found out for herself.

Stan and Eddie formed a partnership to clean windows but were warned off a new estate by the Henshaw brothers. Nevertheless, the round was profitable and Eddie spent twenty pounds of the profits on an Alsatian called Fury. Hoping to hire the dog out, he broke into the yard to prove to Ray Langton that he needed a guard dog. Ray agreed to hire Fury for five pounds a week but soon afterwards both the dog and a large quantity of copper piping was stolen.

Looking into other people's houses proved too much for Eddie and he started to take advantage of his job to case houses for his friend Monkey Gibbons to burgle. The police found out but questioned Stan, suspecting him of the crimes. Hilda put the police on to Eddie and he was arrested after a detective found stolen goods hidden at Minnie's.

2 Murder At No.9

Len Fairclough was flattered when a young blonde housewife sought his help over her violent husband. Lynne Johnson showed Len her bruises and asked him, as her councillor, what she should do. Len advised her to leave her husband, Roy, and became annoyed with her when she refused to and kept turning up on his doorstep for help. Then, one day Jerry Booth and Ray Langton returned home from work to find Lynne dead in the kitchen. The police were called and all three men were taken in for questioning. Witnesses reported hearing Len shouting at Lynne, and Detective Inspector Patterson suspected him of murder. Len spent two nights in police cells and was annoyed when Rita Littlewood steered away from him. However, Bet Lynch paid him a visit and fought for his release. Eventually Patterson got a confession out of Roy Johnson and Len was released.

Business at the yard was bad, and Jerry and Ray nearly came to blows with Len after discovering he had not turned up for the only job on their books. Instead he had spent the afternoon in bed with Bet. She thought it was the start of a brilliant relationship, with someone she knew and trusted, but he made it clear that he was only interested in her for casual sex. Refusing to be used again, Bet finished with him and was at an all-time low when the news was broken to her that her nineteen-year-old son, Martin, had been killed in a car crash in Northern Ireland. Devastated

that the only decent thing in her life was dead, she contemplated suicide but Eddie Yeats took away her tablets and restored her faith in men by washing her tights.

3 A Midnight Flit

Maggie Clegg had been so worried that Gordon might hear from a stranger that she wasn't his mother that she summoned him to Weatherfield to break the news to him herself. She was upset when he immediately got drunk to celebrate that alcoholic Les wasn't his father. Betty hoped that the matter would be kept secret between the family, but when she criticized Granny Hopkins over her stock, Granny wrote to Gordon about his true parentage. Gordon was furious and ordered the

Hopkinses to leave the shop. Granny was all for digging her heels in but Idris and Vera were ashamed of her actions and the family, except Tricia, left under the cover of night.

In order to keep the shop open, Gordon installed Blanche Hunt as manageress and agreed that Tricia Hopkins could stay on and rent the shop flat with her friend Gail Potter. Tricia and Gail were tired of working in offices and sold their belongings to raise the money to enrol on a modelling course with the Jet Girl Agency. After one lesson they discovered that the agency was bogus and their money had disappeared along with the organizer. To pay the rent they took jobs as telephone salespeople for a heating company.

Jerry Booth tried to interest the girls in a biking holiday and borrowed the Ogdens' tandem to take them on a trip. Tricia was bored and came home early, Jerry limped back with a wrecked tandem, and Gail, who had left him to find help, eventually returned two days later having met a man with a Porsche.

4 Mavis Searches for Love

Mavis Riley was delighted when her Spanish boyfriend Carlos proposed to her. She looked forward to a June wedding before he admitted they'd have to marry within the month: he needed an English wife to get a work permit. Distraught that he didn't love her, Mavis broke with him. In an attempt to find Mr Right, she amazed Rita Littlewood by joining a computer dating agency, calling herself Mavis Armitage. Her first date turned out to be Ken Barlow who, after his initial embarrassment, took her to the Roebuck Inn for an evening of good food and fine wine. There was never any question of romance between the two, and Mavis continued to take dates offered by the agency. When one of her dates frightened her by stalking her, Jerry Booth stepped in. As ever, Mavis was grateful for his support but frustrated by the way he wouldn't declare any feelings for her.

She was also frustrated at work: Rita had taken a contract to sing at Ralph Lancaster's club, the Gatsby, and refused to get up early to make up the papers. Mavis found her workload too much and rebelled, accusing Rita of exploiting her. Jerry took her side, calling Rita cruel and bullying. The situation was resolved when Mavis's pay was increased by two pounds a week.

After Jerry's sudden death from pneumonia in November, Mavis found herself without her steadying force and soulmate, and only a month later she got herself into a lather when she caught Eunice Wheeler shoplifting in the Kabin. The police were called and Eunice was charged. Mavis felt guilty when she learnt Eunice had three children and tried to make amends by buying them Christmas presents, which were thrown back in her face.

5 A Change of Career for Ken

Ken Barlow found himself a victim of the recession when Mark Brittain made 20 per cent of the warehouse staff redundant. Ken was the first to go. He surprised the neighbours by taking a job with Weatherfield Cabs as a taxi driver and enjoyed not having a mentally challenging job for a change. One night his fare turned out to be his estranged wife Janet with her boyfriend Vince Denton, and the trio spent a civilized evening together.

In the autumn, three of Ken's former pupils, Chris Ashton and Kevin and Bernie Marsh, roamed the Street causing upset by cheeking the residents and vandalizing property. Albert Tatlock saw them smash a window in the community centre and reported them to the police. The youngsters thought Ken was responsible and wrecked No.11 in revenge.

Later Bernie and Kevin's father offered Ken thirty pounds to keep quiet about the vandalism but Ken refused the bribe. He didn't take the matter to the police as he felt society was to blame for the boys going off the rails.

However, fearing that the police were after them, the boys broke into the warehouse and spent the night in the storeroom. In the morning they left a cigarette burning and a blaze started. Unfortunately the storeroom was Edna Gee's favourite haunt for a cigarette. When she opened the door she was engulfed in flames and died instantly. The fire took hold, spread throughout the warehouse and the workers were evacuated, as were the residents of Coronation Street as toxic chemicals were in danger of igniting. Five fire engines battled the blaze and saved the terraced houses. Edna's husband, Fred, identified her body and was comforted by Ivy Tilsley, who lost her job along with the other warehouse workers.

The fire, and Ken's caring attitude towards the tearaways, convinced Alf Roberts that he was the man to bring the community closer together. Ken was appointed community officer at the centre, with the remit to serve the community. He started with the local youth group, which was dominated by the forceful personality of one teenager, Janice Berry. When Ken discovered she was bullying and blackmailing the others he organized an election to find a youth leader. Janice was humiliated in the polls and quit the centre.

6 Embarrassment for Alf

Eager to impress local businessman Harold Digby, Alf Roberts invited him and his wife to dinner. To round the numbers off he asked Mavis Riley to act as his hostess but

at the last minute she chickened out and Alf was left with her replacement, Rita Littlewood, in a plunging gown. Alf was relieved when the evening proved a success, and the next morning Rita received a see-through nightie as a present. She assumed it was from Alf and worried about his feelings towards her. However, Digby's wife revealed that her husband liked to bestow extravagant presents upon beautiful women.

Alf's head was turned by Donna Parker, who worked in the canteen at the GPO where Alf ran the sorting office. She asked him to help retrieve a letter she'd sent to her sister but he refused: it was against the law to tamper with the post. Instead, he listened to her problems and offered his spare bedroom so that she could escape a violent boyfriend. He became besotted with her and was flattered when she moved into his bed. When she told him about her dreams to open her own hair salon he had no hesitation in handing her five hundred pounds of his savings as a deposit on premises. As soon as she had the money Donna disappeared, leaving Alf feeling rather foolish. He told his friend Len Fairclough what had happened but rather than take his advice to inform the police put the incident down to experience.

7 Ernest Takes On the System

When Weatherfield Council put up the rates by 30 per cent Ernest Bishop refused to let them get away with it. He formed the residents into an action group, Weatherfield's Association of Rate-payers (WARP). After learning of a council plan to spend two thousand pounds on a statue and fountain in the precinct, he argued publicly with councillor Alf Roberts, and swore to oppose the idea. Alf shrugged off Ernest but fellow councillor Len Fairclough was annoyed. To show the residents he couldn't be bossed around, Len announced he was going on an all-expenses-paid trip to Torquay in the mayoral Rolls-Royce. Ernest discovered that the council had contracted to buy

dozens of tractors it didn't need from the brother of a councillor and, enraged, released the details on local radio, accusing the council of squandering rate-payers' money. When the tractors were sold for a huge profit Ernest was left facing a libel action, and saw WARP crumble as, one by one, the residents paid their rates, fearing prosecution.

8 Deirdre is a Bride

Deirdre Hunt was growing restive in her engagement and pressed fiancé Billy Walker into setting a date. He told her he only had £526 in savings and wasn't prepared to marry until he could provide for her. Deirdre insisted she didn't care and was happy to live at the Rovers if necessary. The wedding date was set for 24 May and Annie Walker clashed with Blanche Hunt when they both bought the same outfit.

Just nineteen days before the wedding, Deirdre felt unsettled about marrying Billy and then being stuck in a rut. She asked him for time to think through her doubts but he admitted that he, too, was having second thoughts. He broke off the engagement and left England for a bartending job at the Hotel Carlotta in St Helier, Jersey. Deirdre hit back by going out on the town and getting picked up by oil-rigger Maurice Gordon. When she spent the night with him in his hotel room

Blanche called her a slut and slapped her face. A couple of weeks later, when Maurice pestered her again, Deirdre was amazed when Ray Langton fought him off.

Deirdre and Ray were both troubled by their feelings for each other and she smashed up the yard office when he taunted her over Billy's disappearance. They made up then decided to get married, which amazed all the residents. The wedding took place at a local register office, with Len and Rita as witnesses. After honeymooning in London, the couple moved in with Blanche, and Ray carved the house into two separate flats. Deirdre threw herself into housekeeping and splashed out on a coffee table. A housewarming party ended in disaster when Eddie Yeats turned up with his stripper girlfriend Michelle Turnbull: egged on by the men, she started to strip, and upset Deirdre so much by burning the table with her cigarette that she told the guests to leave.

Towards the end of the year, Tricia Hopkins, who had long had a crush on Ray, saw him in town with a woman and started spreading a rumour that he was being unfaithful. Deirdre thumped Tricia, giving her a black eye. Then Ray introduced her to the woman – a client he had taken to choose tiles for her bathroom – and thanked her for having faith in him.

9 Annie's Darkest Hour

The fire engines attending the warehouse fire used so much water to douse the flames that the cellar at the Rovers Return flooded. Annie Walker was grateful when the residents lent a hand, and several buckets, to form a human chain to bail out the water but afterwards discovered that her nest-egg of thirty gold sovereigns, which had been hidden in the cellar, was missing. She was quick with accusations and embarrassed when Bet Lynch revealed that the coins were safe in the place to which Billy had removed them some months before. Annie was grateful when Bet smoothed out the residents' ruffled feathers but her gratitude didn't last long.

Bet was thrilled when her old flame Frank Bradley turned up, working as a drayman for the brewery. They went out on a date together and Bet hoped for a golden future. She was disappointed, though, by the return of Sean Regan, who still fancied her – despite his marriage to Concepta – and warned Frank off. Bet was furious and slapped Sean before threatening to write to Concepta to tell her of the pass he made at her. Annie was furious when Sean suddenly returned to Ireland, and refused to believe Bet's side of the story: she maintained that he wouldn't sully himself with a slut like her. She fired Bet, but was forced to reinstate her after discovering the truth from Len Fairclough. In order to protect Concepta Annie begged Bet to tear up the letter, which she did.

That night Annie went to bed, glad to have saved Concepta some upset. She was unaware that two youths, Neil Foxall and Les Grimes, were hiding in the toilets. As she slept they ransacked her living quarters looking for valuables. Annie woke to find the youths in her bedroom but they refused to be intimidated by her and threatened her with violence if she didn't hand over her cash.

Annie refused to co-operate and they fled empty-handed when Len Fairclough and Ray Langton, alerted by the light of their torch, arrived and fought them off. The shock was too much for Annie and she fell down the stairs, petrified that the brewery would learn of the break-in and force her to retire. After recovering in hospital, she was flattered when the brewery bosses expressed their continued faith in her.

The year ended with a surprise visit from Concepta, who sadly confided in Annie that she wasn't blind to Sean's faults but was too much in love with him to do anything about them.

10 Betty's Personality Wins Through

Newton & Ridley ran a competition in each of its public houses to find the Personality of the Pub. Annie Walker and Bet Lynch were both put out when they lost in the regulars' vote to Betty Turpin. In her turn Betty nominated Stan Ogden as the company's best customer. The brewery calculated he had drunk more pints in the Rovers than any other customer and awarded him free beer for a week.

When she was looking after the pub one night in Annie's absence, Betty had a shock when she thought she saw Martha Longhurst's ghost in the Snug. A pair of glasses identical to Martha's were found on the bar, and Betty was relieved when an

elderly customer claimed them. Later she was flattered to find herself the object of fishmonger Bert Gosling's desire, although his coarse humour offended her. He gave her half a salmon, hoping she'd invite him to tea, and Betty stored it in the Rovers' fridge. When Annie found it, she assumed Bert was paying court to her and frightened him off by flirting with him.

The moment Betty had dreaded for thirty years finally came when Sophie Edwards, a barmaid picked up by a visiting Gordon Clegg, told the residents that Betty was his real mother. Betty resigned from the Rovers and contemplated moving to London to live with her son, but Annie and Bet made her see no one was judging her and that she was better off staying where she belonged.

11 A Muddled Year for Albert, Minnie and Ena

Albert Tatlock adopted a stray pigeon and named him Gilbert. He had plans to race him and start breeding, and was most upset when Minnie Caldwell's cat, Bobby, killed and ate him. Minnie assured Albert that the bird's death would have been painless, but she was unaware that Albert himself was in constant agony. Shrapnel had entered his body when he was fighting in the trenches in 1916 and nearly sixty years later it was time to have it removed. It had reached his backside after floating all round his body and Albert felt enough was enough. He sought medical help. Weeks later he celebrated his eightieth birthday with a surprise party the residents threw for him in the Street and was grateful to be able to sit down in comfort.

Minnie Caldwell spent much of the year visiting Handel Gartside in Whaley Bridge, and when Ena Sharples returned to the area there was nowhere for her to stay. She dumped herself on Annie Walker, claiming that she was within her rights as the Rovers was an inn, but within a week she'd moved out as she kept getting under Annie's feet. Gail and Tricia took her in above the Corner Shop but eventually Alf Roberts came to the rescue by insisting she be installed once more as caretaker at the centre. Ena was thankful to move back into the flat.

Cinderella

Rita Littlewood turned her hand to theatrical management when she produced *Cinderella* at the community centre. The audience was made up of local children. Rita didn't appear herself but sang all of Prince Charming's songs while Bet Lynch mimed on the stage.

Cinderella...........**Tricia Hopkins**
Prince Charming...........**Bet Lynch**
Buttons...........**Len Fairclough**
Ugly Sisters...........**Hilda Ogden and Alf Roberts**
Fairy Godmother...........**Betty Turpin**
Dandini...........**Deirdre Langton**
Baron...........**Albert Tatlock**
Baroness...........**Mavis Riley**

Costumes and makeup by Blanche Hunt, music by Ernest 'Fingers' Bishop

CAST

Lynne Johnson	Ann Kennedy
Roy Johnson	Roddy McMillan
Harold Digby	Joe Lynch
Ralph Lancaster	Kenneth Watson
Maurice Gordon	Ray Lonnen
Donna Parker	Rachel Davies
Michelle Turnbull	Carolyn Pickles
Monkey Gibbons	Arthur Kelly
Vince Denton	Mike Hayward
Bert Gosling	Meredith Edwards
Chris Ashton	Bryan Sweeney
Bernie Marsh	Sean Flannigan
Kevin Marsh	Kevin Moreton
Fred Gee	Fred Feast
Sophie Edwards	Diana Quiseekay
Janice Berry	Vicky Williams
Neil Foxall	Terence Budd
Les Grimes	Mike Grady
Eunice Wheeler	Brenda Elder

1976

Behind the Scenes

The year started with a change of producer. Bill Podmore arrived as the seventeenth on the show but his reign, until 1988, was to be the longest. His greatest legacy to the show was his insistence on including as much comedy as possible. He had learnt his craft on Granada programmes including *Nearest and Dearest* and one of his first moves was to bring one of the stars of that show, Madge Hindle, across the cobbles to create the character of Renee Bradshaw. Recalling the days of Florrie Lindley and Maggie Clegg, Podmore hoped to make the shop once again the arena for gossip and intrigue.

Patricia Phoenix returned, after three years spent touring the country in stage plays. She explained, 'Somebody caught me on a very cold night in a dressing room in Morecambe and I was fed up and I said "I want to go home." ' Her first scene involved walking down the familiar Street and knocking on Len Fairclough's door. His greeting was, 'Welcome back, Tanner,' but the shot took so many takes that Peter Adamson actually muttered, 'Welcome back, Tanner, why don't you shove off again?' Viewers were thrilled to see the red-headed siren back at No.11, and Ena Sharples returned after Violet Carson's spate of ill health.

Key Dates 1976

Febuary 23	Derek Wilton's first appearance
April 5	Elsie Howard returns after an absence of three years
April 7	Margot Bryant makes her last appearance as Minnie Caldwell, after 986 episodes
May 10	Renee Bradshaw's first appearance
October 11	Mike Baldwin's first appearance

> "The story of my life. Two marriages. Two kids. Several jobs. A variety of dreams and ambitions, some shattered, some just getting a bit tatty round the edges."

Ken Barlow

As well as old faces there were new ones, including the first appearance of Derek Wilton, who started a courtship with Mavis Riley that lasted thirteen years. Johnny Briggs also joined the cast as Londoner Mike Baldwin: he was to be a modern-day Dave Smith, viewed as a villainous employer and treated with suspicion. Johnny had been a boy soprano and had become famous for his action-heartthrob role in the television drama *No Hiding Place*.

Margot Bryant made her last appearance when Minnie Caldwell retired to Whaley Bridge with Bobby the cat. In reality Margot's ailing health caused her to enter a nursing home where she lived until her death in 1988.

Top Twenty

Pos	Character	No of eps	Total	Pos Prev Year
1	Len Fairclough	82	1310	2
2	Bet Lynch	78	506	3
3	Betty Turpin	77	583	4
4	Ray Langton	71	664	1
5	Annie Walker	70	1289	8
6	Hilda Ogden	69	877	6
7	Ken Barlow	66	1101	9
8	Elsie Howard	64	1131	–
9	Alf Roberts	63	390	11
10	Gail Potter	63	109	22
11	Deirdre Langton	60	237	7
12	Rita Littlewood	59	330	5
13	Emily Bishop	58	918	18
14	Ernie Bishop	58	360	10
15	Mavis Riley	57	200	17
16	Stan Ogden	56	833	14
17	Albert Tatlock	54	986	19
18	Fred Gee	52	54	–
19	Terry Bradshaw	49	49	–
20	Ena Sharples	42	1037	20

STORIES

1 Living Over The Brush

Ken Barlow stood in the witness stand and gave a character reference for the Marsh brothers, which upset many of the residents who wanted the lads locked away for killing Edna Gee. Ken blamed their parents publicly and felt sorry for the boys as they were sent to a detention centre for three months.

At the community centre, he threw himself into organizing art classes, in which Albert Tatlock posed as a model, and a literary appreciation class run by market researcher Wendy Nightingale. Ken and Wendy were attracted to each other and he took advantage of her feelings towards him to manoeuvre her into bed. Wendy felt guilty about being unfaithful to her husband Roger and confessed all, leading to him confront Ken at No.11 then knock him, unconscious, to the ground. Wendy's response was to walk out of the marital home, and her Mini was soon parked permanently outside Ken's house.

Albert told Ken he was disgusted with him living in sin, especially as he was still married to Janet, but Ken refused to listen. Content with his personal life, he set about putting together a bank-holiday street party.

When she saw Ken in his natural environment, taking charge of the neighbours, Wendy felt out of place and too middle-class. But after receiving complaints, the centre's committee reprimanded Ken for his personal life. He, of course, refused to be dictated to, and was astonished when Wendy announced that she was returning to Roger after discovering he had paid her car insurance. When his bosses offered Ken their condolences, he told them he had no confidence in the committee and walked out of his job.

While Ken faced a professional and emotional crossroads, Albert was having his own problems. He was struggling on his pension, and the council told him that he was too old to keep his beloved allotment. Ken was moved by Albert's vulnerability and, for his sake, decided to remain in Weatherfield, moving into No.1 as his lodger. He returned to the centre and rallied the locals into helping on the allotment. When Ray Langton got bored with digging, he carved 'Albert rules, OK' on a marrow.

Albert formed a bingo partnership with fellow OAP, Bertha Lumley. They enjoyed two sessions a week at the Alhambra and once split a hundred-pound win 50-50. It all came to an end, though, after Bertha's husband Nat learnt they had exchanged a kiss and threatened to kill Albert.

2 Ernest Signs On

Ernest Bishop's nightmare year started with accusations of embezzlement when he mislaid a five-pound postal order he was holding as treasurer of the Scout fund. Tricia Hopkins spread rumours that the Bishops had been stealing from Mission funds and was shamefaced when, after finding the money, Ernest delivered a sermon on trust and honesty.

There was more trouble in store for Ernest when, forgetting his wedding anniversary, he went to a stag night with Alf Roberts and Ray Langton and ended up on the stage as a stripper's prop. Emily was furious and locked him out of the house. Ernest had to do a lot of begging before she forgave him. Hearing that the Mission superintendent wanted an explanation, Ernest took Ena Sharples's advice and said he'd gone to the party to study filth and obscenity.

The trebling of the Studio's rent forced Ernest into liquidation and he was forced to sign on. When he sold his precious cameras to meet an Inland Revenue demand, Emily upset him by selling her engagement ring. She took a job as an orderly at Weatherfield General but Ernest turned down a porter's job as blood made him faint. Rita Littlewood came to the rescue by securing him a job as the Gatsby's resident pianist but he was forced to play at stag nights and Emily was upset when strippers called to practise their routines at No.3.

3 The Langtons' First Year

Blanche Hunt made a break with the past when she sold her corset business and left Weatherfield to run a country club in Kenilworth. The club was owned by Dave Smith, who caused upset by returning to the area after an absence of five years. He showed an interest in opening a cash-and-carry in the old warehouse but was refused planning permission and had to content himself with rekindling an affair that had ended twenty years before.

Blanche's daughter Deirdre Langton was made to feel unskilled when Ray offered an apprenticeship to teenager Jill Marriott. Jill turned the post down, saying the yard wasn't a proper business, and Deirdre felt all she would be good for was

motherhood. She had a false alarm and then, six months later, told a delighted Ray that she was pregnant. Ray spent months planning for the new arrival and renovated a second-hand pram, which Deirdre promptly gave away. Eager to move out of their cramped flat he hoped to buy a house on Coronation Street but again clashed with his wife, who refused to live anywhere so dingy and common.

4 Hilda's Deli Dash

Hilda Ogden became a granny for the third time following the birth of an eight-pound-five-ounce baby girl named Jayne. After fussing over the baby in Chesterfield, Hilda returned home to find the house suspiciously clean and tidy. Unaware that Minnie Caldwell had been looking after Stan, she automatically assumed he'd found another woman. To win him back she tried to make herself alluring, only to be disappointed when he failed to notice.

Stan panicked when he heard that a TV detector van was roaming the area. He tried to hide the television but bumped into Hilda as she returned from buying a licence and dropped the set. The repairman refused to mend it, saying it had obviously been manhandled so Stan attempted to claim on the insurance by starting a small fire in it. Unfortunately he used too much lighter fluid so an inferno was the result and the rental shop demanded seventy-five pounds to replace the television. Hoping for a change in their fortunes, Hilda started entering competitions and ended up winning a dash around a local delicatessen. Because of Stan's bad back, Deirdre Langton joined Hilda in grabbing £107 worth of goods. The deli owner was happy to exchange the fancy food for cash plus a tin of caviar. Hilda paid off the television rental shop and treated Stan to caviar and chips for supper.

During the bank-holiday street party, Stan tried to win five pounds by letting his escapologist pal Wally Fisher lock him up in chains in a sack. He assured Hilda he could free himself but found he wasn't as nimble as he had been the last time he'd done the stunt. Hilda feared Stan would suffocate, so a search was launched for Wally, who was found drunk in the ladies' toilet.

5 Changes at the Corner Shop

Gail Potter had a nasty experience in her bedsit above the Corner Shop when she

started to receive obscene phonecalls. She was relieved when engineer John Lane arrived to tap the calls but when he was still in the flat after three hours she realized all was not well. He revealed himself to be the caller and swore he loved her. She was petrified, thinking he was going to hurt her, but luckily Emily Bishop grew suspicious and called the police, who arrested him.

Gail and Tricia had given up telesales and had started to run the Corner Shop while still claiming the dole. Gordon Clegg was furious to find they had allowed the stock to run down and had chalked up hefty slates for boys they fancied. He decided to buy the shop from Maggie and give it to his mother Betty Turpin, but she said she didn't want the responsibility. Instead he sold it to supermarket cashier Renee Bradshaw.

Renee's brother Terry was already settled in the area, helping out occasionally in the Rovers as well as labouring at the yard, and Renee hoped to provide a stable home for him. Having bought the shop and evicted Gail and Tricia she thought he could have the bedsit. Tricia remained as her assistant in the shop for a couple of weeks until Renee sacked her over her lax attitude. She left the Street and took a job in a humbug factory. Her parting shot was to report Renee for opening the shop after hours.

To boost trade, Renee applied for a licence to sell alcohol, which infuriated Annie Walker who stood against the application. The matter went to court, with Renee handing in a petition signed by 276 customers. Annie was enraged when she lost the objection, mainly due to Bet Lynch taking the stand and saying an off-licence would be healthy competition for the pub. Ena Sharples was the first customer at the off-licence and, as such, was given two free bottles of ale.

Renee's fiancé, sailor Harry McClean, dropped anchor but only long enough for her to tell him their relationship was over. Instead, she was looking forward to a happy time with Terry but that was denied her: Terry developed a crush on Gail but when she laughed at his advances he slapped her face and left to join the Army. Renee called Gail a trollop.

6 Mavis Meets Derek

Furniture sales representative Derek Wilton was so taken with Mavis Riley after calling into the Kabin for directions that he asked her out for a drink. She was delighted and enjoyed his company so much that she surprised Rita Littlewood by joining him on a weekend's holiday in the Lakes. He bought her a mood-stone ring and after the holiday it shone green for contentment. Eager to progress the relationship, Mavis borrowed Rita's flat to cook a romantic meal, but the evening ended in frustration and tears when Derek failed to take any liberties and shook hands with her. Derek was a shy man and felt he couldn't continue to see Mavis without first consulting his mother. He took Mavis to tea with her but Amy Wilton wasn't impressed by her guest, saying that the pair were too alike. On his mother's advice, he stopped seeing Mavis.

Mavis made the most of her lonely nights to write a novel *Song of a Scarlet Summer*, based on observations from behind the counter. Her heroine, Rosalind Lane, was based on Rita, the hero Lionel Forrest on Len. Rita sneaked a peep at the manuscript and was surprised to find how steamy it was: '. . . she tossed back her chestnut curls and unable to control his passion Lionel bent his strong mouth to her waiting rosebud lips . . .' Mavis sent the finished book to a publisher then panicked in case any of the customers recognized themselves in her work and sued for libel. She was relieved when the novel was rejected and decided not to pursue a career in writing.

7 Stan and Albert's Lock-in

Annie Walker was ordered by the brewery to employ a resident potman after Stan Ogden and Albert Tatlock spent a night locked in the Rovers' cellar, drinking from the barrels. She took in Fred Gee while he was still working as a storeman at a local foundry. He fell for Rita Littlewood, but she wasn't interested in him and told him she was dating Derek Wilton, which didn't go down too well with Mavis Riley. Fred found a more willing girlfriend in the shape of Vera Duckworth. However, Annie didn't approve of her and played gooseberry whenever she was in the Rovers.

When the brewery put on a Superbrain contest, Annie was adamant that the Rovers should win and held a competition to choose who was to represent the pub. She was amazed when Stan Ogden won, answering questions on Manchester United. In the second round he decided to answer questions on the Western Desert, but the residents had no confidence in him. They got him drunk and sent Bet Lynch instead, answering questions on detective novels. She came last in the round but won a date with the quizmaster.

Nellie Harvey surprised Annie by showing off her new white Mini and challenging her to learn to drive in less than eighty-six lessons, the number she had had. Annie rose to the occasion and startled Alf Roberts by asking him to give her lessons. While Annie busied herself with learning correct stopping times, Fred joined up with Alf and Terry Bradshaw and bought a greyhound called Fred's Folly. They housed the dog with Albert and planned to race her. Out driving with Alf, Annie was startled when the dog ran across her path. She swerved to avoid it and crashed into Stan's window-cleaning cart. Accusations flew, with Hilda threatening to sue and Alf facing major car repairs. The dog disappeared and Fred mourned his loss of earnings. Eventually Annie paid for the car to be fixed, and to pacify Hilda Len Fairclough built Stan a new cart.

Annie passed her test after eighty-three lessons, beating Nellie. She bought a Rover 2000 but on her first trip out she was stopped by the police and breathalysed. When the test showed positive she was taken to the police station to give a blood sample.

8 The Return of the Siren

Elsie Howard turned up on Len Fairclough's doorstep with her suitcase and explained that she and husband Alan had reached the end of the road. Rita Littlewood was most put out by her arrival: just days before she had told Len that her old flame Harry Bates had proposed to her, in the hope that Len would declare himself. Instead he'd told her he wasn't bothered whether she married Harry or not. In the event she turned him down and still harboured hopes of becoming Mrs Fairclough, but worried that Elsie's return would ruin her plans.

Elsie lodged in the living quarters at the Corner Shop and took a job as manageress of Sylvia Matthews's lingerie shop, Sylvia's Separates. She employed Gail Potter as her assistant and set about educating the local women in the ways of silk and satin. When Hilda Ogden tried to return a top which was too young for her, Elsie refused to take it back as it had been purchased in a sale. Furious, Hilda told Sylvia that she was employing someone who had been accused of shoplifting. Sylvia assumed that Gail was who she meant but Elsie admitted it and resigned. After acquainting herself with all the facts of the case Sylvia apologized and Elsie was reinstated.

Elsie moved into No.11 and Gail became the lodger. Their first night at the house was interrupted by the arrival of jailbirds Eddie Yeats and Monkey Gibbons, who had been told by Ray Langton that the house was empty. When Ray told Elsie he thought she'd have welcomed male company she set about him with her handbag, weighted down with a glass ashtray.

9 Len Gets It Wrong

Alf Roberts caused a stir when, quite out of character, he started to spend a lot of money on his appearance. Then he received an anonymous letter accusing him of taking backhanders and pinned it to the Rovers' dartboard, protesting his innocence.

Meanwhile, his friend Len Fairclough tracked down Donna Parker and made a play for her, while assuring Rita Littlewood that his interest in Donna was purely in the name of justice: he planned to retrieve the money she had swindled out of Alf. When she began to look for new premises, Len offered Donna the Kabin, and she agreed to buy it from him, giving him a sizeable deposit. Len handed the money over to Alf, only to discover that Donna had already returned the money, with interest, and it had been that he'd been splashing around.

Business at the yard rolled along and in the summer Len and Ray landed a contract at a building site. There, they discovered that the site foreman, Jack Barker, was stealing equipment and selling it. Len refused to keep quiet over this so Barker rigged the scaffolding he was working on. Unfortunately Ray was the one to walk across it when it collapsed. He was rushed to hospital and Len sought comfort by ramming his fists into Barker.

When Elsie Howard challenged him to prove he could still show a girl a good time, he took her to watch Rita singing at the Gatsby. Rita was infuriated when he refused to give her a week's holiday from the Kabin to fulfil a booking in Torquay and hit him: he fell off a bar stool and knocked his head on the floor. While he recovered in bed, Elsie and Rita jostled for the honour of nursing him. Rita gave up Torquay to look after him and was furious to find that he was feigning illness. She poured a pint over him and threw all his clean washing into the Street.

10 Gail Falls in Love

Young Gail Potter enjoyed being mothered by Elsie Howard but objected when Elsie tried to advise her on her love-life. Roy Thornley was a sales representative who

often called at the shop and Gail was flattered when he showed an interest in her. When Elsie warned her off the older man, Gail accused her of being jealous of their love. Gail's bubble burst when Elsie found out that Roy was married. He apologized to Gail but she felt cheated out of her virginity. Then Doreen Thornley filed for divorce, citing Gail, and Roy begged her to lie in court to help him. When Doreen called Gail a trollop and a home wrecker Gail broke down and Sylvia Matthews joined in with the furore by sacking her from the shop. Elsie refused to let Gail take all the blame and secured her job by threatening Sylvia with an industrial tribunal. Then she uncovered the truth: Sylvia was Roy's long-standing mistress and Elsie persuaded Doreen to drop Gail's name in favour of the bigger fish.

11 Albert and Ena Left Alone

Ena Sharples and Albert Tatlock were both saddened to hear that Minnie Caldwell had left for good to live in Whaley Bridge. Handel Gartside removed her belongings and promised Ena he'd take good care of her old friend. To cheer them up, Albert smuggled a bottle of rum into the Snug and he and Ena got quietly drunk together, remembering the good times.

Ena remained as sharp as ever: when conman Frank Holmes attempted to sell her a shower, she alerted Eddie Yeats, for Holmes had said he'd sold one to a woman Ena knew had been dead for five months. Eddie captured Holmes, and was embarrassed to make a citizen's arrest.

12 Eddie's Designs on Chez Ogden

Back in the area and looking for somewhere to lay his head, Eddie Yeats offered himself to the Ogdens as a lodger. Hilda agreed to take him in, on the condition that he helped Stan decorate the living room. Eddie acquired a job lot of half-price wallpaper but half-way through hanging it discovered that several rolls were faded. Hilda fumed at her ruined room but Eddie came to the rescue when he found a mural to hang on the unfinished wall. Hilda fell in love with the scenic vista of the Canadian Rockies and invited the neighbours round to take in the view.

When Hilda suspected local lads of stealing her washing, Stan ended up with a black eye. He retaliated by following them home and stealing theirs. Then Hilda discovered her washing hadn't been stolen at all: Renee Bradshaw had taken it in when rain had started to fall. The lads' father tracked Stan down and thumped him.

Eddie also had trouble with irate parents when he helped out at the community centre's playgroup. He was a natural with the kids and Ken Barlow planned to put him on the payroll, but parents objected to having their children mixing with a jailbird and he had to give up.

Hilda reached her lowest ebb when Bet Lynch found her old mac and gave it to some children to dress their guy. Stan bought it back for 10p but Hilda was too insulted to wear it again. Then when she realized that Stan had stolen half of the Christmas money she snapped: she told him she was sick of him and sick of being the local joke. Then she ordered him out of her sight whereupon he disappeared.

Stan roamed around the country before dumping himself on Hilda's younger brother, Norman Crabtree. Norman ran a fish-and-chip shop in Oakhill with his flirtatious assistant Edie Blundell. When she didn't hear from him for two weeks Hilda feared Stan was dead and was furious to hear that her own brother had taken him in. Eddie Yeats decided to reconcile the couple because Hilda refused to let him stay at No.13 without Stan: it wouldn't be proper, she said. He begged Stan to return, only to find he'd got his feet under Edie's table and had no desire to go back to Hilda. In the end it was up to Hilda to see Edie off and drag Stan home. However, Eddie's hopes for the back bedroom were dashed again when Hilda informed him that she and Stan needed a honeymoon period and he was unwelcome.

13 Baldwin Opens Shop

Londoner Michael Vernon Baldwin arrived in Weatherfield and bought the disused warehouse to open up his second factory manufacturing denim clothes. He employed Ernest Bishop as wages clerk and advertised for people to sew. Ivy Tilsley, Vera Duckworth and flirtatious Marie Stanton were all taken on, and when Annie Walker threatened to cut wages at the Rovers, Bet Lynch and Betty Turpin applied. Annie tried to persuade Ernest only to take on Bet but he refused: Betty was unsuitable for the work but he wasn't going to upset her by saying so. Instead, he turned them both down. In the meantime, Annie employed inexperienced Gail Potter to serve behind the bar but she couldn't cope with the demands of the job and resigned. Annie was forced to drop the pay cut and her faithful staff returned to the fold. Bet, however, had caught Mike's eye and after buying No.5 he modernized it and installed Bet as his live-in lover. He told her that he had a wife in London but needed comforting during the week and she was happy with the arrangement, although Annie insisted Bet referred to herself as Mike's housekeeper.

When Sylvia Matthews decided to sell her shop Elsie Howard suggested that Mike bought it and turned it into an outlet for his clothes. He liked the idea but upset Elsie by making Gail Potter manageress and telling Elsie she was too old to sell trendy gear. Instead he moved Elsie to the factory, and made her sewing-room supervisor. Her management skills immediately ironed out a problem when the girls threatened to strike as Ernest refused to pay them on Thursdays rather than Fridays. Elsie sided with the girls, pointing out the difficulties of shopping, and won Mike round. The girls had their revenge on Ernest at the staff Christmas party when they pounced on him and debagged him. Meanwhile, Marie was busy in Mike's office, getting to grips with an appreciative Len Fairclough.

CAST

Jill Marriott	Julie Shipley
John Lane	Ian Hastings
Terry Bradshaw	Bob Mason
Derek Wilton	Peter Baldwin
Wendy Nightingale	Susan Farmer
Roger Nightingale	Matthew Long
Sylvia Matthews	Rosemary Dunham
Roy Thornley	Sydney Livingstone
Wally Fisher	Michael Ripper
Frank Holmes	Colin Farrell
Bertha Lumley	Nadoline Thomas
Nat Lumley	Eric Longworth
Jack Barker	Sean Lynch
Amy Wilton	Hilary Mason
Doreen Thornley	Jane Lowe
Renee Bradshaw	Madge Hindle
Mike Baldwin	Johnny Briggs
Harry McLean	Richard Moore
Marie Stanton	Lois Baxter
Norman Crabtree	Stan Stennett
Edie Blundell	Avis Bunnage

1977

Behind the Scenes

The curse of the Barlows claimed another victim in the shape of Janet, Ken's second wife. Judith Barker, the actress playing Janet, was pleased to be killed off: although she found plenty of theatre work, television roles had been thin on the ground – producers felt she was still associated with the Street.

The wedding of Rita and Len, four years in the making, was billed as the highlight of the year, although filming didn't go without hitches. Barbara Knox was involved in a car crash just weeks before and Rita was married wearing a brace under the wedding dress and Patricia Phoenix was too ill to attend the ceremony. Photographs had already been taken for a *TV Times* souvenir and the familiar shape of Elsie had to be edited out to match the screened storyline, which involved Elsie being too upset to attend.

Towards the end of the year Stephen Hancock told Bill Podmore that he wanted to leave the show: he was irritated by the cast payment system. That September, he was quoted in the *News of the World* as saying. 'The Street kills an actor. I'm just doing a job, not acting. The scriptwriters have turned me into Ernie Bishop. I've tried to resist it, but it is very hard not to play the part all the time, even at home.' Bill Podmore decided that to save Emily Ernest would have to die, and Bill agreed with scriptwriter John Stevenson that a brutal murder would devastate residents and viewers alike. Although it was not transmitted until January 1978, the death scenes were recorded in December.

Top Twenty

Pos	Character	No of eps	Total	Pos Prev Year
1	Len Fairclough	78	1388	1
2	Elsie Howard	77	1208	8
3	Hilda Ogden	77	954	6
4	Bet Lynch	77	583	2
5	Rita L Fairclough	74	404	12
6	Ray Langton	72	736	4
7	Betty Turpin	67	650	3
8	Annie Walker	66	1355	5
9	Alf Roberts	65	455	9
10	Ken Barlow	64	1165	7
11	Eddie Yeats	64	146	22
12	Mavis Riley	63	263	15
13	Deirdre Langton	62	299	11
14	Renee Bradshaw	61	103	21
15	Fred Gee	61	115	18
16	Gail Potter	60	169	9
17	Stan Ogden	58	891	16
18	Emily Bishop	57	975	13
19	Albert Tatlock	56	1042	17
20	Ernie Bishop	55	415	13

> "We've all had our nightmares. We're all the walkin' wounded. It's just that some of us get more wounded than others."

Rita Littlewood

Key Dates 1977

January 10	Suzie Birchall's first appearance
January 24	Tracy Langton is born
February 21	Janet Barlow dies
April 20	Len Fairclough marries Rita Littlewood
August 17	Edie Riley dies
November 29	Doris Speed invested with the MBE by the Queen at Buckingham Palace.

STORIES

1 A New Life

Deirdre Langton started the year with a dash to the maternity unit at Weatherfield General. However, her contractions stopped, she was sent home shamefaced and locked herself away at home until she went into labour for real a week later. She

gave birth to an eight-pound-four-ouce daughter and clashed with Ray over what to call her. She had decided upon Lynette but Ray had his own favourite name and registered his daughter as Tracy Lynette. Blanche Hunt arrived to make a fuss of the baby and surprised the family by showing off her fiancé, a vet called Steve Bassett. Deirdre was relieved that she'd finished with Dave Smith. Ray bought No.5 from Mike Baldwin and Deirdre returned happily to work part-time at the Yard. She was upset when the vicar at St Luke's refused to christen Tracy because the Langtons weren't churchgoers. The vicar at St Mary's wasn't so strict, though, and Ken, Emily and Betty stood as godparents.

To celebrate the Queen's Silver Jubilee, Ken Barlow organized competitions at the community centre. Tracy was voted the bonniest baby and won her parents a weekend in London. Emily Bishop was hurt when Deirdre refused to leave Tracy with her when they went away and Blanche arrived to babysit. When the Langtons' return train was held up, Blanche was forced to leave Tracy in Ena Sharples's care as she had to return home to the Midlands. However, while she was rushing to answer the phone, Ena tripped and was knocked out. Tracy's cries alerted the Bishops, who comforted her and rushed Ena to hospital. Deirdre apologized to Emily for having doubted her abilities in the first place.

2 Suzie Takes the Street by Storm

Teenager Suzie Birchall talked Mike Baldwin into employing her in his boutique and cheeked her way into sharing Gail Potter's room at No.11. To prove her worth to Elsie Howard, she attempted to clean the chimney by dropping a brick down it. Unfortunately she chose the wrong chimney and the Ogdens' living room ended up covered in soot. Elsie was amused by Suzie as she reminded her of her younger self but she was furious when Suzie brought a stray dog, Albert, into the house only to have him ruin her new dress. At Suzie's suggestion, Mike held a competition for the renaming of his shop and presented Albert Tatlock with a denim outfit for thinking up 'The Western Front'.

When Elsie went away on holiday, Suzie let out her bedroom to make money. The lodger was French student Roger Floriet, who took advantage of his good looks to have the girls running around after him. Both declared love for him but he couldn't choose between them and returned alone to Lyon.

Mike employed Steve Fisher as delivery-van driver even though he had too many qualifications for the job. Gail fell for Steve immediately, but he had eyes only for Suzie. She enjoyed his attention but thought him too immature to bother with. The girls talked Steve into letting them join him on a delivery to Southport. He parked the van on the beach and was stranded when the tide came in and ruined the stock. Mike sacked him but changed his mind when the girls took the blame.

Suzie had moved to the Street because she was on the run from her violent, abusive father, Bob. She was terrified when he tracked her down and insisted she return home because her mother had run away. She refused but he tried to drag her into his car, and Steve had to fight him off. Bob was furious and told Suzie she was no longer his daughter.

Steve was upset to overhear Mike betting that he could take Suzie on a date and tried to warn her. However, she liked the idea and went out with him, allowing him to spend money on her. However, she frustrated his attempts to get her into bed and annoyed him by taking up with Robin Smethurst, who was young enough to be his son.

3 Ken's Troubled Family Life

Janet Barlow returned to the Street and begged Ken to take her back. He refused but allowed her to spend the night at No.1. He wasn't aware that she had split with her boyfriend Vince Denton and was depressed. That night she took an overdose and in the

morning Ken discovered her body. When he was taken in for questioning Emily Bishop collapsed in the Street, feeling guilty for not having had time to talk to Janet.

After the funeral Vince told Ken that he'd put £7,520 into Janet's building-society account as a tax dodge and asked him to return the money. Ken agreed, which upset Albert Tatlock who felt the twins could have had it.

In the summer one of the twins, Peter, visited No.1 and Ken was ashamed to realize he didn't know his son at all. In an attempt to befriend him, he took him walking in the Peak District but Ken fell down a hill and had to lie there all night while Peter ran for help and guided the mountain rescue team to him. Ken was winched to safety by helicopter, with torn ligaments in his leg, and Peter was praised for his bravery.

4 Mike's Troubled Love Life

Meanwhile, Bet Lynch's hold upon Mike Baldwin's affections had been challenged by Marie Stanton, who made a big play for a willing Mike. Bet had fought her off, much to Mike's glee, then threatened to see off any other contenders. She had enjoyed living with him at No.5 but annoyed him by employing Hilda Ogden to clean the house. He pointed out that Bet was his housekeeper, then asked her to provide another tart to help him entertain a business client. To spite him, Bet asked Betty Turpin to make up the foursome but Mike was delighted as the client enjoyed Betty's sense of humour and gave him the contract.

Then Mike told Bet to clear out of the house as his wife was coming for the weekend. When Anne arrived she guessed from the blonde hairs and cheap scent at No.5 that Bet was Mike's mistress and warned her off. Bet was stunned when Anne revealed that she was only Mike's common-law wife – they weren't married. Bet rounded on Mike for lying to her to stop her getting too close to him and finished by slapping his face. He told her they were finished and ordered her out of the house. She refused to go and changed the locks, but was forced to give way when he sold No.5 to the Langtons.

For a while it looked as if Mike would have to put his workers on a three-day week but militant Ivy Tilsley refused to let him take work to his London factory and instead rallied the girls to work harder. Their efforts were spoilt by the arrival of Terri Clayton, whose mother owned the hotel at which Mike had become a resident. Terri was Mike's latest lover and he installed her as a machinist, even though she was useless and held the others up. When Terri started to throw her weight around Mike asked Ivy to sort her out and the poor girl resigned after Ivy and the rest of the girls attacked her.

When Annie Walker went on holiday, Bet was given charge of the pub, along with new barmaid Dawn Perks. She disliked Dawn's flirtatious manner and was furious when Mike took her out to dinner. He made a hasty retreat when Dawn and Bet

squared up to each other behind the bar when Bet insisted she clean the toilets. Dawn resigned and Mike looked around for another conquest.

5 Footloose and Fancy-free

Evicted from No.5, Bet Lynch moved into the flat above Renee Bradshaw's shop. Renee charged her six pounds in rent after doing a secret deal with Mike Baldwin whereby he paid an extra two pounds a week on top so that Bet could afford the flat. On her first night under Renee's roof Bet unplugged the shop freezer, ruining a large amount of uninsured stock.

When two local men, Les Fox and Eric Bailey, chatted up the two women Bet pushed Renee into going on a double date. As the women left the Street to go to Ashton where they were to meet, Eric and Les broke into the shop and emptied it. Renee wasn't impressed with the way Bet kept on costing her money.

6 Emily Fights For Her Man

When Ernest Bishop received a valentine from machinist Thelma James he was surprised that his wife Emily couldn't see the funny side. But Emily had realized that Thelma was after Ernest and launched an attack on her, threatening her with violence

if she didn't leave him alone. Ernest enjoyed being fought over, and Thelma backed off.

To commemorate the Queen's Silver Jubilee, Weatherfield Council announced a carnival with themed carts. Ernest organized the Street's effort, 'Britain Through the Ages', and stood up for Emily against Annie Walker when the two clashed over who should play Queen Elizabeth I. Annie persuaded the brewery to provide a suitable lorry, on the condition that she played the Virgin Queen. Then she studied the role and wrote to Glenda Jackson for tips, but on the day was outshone by Ena Sharples's impersonation of Queen Victoria. The residents enjoyed dressing up:

Annie Walker	Elizabeth I
Ena Sharples	Queen Victoria
Bet Lynch	Britannia
Ken Barlow	Sir Edmund Hillary
Albert Tatlock	Sherpa Tenzing
Fred Gee	Sir Francis Drake
Ernest Bishop	Sir Walter Raleigh
Eddie Yeats	a cave man

However, they never actually entered the carnival as Stan Ogden had left the lorry lights on all night and the battery was dead. He was subjected to a kangaroo court in the Rovers and sentenced to buying drinks all round.

Ernest surprised the regulars by turning violent when Councillor Tattersall attempted to evict Ena from the centre, saying she was useless and too old. The residents, too, turned on Tattersall but he accused them of running things to suit themselves and threatened an inquiry that would result in Ena being put into a home. Alf Roberts came to the rescue when he found out that Tattersall wanted the caretaker's job for his own niece and saw him off.

7 Rita Finally Marries Len

Len Fairclough received a surprise visit from his son, Stanley, who introduced him to his fiancée Liz Brocklebank and made a point of telling Len he wouldn't be invited to the wedding. Len was still recovering from this when he received another blow: Rita Littlewood gave notice at the Kabin to take a four-month singing contract in Tenerife. Desperate to keep her in Weatherfield, he proposed to her but she told him he was three years too late and made plans for her new life. Len took her to the airport and begged her to reconsider and marry him. She allowed the plane to go without her and returned to the Kabin as his fiancée. While being pleased for her, Mavis Riley was put out as Len had made her manageress of the shop after Rita had left. She was forced to stand down in Rita's favour but was given a pay-rise to ease the disappointment.

Len paid off Rita's agent when he threatened to sue her for breach of contract and stunned Rita by insisting on a quick wedding. His friends threw a stag night for him at the Rovers and he surprised them by refusing Marie Stanton's offer to spend his last bachelor night in her bed. He got roaring drunk at the party and fell downstairs, twisting his ankle.

Alf Roberts was best man, Mavis was the bridesmaid and Rita's uncle Sam gave her away when the couple tied the knot at St Mary's. After honeymooning in Tenerife Rita moved into No.9 and set about being a good wife, but Len immediately started to take her for granted and laid down rules. When Terry Bates, the son of Rita's common-law husband, arrived on the doorstep after hitting his father's girlfriend, Rita took him in, only for Len to throw him out into the Street. Ralph Lancaster offered Rita singing work at the Gatsby, but again Len put his foot down and told Rita she had retired from showbusiness. In the end he agreed she could do one last performance, but that was a disaster when the Rovers' bar flap dropped on Ernest Bishop's fingers and his replacement on the piano couldn't read her music.

8 Unlucky Ogdens

Eddie Yeats panicked when Bet Lynch told him that the consignment of watches he was attempting to sell was stolen and that the police were after him. He dropped them down the grate outside the pub then discovered that Bet had been joking, but it was too late to retrieve them as the council had cleaned the drains.

His friend Stan Ogden also fell foul of Lady Luck when Hilda decided their unlucky lives were down to their address at No.13. To please her, Stan bought new numbers and changed the door to read 12a. Hilda was pleased with his handiwork before discovering they were locked out of

the house. Stan had to break a window but not before the roast lamb dinner was burnt. Furthermore, as they didn't have council permission to change their house number, they had to replace the original one.

Mike Baldwin took Hilda on to clean the factory and she experimented with his sewing-machines. Eddie talked her into running up curtains when the place was deserted, planning to sell them on the market, but Mike found out and threatened her with the sack if it happened again.

Stan sold the Ogdens' old tandem to Gail Potter and Suzie Birchall for seven pounds before discovering it was worth a hundred. Eddie bought it back from them for fifteen and promised to go halves with the Ogdens on the profits. On their way to a dealer, Eddie and Stan left the bike against a wall while they nipped into a pub. On their return they found the wall had been demolished and the tandem wrecked.

When Hilda bought Renee Bradshaw's old washing machine she was furious to find Stan taking in washing at a pound a load. She refused to touch the clothes and watched Stan struggling to iron them. For coming up with the slogan 'Be a mistress as well as a wife and your husband'll still be a boyfriend' Hilda won third prize in a competition run by Loving Cup shandy. The prize was a night at Manchester's Midland Hotel, with spending money. Hilda borrowed Rita Fairclough's see-through nightie and got carried away with the romance of her second honeymoon but Stan was only interested in the contents of the mini bar.

9 Romance for the Street's Spinsters

Mavis Riley surprised herself by agreeing to accompany Fred Gee on a fishing trip. Fred panicked about her intentions and invited Alf Roberts along too. Renee Bradshaw made up the foursome, which ended with her and Mavis falling into the water and catching colds. While Renee recovered from her chill Alf ran the Corner Shop and

they both realized they enjoyed the other's company. One evening, while he was drunk, Alf proposed to her but changed his mind the next day when he'd sobered up.

Mavis's love-life was just as frustrating as Renee's. She was pleased when Derek Wilton turned up again and leant on him while being harassed by her domineering aunt Edie Riley and her vicious daughter Ethel Platt. Mavis moved out of her aunt's house and rented the Kabin flat but felt guilty when Edie suffered a heart-attack and returned to nurse her. Edie and Ethel didn't like the prospect of Mavis leaving them to marry Derek so tried to wreck their relationship. Eventually Derek stood up to the pair and insisted Mavis escape Edie's tyranny. He took her out for dinner but on their return they found the old woman had died of another heart-attack. Mavis was racked with guilt but was pleased that Edie had left her the house. However, she had borrowed heavily and the bank seized the house, leaving Mavis with a couple of china dogs as her inheritance. Derek offered Mavis financial support in buying a house of her own and Mavis hoped that, in making this gesture, he was planning to propose. She was left disillusioned once more when his mother intervened and forbade the venture. Derek left the area and Mavis settled into the Kabin flat.

10 Broke Betty and Annie's Anniversary

Struggling to make ends meet, Betty Turpin decided to sell a treasured china cabinet. She asked Alf Roberts to ensure that no one took advantage of her but the buyer turned out to be Arthur Stokes, a councillor friend of Alf's, who jumped to the conclusion that Betty and Alf were lovers. Betty was embarrassed when Stokes spread rumours to this effect until Alf sorted him out.

Annie Walker decided to have the Rovers decorated, but the brewery decorator, Maurice Allen, neglected the pub and used company materials to decorate for Ernest Bishop. He was reported to the brewery and sacked, causing the draymen to go out on strike. Annie was forced to ration beer, which panicked Eddie Yeats and Stan Ogden into brewing their own in the bath, until, fearing it was illegal, Hilda pulled out the plug.

Annie was relieved when the strike ended but then discovered money had been stolen from her sewing basket. Remembering that Betty was hard up she accused her of the theft, and Betty walked out. She went to work at the Corner Shop. Annie was embarrassed when Maurice confessed to stealing the money but by then she had told her friends that Betty was dishonest. Betty threatened to sue Annie for defamation of character but in the end common sense brought the women back together and Betty returned to the Rovers in time for Annie to celebrate her fortieth anniversary at the pub. The residents threw a party for her, and her son Billy delighted her with a surprise visit.

Shortly afterwards Annie received a visit from her cousin Charles Beaumont. He borrowed heavily from Alf Roberts and Len Fairclough before Annie discovered he was an experienced con-man. She was forced to give him money to pay back her friends then sent him away.

Annie's vanity pushed her into buying an expensive carpet from Eddie Yeats because it was woven with her initials. She had it laid in the living room and invited all her fellow landladies round for a sherry morning before Hilda Ogden dropped the bombshell that it was an off-cut from the bingo hall – the Alhambra Weatherfield.

11 The End of Marriage No.3 for Elsie

Elsie Howard was too upset at the thought of Len marrying to attend the Fairclough wedding, but she did turn up at the reception and forced herself to wish Rita well. It was held at the Greenvale Hotel and Elsie was flattered when the owner,

CAST

Stanley Fairclough	Jonathan Coy
Liz Brocklebank	Diane Grayson
Suzie Birchall	Cheryl Murray
Thelma James	Mary Healey
Tracy Langton	Christabel Finch
Steve Bassett	Dennis Chinnery
Anne Woodley	Carole Mowlam
Vince Denton	Constantin de Goguel
Sam Littlewood	Harry Littlewood
Ted Brownlow	Barrie Cookson
Elaine Dennett	Valerie Georgeson
Maurice Allen	Peter Armitage
Arthur Stokes	Stan Richards
Councillor Tattersall	George Waring
Les Fox	Eric Allen
Eric Bailey	Geoff Hinsliff
Roger Floriet	Benjamin Feiltelson
Edie Riley	Marjorie Sudell
Ethel Platt	Julia Lang
Peter Barlow	Joseph McKenna
Steve Fisher	Lawrence Mullen
Dawn Perks	Jeanette Wild
Terri Clayton	Jenny Edwards
Bob Birchall	David Hargreaves
Charles Beaumont	Derek Francis
Robin Smethurst	Andrew Beaumont

Ted Brownlow, sought her out. He became a regular caller at No.11 but was frightened off when Rita told him that Elsie had been married three times.

Any hopes Elsie might have had of getting back together with her estranged husband, Alan, were dashed when his girlfriend Elaine Dennett turned up and pleaded with her to divorce him. Elsie refused to agree until Alan sent her a letter insisting that their marriage was over. In times of trouble Elsie had always fallen back on Len and she saw no reason to stop now that he was married. She started to spend more and more time in his company, which upset Rita as the gossips got to work. Fred Gee took Rita's side and accused Len of neglecting his wife. The men ended up fighting at a party held by the Langtons and smashed Deirdre's precious coffee table.

12 Viaduct Violation

Deirdre Langton caused trouble for husband Ray when she discovered his partnership with Len Fairclough was 60–40 in Len's favour. She insisted that Ray deserved 50 per cent and threatened to persuade him to set up in competition with Len, but Rita Fairclough refused to allow Len to give Ray more of the business. The two wives fell out, but Len and Ray finally sorted the matter out by deciding new terms and refusing to tell their wives what they were.

On her way home from her keep-fit class at Bessie Street School, Deirdre was molested under the viaduct by a man intent on rape. She struggled free and ran home, but would not report the matter to the police. She suffered a breakdown over the incident and refused to let Ray touch her. He felt helpless, and accused her of shutting him out. This led to Deirdre abandoning Tracy and disappearing. Ray called in the police. Deirdre was contemplating suicide by jumping off a motorway bridge, but she was distracted by a passing lorry driver seeking directions and made her way home for an emotional reunion with Ray.

1978

Behind the Scenes

Street fan Lord Laurence Olivier had long been vocal in his respect for Jean Alexander's portrayal as Hilda Ogden and agreed to be written into an episode. A part was created for him, as a tramp spending the night outside a department store with Hilda, but reshoots for the film *Marathon Man* clashed with the recording date and the part went to another actor.

Neville Buswell sent the writers into a panic when he announced his decision to quit the Street and acting and leave the country. Anne Kirkbride feared she would lose her job – Ray and Deirdre were a strong partnership – but Bill Podmore decided to give her character a lifeline and explore the struggles of a single mother, after Ray had emigrated. It was hoped that he would return eventually but he never did. While filming a one-off video in Las Vegas in 1997, the Street production team tracked down Neville to the bank he managed and persuaded him to make a cameo appearance as Ray.

Coronation Street came of age in December 1978 with Violet Carson, at the age of eighty, giving an unguarded interview about her relationship with Ena Sharples: 'I'm in two minds about this celebration. I realize that *Coronation Street* has made me, but it's also destroyed me. I've played a marvellous character who has become a household name, but let's face it, it's Ena Sharples who's famous, not Violet Carson. She's taken over. She rules my life. I've begged them to bury the old girl and let me go, but they won't hear of it.'

Key Dates

1978

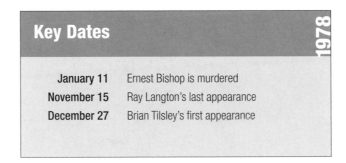

January 11	Ernest Bishop is murdered
November 15	Ray Langton's last appearance
December 27	Brian Tilsley's first appearance

Top Twenty

Pos	Character	No of eps	Total	Pos Prev Year
1	Len Fairclough	73	1461	1
2	Bet Lynch	69	652	2
3	Hilda Ogden	68	1022	2
4	Ken Barlow	67	1232	10
5	Annie Walker	65	1420	8
6	Elsie Tanner	64	1271	2
7	Rita Fairclough	62	466	5
8	Mike Baldwin	62	133	21
9	Steve Fisher	61	75	27
10	Betty Turpin	60	710	7
11	Deirdre Langton	59	358	13
12	Mavis Riley	59	322	12
13	Gail Potter	59	228	16
14	Emily Bishop	58	1033	18
15	Ray Langton	58	794	6
16	Renee B Roberts	56	159	14
17	Fred Gee	56	171	14
18	Suzie Birchall	55	107	22
19	Stan Ogden	54	945	17
20	Alf Roberts	50	505	9

"I was really something when I was young. A different lad every night of the week, they queued up just to walk me 'ome from work. An' then the dance 'alls . . . 'Ow I come to throw meself away on a nothin' like Arnold Tanner I'll never know. I could 'ave done anythin'. Got anywhere. I don't just mean fellers. I mean life generally. I was a fighter . . . I walked down this street last night in the pourin' rain an' cried . . . for a girl 'oo once 'ad guts, and hope . . . only she's dead now. I'm not sure just when it was she died."

Elsie Howard

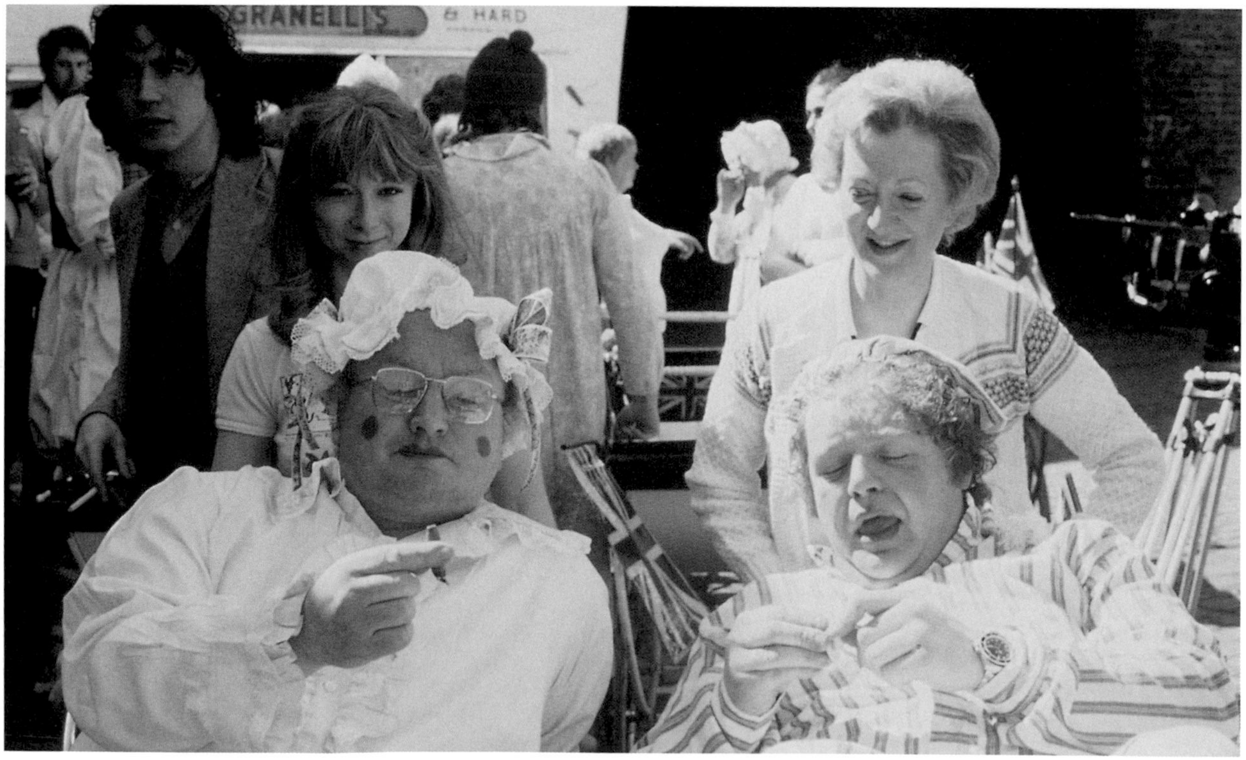

STORIES

1 Cold-blooded Murder

As Ernest Bishop made up the wage packets at Baldwin's Casuals, two youths, Tommo Jackson and Dave Lester, burst into his office with a shotgun intent on stealing them. They were disturbed by Mike Baldwin entering the office, and the gun went off. Ernest was shot in the chest. He was rushed to hospital but died on the operating table. When she heard the news Emily fainted in the Street. As a mark of respect, Annie Walker closed the Rovers on the day of the funeral and the residents rallied round Emily, but it was playing with little Tracy Langton that eventually brought her out of herself.

Ivy Tilsley started up a petition to bring back hanging and was surprised when Emily refused to sign it. The police caught the murderers and Emily went to court to see them sentenced to life imprisonment. Then she immersed herself in voluntary work at the hospital and took in battered wife Brenda Summers, urging her to leave her violent husband. Brenda was glad of Emily's help but refused to give up her marriage and, to Emily's astonishment, returned to her husband.

2 Hilda Embraces Technicolor

Determined to buy a cheap colour television set Hilda Ogden camped out all night to be the first in the queue at the Perkins sale. It wasn't a pleasant experience: she had to share the doorway with a meths-drinking tramp. Then she was so busy being interviewed by the local radio reporter that she lost her place in the queue and was pushed back when the doors opened. Frustrated at not securing the television, Hilda asked Eddie Yeats to buy her one, but he produced a blue and green screen to put in front of an ordinary black and white set. Hilda turned it down, saying that it was as useless as everything else he produced.

A blast from the past made Hilda reassess her life. Her wartime sweetheart, GI Ralph Curtis, spent an evening reminiscing with her at No.13. Stan was hostile towards the American but fell asleep while Ralph told Hilda all about his home in the States. To recapture her youth, Hilda jived with him and allowed herself to think of how different life would have been if she had married him instead of Stan.

Hoping to branch out in the window-cleaning world, Stan and Eddie spent a day cleaning the stained glass at St Margaret's, only to have the vicar thank them for their charity. Stan had only just recovered from this shock when Hilda delivered another. She had discovered they paid more in water rates than Elsie Howard and told him he would have to start bathing every week to get their money's worth. The plan backfired when he fell asleep and let the bath overflow, ruining the wallpaper in the living room below, including Hilda's precious

mural. Rather than see it go altogether, Hilda replaced the Rockies with a new vista, this time a seascape.

3 Crippled Mavis

Mavis Riley celebrated her fortieth birthday with a visit from Derek Wilton. She was amazed by his cheek when he sought her help in freeing him from his engagement to domineering Beryl Challis whom his mother had chosen as his bride. Mavis advised him to stand up to her but they were interrupted by the arrival of Beryl, who accused Mavis of being Derek's mistress. Beryl finished with Derek, telling Mavis she was welcome to him. Mavis was pleased but Derek had no interest in more romance and slipped away.

Always eager to help charity, Mavis agreed to take part in a sponsored pram race, to raise funds for the hospital's kidney-machine appeal, in which the women had to push men around eight local pubs and the men had to drink a pint in each. Gail Potter pushed Fred Gee and Suzie Birchall had Steve Fisher but Mavis was stuck with bouncing baby Eddie Yeats. She found it impossible to move the pram under Eddie's considerable weight. Suzie and Steve won, but were disqualified as Suzie drank half of the last pint.

When her back gave way at work, Mavis was relieved when customer Sid Garfield managed to sort it out by applying pressure to certain parts of her spine. Hearing of his healing hands, Annie Walker invited Mr Garfield to work miracles on her back. Her delight at the result changed to horror when she discovered that although he worked at the hospital it was as a porter, not as a consultant.

4 A Marriage of Convenience?

When Alf Roberts proposed, Renee Bradshaw was torn: she loved him but

needed to make sure he wanted her and not just the idea of a wife. After he assured her of his love she accepted and they married three weeks later at the local register office. The wedding was not without complications. During the stag night, Len Fairclough got roaring drunk and ended up spending the night in a cell after his disgusted wife Rita disowned him, and the reception was spoilt by another drunk: Renee's stepfather, Joe Hibbert, offended her by accusing Alf of marrying her for the shop, because she was no beauty. Alf hit him and marched Renee off to their honeymoon in Capri.

Len was annoyed when the leader of the council, Alderman Chapman, asked for his resignation over the drunk and disorderly charge. He refused but was then dropped as a candidate by the Rate-payers Association. Having lost his seat on the council, Len had then to endure a court case in which the arresting policewoman testified that he had made advances towards her. Len was let off with a fine, but a furious Rita locked him out of her bedroom.

At the Corner Shop, the newlyweds' married bliss was disturbed by the presence of lodger Bet Lynch. Alf insisted that she leave, and Renee told her of how Mike Baldwin had been subsidizing her rent. Rather than leave, Bet told Renee she didn't mind if the rent was increased in future. In fact, she enjoyed making Alf feel uncomfortable, and when Renee went to look after her mother, Daisy, because Joe had left her, she made a big deal of being alone with Alf. Her flirting upset him so much that he moved back into his old house on Park Road until Renee came home.

5 Albert and Ena Clash

When Albert Tatlock moved the British Legion Dominoes Committee into the Rovers Return Snug Ena Sharples declared war on him for infiltrating her lair. She squatted in the bar and saw off the committee one by one by making them fall out with each other.

She also won the second round, when the brewery offered a free drink each day for life to its longest-serving customer. Albert announced he'd first drunk at the Rovers during a Whit Week Walk in 1919, but Ena produced a very old friend who told everyone that she and Ena had first entered the Rovers on Christmas Eve 1918:

she remembered the night as it was the first and last time she'd drunk alcohol. Ena was awarded the free drink while Albert sulked. The brewery caused more disruption at the Rovers when it launched its own magazine,

Over the Bar. Annie Walker assumed she would feature on the front cover of the first issue, and joined Albert's sulk when a picture of Betty Turpin serving Eddie Yeats was used instead.

A run of food poisoning in the area caused Albert to accuse Annie of selling dodgy pies. When they were analysed and cleared, the finger of suspicion moved to Renee Roberts's salad selection. She revealed that she bought it all from Albert, and the tables were turned on him because he had to confess that he had used a new chemical spray on his produce to make it look fresher.

6 Hilda Fights Back

Elsie Howard was disturbed to hear noises above her bedroom at night. Investigating in the loft, Suzie Birchall discovered that a pigeon had got in through a hole in the Ogdens' roof. While she was trying to catch it, Suzie lost her balance and her foot went through the Ogdens' bedroom ceiling. Hilda grabbed her shoe as evidence and, recognizing it as one of Suzie's, climbed into the loft and stuck her broom handle through Elsie's ceiling. Elsie and Hilda embarked on a tit-for-tat vendetta, playing loud music, beating dirty carpets over washing, tipping rubbish over walls and making life miserable for each other. Eventually they agreed to go to a small claims court. After listening to both sides the arbitrator suggested they paid for their own repairs. Elsie was happy with the outcome as Len Fairclough had already told her he would charge Hilda twice as much as he would her for the repairs.

Later on in the year, Hilda found herself in trouble with the police after she discovered Stan's window-cleaning cart abandoned down a back alley. She decided it must have been stolen so she wheeled it away, only to be stopped by the police who discovered it was full of stolen lead. Rather than tell Hilda he and Eddie Yeats had lent the cart to petty thief Tiny Hargreaves, Stan let her believe it had been stolen, but when the police investigated the lead Stan and Eddie became their prime suspects. Faced with the prospect of Stan being sent to prison, Hilda forced Eddie to tell the police the truth, and to squeal on Tiny.

Eddie kept refusing jobs so his social security benefit was cut. Then he took possession of a one-armed bandit and stored it overnight at No.13. Stan was unaware that it was empty, and fed all the housekeeping money into the machine but won nothing. Hilda was outraged when Bet Lynch used the machine once and won the jackpot. She demanded the money back but Bet laughed in her face.

7 Fred Causes Problems at the Rovers

When Annie Walker's Rover 2000 failed its MOT she blamed her potman Fred Gee for not taking better care of it. He couldn't understand why she thought it was his fault and, as a joke, dressed up as a chauffeur the next time he took her for a drive. However, Annie approved of the uniform and insisted he wore it all the time. During a party at the pub, in Annie's absence, the car was stolen. When the police arrived they found drinking in progress after hours. The Rover turned up without a scratch but the thief left a note, saying the tappits needed adjusting.

Annie was horrified when she heard the brewery were facing a takeover bid from rival firm Morley's. Fearing she'd be forced to retire by a new firm, she summoned her children. Joan Davies told brother Billy that, whatever happened, she wasn't prepared to have their mother living with her, but he was more supportive and told the brewery he'd take on the tenancy if necessary to secure Annie's future. She was grateful for his support, but was thrilled when the takeover fell through and she was

assured her position was secure. Billy returned to Jersey, relieved that he didn't have to waste away at the Rovers.

Although Billy didn't want his own Weatherfield pub, Fred Gee did. The brewery offered him the tenancy of the Mechanics but on the condition that he got married. He wasted no time and proposed to Betty Turpin, who said she could never marry again. Then he moved on to Bet Lynch, who carefully refused his proposal, pointing out that when she married it would have to be for love. Flying Horse barmaid Alma Walsh was next on Fred's list and she was more receptive, but Fred decided he couldn't be bothered with marriage and gave the idea up. Shortly afterwards he was bothered by the unwelcome advances of a local woman, Wendy Williams, who left her husband for him. Fred convinced her to return home, much to her husband's annoyance.

8 Strike!

Eager to clinch a business deal, Mike Baldwin asked Bet Lynch to charm a buyer into giving him an order. Bet was indignant until she met George Livesley and decided that an evening in his company would be fun. After a meal in town she was alarmed when, despite having drunk three bottles of wine, he insisted on driving her home. Her fears were justified when he knocked a man over and refused to stop. The next day she told Mike but Livesley refused to let them call the police and threatened to take his order elsewhere. Mike called his bluff and secured the business by threatening to inform his wife about his night out with Bet, who felt sick about being used by Mike once more.

Mike continued to be obsessed with work, and when cleaner Hilda Ogden asked for money to buy a new broom he refused, accused her of maliciously ruining her old one and sacked her. Ivy Tilsley was infuriated over Hilda's treatment and called the rest of Mike's workforce to strike. Trade unionist Ida Clough backed the proposal, although the union refused to acknowledge the action as Hilda wasn't a member. The girls stopped working and picketed the factory. Hilda was amazed that the action was in response to her sacking but refused to join it. Instead she secretly took a job cleaning at the abattoir. The picket turned violent when Steve Fisher tried to transfer the denim to Mike's London factory: the women mobbed him and Vera Duckworth smashed the van window. Steve ran for safety but the same thing happened when Mike tried to bring in non-union workers.

The black-legs, too, were mobbed, and the police had to be called to rescue them from the factory. Eventually Mike was forced to reinstate Hilda, who wasn't happy to leave her new job as the pay was better.

Ivy, Ida and the rest of the girls returned to work pleased with themselves for beating Mike, but a few months later, in December, they were shaken when one of the strikers, Eileen Tibson, disappeared with the Christmas club money. She was only gone a day but in that time spent £240 on presents for her children. She was diagnosed with clinical depression, and had suffered a breakdown brought on by her husband leaving her. Ivy refused to bring in the police and Mike replaced the money out of the workers' bonuses.

9 The Return of the Tanner

Elsie Howard celebrated her birthday with the arrival of her decree absolute. Depressed by the failure of her third marriage she decided to hit the town, only to be mistaken for a prostitute. She felt she'd reached an all-time low and left the area to stay with her daughter Linda Cheveski in Birmingham.

Three months later she returned and announced she was changing her name back to Tanner. Times had changed and Elsie had difficulty adjusting: when she hit a boy for cutting down her washing-line she received a visit from the police, who warned her it was an offence to hit a child. Some things, however, had not changed, and after a night out Elsie found herself unable to pay the taxi-driver's fare. She invited him in for a cup of tea instead, and was soon embarking on yet another romance. The driver's name was Ron Mather and he fell for Elsie as much as she did for him. She was amazed that he wasn't married, although he did have an over-possessive ballroom-dancing partner, who thought Elsie was a rival dancer and warned her off.

In order to get to know each other on neutral ground, Elsie and Ron took a two-week holiday in Majorca and returned a united couple. The only blot on the landscape was tax exile Harry Payne, whom they'd met in Spain and who tracked them down in England to court Elsie. She was flattered when he threw his money at her but Ron took offence and got rid of him.

10 The End of the Line for Fairclough and Langton

Len Fairclough and Ray Langton started work on a big construction job, converting an old house into a hotel. To raise funds

Len secured a loan against the Kabin and bought three thousand pounds' worth of material which he stored at Clayton's warehouse. When the warehouse burned to the ground Len was staggered to discover Clayton wasn't insured for its contents. Desperate to save the job, Ray offered to take out a mortgage on No.5, but his wife Deirdre refused to let him. Rita asked her sugar daddy Eric Summers for a loan but Len refused his terms and talked the bank into lending the money. Rita found it ironic when Len asked her to return to singing to help with funds, and was forced to perform at second-rate working-men's clubs. The hotel development went bust leaving the firm six thousand pounds in debt. The bank agreed to accept sixty pounds a week over a two-year period, and to make quick money Ray and Len entered the emergency call-out business, working around the clock.

Len's finances weren't improved by the arrival of baker Joe Dawson who bought the shop next to the Kabin and announced his intention of opening a café. He reported the Kabin café to the authorities as having inadequate toilet facilities, and Len was told to stop serving food and drink in the tiny back room. Rita stopped Len attacking Dawson, fearing the police would get involved, and took up Mavis Riley's suggestion to start selling records instead.

Fed up at work, and bored with his domestic life, Ray fell for Dawson's waitress, Janice Stubbs. They embarked on an affair, much to the horror of Dawson's manageress Emily Bishop, who uncovered their relationship. When Deirdre grew suspicious Emily was forced to tell her all she knew and Deirdre confronted Ray. He was repentant and talked her out of leaving him by promising a new start. She agreed to emigrate with him, alarming her mother, Blanche Hunt, who hit him for being unfaithful. After their leaving party at the Rovers, Deirdre realized she didn't trust Ray enough to start afresh in Amsterdam and refused to go. He left her and Tracy, and headed off to Holland.

11 Teenage Angst for Ken

Albert Tatlock took up matchmaking after discovering that his chiropodist, Sally Robson, was single. He pushed Ken Barlow into taking her to see *Star Wars* and encouraged them to spend time together. Both Ken and Sally were interested in each other, and Sally found Albert amusing. However, Albert's approval of Sally diminished when it was revealed she was divorced with a thirteen-year-old daughter, Philippa. Ken wasn't keen on becoming a father figure and by mutual consent the couple stopped seeing each other.

Later on in the year, Ken's own son Peter turned up on the doorstep, having run away from Glasgow following his appalling O Level results. Ken didn't know how to relate to his son and Peter felt more at ease with Albert than with his father. He was annoyed when Ken insisted he retook his exams in Weatherfield where he could supervise his son's studies. Edith Tatlock arrived to find out why Peter wasn't being allowed to come home and plotted with him to run away back to Scotland. Ken uncovered the plan and made Edith see that Peter couldn't leave against his wishes. When Peter announced his intention to join the navy, Ken arranged for a chief petty officer to give him a pep talk. Peter saw the sense in gaining qualifications and persuaded Ken to let him retake his exams in Scotland where his friends were.

Although he didn't have Peter to tutor, Ken wasn't without a pupil: towards the end of the year illiterate Karen Barnes asked him to help her to read and write. Knowing her husband was on remand in Risley, Ken agreed to teach her, although Albert warned him to have nothing to do with her.

12 Mike Deals with Suzie and Gail

Steve Fisher grew tired of van-driving and applied for an electrician's job at a local dairy. Mike Baldwin wrote him an appalling reference and told him he didn't want him to leave, then offered to train him up as his right-hand man. Steve readily agreed to this and started to flex his managerial muscles after discovering that Suzie Birchall had run up a large telephone bill ringing Roger Floriet in France. He told Mike to sack her, but Mike let her off with a warning and the demand that she repay the twenty pounds.

When Elsie Howard left the area for three months Steve was made supervisor of the sewing room, and Ivy Tilsley was given an extra five pounds a week to serve as senior machinist. Steve continued to fancy Suzie and seemed blind to the way Gail Potter threw herself at him. Gail was distraught when Suzie took Steve to bed, to prove she could have any man she wanted. She hoped that afterwards he would treat her better than the rest of the staff and was insulted when, having slept with her, his interest waned.

Mike took a fancy to a rival buyer Carole Gordon and offered her a 10 per cent pay increase if she worked for him as a sales representative. She turned down his offer but agreed to go out with him. During their brief liaison she told him that his rivals were opening a large fashion boutique that would rob all the Western Front's trade. Mike thanked her for the advice and decided to close his shop. When he caught Suzie and Gail closing the shop early he sacked them on the spot, pleased that he wouldn't have to bother with redundancy. However, Steve felt the girls had been mistreated and told them they had grounds to claim unfair dismissal. They threatened Mike with an industrial tribunal, which forced him to pay them a hundred pounds each in compensation. The girls decided to use the money to start new lives in London, but at the last minute Gail got cold feet and Suzie went alone. Gail's future looked bleak until at a Christmas party she met biker Brian Tilsley and agreed to a date.

CAST

Tommo Jackson	Dave McEale
Dave Lester	Tony Parke
Sally Robson	Susan Farmer
George Livesley	Graham Weston
Daisy Hibbert	Pearl Hackney
Joe Hibbert	Norman Bird
Ida Clough	Helene Palmer
Beryl Challis	Miranda Forbes
Wendy Williams	Mary Wray
Joan Davies	Dorothy White
Ralph Curtis	James Berwick
Sid Garfield	Barry Jackson
Alma Walsh	Joyce Kennedy
Eric Summers	Bill Waddington
Eileen Tibson	Muriel Rogers
Brenda Summers	Anita Carey
Joe Dawson	Peter Schofield
Janice Stubbs	Angela Bruce
Ron Mather	Joe Lynch
Tiny Hargreaves	Jimmy Gardner
Carole Gordon	Louisa Rix
Harry Payne	Max Wall
Karen Barnes	Catherine Neilson
Brian Tilsley	Christopher Quinten

1979

Behind the Scenes

The cast were delighted with the arrival of actor Peter Dudley to play Ivy's long-suffering husband, Bert. Peter had worked with many of the actors before at Oldham Repertory Theatre and for him coming to work on the Street was like turning up at a family reunion. The Tilsleys were the first family to move into the Street since the Hopkinses in 1974, but they were already more firmly rooted in the series than the Welsh family. Ivy had worked in the Street for eight years and Brian was already taking Gail Potter out before the removal vans moved in. The only hiccup was having to change Mr Tilsley's name. In 1975 Ivy's husband, Jack, had appeared in two episodes but as Vera Duckworth had always referred to her never-seen husband as Jack the decision was made to call him Bert.

By the end of the year Vera also acquired a husband in the shape of work-shy Jack. William Tarmey had been an extra on the Street (in 1977 it had been he who dropped the Rovers' bar flap on Ernie Bishop's fingers, causing him to miss Rita's come-back at the Gatsby): 'I'd worked on *Coronation Street* for about ten years throwing darts in the background and while I was doing that I was also doing little cameo parts on other programmes. I was either the policeman, or the guy who got shot, or the one with the mad dog.' His first scene found him in the Rovers, and he was so petrified that he couldn't hold his pint pot because his hand was shaking so much.

> "There've bin times when Elsie Tanner's life's kept mine going. I've a lot to thank her for."
>
> **Ena Sharples**

Another new face was that of RADA-trained actress Sue Nicholls, who had become famous as waitress Marilyn Gates in *Crossroads*. She was cast as Gail's man-mad mother Audrey Potter. She was only meant to appear in two episodes but fitted in so well that the writers kept asking to see more of her.

There were double celebrations when the Variety Club of Great Britain joined forces with Pye Television to throw a dinner in the Street's honour. During the evening the Poet Laureate, Sir John Betjeman, presented Doris Speed with a life-time achievement award, and toasted the success of the programme. He likened it to the work of Charles Dickens and said it was the best-written and -crafted programme on television.

Key Dates 1979

April 14	Audrey Potter's first appearance
August 8	*Coronation Street* taken off air as part of ITV strike
September 7	Alan Browning dies of a liver complaint six years after his last appearance as Alan Howard
October 24	*Coronation Street* returns to the screen
November 28	Gail Potter marries Brian Tilsley; Jack Duckworth's first appearance

Top Twenty

Pos	Character	No of eps	Total	Pos Prev Year
1	Gail Potter Tilsley	61	289	11
2	Elsie Tanner	60	1331	6
3	Len Fairclough	60	1521	1
4	Hilda Ogden	57	1079	2
5	Ivy Tilsley	56	129	26
6	Suzie Birchall	55	162	18
7	Rita Fairclough	54	520	7
8	Stan Ogden	52	997	19
9	Betty Turpin	52	762	10
10	Deirdre Langton	51	409	11
11	Brian Tilsley	51	53	–
12	Annie Walker	49	1469	5
13	Ken Barlow	47	1279	4
14	Alf Roberts	47	552	20
15	Bert Tilsley	46	46	–
16	Fred Gee	45	216	16
17	Eddie Yeats	44	237	22
18	Bet Lynch	43	695	2
19	Mike Baldwin	42	175	8
20	Emily Bishop	41	1074	14

STORIES

1 Ken the Brave

Dave Barnes warned Ken Barlow to stop teaching his wife Karen to read and write, but Ken refused, guessing correctly that Dave was scared she would discover he was also illiterate. Then Dave broke into Ken's

house, frightening Albert Tatlock and threatening to kill Ken. Somehow Ken caught him off-guard and knocked him out with a punch to his face. Albert was disappointed when Ken refused to call the police and tried to forget the whole incident. His next venture was to organize a jogging class at the community centre, but only Mavis Riley turned up.

2 Tracy's Narrow Escape

Deirdre Langton faced hardship as she struggled with life as a single parent. When Rita Fairclough refused to let Len employ her as his secretary she was forced to break into baby Tracy's piggy-bank for food money. As Ray needed funds in Holland she was forced to sell the family home but rather than move into a high-rise flat she became Emily Bishop's lodger at No.3. Then she met up again with Sally Norton, who had been in the same maternity ward back in 1977. Sally's son had been taken into care and she hung around Deirdre, making a fuss of Tracy.

One day in March a lorry-driver suffered a fatal heart-attack while turning into Coronation Street. His lorry overturned and his cargo of timber shot through the Rovers' windows. Deirdre was in hysterics – she'd left Tracy in her pushchair outside the pub door, which was now hidden by wood. The emergency services were quickly on the scene but Deirdre disappeared, fearing Tracy was dead. After moving all the timber the police were surprised to see no sign of the pushchair and started searching for her. She was found with Sally who had taken her for a walk, seconds before the crash.

Deirdre was located contemplating suicide once again on the canal bank, so mother and daughter were reunited.

Ken Barlow had tried to take charge of Deirdre during the crash and afterwards he provided a shoulder to lean on. Deirdre went to a disco he organized at the community centre and was surprised at the depth of her feelings for him.

3 Alf's Split Personality

Alf Roberts had been sitting in the Rovers' window at the time of the lorry crash and was rushed unconscious to hospital. Renee kept a bedside vigil, upset that their last words had been spoken in anger: she hadn't wanted him to give up the post office to work in the shop with her. She was relieved when he regained consciousness after three days, but as soon as he was back on his feet she discovered the crash had affected his brain: now he would erupt suddenly into uncontrollable anger. Alf refused to believe anything was wrong with him until Renee threatened to leave home

unless he saw a psychiatrist. Slowly, with the help of tranquillizers, he returned to his normal, easy-going self, and retired from the Post Office with six thousand pounds plus a pension of two thousand pounds a year for life. He was happy with that, and with the eight hundred pounds he received in compensation for his injuries, until he learnt that Betty Turpin had received three hundred pounds and she'd only received a cut to her arm.

When Renee had to be away for a couple of weeks Alf decided to turn the tables on Bet Lynch. Fed up with her flirting, he frightened her by making a play for her. Bet locked herself in her bedroom and didn't know how to cope with him, but he had a whale of a time.

4 The Course of True Love . . .

Throughout 1979 a romance was played out for all the residents to observe. It started when Gail Potter was stood up outside a cinema having arranged a date with Brian Tilsley at a Christmas party. He didn't turn up because he was so drunk at the party that he hadn't remembered making the date. Gail forgave him, and the pair started going out together. Brian's mother, Ivy, took against Gail as she wasn't a Catholic and did all she could to put Brian off her. Gail was upset when the Tilsleys bought No.5 and moved in, just three doors away. Brian's father, Bert, warned Ivy not to turn against Gail as she might lose Brian but Ivy was determined that he would not marry out of the faith. When the youngsters announced their engagement Ivy refused to congratulate them or attend

the party Bert threw in their honour. However, Gail's mother, Audrey, was delighted and embarrassed her daughter by dancing with all the men at the party

Gail pushed Brian into selling his motorbike and buying a car, then broke off their engagement after catching him dancing seductively with Suzie Birchall at a disco. Ivy was pleased that the romance was off, but Gail's landlady Elsie Tanner was annoyed on her behalf and argued with Ivy at the factory. Then Steve Fisher accused Brian of being a mummy's boy, at which Brian took offence and the pair brawled in the Street. Gail nursed Brian's wounds and the engagement was back on, only to suffer another setback when Ivy told Brian about Gail's affair with Roy Thornley. He was upset to discover Gail wasn't a virgin but Bert told him not to be a hypocrite and urged him not to let the news put him off her. Instead of dumping Gail, Brian turned on his mother for carrying malicious gossip and left home. Ivy collapsed.

Bert accused Ivy of ruining their marriage with her selfishness and warned her against ruining Brian's life. She begged Brian's forgiveness and was relieved when he returned home. She started to view the marriage more positively and was grateful when Gail took instructions to become a Catholic and agreed to marry at St Boniface. However, Ivy's plans for a big wedding clashed with Audrey's ideas, and the two mothers locked horns until Gail walked down the aisle to be given away by Mike Baldwin. The wedding went without a hitch, although the reception was spoilt when Vera Duckworth fought with her husband Jack after he had told the priest some dirty jokes. The Tilsleys honeymooned in the Isle of Man, and afterwards Gail moved bravely into No.5, sharing a kitchen with Ivy.

5 Eddie Finds Employment

After collapsing from overwork, Len Fairclough was warned by the doctor to take things easy and employed Eddie Yeats as a labourer. Eddie landed Len in trouble when he vandalized property in order to win the job to repair it. Len put it down to over-enthusiasm.

Not content with having a wage packet, Eddie took a weekend job manning an ice-cream van for Pagliaci's. Stan Ogden couldn't see why he wanted to do this job until Eddie revealed his plan to use the van as a cover to sell beer. Hilda forbade Stan to have anything to do with it, and when the police started asking questions Eddie dropped his scheme.

While he was insulating Betty Turpin's loft, Eddie found ex-con Herbert Cook sleeping rough. He made him a cup of tea at Betty's and felt pleased with himself for a small act of charity, but Herbert stole Betty's

prize carriage clock. Eddie pleaded with her not to call in the police – he didn't want to see Herbert back in prison. Betty agreed unwillingly to keep them out of the matter but told Eddie she'd never trust him again.

6 Fred's Vanity Goes To His Head

Fred Gee branched out into book-making by taking bets over the Rovers' bar. He didn't bother phoning them through to the bookie's and found himself owing Mike Baldwin forty pounds when his horse raced home at 20/1. He was forced to take money from the till to pay Mike, then faced Annie Walker's wrath. She continued to treat him as a chauffeur-cum-footman and annoyed him by sending him on an errand to purchase wood-pigeon for a dinner party. He had no luck tracking it down, and was horrified when the police impounded the Rover, which he had parked illegally. Annie said she would dock his wages to pay the fine, and decided she no longer wanted Fred in her service. When Billy arrived on a visit she hoped he would replace Fred but he had no intention of staying in Weatherfield and gave Fred the

money to pay Annie back for the fine. When Fred gave it to her, Annie was so touched that she told him she would pay half. Fred could hardly believe his luck.

After Audrey Potter had laughed about his bald patch, Fred bought a hair piece. Annie realized it was a touchy subject and asked her customers not to mention it. However, Albert Tatlock refused to remain silent and told him he looked a joke. Upset by the regulars' laughter Fred threw the wig in the bin.

7 Deidre's Emotional Roller-coaster

Back in Weatherfield, Billy Walker was pleased to discover that Deirdre Langton was single once again, and after Ken Barlow assured him he had no strong feelings for her he made a play for her. Emily Bishop was annoyed when Deirdre started dating Billy: she thought Ken was a better prospect for her and Tracy. Deirdre told her to mind her own business and was thrilled when Billy invited her to live with him in Jersey. He had plans to buy a wine bar in St Helier and asked his mother for a loan. Annie told him she would give him the money, but only on condition that he dropped Deirdre. Billy refused to comply until Deirdre confessed that he didn't excite her as Ray had. Then he took the money and left.

Ken stepped out of the shadows, declared his feelings for Deirdre and took her with Tracy on holiday to the Lakes. On their return Deirdre received a letter from Ray asking for a divorce and threatening to cite Ken as co-respondent. Len Fairclough said that he had told Ray about their relationship and that Ray wanted to marry his Dutch girlfriend who was pregnant. Ken panicked and begged Deirdre to keep his name out of the divorce, but his lack of concern at her name being dragged through the mud upset her. Then Ken saw that he was acting like a heel and apologized. The pair were reconciled in time for Christmas and a visit from his daughter Susan. She got on well with Deirdre, but Ken became anxious when he realized she had grown into a young woman.

8 Derek's Chocolate Novelties

While Alf Roberts was in hospital, Mavis Riley helped out at the Corner Shop and was thrilled to receive a visit from Derek Wilton. He told her he had started work at Sandicroft's Confectioners and needed her help in winning the salesman-of-the-month award. Eager to please, Mavis ordered a gross of Easter bunnies for the shop and another gross for the Kabin. Derek won a canteen of cutlery as third prize, and hurt Mavis by giving it to his mother instead of her. Stuck with a load of bunnies no one wanted, Rita Fairclough told Derek he was a louse.

Noises in the night disturbed Mavis, who sought help from Eddie Yeats. Rita was titillated when he spent the night in Mavis's flat and located the source of the noises as the fireplace. Fearing a bird was trapped, Mavis phoned the RSPCA and Inspector Harry Scott arrived to free a budgie. Mavis gave the bird a home and named it Harry after its saviour. She was thrilled when Harry the man invited her to dinner.

9 Bet and Rita's Adventure

To help local students, Bet Lynch volunteered to be kidnapped from the Rovers during Rag Week. She made a big drama out of the capture and spent a day

with the students in a run-down flat until she heard the humiliating news that only four pounds had been raised as a ransom. Annie Walker added insult to injury by docking her pay because she was annoyed that her barmaid had missed a day's work.

Rita Fairclough looked forward to a caravanning holiday in Morecambe and was annoyed when Len told her he couldn't join her as he was working. Instead she took Bet and immediately regretted inviting her as she made a play for two men in the neighbouring caravan, Alec Keegan and Tony Ball. Rita made certain that Alec knew she wasn't after an affair but Bet threw herself at Tony. Len arrived unexpectedly and caught the four together but, to Rita's annoyance, he showed no jealousy and instead joined the men in their fishing trip.

10 Hilda's Talents Put To the Test

While she was painting a skirting-board, Hilda Ogden discovered a talent for copying abstract art. She was amazed when Eddie Yeats framed a piece and sold it to

that patron of the arts Annie Walker for twenty pounds. Annie was proud of the painting until she reframed it and discovered a message scrawled on the back from Hilda to Stan. Then she binned it, telling Hilda she had sold it on to an art collector for a huge profit. When Hilda turned her attention to music Annie banned her from playing the Rovers' piano as the din was too awful.

Eddie turned his hand to farming when he bought six hens and installed them in the Ogdens' back yard, naming them after the Street's womenfolk. At first Hilda hated them and looked upon them as vermin, but gradually she grew fond of them, especially Little Hilda. However, she insisted they earned their keep so Eddie began buying eggs from the corner shop and placing them under the birds for Hilda to find. It was a cunning plan, but when Eddie told Suzie Birchall she had a fat bottom, she took revenge by planting hard-boiled eggs in the hen coop, then watched in delight as Ena Sharples confronted Hilda in the Rovers and cut up an egg she'd bought from her to prove that it wasn't raw. Furious, Hilda insisted the birds were removed and Albert Tatlock wrung Little Hilda's neck. Hilda cooked the chicken for Stan's birthday dinner but neither could bring themselves to eat their pet and they gave the whole meal to Albert.

Albert continued to take advantage of Eddie and the Ogdens when he told them he'd found a valuable old coin on his allotment. Using a metal detector the trio dug for buried treasure and only realized they'd been conned when they'd turned over all the earth and it was ready for planting.

11 Elsie Moves to Torquay

After being beaten up by a customer who refused to pay a fare, Ron Mather decided to give up taxi-driving and took a job as a chauffeur to a wealthy gent, Mr Pickering, in Torquay. He asked Elsie to move with him, saying that Pickering was looking for a

housekeeper, but Elsie didn't want to become a servant. However, after seven months without Ron Elsie had second thoughts and he was delighted when she moved south, leaving the sale of No.11 in Suzie Birchall's hands. Suzie had no intention of helping with the sale and did all she could to put off the prospective buyers. Elsie returned to Weatherfield after Ron had stood by while Pickering made a pass at her. Having given up her job at Baldwin's she faced an uncertain future.

12 Suzie and Steve Bow Out

Suzie Birchall had returned from London full of talk about the high life. However reality was grimmer: forced to find the rent money she signed up with Paul Stringer's modelling agency. Stringer was fifty-two and threw presents at her in exchange for sex. Elsie Tanner accused her of being a slut, but Suzie refused to see herself like that and insisted she was a model, but the only work she was given was demonstrating German sausages in a supermarket. Desperate for stability, she was grateful when her old friend Steve Fisher took her on as a machinist at Baldwin's.

After the Rovers crash Mike Baldwin was forced to stay in hospital with broken ribs and a fractured ankle. In his absence Steve managed the factory, but the girls threatened to strike when he introduced a time-and-motion study. Mike discharged himself to sort out the mess. Then the denim trade hit a slump and he threatened his workers with a three-day week when orders were cancelled. Vera Duckworth took a job as a cashier at a local supermarket but returned quickly when Mike secured a huge order by bedding a buyer.

The trade council organized an exchange trip between Weatherfield and its French twin town, Charlesville. Mike agreed that Ivy, Vera and Hilda could go on the trip if they could raise the money they needed for the journey. Hilda sold her old clothes, having found that they were now fashionable again.

Mike decided that Steve was too naïve to run the factory so ordered him to take over at the smaller one in London. Steve wasn't keen on the move but had little choice.

Mike attempted to rekindle his affair with Suzie, but she told him he was too old for her and flaunted her relationship with punk rocker Norman Mannion. After catching her using his office phone for a personal call, Mike sacked her. Suzie decided she'd had enough of Weatherfield and left town.

CAST

Dave Barnes	Russell Dixon
Bert Tilsley	Peter Dudley
Paul Stringer	John Collin
Sally Norton	Yvonne Nicholson
Audrey Potter	Sue Nicholls
Alec Keegan	Geoffrey Wilkinson
Tony Ball	Brian Peck
Herbert Cook	Anthony Pedley
Jack Duckworth	William Tarmey
Norman Mannion	Andrew Schofield
Susan Barlow	Suzie Patterson

1980

Behind the Scenes

What should have been the biggest news of the year, if not of the programme's twenty-year history, passed without comment. Since the early seventies Violet Carson's health had been deteriorating and her appearances as Ena Sharples, at one time the programme's central character, had become scarce, with months separating them. When, in March, she recorded scenes in which Ena said she was going to stay in St Anne's, the writers, cast and viewers all expected to see the famous hairnet again. Unfortunately they didn't. From this point onwards, all the stories plotted to bring Ena back to the Street had to be shelved as Violet was simply too ill to appear. She became a recluse at her Blackpool home where she lived with her sister, and slowly Ena's presence left the Street. One of the last times she pulled on the famous raincoat was to pose for photographs to be included in a special *TV Times* souvenir magazine celebrating the show's two-thousandth episode. The cast were photographed feeding local children in a glorious street party.

Bill Podmore had to tell Madge Hindle, who had been in the show as long as he had, that her character, Renee Roberts, was to die. The writers felt that Alf and Renee were a mismatched couple and research showed that the public agreed. After Renee's death, as Podmore put it, 'Alf emerged into the sunlight from the shadows of a rather humdrum marriage.'

Renee died as a new character moved into the Street. He was sixteen-year-old Martin Cheveski, brought in to appeal to teenagers and to become a heart-throb. Unfortunately the actor cast for the role was older and never managed to look sixteen. Also, Martin, who was Elsie Tanner's grandson, sprang out of nowhere; the Cheveskis had had a son, Paul, who at this stage would have been nineteen. The actor would have been perfectly cast as him, but the writers wanted a younger character so a second grandson was invented.

Top Twenty

Pos	Character	No of eps	Total	Pos Prev Year
1	Len Fairclough	83	1604	2
2	Annie Walker	75	1544	12
3	Hilda Ogden	74	1153	4
4	Eddie Yeats	74	311	17
5	Elsie Tanner	73	1404	2
6	Ivy Tilsley	72	201	5
7	Emily Bishop Swain	65	1139	20
8	Mavis Riley	65	427	22
9	Alf Roberts	65	617	13
10	Rita Fairclough	64	584	7
11	Fred Gee	64	280	16
12	Bet Lynch	62	757	18
13	Deirdre Langton	61	470	10
14	Bert Tilsley	61	107	15
15	Gail Tilsley	61	350	1
16	Betty Turpin	60	822	8
17	Stan Ogden	59	1056	8
18	Ken Barlow	58	1337	13
19	Mike Baldwin	51	226	19
20	Brian Tilsley	49	102	10

Key Dates

1980

April 4	Violet Carson makes her last appearance as Ena Sharples after 1148 episodes
June 2	Two-thousandth episode transmitted
July 30	Renee Roberts killed
September 10	Emily Bishop marries Arnold Swain
December 9	Twentieth birthday of *Coronation Street*
December 31	Nicky Tilsley is born

> "I were fourteen when I first decided me face didn't suit me."
>
> **Hilda Ogden**

STORIES

1 Rita Makes a Stand

Rita Fairclough had had enough of living in a pigsty and put together a list of alterations she wanted made to the house but Len tore it up. She packed her bags and walked out. She found digs in a theatrical boarding-house and took cabaret work. Gatsby manager Ralph Lancaster offered to set her up in a luxury flat, but she turned him down, knowing there would be strings attached. At first Len waited impatiently for Rita to return home but as the days passed and he missed her, he took Elsie Tanner's advice and decided to seek her out. Finding Rita with Ralph he jumped to the wrong conclusion and demanded her return. When she accused him of treating her like a housekeeper, not a woman, he slapped her across the face and wrote off his marriage. He tried the strong-arm tactics again when Ralph, enjoying his discomfort, offered him the use of a prostitute. Ralph hit him and had him thrown out of the Gatsby.

Len was lonely sitting at home and, two months after she'd left him, he tracked Rita down again, this time to a Blackpool launderette where she worked. He begged her to return and, with nothing else on the horizon, she moved back.

In Rita's absence Mavis Riley had taken charge of the Kabin and promoted paper-girl Louise Clayton to be her assistant. Rita assured Louise her job was safe as she intended to be a full-time housewife. To please Rita, Len agreed to buy a semi-detached house in Handforth but was relieved when she decided she wanted to stay at No.9, so long as he modernized it. After a few weeks she missed the Kabin and returned to work, making Louise redundant.

2 Newlywed Bliss

No.5 was not a happy home. While Brian Tilsley was content to continue living with his parents Gail struggled for independence, upsetting Ivy by insisting on cooking all Brian's meals herself. When Brian spent money on records rather than saving for a deposit on a house Gail threw him out of her bed and he was forced to sleep on the sofa. He accused her of turning into a nag but she finally convinced him that No.5 was too small for two couples to live in harmony. A new estate was built on the other side of town, and Gail was thrilled when Brian promised to buy a sixteen-thousand-pound house on Willow Crescent. The bank offered a 95 per cent mortage but they were still short of the deposit so Ivy gave them three hundred pounds. Brian took the money for granted until Bert told him it was their holiday fund and that Benidorm was now out of the question. The celebrations were cut short when Gail discovered she was pregnant – she had forgotten to take the Pill. The Tilsleys pulled out of the house purchase, knowing they'd need all their money, but Ivy suggested they bought a terraced house in nearby Peterloo Place. However, when a bijou home came available in Buxton Close for thirteen thousand Gail talked Brian into buying it, even though it had only one

bedroom. Ivy was put out as it was two bus rides away, but she was determined never to be off the doorstep. Anxious to be the first person to be entertained by the young couple, she put off Audrey Potter from calling, which upset Gail who banned Ivy from the house.

Audrey did more than call at Buxton Close: when her boyfriend threw her out she moved in, sleeping on the sofa. Eager for a fun night out, Audrey persuaded Brian to borrow a car from the garage where he worked to take them out on the town. The customer spotted the trio and garage boss Ron Sykes sacked him. Gail had been forced to give up work because of the baby and broke down, fearing life on the dole. Sykes felt sorry for her and took Brian back. The Tilsleys were relieved, until Bert was made redundant by Livesley's Foundry. On New Year's Eve Gail went into labour in the Rovers and was rushed to hospital.As the regulars sang 'Auld Lang Syne', news reached Audrey and Ivy that they were grandmothers.

3 Elsie's Lodgers

The council decided to rebuild the frontage of the community centre, which meant that Ena Sharples had to move out. Elsie Tanner gave her a bed for a week, but Ena realized she couldn't lodge at No.11 for ever as she'd soon start criticizing her old enemy. Annoyed that no one else was prepared to take her in, Ena packed her bags and moved to St Anne's to housekeep for Henry Foster.

Elsie didn't stay alone for long at No.11. Confident lorry-driver Dan Johnson talked her into giving him bed and breakfast, but insisted on sleeping in her bed rather than in the back room. Elsie enjoyed having a man about the house again and took no notice when friends

warned her that Dan had a roving eye. He was content at No.11 but found Elsie a touch too old for his tastes. When Bet Lynch made it clear she was interested in him he was happy to take her out, with the result that Elsie threw his belongings into the Street and had to be restrained from clawing Bet's eyes out.

Dan moved into Bet's bedsit above the Corner Shop, upsetting Alf and Renee Roberts, who gave Bet notice to quit. She moved into another bedsit in Leyland Road, and set about turning it into a love-nest for two. Although he had a woman in every city, Dan was a possessive man and saw red when he caught Bet chatting to a neighbour. Keith Sadler was only borrowing Bet's iron but Dan punched him in the stomach. When Bet complained about his behaviour Dan walked out, saying that he didn't like his tarts to criticize him.

4 Hilda Ogden – Scarlet Woman

Representing the Great British Worker in France, Hilda Ogden, Vera Duckworth and Ivy Tilsley were caught up in an international row after taking part in a drinking orgy with a group of ex-paratroopers during which Vera's knickers were flown from the Town Hall flagpole. Desperate to keep the incident from their husbands, the trio agreed to stay quiet about their exploits.

When Hilda got home she was outraged to discover that Stan had been renting the house to local men and their girlfriends. She had only just forgiven him when he learnt that a woman called Dora Entwistle had left him a hundred pounds and two china dogs in her will. Hilda accused Stan of having relations with Dora, before a solicitor revealed that she had been an elderly woman who had always found Stan a cheerful window-cleaner.

After seeing money in Stan's tea-leaves, Hilda dragged him to bingo but he escaped, leaving her with two cards to fill in. When Vera won the jackpot – a holiday for two in Blackpool – Hilda declared the winning card had been Stan's but Vera wouldn't believe her and took the holiday. The relationship between the two women collapsed completely when Hilda grew annoyed over Vera's refusal to let her join the factory girls' pools syndicate. In revenge Hilda copied the winning numbers on to

Vera's coupon then looked on in horror as the factory workers celebrated a huge win. Believing she was about to receive twelve thousand pounds, Vera splashed out on a fur coat, and Hilda was forced to come clean. The girls refused to talk to her and she was sacked from the factory.

Stan panicked when he developed an itchy rash, which the doctor suggested was an allergy to beer. While his mates fell about with mirth and Annie Walker feared a fall in profits, Stan mused that life wouldn't be worth living without a pint in his hand. He was relieved when tests showed it was eggs to which he was allergic.

As a Christmas treat for herself, Hilda employed Brenda Palin to clean No.13. Stan thought it was a waste of money for a char to have a char, but Hilda was delighted not to have to sweep and polish at home for a week.

5 Emily Marries a Bigamist

Deirdre Langton took a full-time job in the offices of Weatherfield Rainwear, taking it for granted that Emily Bishop would look after Tracy. Emily objected to this, and the women decided that their best option would be to go into business together. They opened the Coronation Street Secretarial Bureau, with Deirdre taking in typing and Emily bookkeeping. One of their first clients was pet-shop owner Arnold Swain, who took an interest in Emily but scared her off by asking questions about her finances. Deirdre turned private eye to look into Arnold's finances and discovered he was well provided for. Arnold proposed to Emily but she turned him down, feeling she was too old to be someone else's wife. However, he persisted, and on his second attempt she agreed, realizing he genuinely cared for her.

News of Emily's engagement sent Mavis Riley into a depression and, rather than be a bridesmaid and witness the union, she went on holiday. Deirdre and Tracy stood as Emily's attendants during the register-office ceremony and Emily was touched to receive a telegram from Leonard Swindley wishing her well. The Swains honeymooned in Shanklin, on the Isle of Wight, and afterwards Arnold startled his bride by announcing his intention for them to move to rural Derbyshire. To aid the sale of No.3, he asked Len Fairclough to replace the dull front door with a glass-panelled one. The new door kept sticking, and in trying to open it, Emily pushed her hand through the glass and needed stitches. Arnold blamed Len and refused to pay, but Emily went against his wishes and settled the account.

While Arnold was away on business Emily received a visit from an insurance man enquiring after a Mrs Margaret Swain. She was stunned to discover that Arnold had another wife to whom he was still legally married. When he returned he couldn't deny it and tried to explain that his first marriage had, in his eyes, only lasted as long as the honeymoon fifteen years beforehand. Disgusted with him and herself, Emily threw Arnold out of the house, refusing to accept that he still loved her. After scrubbing the house clean, she reported the matter to the police and struggled to convince them that she wasn't making the story up.

6 Deirdre on the Move

After being taken on as Alf Roberts's resident assistant Deirdre Langton left No.3 and moved into the Corner Shop flat. Little Tracy caused anxious moments when she locked herself into the toilet. Alf had to rescue her through a small window. Deirdre's romance with Ken Barlow died after he decided not to risk a third marriage: he was still experiencing difficulty in adjusting to his daughter Susan being a young woman, and especially when she introduced him to her nineteen-year-old boyfriend Duncan Craig. He was even more put out when sixteen-year-old Susan went camping with Duncan, sharing a small tent.

Albert Tatlock was glad to see Ken finishing with Deirdre as he thought her unsuitable for him. Then he faced a dilemma when an old friend, Monty Shawcross, invited him to join their regiment in marching to the Cenotaph on Remembrance Sunday. Albert refused on the grounds that no one was interested in old soldiers, but then felt guilty when Monty died of a heart-attack. To honour him, and their fallen pals, he sold his military medal and bought a wreath with the proceeds to lay on the steps of Manchester's Cenotaph. Ken bought back the medal for him and told him to treasure it as a link to his friends.

7 Telephone Menace

Mavis Riley was tormented by a man who telephoned her at the Kabin, made obscene remarks about her and told her how much he wanted to see her in her nightie. She called the police, who set her up to meet him in the shopping arcade, but things went horribly wrong when Eddie Yeats saw her and stopped for a chat. The police pounced and Eddie was arrested. The caller had watched the incident and phoned Mavis to say she had upset him and that he wouldn't be calling again. Eddie was released without charge.

A few weeks later he re-entered Mavis's life when she bought a hanging chair from him. He erected it in the Kabin flat but when she sat on it the ceiling fell down as the joists were rotten.

While her flat was repaired Mavis lodged with the Faircloughs, who were having problems as Rita had hired Hilda Ogden to clean the house. Len refused to pay her, saying that housework was Rita's job. At Rita's insistence the couple swapped jobs, with Len selling papers in the morning and spending the afternoons in the pub. Rita enjoyed herself at the yard until a customer made advances to her and she had to ask Len to sort him out.

8 Mike's Supervisor Rows

Elsie Tanner asked Mike Baldwin to give her the vacant post of supervisor at the factory. When he refused she was forced to take the job of manageress at Dawson's Café, now under new management and called Jim's Café after its owner Jim Sedgewick.

Mike employed a buyer from a rival firm, Pauline Stringer, as production controller and was shocked to discover she was a trade unionist. She found out that Ivy Tilsley was not an official Garment Workers Union shop steward and insisted on an

election. Ida Clough stood against Ivy, and won fourteen votes to her seventeen. Pauline pointed out to Mike that the election had split the workers and had broken Ivy's confidence. Mike and Pauline became lovers but she quit after he undermined her authority by refusing to allow the girls a shopping hour. Then Ivy was made supervisor and, because she couldn't serve management and workers, Ida was given the role of shop steward.

Mike's problems with women didn't stop at the factory gates. Ken Barlow organized a raffle to raise funds for OAPs in which the first prize was a date with Mike. Hilda Ogden was delighted to win, but Mike couldn't contemplate the idea of spending an evening with her and offered her forty pounds to forgo it. She won him round by saying how special she would feel if he treated her like a lady.

Mike was stunned to receive a visit from his estranged father, Frankie, who asked him to invest in a video business. Suspicious, Mike refused but gullible Fred Gee gave him seventy pounds then panicked when he disappeared back to London with the money.

9 Bar Wars

Annie Walker started serving soup and sandwiches at the Rovers and had a bell installed to summon her staff – one ring for Betty, two for Bet, three for Fred.

Then she planned to show off to friend Olive Taylor-Brown by taking her to an exclusive gala dinner but dropped her handbag on the way. Hilda Ogden saved the night by retrieving it – it contained the dinner tickets – but Annie was furious when Olive insisted she gave Hilda a five-pound reward.

Another Ogden caused trouble when, angered by a price increase, Stan pinned the Labour Club's price list to the Rover's wall. Annie barred him but in response Ken Barlow threatened to lead a boycott so she backed down.

Fred started up a barber-shop quartet to compete with the Flying Horse, with Alf, Bert and Eddie, but was dropped by the others as he sang off-key. Renee Roberts dressed as a man to replace him but the Rovers lost the contest anyway. Months later Fred fell for relief barmaid Arlene Jones and wondered why she kept avoiding him. He did not know that Bet had told her Fred had startling habits. He decided to make a pass at her and was stunned when she told him the Rovers was grotty and set her husband on him.

Betty also had a troubled year. She felt sorry for local latch-key children, Wayne and Sharon Fletcher, and reported their mother to the NSPCC for neglect. Their mother's boyfriend threatened her with violence but Eddie Yeats saw him off, and Mrs Fletcher was left to accuse Betty of ruining her life when he abandoned her. Nevertheless the NSPCC assured Betty she'd done the right thing.

Bet lost her handbag in the sales and ended up having her bedsit ransacked. All her belongings were either stolen or trashed, including her only photograph of her son. The residents organized a whip-round and Annie gave her an evening dress to wear behind the bar. She was horrified when Bet wore it back to front, to create a plunging front.

10 Forbidden Love

Elsie Tanner gave her back room an airing when her sixteen-year-old grandson, Martin Cheveski, came to stay. Len Fairclough took him on as an apprentice, sacking Eddie Yeats in his favour, and Martin quickly fell in love with Karen Oldfield, a trainee machinist at Baldwin's. He was out with her one night when Elsie fell asleep on the sofa with a cigarette. Luckily, Hilda Ogden called round to borrow some sugar and found No.11 full of smoke. She dragged Elsie to safety then hounded her for days afterwards, reminding her of how she'd saved her life. Eventually Elsie told her not to bother the next time the house was on fire.

Elsie was furious when Martin got Karen drunk on her gin and the couple had their ears pierced. Karen's father, a police sergeant, ordered Martin to stay away from her but Martin proved his love by threatening to return to his native Birmingham if he wasn't allowed to see her again. Wanting to make a commitment to Karen, Martin proposed to her but she felt they were too young and split with him. He returned to Birmingham broken-hearted.

11 Bin Warfare

After Eddie Yeats had nursed the Ogdens through a bad case of flu, Hilda agreed to take him in as a lodger, but only on condition that he was in full-time employment. He took a job on the dustbin lorry, earning eighty pounds a week, twenty of which he gave to Hilda for his bed and board. When Hilda spent a few days visiting her brother Eddie talked Stan into taking in fellow binman Johnny Webb. All went well until Hilda's return, when mischievous Vera Duckworth told Johnny's wife Maureen that he had been sharing Hilda's bed. Hilda was astonished when Maureen confronted her in the street and accused her of being a trollop.

Annie Walker wasn't pleased when she caught Eddie and Johnny discussing the contents of her bins in the Rovers, and when Eddie told everyone her hair colour came from a packet she phoned the council and demanded that a different crew emptied her bins. However, all the bin crews sided with Eddie and Johnny and boycotted the Rovers' rubbish. Annie refused to back down, and the stench of rubbish filled the area around the Street. The local press became interested in the story and Bet Lynch was photographed sitting on top of a bin and was quoted criticizing Annie. The row was eventually sorted out by Alf Roberts, who urged Annie to be bigger than the binmen and apologize. She invited them in for a sherry and was forced to crawl.

12 A Tragic End to Renee

After holidaying in Grange-over-Sands Alf and Renee Roberts decided to sell up and open a sub-post office in Cumbria. They found buyers for the Corner Shop and put down a deposit on a shop in a small village. Renee started driving lessons, and after a drink to celebrate the acceptance of their offer, she said she would drive Alf home. The car stalled in a country lane and Alf got out to take the wheel. At that moment a lorry sped round the corner, hit the car and Renee flew through the windscreen. She was rushed to hospital but her spleen and liver were ruptured and she died on the operating table. Devastated, Alf was breathalysed and broke down when he couldn't remember what Renee looked like when she smiled. At the funeral Daisy Hibbert accused Alf of murdering her daughter, and would not believe that the breathalyser test had been negative.

CAST

Jim Sedgewick	Michael O'Hagan
Dan Johnson	Richard Shaw
Louise Clayton	Janet Rawson
Olive Taylor-Brown	Paula Tilbrook
Pauline Stringer	Patricia Browning
Duncan Craig	Gary Stewart
Arnold Swain	George Waring
Keith Sadler	Richard Kay
Martin Cheveski	Jonathan Caplan
Wayne Fletcher	Martin Bacon
Sharon Fletcher	Wendy Bacon
Arlene Jones	Geraldine Moffatt
Karen Oldfield	Sally Jane Jackson
Sergeant Oldfield	Michael Lees
Johnny Webb	Jack Smethurst
Maureen Webb	Eileen Kennally
Monty Shawcross	John Barrett
Ron Sykes	Bobby Knutt
Frankie Baldwin	Sam Kydd
Brenda Palin	Sandra Voe

1981

Behind the Scenes

Wedding fever gripped the nation as preparations were made for Prince Charles's wedding to Lady Diana Spencer. Down on the Street another royal couple, Ken and Deirdre, pushed ahead with their own nuptials, timed by the writers to take place just two days before the event at St Paul's Cathedral. Both William Roache and Anne Kirkbride were delighted with the idea of their screen characters marrying, knowing they worked well together and that each character had enough past history to ensure dramatic storylines in the future. Worries that, at twenty-six, Deirdre was too young to be married to forty-two-year-old Ken were swept aside and Wardrobe were instructed to dress her in dowdy outfits that would blur the difference in their ages. The press jumped at the titbit that the actor marrying the Barlows was an actual vicar, and there was much speculation as to whether the actors would be married in real life or not.

Two new faces were introduced to the show, both respected actresses. Meg Johnson, a stalwart from Oldham Repertory Theatre, was brought in as Fred Gee's love interest, while star of West End and sixties films Amanda Barrie first appeared as café-owner's wife Alma Sedgewick. The only note Amanda had on which to hang the character of Alma was 'She's a lazy slut with a roving eye.'

> "You could meet Alf Roberts riding on a horse in the middle of the Sahara Desert and still know he's a grocer."
>
> **Audrey Potter**

Top Twenty

Pos	Character	No of eps	Total	Pos Prev Year
1	Elsie Tanner	88	1492	5
2	Fred Gee	82	362	10
3	Len Fairclough	79	1683	1
4	Rita Fairclough	77	661	10
5	Bet Lynch	74	831	12
6	Ken Barlow	73	1410	18
7	Deirdre L Barlow	71	541	13
8	Alf Roberts	71	688	7
9	Annie Walker	68	1612	2
10	Hilda Ogden	68	1221	3
11	Bert Tilsley	68	175	13
12	Mike Baldwin	65	291	19
13	Mavis Riley	62	489	7
14	Ivy Tilsley	60	261	6
15	Albert Tatlock	59	1224	21
16	Eddie Yeats	59	370	3
17	Stan Ogden	58	1114	17
18	Betty Turpin	58	880	16
19	Eunice Nuttall Gee	56	56	–
20	Emily Bishop	54	1193	7

Key Dates

1981

May 13	Fred Gee marries Eunice Nuttall
June 22	Alma Sedgewick's first appearance
July 27	Ken Barlow marries Deirdre Langton

STORIES

1 Temptation for the Tilsleys

Ivy Tilsley was outraged when she learnt that Elsie Tanner was going to be her grandson's godmother. Gail and Brian decided to call their son Daniel David, but on realizing that if they did his initials would be DDT, changed their minds at the font and he was christened Nicholas Paul. Brian annoyed Gail by acting as if he were single and she urged him to take more responsibility. Bert lectured his son after hearing him say he wished he'd never married as he had no money and the bills kept coming in. Despite their financial

problems, though, Brian refused to let Gail return to work and told her that mothers who worked were sluts. Instead he took a night job at Ron Sykes's filling station. He was hardly at home so Gail befriended the neighbours, only to have one, Colin Jackson, make a pass at her. She told Brian, who told the terrified Colin that he would thump him if he called again.

Brian wasn't so restrained when wealthy customer Glenda Fox made a play for him. He found the experience exciting but slipped up when Gail found one of Glenda's handkerchiefs in his overall pocket. Again it was up to Bert to sit Brian down and order him to put his family first. The Tilsleys were reconciled and went on to win the Mr and Mrs contest held at the Rovers. Brian was soon in trouble again, though, after being caught up in an attempted robbery at the filling station. He knocked the thief, Ronnie Burgess, unconscious, but ended up in court on a charge of unlawful wounding. Ron Sykes paid for the best solicitor and Brian's name was eventually cleared.

2 The Vice Man Cometh

Frankie Baldwin returned to the Street on the run from the Vice Squad. He told his son Mike that his video-company partner had been producing blue movies. Business was good, though, and he gave Fred Gee a hundred and fifty pounds on his investment. Fred gave him another fifty and persuaded Alf Roberts to invest too, before he discovered that Frankie's cheque had bounced. Frankie disappeared again, leaving the police to question Fred as a shareholder in Gee Whizz Videos. Three months later Frankie returned and repaid Alf and Fred in cash, and showed off his twenty-year-old girlfriend Sylvia Hicks, to whom Mike took an instant dislike, seeing her as a gold-digger.

Mike's business didn't do as well as his father's. An important buyer, Johnson's, went bust, leaving Mike with a load of stock. He told Ivy Tilsley that he was going to make a third of his workers redundant and asked her to come up with twelve names. She fell into his trap and begged him to put them all on a three-day week rather than lose jobs. To help shift the unwanted stock, Mike hired a market stall and ordered his staff to man it, putting them on 5 per cent commission. Ivy and Ida Clough weren't successful as they were too timid, but Elsie Tanner and Vera Duckworth took to it like ducks to water and soon sold the stock.

3 The Courting of Deirdre

Ken Barlow's year started with trouble from the police when Albert Tatlock objected to

him parking his new car – a German Volkswagen – outside No.1. The police followed up Albert's complaint and, taking their advice, Ken rented a garage on Viaduct Street. He started to show renewed interest in old flame Deirdre Langton, but stood aside when she dated Dirk van der Sterk, a Dutch colleague of her estranged husband Ray. Deirdre enjoyed seeing Dirk, but he wasn't in the country long so she decided to make a move towards Ken. They arranged another date but his car broke down and Deirdre, thinking she'd been stood up, went for a meal with Mike Baldwin. Mike made the most of the situation and told Deirdre he wanted to see more of her. They started to date, causing Ken to react jealously and Emily Bishop to beg Mike to stay away from Deirdre – she feared for Tracy's emotional state at having too many 'uncles'. Deirdre told Ken he'd proved himself too unreliable in the past and finished with him. Mike bought a luxury apartment at 46b St Mary's Place and Deirdre helped him move in. Ken started a relationship with beautician Sonia Price and took her to Mike's flat-warming. At the end of the evening Ken and Deirdre found themselves washing up together and realized they were made for each other. Mike gave Deirdre his blessing and promptly started taking Sonia out.

4 Elsie Hits Rock Bottom

Elsie Tanner had struggled in her position as manageress at Jim's Café with the help of Johnny Webb's niece Sandra but resigned when Jim Sedgewick's wife Alma took over the business: Alma had been pulling rank over Elsie and refused to lift a finger so that Elsie had to do all the donkey work. Before leaving the café, Elsie fell for handsome customer Wally Randle and threw herself at him, only to be rejected when he broke the news that she was far too old for him. Bet Lynch tried to cheer her up by taking her on the town for the night and Elsie ended up sharing her bed with Bill Fielding, a guy she picked up in a pub.

In the morning she went to work leaving him in the house and returned to find that the place had been ransacked by his wife, who had tracked him down. All Elsie's clothes were slashed to pieces and her furniture had been smashed up. After spending a few weeks with her daughter Linda Cheveski in Birmingham sorting out her life she returned and surprised everyone by taking a machinist's job at Baldwin's Casuals.

5 The Faircloughs' Problems with Kids

The paper-boys and -girls were causing havoc at the Kabin. Neil Grimshaw was found to be throwing away papers and when Mavis Riley reprimanded him he answered her back and threatened the rest with violence if they turned up for work. At this point Eddie Yeats stepped in and threatened to thump the lad unless he dropped the revolt. Neil apologized meekly, but not long afterwards another paper-boy, Richard Dickinson, brought the gang out on strike when Len refused to give them an extra pound a week. After delivering the papers himself Len was forced to back down and agreed on a 65p increase.

When Rita announced that she wanted to adopt a child, Len wouldn't even consider the idea – he said he had been a bad father to Stanley. However, Rita wore him down and they went to an adoption agency where they were told that they were too old. Determined to have a child, though, Rita offered to take on a local girl's

unwanted baby but that also fell through. Finally the Faircloughs were accepted as foster-parents, and social worker Donald Worthington entered their lives. He sent thirteen-year-old John Spencer to them, together with his rabbit George. The couple enjoyed his company but worried because his best friend was a punk and had encouraged him to rebel against them. After his mother came out of hospital John returned home but when her boyfriend hit him he ran away and hid at No.9. His mother found him there and refused to let him see the Faircloughs again.

6 Vera Plays Around

After being unemployed for six months, a depressed Bert Tilsley saw his benefits cut. He was offered a three-month contract in Holland but, knowing Ivy didn't want him to leave the country, turned it down. He took on little jobs – labouring for Len, decorating for Ken – then found himself the subject of a DSS investigation for illicit earnings. The neighbours offered to lie for him but Bert admitted the offence and broke down when he realized he'd applied for sixty jobs and hadn't had a single interview. His sixty-first was for the job of van-driver at Baldwin's Casuals. Mike wanted to give him the job but couldn't cope with the idea of employing a husband and wife. Instead the job went to Ida Clough's son, Bernard.

Another person in the running for the job was Jack Duckworth, who had lost his job driving lorries. Unlike Bert, he enjoyed being unemployed and supplemented his benefit by moonlighting as a taxi-driver. The Duckworth marriage hit a bad patch when Jack threw Vera out after discovering she was being unfaithful to him with a bricklayer called Harry. Vera dumped herself on the Tilsleys, and upset Ivy by entertaining Harry in their house. Bert begged Jack to take her back but he was enjoying his freedom too much and refused. Ivy finally persuaded Vera to go home by pointing out that she was playing into Jack's hands by staying away.

7 The Wedding of the Decade

While the residents celebrated Ken and Deirdre's engagement, Albert Tatlock feared for his own future. Deirdre made it clear that she wasn't prepared to live at No.1, and wanted a house with a garden for Tracy. Albert's daughter, Beattie Pearson, arrived, argued with Ken and refused to take Albert in. Albert wept, feeling no one wanted him, then collapsed in the street. The doctor told Ken that Albert was too old to live on his own so Deirdre agreed to move to No.1 as long as Albert slept in the front parlour so that Tracy could have his bedroom.

The vicar at St Mary's refused to marry the couple because Deirdre was divorced, so the ceremony took place at All Saints. Alf Roberts gave Deirdre away, Emily Bishop was matron-of-honour, Len Fairclough was best man, while Tracy and Ken's daughter Susan were bridesmaids. Annie Walker laid on a reception at the Rovers, and Ray Langton sent a telegram congratulating the couple. After honeymooning in Corfu the Barlows came across their first hurdle when Tracy started at Bessie Street School and asked why she was still called Langton. Deirdre wrote to Ray asking for permission to change her name but he refused.

8 Big Tips and Cheap Beer

Annie Walker treated herself to a winter cruise, but decided she didn't trust her staff to run the pub while she was away. The brewery sent relief manager Gordon Lewis

to take over in her absence, and he soon showed himself to be a Jekyll and Hyde character. Betty Turpin was furious when he sided with Stan Ogden who had accused her of short-changing him, and Fred Gee smarted when he ordered a complete change-around in the cellar. Then Gordon suspended Fred for helping himself to a short, and Bet and Betty walked out in sympathy.

Annie returned from Casablanca to find two strange barmaids in place and her staff taking jobs at the Rifleman's. Annie was furious and reported Gordon to the brewery after he told her she was too old to run a pub. She had to beg her staff to come back, and promised that when she next went on holiday Betty would be in charge.

A few months later she was annoyed by the amount of petty squabbling that went on over tips. Insisting that she got the most tips, Bet challenged the others to a tip contest, providing individual glasses for them to keep their money in: hers was a pint pot, Betty's a half-pint and Fred's a sherry glass. Annie put a stop to the contest by insisting that all tips were shared equally.

After hearing that London pubs operated a Happy Hour, Annie decided to take up the practice, serving beer 10p cheaper and spirits half price between five thirty and six thirty. She soon stopped this as the customers all left at six thirty to go to Nellie Harvey's cocktail hour, which ran until seven thirty.

9 April Fools

No.13 was filled with music when Eddie Yeats swapped a washing-machine he had found on the rubbish tip for an accordion. He threw himself into his job as binman and lovingly cleaned the lorry, winning a couple of cup-final tickets in a local competition for the cleanest dustcart.

Unfortunately not all his associations with the refuse department were so happy. When Stan Ogden mistook the laundry for the rubbish as both were in bin bags Eddie threw the household's clothes and bed-linen away. Hilda insisted they search the tip but nothing turned up, and Stan played an ill-judged April Fool joke by pretending to have found the bag. Hilda continued to suffer at the hands of her menfolk when they stayed out until three a.m. having told her they were going to the Legion. Hilda convinced herself that Stan had spent the night with the Legion barmaid Freda Woods. She confronted Freda, who admitted that so many men took her home that she couldn't remember who they were. Hilda introduced her to Stan and was insulted when Freda said there was no way she would ever have spent the night with him. In the end Stan was forced to admit he'd been at a strip-club all night. Hilda gave up cleaning for the Faircloughs in favour of doing Mike Baldwin's flat. When she saw a window-cleaning round advertised, she planned to buy it for Stan, before discovering it was his round that he had put up for sale, planning to live off social security.

After visiting her brother, Hilda announced that No.13 was a dump and determined to buy a new house on the River Park Estate. The Ogdens agreed to sell No.13 to the Bells, but were denied a mortgage as they couldn't include Eddie's rent in their application. When the Bells gave them a down payment, Stan decided to sell No.13 anyway and take a council house. Hilda was delighted at this idea until she found that the house offered to them was in a rough area. Stan was mortified when she returned the cheque to the Bells.

10 Freddie the Groom

The residents had a surprise when Fred Gee introduced his girlfriend Eunice Nuttall to them; after years of wooing common or desperate women he had finally found a looker. Having been told by the brewery that he'd be entitled to his own pub if he was married, Fred proposed and Eunice accepted. Before the register-office ceremony, Eddie Yeats booked a stripper to appear at Fred's stag night, but Fred refused to let her perform and took her home. Then he had to spend the night on her floor as he couldn't get a taxi.

After the wedding ceremony the Gees went on a pub crawl before honeymooning in Rhyl. Annie Walker's pleasure at seeing Fred happily married was cut short when Eunice moved into the Rovers and promptly took over. The Gees were interviewed by the brewery but were turned down as landlords when it was discovered that as a barmaid Eunice had once been sacked on suspicion of stealing from the till. The couple sank into despair but Annie refused to be treated as a lodger in her own home and tried to find someone to replace Fred.

Eunice fought Annie to save Fred's job, and persuaded her to raise his salary. Then the unhappy couple moved out of the pub and into her father's spare room. At this point they alarmed Alf Roberts by asking him to let the Corner Shop flat to them. In order to put them off the idea he pulled strings at the Town Hall and had Eunice appointed caretaker at the community centre, a job that came with a flat. The Gees' domestic bliss was short-lived, though, because Eunice's teenage daughter Debbie arrived to stay.

Councillor Ben Critchley received complaints from residents over Fred's bolshy attitude and demanded an investigation when he discovered that Eunice's appointment hadn't gone through the official channels. He requested the Gees' removal but then took a fancy to Eunice and offered the couple jobs at his hotel. Fred refused to work for him, but Eunice decided to take the opportunity and walked out on her marriage. Fred left the centre and returned to Annie's back room.

11 Flighty Audrey

Gail Tilsley's mother, Audrey Potter, turned up on her doorstep with a black eye and announced that she had finished with boyfriend Tony Ditchburn. Gail secured her a bed at Elsie Tanner's, and Audrey was delighted when Tony tracked her down but he had only come to take back the car he'd bought her. Alf Roberts took her on to run the shop while he went on holiday, but Audrey neglected the business and started up a hair-salon in the back-room. On his return Alf surprised everyone by not minding and confessed to Len Fairclough that he had designs on bubbly Audrey. They set tongues wagging by painting out Renee's name from over the shop and he let her talk him into buying a sporty black MG. Alf built up his courage to propose, which alarmed Audrey, who packed and fled the Street to return to Tony.

12 Brief Encounters for Mavis and Emily

Emily Bishop had a traumatic year, which started with the return of her bigamist husband Arnold Swain. He held her at No.3 and told her that God had instructed him to lead them in a suicide pact. She had to fight for her life and managed to escape. Then the police used her as bait to capture Arnold, who was sent to a psychiatric hospital where he died at the end of the year. She was sickened when she found he had left her a legacy of two thousand pounds.

In the summer Emily holidayed in Malta with Mavis Riley, then travelled to London with her to cheer as Prince Charles married Lady Diana.

Mavis's love life had a boost when decorator Maurice Dodds encouraged her artistic endeavours. The relationship turned sour when he asked her to pose for him in the nude. Initially she agreed to his request but then took flight and ended their relationship. She didn't fare any better when sales representative Bobby Simpson asked her out – they had never met before as they dealt with each other exclusively on the telephone. Mavis got cold feet and decided to back out of the blind date, so Bet Lynch went in her place. Bobby was shocked to meet his quiet Mavis in the flesh.

CAST

Nick Tilsley	Warren Jackson
Neil Grimshaw	Michael Le Vell
Dirk Van Der Stek	Lex Van Delden
Gordon Lewis	David Daker
Sandra Webb	Shelagh Stephenson
Wally Randle	Mark Eden
Sonia Price	Bridget Brice
Eunice Nuttall Gee	Meg Johnson
Debbie Nuttall	Gina Maher
Richard Dickinson	Gary Carp
Bill Fielding	John Junkin
Colin Jackson	Paul Lowther
Freda Woods	Rita May
Alma Sedgewick	Amanda Barrie
Don Worthington	Brian Capron
Maurice Dodds	Gilbert Wynne
John Spencer	Jonathan Barber
Glenda Fox	Hazel Clyne
Tony Ditchburn	Barry Stanton
Sylvie Hicks	Debbie Arnold
Ronnie Burgess	Ian Burns
Ben Critchley	Allan Surtees
Bobby Simpson	David Simeon
Graham Bell	Max Smith

1982

Behind the Scenes

> "Bet Lynch'll have sequins on her flippin' shroud."
>
> **Hilda Ogden**

In the summer of 1981 building work had started on the construction of a new outside Street set. The one used by the crew had been built in 1968 and was falling to pieces, and its position, in an old railway yard, was at some distance from the studios. Granada had purchased land in a neighbouring area, Castlefield, when three rows of terraced housing were demolished next to the old Liverpool Street railway station (the first passenger railway station in the world). With the discovery of a ruined Roman fort and the planned opening of a huge industrial museum, the whole area was to be renovated. The Queen and Prince Philip were invited to tour the area and workmen rushed to finish the new *Coronation Street*; 49,000 bricks and 6,500 roofing slates were reclaimed from Salford streets to give the new Street the right period look.

The visit took place on 5 May, with all the cast dressed in character and standing in front of their houses. The royal party walked down the Street, chatting to them, then drove off to tour the rest of the area. Julie Goodyear wore earrings bearing cut-out photographs of Charles and Diana. As the Queen passed, Julie pointed to them and said, 'See? I even know which side of the bed they sleep on.'

In the autumn, Bill Podmore decided to take a step back from the programme and was made executive producer, to allow him to work on other projects. Mervyn Watson was taken on as producer with day-to-day control of the show. One of his first jobs was to push through writer Adele Rose's staggering idea that Deirdre Barlow should have an affair with Mike Baldwin. No one had any idea of just how strongly the story would grab the attention of the public and the press.

Key Dates

1982

July 4	Frankie Baldwin dies
September 20	Phyllis Pearce first appears

Top Twenty

Pos	Character	No of eps	Total	Pos Prev Year
1	Len Fairclough	81	1764	3
2	Elsie Tanner	76	1568	1
3	Annie Walker	75	1687	9
4	Hilda Ogden	70	1291	9
5	Bet Lynch	70	901	5
6	Eddie Yeats	70	440	15
7	Ken Barlow	69	1479	6
8	Ivy Tilsley	68	329	14
9	Rita Fairclough	66	727	40
10	Fred Gee	66	428	2
11	Mavis Riley	63	552	13
12	Stan Ogden	62	1176	17
13	Gail Tilsley	60	460	21
14	Deirdre Barlow	59	600	7
15	Betty Turpin	58	938	17
16	Emily Bishop	57	1250	20
17	Mike Baldwin	56	347	12
18	Alf Roberts	52	740	7
19	Marion Willis	50	50	–
20	Albert Tatlock	48	1272	15

STORIES

1 Elsie Rocks the Boat at Baldwin's

To help clinch an important order, Mike Baldwin asked Elsie Tanner to sweet-talk buyer Wilf Stockwell. She was indignant until she met Wilf and embarked on a passionate affair with him. He admitted he had a wife but swore the marriage had been over for years, until Dot arrived at the factory and stopped production, demanding to know who was sleeping with her husband. Elsie stood up to her, saying that she loved Wilf and knew their marriage was over. Furious, Dot complained to Wilf's bosses and the order was cancelled.

Mike was appalled as no work was coming in, and the girls sent Elsie to Coventry. She was amused by their refusal to talk to her and took the opportunity to insult them to their faces, knowing they couldn't retaliate. Wilf refused to let Elsie take the blame and resigned from his job, left Dot and turned up on Elsie's doorstep. However, she panicked and refused to take him in, ending their relationship.

Mike managed to get his workers back on a four-day week but his business hit a recession and he commissioned a time-and-motion study to find out which of his two factories – in Manchester and London – was the most cost-effective. He was amazed to find the Weatherfield factory made the most money and decided to make 25 per cent of his London staff redundant. The London workers appealed to Ivy Tilsley to bring her girls out on strike to support them but the Weatherfield workers feared for their own jobs and refused.

Emily Bishop became Mike's new wages clerk after he discovered he had given the girls an extra four pounds in the wage packets. On her first week she struggled to cope with the disruptive influence of Cleo, the factory cat, who spilt coffee over her spreadsheets. Mike took the cat to the RSPCA but Vera Duckworth rescued her and made her a union member. Mike retaliated by including the cat in the bonus shareout, saying the money she earned would 'go in the kitty'.

2 Hilda's Funny Valentine

To make up for forgetting her birthday, Stan Ogden decided to send his wife Hilda a Valentine. In order to keep her guessing who it was from he asked Alf Roberts to write the card and post it. Hilda was thrilled with the card and convinced herself she had a secret admirer. Then, after seeing Alf's writing in the shop, she realized he had sent the card and told him that, while she was flattered, she could never leave Stan. Alf was bemused until she told him she knew he had sent the card, at which he told her it had been Stan's idea. She was very embarrassed but worse was to follow when Eddie Yeats sat on her favourite chair and it collapsed under his weight. Fed up with living with tat, Hilda demanded a new three-piece suite but was ashamed to be denied HP: the Ogdens were on a credit blacklist. Eddie came to the rescue with a suite from the bin round.

After deciding she wanted the house freshening up, Hilda gave Stan money to have the exterior woodwork repainted. He spent it on beer then mixed up a load of paint Eddie brought home from the tip, concocting a shade of brown they called 'Jamaican Sun'. When Hilda discovered the paint's origin she demanded that the work be redone with proper shop-bought purple paint. The year's misfortunes were forgotten, though, when Hilda achieved an ambition and was employed to clean a detached house in Oakfield Drive by doctor's wife Joan Lowther.

3 Homeless Bet and Randy Jack

Taxi-driver Jack Duckworth turned his attention to Bet Lynch and, telling her he was attracted to her like metal to a magnet, talked her into bed. Bet questioned her sanity in falling for the cheap line of a married man but recovered her sense of humour when his wife Vera confided in her that she was seeing a construction worker

called Vic. Vera used Bet as an alibi to see Vic, which backfired on her when Jack announced that he knew she was lying as he'd spent the night with Bet. Vera went for Bet in the Rovers then threw Jack out. Bet refused to have anything more to do with him so he planted himself on the Tilsleys. However, Ivy refused to let him stay and forced Vera to take him back.

When her landlord told her he needed to undertake roof repairs at her flat, Bet sought lodgings with Alf Roberts at the Corner Shop. She was aghast to find that the repairs had been a ploy to get rid of her when the house in which she lived was knocked to the ground in a redevelopment scheme. Alf agreed to let Bet stay on at the shop but his kindness was used against him when, as a member of the watch committee, he refused to allow a blue movie to be shown in Weatherfield. The cinema manager insisted on an investigation, which led to reporters calling at the shop and taking photographs of the blonde barmaid who was living rent-free with Alf. The story hit the local papers and Alf ordered Bet to leave, until he realized that the press would follow up the story if he threw her out. He agreed that she could stay, but insisted that she paid rent.

Alf's life lifted romantically when Joyce Lomas entered it. She was an old friend of Annie Walker, who enjoyed a spot of matchmaking between the two. However, Joyce was more interested in the shop than she was in Alf, and told him of her plans to turn it into an off-licence. Alf was frightened by the speed at which she planned things, and they parted company.

4 Work for the Tilsleys

Bert Tilsley finally landed a job, at Longshaw's Foundry, but nearly lost it when his start date clashed with his court appearance on an illicit earnings charge. He came clean to his new boss, who admired his honesty and kept the job for him. In court he was fined ninety pounds and ordered to pay back two hundred pounds dole money. His son Brian faced redundancy when Ron Sykes sold his garage and took a job in Qatar. Brian talked Ron into taking him with him, on a six-month contract to service the government's motor fleet. Gail was distraught at the idea of Brian working overseas for six months but agreed that they needed the money so he headed off to the sun.

Left alone with baby Nicky, Gail had a phone installed and, spurred on by her neighbour Jackie Moffatt, applied for a secretarial job. This annoyed Ivy, who knew she didn't need the money, and Gail tried to make her see that boredom was driving her out of the house. At interview Gail was humiliated when she had to confess that Jackie had typed her application letter, and as no one else would employ her she took a waitressing job at Jim's Café, working under Alma Sedgewick. It was here that lorry-driver Les Charlton fell for her and, angry that Brian had spent his leave in Cairo rather than returning home, Gail agreed to go out with him. Their date was ruined when Nicky disappeared while he was with his child-minder. The residents turned out to search for him and he was eventually found at No.7 having wandered into the empty house.

Gail cut down her hours and went part-time and as soon as Brian returned Ivy made certain he knew what had been going on in his absence. Brian thumped Les Charlton and accused Gail of being unfaithful, telling her he didn't care as he had had a relationship with a nurse while he was abroad. However, Brian grasped that his family needed him in England, and broke his contract with Ron, who offered him a partnership in a new garage venture. Brian agreed to spend his savings on a 40 per cent share of the business, which opened in Albert Street. Gail was proud of Brian until she saw him bullying a complaining customer over a botched job.

Ivy lost her job at Baldwin's for two days, when Mike found that the factory girls were using his time and machines to sew denim handbags to sell on the market. He reinstated her when the others convinced him she had tried hard to stop them making the bags.

5 The Baldwin Clan

When Mike Baldwin's father Frankie heard that his son had spent time alone with Sylvie Hicks, he accused him of trying to steal his girlfriend. Mike insisted that they had never gone to bed together and appeased Frankie by paying off his tax bill. Just a couple of months later, Mike heard that Frankie had died of a heart-attack, leaving him three thousand pounds, which he insisted on splitting with Sylvie, acknowledging that she had loved the old man. Mike's own love life took off when he fell for florist Maggie Dunlop and talked her into moving in with him. His cleaner Hilda Ogden was horrified at charring for unmarried lovers, until he agreed to pay her an extra pound per day.

Maggie had grand plans to open a second flower shop and asked Mike to lend her the money she needed for the venture. She was outraged when he refused, saying she was a bad risk. Instead she got the money from an old friend, Harry Redman. Just days afterwards she discovered she was pregnant, delighting Mike who looked forward to being a father, but she refused to commit herself to him and reminded him that he had said she was a bad risk. He was devastated when she walked out on him and married Harry.

6 Annie's Troublesome Cellarman

Newton and Ridley marked their bicentenary by throwing a lavish ball for all their licensed victuallers. When Annie Walker's date let her down she was forced to accept Fred Gee as her escort, but lived to regret it. He got terribly drunk, ordered a new car, a Space Invaders machine and offered a waitress he fancied a job as a Rovers' barmaid. A couple of months later, he brought on more headaches when he fell down the cellar steps and was told to rest in bed. His back healed quickly but Fred decided to make the most of the situation and threatened to sue Annie for neglecting the steps. To get him back on his feet, Annie called in the rugby club physiotherapist, which jolted Fred, who had been led to believe by Bet Lynch that he was getting a Swedish masseuse.

Fred's luck on the horses had never been good but in the summer he found himself owing the local bookie eighty-five pounds. To pay off the debt he took advantage of Annie being absent to lend her car to Mrs Chadwick, the bookie's wife. The deal worked like a charm and Fred's debts were cleared, but then Mrs Chadwick found she had left her gold lighter in the car. Fred feared he would have to admit all to Annie but she stunned him by assuming he had got a classy new girlfriend and returned the lighter, with her blessing.

However, there was no girlfriend on the scene, only the fleeting return of Fred's estranged wife Eunice. She turned up with a black eye and begged him to help her flee her boyfriend Ben Critchley, who had turned violent. Fred helped her remove her belongings from the hotel but refused to take her back and filed for divorce.

7 The Faircloughs' Little Girl

Tomboy Sharon Gaskell moved into No.9 as the Faircloughs' foster-child and overnight their quiet lives were turned upside down. She threw a boisterous seventeenth-birthday party for herself and fell out with Len when he stopped her sleeping with her boyfriend, Steve Dunthorne. Sharon maintained she was old enough for sex and considered going on the pill, at which point Len found himself out of his depth and handed her over to Rita, who lectured her on self-respect. Rather than work in the Kabin all day, Sharon proved her worth with a tool-box and helped Len build a new house in the gap between Nos.5 and 9.

He had bought the land and planned to build a modern home to be sold at a good profit.

Sharon was horror-stricken when she was reallocated to the Boltons, who were to be her long-term foster-parents. After a couple of months with them she ran away and returned to the Fairclough, begging them to take her in. Social worker Donald Worthington warned them that if they agreed to keep Sharon they'd have to do so until she was at least eighteen. Thrilled at the prospect they readily agreed.

All was well in the new family until Sharon clapped eyes on Brian Tilsley and fell for him. She started to babysit for the family and eventually threw herself at him. He was flattered by her attention and, drunk, responded. He tried to tell her that he would never leave Gail for her, but she insisted she was happy to share him. When Gail discovered what was going on she believed Brian when he said he hadn't encouraged Sharon and told Rita. Together they confronted Sharon, but Sharon told Rita she was a hypocrite for lecturing her about married men and Rita slapped her. Sharon insisted she loved Brian, and it was only when he told her she was young and silly that she got over her infatuation. However, she found it hard to live near him and when she was offered a job as a kennelmaid in Sheffield she left the Street.

8 Slim Jim and Stardust Lil

Eddie Yeats became a CB enthusiast, adopting the handle 'Slim Jim'. He made contact with 'Stardust Lil' and they arranged an eyeball. Lil turned out to be florist's assistant Marion Willis, and Eddie fell head over heels in love with her. To impress her he 'borrowed' the keys to Mike Baldwin's flat from Hilda Ogden's handbag and entertained Marion there, telling her he was a businessman. When Mike found out he threatened to call in the police, but decided that Eddie was too pathetic to bother with. Eddie told Marion the

truth, which thrilled her as she had felt uncomfortable to be going out with an affluent man. She was delighted to hear that he was really a binman.

Marion moved into No.11 as Elsie Tanner's lodger, and shortly afterwards the couple threw an engagement party, which ended in police intervention after the Rovers' piano was rolled out on to the cobbles. Eddie's happiness was short-lived, though: when Marion's old flame Phil Moss tracked her down and begged her to return to him, Eddie called off the engagement to give Marion space and she left the Street to move in with Phil. However, her attempt to rekindle an old affair failed and she soon returned, realizing that Eddie was her one true love. Hilda Ogden and Elsie Tanner joined forces to bring the couple back together, and the engagement was on again.

Soon afterwards, one of Eddie's jailbird friends, Billy Nelson, sought him out and sweet-talked Hilda into letting him sleep on the sofa. Eddie and Stan were stunned when he admitted he had escaped custody and that the police were on his trail. Their atempts to get rid of him were frustrated by Hilda who, kept in the dark, accused them of picking on Billy. Billy disappeared at the same time as Annie Walker's wristwatch and Marion's engagement ring, but Eddie found them with Billy's fence, Monkey Gibbons, and returned them before their owners had realized they had been stolen.

Elsie's new boyfriend, salesman Geoff Siddall, caused the couple more heartbreak when he talked Eddie into investing their savings in a car-import scam, then disappeared with the money. Marion was furious and ordered Eddie out of her life. He was devastated and ran away to Liverpool. Upset and wanting a reconciliation, Marion tried to find him. They were reunited when he saw off a Scouser who had mistaken her for a prostitute. In an attempt to save more money, Eddie gave up drinking and smoking, his two main pleasures in life.

9 A New Family

When Len finished building No.7 he planned to sell it but Rita told him she wanted to move into it herself: it was modern and a vast improvement on No.9. Len refused to consider the idea, so Rita found a buyer for No.9 on her own. Binman Chalkie Whitely offered ten thousand pounds for the old house, and Rita wore Len down into agreeing. Rather than have a housewarming in No.7, Len threw a leaving party at No.9, infuriating Chalkie who accused him of wrecking the place.

Chalkie moved in with his young grandson Craig, who made a nuisance of himself with his drum-kit. Together they built a pigeon coop in the backyard, which annoyed Len – the birds' cooing got on his nerves. Len lost a job when Chalkie failed to give him mail delivered to No.9. The men ended up at each other's throats.

When Craig's maternal grandmother, Phyllis Pearce, tracked the family down after Chalkie had moved without telling her where they were going, she remonstrated with Chalkie over the way he was bringing Craig up and caused havoc by releasing the pigeons.

Craig's father, Bob, returned from five months in the Gulf and proved an instant hit with Bet Lynch. She threw herself at him only to have him announce that he was emigrating to Australia and taking Craig with him. Chalkie and Phyllis looked on helplessly as Bob took the boy away from them to live on the other side of the world.

10 Mavis Meets a New Man

Emily Bishop faced a dilemma at the start of the year in the form of an inheritance from Arnold Swain, which she did not want. She decided to spend the money on a new trampoline for the community centre and a bed for the hospital in the name of Ernest Bishop. No sooner had she written the cheques than Arnold's real wife Margaret turned up on her doorstep. Emily felt so sorry for her tale of woe that she wrote another cheque on her own account and gave it to her, saying it was hers by rights.

Mavis Riley celebrated her forty-fifth birthday with the reappearance of her old flame, Derek Wilton. Before he told her that his mother had died she told him to leave her alone and go back to his interfering mother. She felt sorry for her harsh words and agreed to a date, during which he gave her cruise brochures and asked for her opinion on them. Mavis was thrilled by the thought of holidaying with Derek and dreamt of little else for a week, only to be told that he was taking his sister who had nursed their mother until the end.

Excitement ran high in the Kabin when Mavis discovered that her budgie Harry had laid an egg. She promptly changed the bird's name to Harriet and carried the egg around in her bra in the hope it would hatch. The RSPCA told her it wouldn't but offered to loan her a cock bird to mate with Harriet. Mavis turned down the offer, as she didn't want Harriet bothered by a stranger she might not like. To get herself out of the flat, Mavis enrolled on an English literature course and promptly fell for fellow student Victor Pendlebury. Together they collaborated on a short story entitled 'A Night to Forget' and entered it in a local radio competition. It won, and was read on the air, which embarrassed Mavis as it had a racy plot. Victor escorted her to the community centre Christmas dance but as she didn't want to dance he spent the entire evening on the floor with Emily. Furious, Mavis told him not to call on her again, and added that he was a rotten writer.

11 A Year of Shocks for Betty

Gordon Clegg arrived in Weatherfield to introduce his fiancée Caroline Wilson to his mother Betty Turpin. Caroline was shocked by his northern working-class roots and made it clear that she disapproved of Betty working in a pub. Looking forward to the wedding, Betty bought a new outfit for the occasion and was hurt when Gordon sent a telegram to say they had married quietly in a register office.

To help take her mind off the snub, Betty took in travelling electrician Alec Hobson as a lodger. He usually slept in his van but was glad of Betty's home comforts. However, the Street's residents refused to give him their appliances to mend after he 'fixed' Vera Duckworth's sewing-machine, which then gave her an electric shock. Alec planned to move on but the wheels on his van were stolen. Eddie Yeats offered him a set for fifty pounds but Alec recognized them as his old ones and refused to pay. When Eddie complained to the dealer from whom he'd bought them he earned himself a black eye. Disgusted with the locals, Alec left town.

Weeks later Betty was shocked to receive a visit from Ted Farrell, the man with whom she had had an affair after the war. She confided in Annie Walker that he had no idea he was Gordon's father. Now, as he was married with children, she decided not to tell him. By far the most unpleasant shock occurred when Betty was walking home from work and was set upon by a couple of teenagers, who snatched her handbag and left her battered, bruised and with a broken arm. Deirdre Barlow was furious to hear of the attack, the latest in a run of muggings. She upset husband Ken by telling the police that she suspected local boy Raymond Attwood of being the perpetrator: he was spending more money than usual. Attwood was arrested and confessed.

The Barlows' first year of marriage was not very happy. Deirdre smarted when Ken refused to consider having another child and told him he had married her under false pretences. Her life revolved around serving at the shop and cooking for the family, and she grew bored and frustrated when Ken refused to spend Christmas at her mother's country club. Perhaps unwisely, she accepted an invitation from Mike Baldwin to go with him to the pictures, and at the end of the evening allowed him to kiss her.

CAST

Wilf Stockwell	Terence Longden
Caroline Wilson	Elaine Donnelly
Alec Hobson	Tom Price
Margaret Swain	Charlotte Mitchell
Chalkie Whitely	Teddy Turner
Marion Willis	Veronica Doran
Jackie Moffatt	Jacqueline Tong
Dot Stockwell	Barbara Young
Sharon Gaskell	Tracie Bennett
Steve Dunthorne	Howard Grace
Raymond Attwood	Joe Searby
Maggie Dunlop	Jill Kerman
Les Charlton	Graham Fellows
Ted Farrell	Gerald Sim
Craig Whitely	Mark Price
Mrs Chadwick	Sue Johnston
Phil Moss	Ken Kitson
Billy Nelson	Chris Darwin
Phyllis Pearce	Jill Summers
Joyce Lomas	Shirley Dixon
Joan Lowther	June Broughton
Geoff Siddall	Edward Judd
Bob Whitely	Freddie Fletcher
Victor Pendlebury	Christopher Coll

1983

Behind the Scenes

Key Dates

1983

January 1	Jack Howarth awarded the MBE in the New Year's Honours List
May 11	Peter Adamson makes his last appearance as Len Fairclough, after 1797 episodes
July 11	Curly Watts's first appearance
August 1	Terry Duckworth's first appearance
August 22	Percy Sugden's first appearance
October 19	Kevin Webster's first appearance
October 12	Doris Speed makes her last appearance as Annie Walker, after 1746 episodes
October 31	Eddie Yeats marries Marion Willis
December 7	Len Fairclough dies in a car crash
December 26	Violet Carson dies aged eighty-five

When he read scripts that showed his screen wife embarking on a passionate affair with another man Bill Roache was horrified. He reminded producer Mervyn Watson that the Barlows had been married less than two years and said he was worried that all the work he and Anne Kirkbride had put in to make the marriage credible would be wasted. Mervyn tried hard to assure Bill this wouldn't be the case, without revealing that the writing team had no idea which of the men Deirdre would choose: 'Some actors become very disturbed by the prospect of what their character is about to experience and find it uncomfortable. But then if they bite the bullet and get on with it, they turn in probably the best performance of their careers. I think certainly that was the case for Bill.' As soon as Deirdre slipped her coat off in Mike's flat and planted a smacker on his lips the British public were glued to their television screens and tabloid newspapers as the 'will she, won't she' debate started. Sir John Betjeman stood by Ken, 'He's a nice man and he deserves better,' but a woman walked around the Granada studios with a banner that read, 'Go with Mike – I would!' For two months the story rolled along, gathering momentum and the three actors involved were hounded wherever they went. After a heated story conference the writers decided to let Deirdre remain at No.1 and Ken slammed the front door in Mike's face. The reconciliation between the Barlows took place on the same night as Manchester United played Arsenal at Old Trafford. The *Daily Mail* hired the electronic scoreboard, and at eight p.m. flashed up the news 'Deirdre and Ken united again!' The roar from 56,000 fans filled the Manchester air, and later in the year, when picking up their joint *TV Times* awards for television personalities of the year, Bill, Anne, and Johnny Briggs were given a standing ovation in recognition of their spectacular work.

1983 was a year of change for the programme: Peter Adamson was sacked for breaking his contract by telling his life story to a newspaper; Doris Speed left because of illness; and Pat Phoenix announced that she was quitting. Doris collapsed after a national newspaper printed her birth certificate, disclosing her true age as eighty-three rather than the seventy-four she claimed. Shortly afterwards her house was burgled and she was admitted into a nursing-home. Public opinion urged Granada to have Len and Elsie run off together, but the writers chose to bring back Bill Gregory, Elsie's old flame, and for Len to die without Peter Adamson being brought back to record any last scenes. Younger characters were created in the hope that Kevin Webster, Curly Watts and Terry Duckworth would still be around in fifteen years' time.

> "Maggie Thatcher's a Cub mistress compared to our Annie when she's got her warpaint on."
>
> **Bet Lynch**

Top Twenty

Pos	Character	No of eps	Total	Pos Prev Year
1	Bet Lynch	85	986	4
2	Fred Gee	82	510	9
3	Deirdre Barlow	77	677	14
4	Alf Roberts	72	812	18
5	Elsie Tanner	71	1639	2
6	Rita Fairclough	70	797	9
7	Vera Duckworth	70	247	23
8	Betty Turpin	68	1006	15
9	Ivy Tilsley	68	397	8
10	Eddie Yeats	68	508	4
11	Ken Barlow	66	1545	7
12	Hilda Ogden	66	1357	4
13	Mavis Riley	66	618	11
14	Mike Baldwin	65	412	17
15	Annie Walker	59	1746	3
16	Stan Ogden	58	1234	12
17	Brian Tilsley	57	240	24
18	Gail Tilsley	57	517	13
19	Emily Bishop	55	1305	16
20	Marion Willis Yeats	53	103	19

STORIES

1 Deirdre's Bit On the Side

Deirdre Barlow found herself surrounded by intrigue when she embarked on an affair with Mike Baldwin. Her husband Ken had been preoccupied with getting a new job as deputy director of Social Services, and all Deirdre seemed to do was keep house, serve at the shop and look after the family. She felt as if she'd been married for twenty years, rather than two. Mike treated her like a lady and urged her to leave Ken and live with him. When Emily Bishop guessed her boss was having an affair with her best friend she begged Deirdre not to throw her marriage away but Deirdre had decided it was already over. She planned to leave Ken, until he was told he was too boring for the new job. She confessed her affair, and he ordered her out of the house but she broke down, unable to leave, and begged Ken to forgive her. The Barlows were reconciled and flew off to holiday in Malta after Ken warned Mike to stay away from his family.

The tension at No.1 upset Albert Tatlock and the Barlows decided to move to a bigger house to start afresh. Albert felt he was too old to live anywhere else and pleaded with them to stay, offering to give them No.1. Ken refused to accept the house for nothing and, with Deirdre's consent, bought it from him at a reasonable price. Albert's daughter, Beattie Pearson, was furious and spoiled Albert's eighty-eighth birthday celebrations by accusing Ken of conning her out of her inheritance.

2 A Rovers Outing

On hearing that Nellie Harvey was throwing a New Year party for her staff, Annie Walker laid on a spread for hers. The evening went without mishap until cellarman Fred Gee commented on the size of Betty Turpin's backside and then on the state of her morals in having had an illegitimate son. Insulted, Betty resigned and only returned when Annie forced Fred to apologize.

A month later Betty was off work with a virus so Annie took on Suzie Birchall as barmaid, upsetting Bet Lynch who found her too popular with the male customers. The stituation worsened for Bet after her landlord Alf Roberts tripped on one of her shoes and fell downstairs. Annie told Bet to

take his place behind the bacon-slicer while his twisted ankle healed. Frustrated, Bet tried to have Suzie sacked from the Rovers by persuading Jack Duckworth to complain she'd short-changed him, but he fell for her and gave her free lifts in his taxi. Bet was relieved when Alf was back on his feet and Suzie relinquished her job, but Annie's staff troubles were far from over.

Fred parked Annie's beloved Rover 2000 outside the pub, just in time for Eddie Yeats to reverse the council bin lorry into it. The car was a write-off so Annie accepted the insurance pay-out and started to use taxis. She was appalled when Fred borrowed £250 from a money-lender to buy the wrecked car himself. Annie told him furiously that he was beneath contempt, until she realized she could use him as a free chauffeur.

Fred wasted no time in using his new wheels to attract women and took up with Maureen Slater from Warrington. He soon tired of driving her to and from Manchester and dumped her when all she offered him was a kiss. Next he turned his attention to Bet, and took her to Tatton Park for the day. She cooled his passion by bringing Betty along to play gooseberry. Unfortunately, the car's handbrake failed and the car – with Bet and Betty inside – ended up in the middle of a lake. Fred was forced to carry the ladies to safety and meet their demands for compensation.

3 Brian Flexes His Business Muscles

Brian Tilsley found running a garage single-handed too much, so he bought Ron Sykes out of the business and took control. Then his father, Bert, suffered a mini-stroke and lost his job. When he recovered he started helping Brian at the garage but one day he over-inflated a tyre which exploded, knocking him unconscious. He was on a

life-support system for a time, and his recovery was slow. After returning home he disappeared with the holiday money and turned up in a Bristol hospital. Finally he was admitted to a psychiatric hospital in Southport but failed to recognize any members of his family. The doctor told a distraught Ivy it was best that she stopped visiting him. Brian and Gail sold their Buxton Close house, invested the money in the business and moved back into No.5 to keep Ivy company. Gail took driving lessons to be of more help to Brian but he wasn't supportive. After failing her test she gave up. Brian took on eighteen-year-old Kevin Webster as his apprentice. Kevin had been struggling to find employment after completing a Youth Opportunity Scheme.

4 Elsie's Warring Lodgers

After an absence of three years Suzie Birchall returned from London. Delighted, Elsie Tanner took her in at No.11, persuading Marion Willis to share her room by knocking six pounds off her weekly rent. Marion took an instant dislike to Suzie,

thinking her a cheap tart who reduced their bedroom to the state of a tip. She moved into the front parlour and turned it into a love-nest for her and Eddie Yeats. Suzie told Elsie she'd had a disastrous time in London, moving from job to job and having a three-week marriage to a violent man. Elsie didn't believe her until Suzie's husband Terry Goodwin turned up and gave Suzie a beating. He threatened to kill himself unless she returned to him but Elsie stood up to him and saw him off with the threat of police intervention. Suzie filed for divorce and took a bar job at the Lord Nelson. She grew annoyed when Gail Tilsley boasted she had the perfect marriage and set out to prove her wrong, attempting to seduce Brian. She thought Brian would be a walk-over and wasn't prepared for him to tell Gail. Both she and Elsie rounded on Suzie and drove her out of the Street.

When Marion discovered she was pregnant, she and Eddie brought forward their wedding and found themselves at loggerheads with her mother, Winifred, who demanded a white wedding rather than a quiet register-office affair. Marion bowed to her mother's wishes and booked All Saints Church. During the stag night at the Rovers, Fred Gee guessed that Marion was pregnant and ended up in a fight with Eddie, blackening his eye. With the secret out, Marion confessed to Winifred just hours before she exchanged vows with Eddie. The couple honeymooned in Benidorm and planned to live together at No.11, but over in Bury, Winifred had a stroke and the newlyweds moved away to look after her.

5 Bet and the Cheats

Fed up with the sight of the local fatties, Bet Lynch challenged the regulars to lose weight. Stan, Alf and Fred put five pounds each into a kitty and Alf won after losing three pounds. Stan put weight on and Fred was declared a cheat for putting bags of coins in his pockets at the first weigh-in.

Alf might have come up smiling from his lodger's scheme but she was soon

causing him grief by falling for his fellow councillor, Des Foster, a married man. Bet didn't care that he was married – she was just taking pleasure where she found it. Alf refused to let the couple make love in his flat so Bet agreed to move in with Des until he admitted he had no intention of leaving his wife for her. Then he changed his mind and left Edith, saying it was Bet he loved. Bet was thrilled until Edith called at the shop and told Alf that Des had left her for his mistress who had two children. Bet called him a rat and finished the relationship. Months later he turned up again, decorating the Rovers, and tried to rekindle the affair. She let him think he had a chance then firmly turned him down.

6 A Randy Encounter for Mavis

Mavis Riley's heart fluttered when Victor Pendlebury took her camping in the Lakes for her birthday. The excitement soon died when she saw the tiny tent. She hated it so much that they ended up sleeping in a youth hostel. Bohemian Victor announced that he was buying a cottage in Saddleworth and asked Mavis to move in with him in a trial marriage. She was tempted but decided that if he wasn't willing to marry her without a trial he wasn't worthy of her

because he wasn't offering her any security. Victor moved into his country home and a few months later Mavis, calling on him, was shocked when a woman calling herself Mrs Pendlebury opened the door. Flustered, Victor explained that she was his sister-in-law.

Percy Sugden moved into the Street as caretaker at the community centre and quickly set his cap at Emily Bishop. Together they organized an Autumn Fayre in which Victor's prized pottery was smashed and no one wanted Mavis's 'mystery' cake when they discovered that the secret ingredient was sage. Percy alarmed Mavis by attempted to mate his budgie, Randy, with her Harriet. Mavis refused: she thought that Harriet might not like Randy but be unable to escape his advances.

Percy was very disapproving when Emily took in binman Curly Watts as a lodger, telling her she would regret giving house room to a member of the younger generation.

7 Chalkie's Accumulator

When Phyllis Pearce's terraced house was demolished she hoped Chalkie Whitely would take her in at No.9, but he put the house on the market as his son Bob needed the money in Australia. Phyllis was allocated a bungalow in Gorton Close and offered Chalkie her spare room, but he set his sights on flighty widow Alice Kirby until she dumped him in favour of a retired all-in wrestler. Fearing she might never see her grandson Craig again, Phyllis tried to stop the sale of No.9 by putting off prospective buyers, but Chalkie's concerns over the house sale faded when he put ten pounds on a five-horse accumulator and won £3,543.75. He gave up his job, packed his bags and headed off to Australia to live with Bob and Craig, leaving Phyllis alone and in tears.

8 New Ventures for Ken and Mike

The year offered new business ventures for Mike Baldwin. He sidelined into making denim handbags and hosted a trade delegation from Russia before turning his attention to the entertainment industry. With business partner Alec Yardley, he applied for planning permission to turn the warehouse at the end of the Street, on Rosamund Street, into a nightclub. Ken Barlow and Annie Walker led the local

opposition to the venture but Alf Roberts supported it and pushed the application

through at the Town Hall. Ken wrote in fury to the *Gazette* suggesting that Alf was more interested in business than voters.

When they were drunk, Stan Ogden and Eddie Yeats decided to strike their own blow against the disco by painting orange lines down the Street to put paid to extra parking, but Hilda made them scrub it all off as Mike had offered her the position of cloakroom manageress. Mike was delighted when the Graffiti Club opened, but wasn't pleased when Alec made his nephew Don Watkins manager.

Reporter Pam Mitchell had covered the disco protest for the local free paper, the *Recorder*. Ken had impressed her and she encouraged him to use the paper as a soap-box to complain about local bureaucracy. She also made him the paper's agony uncle, much to Deirdre's amusement. When he discovered the council were planning to close local youth clubs and were fabricating attendance figures, Ken passed a confidential report to Pam. She ran the news in the paper, which sparked a public outcry. Questioned by his bosses, Ken admitted to being the mole but would not promise not to do the same again. He was sacked from his job, which upset Deirdre who accused him of putting his principles before his family. Pam left the area for Nottingham and suggested to the paper's owner, Bob Statham, that he employed Ken in her place. Bob refused, saying he wanted a partner, so Ken bought a third of the paper with his savings. He became its editor and main reporter, and enjoyed writing a piece condemning the Graffiti. Bob made him rewrite the piece, pointing out that Mike was a good advertiser. The rewritten piece, in which Ken referred to Mike as 'the Debonair Dynamo of Denim' caused his friends to accuse him of selling out to the enemy.

9 The Duckworths Move In

Bet Lynch had a shock when she viewed the video collection of eligible gents at the Bill & Coo Dating Agency. Staring out from the screen in a cream jacket and with a mock-American accent was Jack Duckworth, calling himself Vince St Clair. Bet wasted no time in setting Vera on the trail and encouraged her to make a date

with 'Vince' under the name Carole Monroe. She donned a red wig for the date, which was set for the Rovers, and Jack walked straight into her trap. To the cheers of the regulars, Vera attacked him and chased him home.

No.20 Inkerman Street stopped being the family home when the landlord sold the block to developers and paid off the Duckworths with a thousand pounds in compensation. Jack was keen to use the money to buy a new car but Vera announced that she wanted to buy No.9 and put down the money as a deposit against the eleven-thousand-pound asking price. The sale went without a hitch, much to the horror of the neighbours, but Vera nearly lost her furniture: she had stored it at No.9, unaware that auctioneers were clearing the house of all Chalkie Whitely's possessions. She had to fight in the Street to hang on to her bits and pieces. The Duckworths' son, Terry, fresh from the Paras, took a job at the abbatoir, but soon got tired of supporting his work-shy father. With the house, the Duckworths inherited Chalkie's pigeons and Fred Gee challenged Jack to race a couple. The race ended with Fred's bird winning while Jack's died.

10 The Ogdens Come Into Money

Stan Ogden was worried when he found he was too old to climb his window-cleaning ladders. Rather than admit this to Hilda he borrowed from money-lender Syd Kippax but couldn't earn anything to pay him back. Syd threatened the Ogdens with legal proceedings unless he was repaid and Hilda broke down. Stan felt useless but Eddie Yeats came to the rescue, using his savings to buy Stan's round from him then employing Stan himself.

When Hilda's brother, Archie Crabtree, died of a heart-attack, she found herself fighting a certain Avril Carter who had worked in Archie's chip shop and who claimed to have been his common-law wife. Hilda took on a community solicitor to challenge Avril's claim to the chip shop but it was through Eddie that she discovered Avril was actually someone else's lover. Defeated, Avril handed over the shop but

Hilda's victory was short-lived: it had to be sold to pay off Archie's debts and she was only left with fifteen hundred pounds. When Trevor Ogden heard about the money he came calling with his son Damian to butter up his parents before asking for a loan. Stan refused to give him a penny and told him to leave. Then Hilda started to receive begging letters from local woman Kitty Earnshaw, who read of the inheritance in the paper and told Hilda sob stories about her own miserable life. Hilda gave her five pounds before discovering she was a fraud.

Delighted, Stan discovered that, due to a mix-up years before, he was actually three years older than he'd thought and that his next birthday would see him drawing his pension. The celebrations were doubled when, in December, the Ogdens celebrated their ruby wedding anniversary with a party thrown in the Rovers' Select.

11 Len's Farewell

Len Fairclough continued to blame Brian Tilsley for Sharon Gaskell's speedy departure to Sheffield. When Brian called in a favour and asked Len to repair his leaking garage roof Len refused to mend it. Brian was angry and invoiced Len for repairs he had made to his van but Len tore up the bill. Brian removed the battery from Len's van and held it until Len paid up.

After taking on a contract in Ashton, Len spent much of the year working away. During the Ogdens' fortieth wedding anniversary party the news was broken to Rita that he had fallen asleep at the wheel of the van, which had crashed into a bridge and killed him. It wasn't until after the funeral, where she was supported by Sharon, that Rita discovered Len had been seeing another woman. When Marjorie Proctor called on Rita, the two mourned together. Len's death also united another couple. His old friend Bill Gregory heard the news and called at the Street to offer his condolences. While he was there he discovered that his old girlfriend Elsie Tanner was still living at No.11. She couldn't believe her eyes when he walked through the door.

CAST

Syd Kippax	Brian Lawson
Alice Kirby	Jean Heywood
Maureen Slater	Carol Kaye
Pam Mitchell	Prim Cotton
Alec Yardley	Harry Beety
Terry Goodwin	Terence Hillyer
Avril Carter	Jean Rimmer
Damian Ogden	Neil Ratcliffe
Curly Watts	Kevin Kennedy
Des Foster	Neil Philips
Edith Foster	Linda Beckett
Terry Duckworth	Nigel Pivaro
Kitty Earnshaw	Lorraine Peters
Percy Sugden	Bill Waddington
Don Watkins	Kevin Lloyd
Bob Statham	Michael Goldie
Winifred Willis	Joan Scott
Kevin Webster	Michael Le Vell
Marjorie Proctor	Eileen O'Brien

1984

Behind the Scenes

The year started with a memorial service in Manchester Cathedral to celebrate the life of Violet Carson, whose death the previous Boxing Day had grieved those actors who had spent so many years working with her. During the service, Bill Roache quoted Violet's reply when she had been asked if Ena controlled her: 'Good Lord, no. I can lock her away in the vestry and walk away from her any time I like.'

Death claimed two more Street favourites this year. First Jack Howarth died of a stomach complaint and then, in the summer, Bernard Youens died after a series of strokes and a heart attack. In the programme, Albert and Stan died with dignity, and the credits rolled over the image of the widowed Hilda weeping over Stan's spectacle case. For Jean Alexander, losing her screen partner of twenty years, they were real tears of grief.

"I'm the local expert on broken hearts; I've had more of them than other people have heated arguments."

Bet Lynch

Key Dates 1984

January 4	Elsie Tanner leaves the Street to live in Portugal
January 16	Bert Tilsley dies of a mental illness
April 1	Jack Howarth dies, aged eighty-eight. He appeared as Albert Tatlock in 1322 episodes
May 14	Albert Tatlock dies of old age
August 27	Bernard Youens dies, aged sixty-nine, after appearing in 1246 episodes as Stan Ogden
November 21	Stan Ogden dies in hospital

Top Twenty

Pos	Character	No of eps	Total	Pos Prev Year
1	Betty Turpin	86	1092	8
2	Jack Duckworth	84	148	26
3	Bet Lynch	83	1069	1
4	Alf Roberts	77	889	4
5	Hilda Ogden	76	1433	11
6	Mavis Riley	75	693	11
7	Rita Fairclough	75	872	6
8	Deirdre Barlow	69	746	3
9	Vera Duckworth	67	314	6
10	Billy Walker	66	408	-
11	Percy Sugden	66	80	33
12	Ken Barlow	64	1609	11
13	Emily Bishop	64	1369	19
14	Mike Baldwin	63	475	14
15	Ivy Tilsley	62	459	8
16	Bill Webster	62	62	-
17	Gail Tilsley	61	578	17
18	Terry Duckworth	61	71	36
19	Kevin Webster	61	65	38
20	Brian Tilsley	57	297	17

STORIES

1 Elsie's Farewell, the Websters' Arrival

Elsie Tanner bade farewell to Coronation Street to start a new life in Portugal with Bill Gregory at his wine bar. She left suddenly at night, leaving the sale of No.11 to her daughter, Linda Cheveski, who was in the throes of divorcing her husband and took the opportunity to stay at the house. Builder Bill Webster was interested in buying No.11 in an attempt to provide a settled home for his children, Kevin and Debbie, following the death of their mother, Alison. Linda took a fancy to Bill and hoped he would invite her to live with him but he wasn't attracted to her. After he bought the house, she returned to Birmingham. As well as buying a new home, Bill started up a new business and rented the building yard from Rita Fairclough. The first big job he took on was repairing the roof at Mawdsley Street chapel. Rita lent him money to buy material for the job and was furious when lead was stolen from the roof. The police suspected Bill of having taken it himself as he'd been sacked from the council for a similar crime, but when the real thieves were caught, Rita was forced to apologize for doubting him.

Sixteen-year-old Debbie caused upset when she failed her CSEs and told Bill she was leaving school. He tried to force her to retake her exams but she refused and took a waitressing job at Jim's Café. Then she fell for biker Dazz Isherwood, which alarmed Bill. After a motorbike accident, which left Debbie with a sprained ankle, Dazz decided he'd had enough of the teenager and dumped her for an older girl. Debbie was heartbroken – but Bill had more success romantically: he fell for Percy Sugden's niece, Elaine Prior, and after a weekend away together the couple decided to get married. This upset Kevin, who refused to accept Elaine as a substitute mother.

2 Turmoil at the Rovers

Fred Gee had a terrible year. To begin with, his Rover broke down and he couldn't afford to repair it. Hoping to claim on the insurance he persuaded Jack Duckworth to take away the car then reported it stolen. The plan was stymied when the car ran out of petrol and a policeman stopped Jack while he was refilling it. Then, still in the hope of raising money on the car, Fred decided to raffle it but no one was interested and Percy Sugden won it for a pound. Fred fumed when he heard that Percy had sold it to Kevin Webster for fifty. Kevin used the car for banger racing, which would have horrified Annie Walker but she wasn't around to hear of it, having retired to Derby.

The brewery appointed Fred as temporary manager and he immediately started to cut corners, buying in cheap pies. He invited Ken Barlow to write an article for the *Recorder* on the Rovers' cuisine and Ken didn't mince his words over how awful it was. When Percy and Mavis Riley agreed with what the article had said, they were both barred from the pub, which led to a mass boycott. Then Fred took on Kath Goodwin as barmaid and after being invited to a brewery bash, played off her and Bet Lynch against each other. In the end he didn't go; pneumonia sent him away to be nursed by his sister and relief manager Frank Harvey took over. He ordered Bet to go to the dance with him but she didn't like his attitude and, to spite him, turned up dressed as a tramp.

Billy Walker returned to the pub to sort out the mess. He started poker games in the back-room but when he was drunk he made a pass at his old flame Deirdre Barlow. When Mike Baldwin warned him off her he guessed that they had had an affair. Later, his girlfriend Samantha Benson arrived from Jersey to warn him that creditors were after him. Desperate to pay them off Billy was intrigued to hear that Emily Bishop had received a huge amount of compensation following Ernie's death. To please her he organized an inter-pub Olympics with the Flying Horse – the highlight of which proved to be Hilda Ogden winning the egg-and-spoon race – and a talent show in which Percy performed his farmyard impressions. The events raised three hundred pounds for Emily's charity and she was thrilled – until Billy asked for a six-thousand-pound loan, making it clear that he knew all about Deirdre's affair with Mike. Emily was willing to pay up to keep him quiet but Mike threatened to tell the police of the dodgy deals in which Billy had been involved, which Samantha had told him about. In the end, Annie paid Billy's debts, in return for him taking over the licence of the pub. To avoid paying Fred redundancy, Billy goaded him into thumping him then sacked him. His responsibility for the Rovers made Billy feel trapped, and after just a few months he handed the pub back to the brewery and returned to Jersey. The Walker empire was at an end and the regulars urged Bet to apply for the job of manageress against relief manager Gordon Lewis, who planned to turn the pub into a more lively place.

3 Ken's Troubles at the Recorder

Agony uncle Ken Barlow started to receive letters from a Christine Glover, who told him of the break-up of her marriage and her pregnancy. Ken was alarmed as she became obsessed with him and started to stalk him, saying she loved him. Eventually she was admitted to a psychiatric hospital and Ken learnt that all the events she'd described to him had happened three years previously.

The Barlows had their own tragedy when Albert Tatlock died in his chair during a rare visit to his daughter, Beattie Pearson. She gave Ken her father's military medal, saying Albert had always looked upon him as the son he'd never had.

Ken's assistant, Sally Waterman, caused him plenty of trouble. When she discovered Alf Roberts had voted against a shopping plaza as it might affect his own business, she wrote a critical piece about him for the paper. Ken refused to print it as Alf was a friend, so Sally gave it to the *Gazette*. Billy Walker took a fancy to Sally and the gossips had a field day when he took her as his lover. Ken disapproved of the union but was forced to admit he had feelings for her too.

She encouraged him to express them, and was pleased when he kissed her. He swore he couldn't be unfaithful to Deirdre and she accepted that, but finished with Billy anyway. Deirdre was suspicious of the situation, even though both Ken and Sally assured her they had only exchanged just one kiss.

4 A Death in the Family

Ivy Tilsley upset her son Brian by starting a friendship with fellow bingo enthusiast, Arthur Whittaker. She saw Arthur as a friend but Brian felt he wanted more from the relationship. Then the Tilsleys' world collapsed when Bert died in a Southport

hospital. Embittered by his father's death, Brian became over-protective of Ivy and when Arthur came calling he saw him off. Ivy bowed to Brian's wishes and restricted her social life to drinking in the Rovers. Brian, on the other hand, developed a buzzing social life, taking up squash and spending evenings out with a set of new wealthy friends. Gail felt uncomfortable with them and was horrified when Brian suggested leaving Nick with Ivy so that they could all spend a fortnight tanning themselves in Spain. After a night out at a casino she forced Brian to see he was out of his depth.

Gail's mother, Audrey Potter, made a big thing of showing off her fiancé, George Hepworth, to the family. He seemed like a nice man until, alone with Gail, he attempted to rape her. When Gail told her mother what had happened Audrey decided to turn a blind eye as she was desperate to marry. However, a few months later she finished with George because of his interest in younger women. When George demanded his ring back, Brian went for him over his attack on Gail, then proceeded to upset Gail by wondering if she'd encouraged George, and continued to upset her when she decided to return to work full-time. Alma Sedgewick had decided to live in Spain with her boyfriend and offered Gail the position of manageress at the café. Gail talked Brian round with the prospect of the extra money: she longed to save enough money to buy a house of her own away from Ivy, and she set about making the café a thriving business, with Phyllis Pearce to wash up.

5 Mike's Son and Heir

After seeing Maggie Redman, née Dunlop, with their son Mark at the Yeats wedding, Mike became obsessed with the baby. He started to trail Maggie, spying on her every move. He accused her of being a bad mother for continuing to work at her florist's shop and threatened a court battle to win custody of Mark. Maggie was forced to tell her husband Harry that Mike was Mark's father and then instructed her solicitor to threaten Mike with the police unless he stayed out of her and Mark's life. Mike was forced to agree to this, and took out an endowment policy to mature when the boy was eighteen. (In 1992 these events were brought forward two years as the

producers of *Coronation Street* decided to make Mark two years older than he was. History was rewritten to the effect that Mark Redman was born in 1981, not 1983.)

Mike's business life was as disastrous as his private one. He was forced to close the Graffiti club after manager Don Watkins ran off with the profits. Then he toyed with the idea of introducing Japanese business practices at the factory but eventually embraced the computer age by installing a PC in his office. He teased the workers that he was going to have bar-codes tattooed on their arms for clocking in and out, but his main reason for having the computer was that he wanted to play games on it when he was bored.

6 Mavis the Reluctant Bride

Derek Wilton re-entered Mavis Riley's life and presented her with the canteen of cutlery she'd helped him to win five years before. She was pleased to see him but was stunned when he proposed to her. Uncertain of her feelings, she decided to turn him down until Rita Fairclough told her she was lucky that someone loved her. Derek and Mavis celebrated their engagement by throwing a party, which was spoilt by the arrival of Victor Pendlebury, who immediately proposed to her himself.

Mavis was tempted by Victor's offer until he accused her of having accepted Derek because she was on the rebound from the failure of their relationship. She stood by Derek but was upset when he couldn't bring himself to send Victor packing and the job fell on her shoulders. Mavis's hen party ended with her weeping in solitude, and on her wedding day she

broke down and told Rita she couldn't go through with it. Rita had to go to All Saints Church to break the news to Derek, only to discover that he, too, had had cold feet and was jilting Mavis. When Rita broke the news to her, Mavis was angry: she felt that Derek had made her a laughing-stock by jilting her.

7 Hilda Left Alone

Stan Ogden became a laughing-stock after stubbing his toe on a paving stone but Hilda decided to sue the council and called in the *Recorder* to cover the story, with a huge blow-up of the injured digit on the front cover. The council settled with a two-hundred-pound pay-out, which Stan soon spent, stealing Hilda's bank card to withdraw cash behind her back.

Over the year Stan's health declined, and Hilda struggled to look after him. He became bedridden and Hilda wore herself out providing for them. After she collapsed with exhaustion the doctor insisted that Stan be admitted to hospital, and a couple of weeks later Hilda heard that he had died. Trevor tried to talk his mother into having

Stan cremated as it was cheaper, but she insisted on burying him, buying a plot with room for her to follow. Hilda kept her dignity throughout the funeral service but later, alone at No.13, she wept.

8 The Warring Duckworths

Jack Duckworth showed wife Vera the true extent of his feelings towards her when they were caught with an out-of-date TV licence. As it was in Vera's name Jack insisted she took the blame, although he had spent the money she had given him to buy a new one. Vera went to court and was fined a hundred and fifty pounds, and Jack got drunk to celebrate that she hadn't been sent to prison then fell over the TV set, smashing it.

During the year Jack suffered two blows in his job as a taxi-driver. First, Mavis Riley, having just passed her driving test, reversed into his car, causing significant damage. Brian Tilsley fixed it but when Mavis refused to pay for damage done before the accident Brian kept the car because Jack had no money to pay the extra. Jack was happy with the situation as it meant he couldn't work but eventually Vera had enough and paid the bill herself. The car was released in time for Jack to pick up Vera and Ivy from bingo one night. As they'd won the jackpot the trio celebrated, and Jack was stopped by the police and breathalysed positive. He was fined two hundred pounds and banned from driving for a year.

While Vera worried about making ends meet, Jack looked forward to a life of leisure. In order to get as much cash as possible from the DSS he removed all the family's belongings from the house and told an official how him caring for his sick family meant he couldn't work. Unfortunately the official called back unexpectedly and found the house full of furniture and the family looking boisterous. His claim for an allowance denied, Jack started selling shirts on the market in partnership with Fred Gee, who was now employed as Mike Baldwin's van driver. The men agreed a deal with a businessman and, to impress him, Fred posed as Mike. The deal was successful but the payment was a cheque made out to 'M. Baldwin'. When Mike discovered that Fred had been posing as him he sacked him and Fred left the area.

Vera decided to make Jack settle down by buying him Stan Ogden's old window-cleaning round. Jack was appalled at the idea of cleaning windows until he came across friendly housewife Dulcie Froggatt, who offered to fill his bucket.

9 Undercover Percy

Percy Sugden suffered a blow when his budgie Randy escaped and flew free. He offered a ten-pound reward, which Jack Duckworth tried to win by passing off another bird as Randy. However, Percy saw through the deception, mainly because his bird had returned home of its own accord.

After the Corner Shop was broken into and a woman attempted to steal Deirdre Barlow's underwear from her washing line, Percy set up a Home Watch scheme. He attempted to rally public interest but his only willing disciple was Phyllis Pearce, who found him dashing and attractive. Soon, though, Terry Duckworth had become fed up with the way pompous Percy patrolled the area at night. To teach him a lesson he reported him to the police as a peeping Tom. Percy was arrested but later let off with a caution.

10 Terry's Threesome

Terry Duckworth, Kevin Webster and Curly Watts formed an unlikely trio, taking over the Rovers' Snug. Their main interest was girls, and Curly soon fell out with Terry after Sharon Gaskell turned down his offer of tea to go to see U2 in concert with Terry. When Terry and Kevin started double-dating, their girlfriends asked them to find a lad for their friend Elaine Pollard. Curly was roped in and became smitten with Elaine, who thought him too boring to be attractive. When Curly borrowed a friend's boat to take the gang on a trip down the Mersey, the dullness of the landscape had

most of them jumping ship and returning by bus to Manchester. However, Elaine decided to stay with Curly, and when the engine failed they were forced to spend the night together.

The rows at No.9 finally got to Terry and he moved out to live with the Ogdens at No.13. Hilda delighted in spoiling him

but Vera accused her of stealing her son. Terry's stay chez Ogden was short: he soon tired of running errands for Stan and returned home.

Down the Street at No.3, Curly hit the newspapers after spotting a UFO through his telescope. While his mates thought he was stupid, Elaine and the other girls admired the fame the story brought Curly and he enjoyed being the centre of attention, until a UFO enthusiast called and asked if the aliens were in contact with him too.

11 Rita's New Life

Rita Fairclough attempted to rebuild her life without Len. She leant on Alf Roberts until she became worried that he was reading more into their friendship than she intended. She also paid for Mavis Riley to have driving lessons so that she could take on more in the business.

Eleven months after Len's death she started nervously to date again when Betty Turpin's policeman lodger, Tony Cunliffe, asked her out. Rita found him attractive but was confused by her feelings, and more so when Bet Lynch rounded on her, saying that Tony was her fella. Tony assured Rita that Bet meant nothing to him; that he'd only gone out with her for sex. Bet was mortified but stood aside to let Rita have a chance of happiness, wishing her well. Rita enjoyed being courted again but couldn't bring herself to allow Tony into her bed. She asked him to be patient but he accused her of wanting to live with the dead and departed, leaving her to face another lonely Christmas.

Bet's love life was just as bleak: apart from Tony, the only man she had had anything to do with was Vinny Morris, a convict Eddie Yeats asked her to meet from Strangeways and help on his way. She was taken by him and felt sorry for him, laying on food, money and herself, until Eddie phoned to complain she hadn't met Vinny – the man she had been with was just a lucky imposter!

CAST

Arthur Whittaker	Trevor Martin
Bill Webster	Peter Armitage
Kath Goodwin	Lori Wells Keefe
Frank Harvey	Nick Stringer
Christine Glover	Bridget Ashburn
Elaine Pollard	Janette Beverley
Vinny Morris	Peter Lorenzelli
Sally Waterman	Vikki Chambers
Debbie Webster	Sue Devaney
Samantha Benson	Susan Kyd
George Hepworth	Richard Moore
Dazz Isherwood	Paul Elsam
Tony Cunliffe	Jack Carr
Elaine Prior	Judy Gridley
Dulcie Froggatt	Margi Campi

1985

Behind the Scenes

Mervyn Watson left *Coronation Street* to become producer of *First Among Equals*, the political drama that brought many awards to Granada's trophy cabinet. He was replaced by a Scot, John Temple, who brought in new characters to fill the gaps left by old favourites. Unfortunately attempts to create a 'normal' family failed as, after only eight months, writers and viewers failed to warm to the Claytons and the clan was written out. Café boy Martin Platt, however, proved a hit and remained. Sean Wilson won the role after auditioning for both Terry Duckworth and Kevin Webster. He'd always been interested in *Coronation Street* and had longed to be part of it: 'When I was a kid, my dad took me to Granada to look through the gates and see where *Coronation Street* was made. It felt like fate, coming back.' Sean had trained at Oldham Theatre Workshop, alongside a young actress called Sally Whittaker. She failed to get the part of Sue Clayton and Kevin's girlfriend Michelle Robinson. However, John Temple was determined to see her in the programme and the writers were instructed to create a chirpy, confident girl who would steal Kevin Webster's heart.

February saw the launch of the BBC's first real soap, *EastEnders*, and the London-based press took it straight to their hearts, predicting that the Street was going to be swept under the carpet by the newcomer.

Key Dates 1985

January 5	Bill Webster marries Elaine Prior
January 28	Sean Wilson first appears as Martin Platt
December 23	Alf Roberts marries Audrey Potter

"Them Duckworths are like stray cats. Invite 'em in for a saucer of milk and they're asleep in your best chair in front of the fire before you can blink."

Hilda Ogden

Top Twenty

Pos	Character	No of eps	Total	Pos Prev Year
1	Ivy Tilsley	89	548	15
2	Vera Duckworth	83	397	9
3	Bet Lynch	82	1151	3
4	Deirdre Barlow	79	825	8
5	Terry Duckworth	77	148	17
6	Hilda Ogden	75	1508	5
7	Jack Duckworth	75	223	2
8	Ken Barlow	73	1682	12
9	Mavis Riley	72	765	6
10	Betty Turpin	71	1163	1
11	Mike Baldwin	70	545	14
12	Emily Bishop	69	1438	12
13	Alf Roberts	69	958	4
14	Gail Tilsley	69	647	17
15	Kevin Webster	68	133	17
16	Brian Tilsley	68	365	20
17	Curly Watts	66	125	22
18	Percy Sugden	62	142	10
19	Rita Fairclough	61	933	6
20	George Wardle	52	52	-

STORIES

1 Bet Goes Up in the World

The regulars at the Rovers Return celebrated when barmaid Bet Lynch was made the brewery's first unmarried manageress. Unlucky candidate Gordon Lewis was given the licence of the rough Docker's Arms and Bet gladly vacated the flat over the Corner Shop to move into the pub, her first real home. While she was trained in the art of management, temporary manager Frank Harvey ran the pub and employed out-of-work secretary Gloria Todd to pull pints. She had no talent but Frank took her out and spent the night with her. On her return from training, Bet took one look at the blonde and sacked her. Other new faces entered Bet's life: she employed Wilf Starkey as cellarman and became friendly with acid-tongued landlady Stella Rigby from the White Swan. Eager to prove her worth to Stella, Bet enlisted the Rovers in the brewery's Brainiest Pub contest. Her team consisted of Ken, Mavis, Curly and Percy, but they failed to get past the first heat as Percy answered incorrectly on a tie-breaker.

Bet's 1985 summer holiday was a week in Blackpool with Rita Fairclough and Mavis Riley. The women were all picked up by sales representatives but to Bet's disgust hers burst into tears when she tried to bed him. Also during the holiday Bet befriended the hotel barman, Frank Mills, and was pleasantly surprised when he followed her back to Weatherfield. She talked him out of working in a posh hotel and instead made him barman at the Rovers, replacing Wilf. The bar buzzed with sexual chemistry between the two and it wasn't long before he was sleeping in her bed. However, when the pair went on an impromptu Norwegian cruise together, the brewery made Betty Turpin manageress. Following the birth of Peter Clegg in London, she had just become a grandmother but her celebrations were marred by concern for Bet. On her return Bet was mortified to be told she was on probation and that the brewery had reinstalled Gloria as a permanent barmaid having gained more bar work experience. Bet was forced to swallow her pride and behave herself.

2 A Blackleg in the Street

Lonely Hilda Ogden advertised for a lodger and took in Henry Wakefield, whom she believed to be a railway ticket collector. It wasn't long before he confessed he was merely a railway enthusiast who had lost his job at a local factory for breaking a strike when his mother was dying. Hilda talked Mike Baldwin into employing him as a van driver, but shop-steward Ida Clough received an anonymous letter tipping her off that Henry was a blackleg. She threatened to bring the girls out on strike, which forced Mike to reluctantly sack Henry. Hilda was devastated when he moved on and accused the factory girls of ruining her chance to take her mind off Stan's death.

Hilda's woes continued when No.13 was burgled while she house-sat for the Lowthers, who had feared burglary in their absence. Her luck improved slightly when she gave Jack Duckworth Stan's old racing formula, as patented by Captain Carstairs. Jack enjoyed a couple of wins but Vera grew suspicious of his involvement with Hilda and tore up the formula book.

Jack's dreams came true when he landed the job of cellarman at the Rovers. He celebrated by giving Dulcie Froggatt's windows one last clean. Unfortunately he was drunk at the time and fell off the ladder, broke his ankle and earned himself a stay in hospital.

3 Kevin Strikes Out Alone

Kevin Webster was left alone when his father Bill married Elaine Prior and moved to Southampton with daughter Debbie. Emily Bishop took pity on Kevin and took him in at No.3, to share Curly Watts's bedroom. However, as a binman Curly woke each morning at five, and Kevin found Emily's strict routine suffocating anyway, so he became Hilda Ogden's lodger at No.13. Later, he fell deeply in love with posh Michelle Robinson, and fought off her tennis-playing boyfriend Malcolm Nuttall to prove his intentions to her. Hilda approved of Michelle and encouraged Kevin to think they might have a future together but Michelle got upset when, eager to lose his virginity, he tried to seduce her. She accused him of rushing her and finished with him.

Curly and Terry clubbed together to buy Jack Duckworth's car for five hundred and twenty-five pounds, planning to start

up their own removal business. Kevin made it roadworthy in exchange for a part-share in it but before long he and Curly sold it behind Terry's back, fed up with the way he treated it as his own. Terry and Curly decided they wanted to make a go of the business so they bought Mike Baldwin's factory van for eight hundred pounds, rented the building yard from Rita Fairclough and called the business Cheap and Cheerful.

4 Mavis's Win

Mavis Riley was sent into a dither when she won a second honeymoon in Capri in a magazine called *Modern Bride*. She was embarrassed to have to notify the magazine that she had never had a first honeymoon as her wedding had not taken place. She made the mistake of telling her sorry tale to Sally Waterman, who resigned from the *Recorder* and used the story to get a job on the *Gazette*. Suddenly Mavis was besieged by the national newspapers and her double jilting was splashed over them all. The news brought Derek Wilton out of the woodwork and the couple found themselves arguing on consecutive days in print.

5 A Watery Grave

Mike Baldwin's business started a new chapter when he began to manufacture jumpsuits designed by Christine Millward. The factory girls decided he had designs on Christine but, whatever his plans were, she kept him at arm's length and made it clear she was happily married. The jumpsuits were a success and business boomed for Mike. He invested four thousand pounds in a crooked deal with old friend Don Ashton, only to have Don get drunk at the Rovers and die when his car swerved into the canal.

Don had left his briefcase in the pub and Mike was shocked when he opened it to find the cash missing. He threatened Bet Lynch with a brewery investigation and upset Emily Bishop, too, by lying to the police, saying he had had no dealings with Don. She decided to resign but he blackmailed her into staying by telling the girls there would be no bonuses if Emily left as no one else could calculate the money. Meanwhile Bet launched her own investigation into the mising cash and discovered that her cellarman, Wilf Starkey, had purloined it. He returned it all, confessing he hadn't been able to stop himself taking it.

6 Families At War

A new family arrived in the Street when milkman Harry Clayton bought No.11 and his wife Connie set up a dressmaking business in the front parlour. Eighteen-year-old Andrea, studying for her A Levels, soon became distracted by Terry Duckworth while her younger sister Sue became the object of desire for Martin Platt, recently employed to wash up at the café. Andrea's mock exam results were so bad that she decided to leave school, but a worried Harry brought in Ken Barlow to talk to her about qualifications and she

agreed to stay on. The Claytons, though, disapproved of Andrea's association with Terry as they felt she wasn't spending enough time on revision.

When Terry's mother Vera asked for a dress to be made up Connie agreed, thinking it would be an easy job. The occasion was the Duckworths' twenty-eighth wedding anniversary and Jack had acquired a length of silver lurex. Vera bought tickets for a posh dance at the Town Hall and had the dress made to her specifications. The finished piece looked awful, and made her look old and fat. She refused to pay Connie's bill, and the result was a feud between the two families, which drove a wedge between Terry and Andrea. In the end, he paid the bill to get some peace.

When Andrea finished their relationship he was stunned, and especially when she confessed she was pregnant with his child. A fight in the Rovers ensued when Jack refused to accept that the baby was Terry's and insinuated that Andrea had been sleeping around. However, Connie assured Andrea she'd help her with the baby, and after she got her exam results – two Bs and a C – the family decided to move away from the Duckworths and start afresh, allowing Andrea the chance to study in Sheffield. Distraught at being cut out of his baby's life, Terry decided to run away but he was mugged at the station and returned home in time to see the removal van leave No.11.

7 Romancing Percy

Percy Sugden organized a Valentine's Day disco at the community centre but was horrified when a DJ calling himself Kaiser Bill turned up to provide the music. However, the dance turned out to be a success, and Curly Watts screwed up the courage to walk machinist Shirley Armitage home, while Phyllis Pearce grabbed Percy for the ladies' excuse me. Then she looked to Percy to be her champion when Sam Tindall at the bowls club took a fancy to her. He wagered Percy that the best bowler would win her hand, but Percy was not interested in Phyllis's hand, or any other part of her anatomy, although pride prevented him from throwing the game. Delighted, Phyllis accompanied Percy on the bowls club outing to Southport and stole his shoes while he went paddling so that they missed the coach home.

Sam decided to hang around on the sidelines, in the hope that Phyllis would look his way one day, and became a regular sight, along with his dog, Dougal, which he carried around in a bag.

8 Troublesome Daughters

A familiar landmark left the Street when the Barlows sold Albert Tatlock's old

sideboard to an antique dealer. They replaced it with modern units, which they had to construct themselves. Tracy caused waves when she demanded to know once again why she was still called Langton, and Deirdre explained about Ray and the divorce. However, Ken decided he wanted to adopt her legally and make her a Barlow.

When Tracy was refused permission to have a dog, she ran away from home and took a train to Newcastle to visit Ken's daughter Susan, who brought her home and stayed for an extended visit, expressing an interest in the *Recorder.* Ken encouraged her to give up her market research job in Newcastle and to join him as a reporter. He was happy when she moved into No.1 – but thunderstruck when she started to go out with Mike Baldwin.

9 Ivy's Crisis of Faith

Romance blossomed for Ivy Tilsley when George Wardle became the new van driver at Baldwin's. They both worshipped at

St Luke's where George also coached the junior rugby team. When the church minibus broke down Ivy used her master key to get out the works' van and joined George to drive the lads to a fixture. The game ended in violence, the van was covered in graffiti, and Ivy was given a black eye. Furious, Mike threatened to sack both George and Ivy, but then let them off. He deducted three hundred pounds from their wages to have the van resprayed.

Ivy surprised her friends by going on holiday to the Isle of Man with George, but insisted on separate rooms and on her return accused him of taking her for granted. To prove his love, George proposed to her and, delighted, Ivy accepted. Her joy changed to sadness when George confessed he couldn't marry in church as he was divorced. She insisted that he was still married in the eyes of God, and returned his ring. Less than a month later she decided she had made a mistake and begged him to have her back, at which Brian called her a slut. However, George couldn't be bothered and started to take out Pauline Walsh from packing. Distraught, Ivy contemplated giving up the church.

Brian's love life was just as rocky. He and Gail were arguing over who should give up work to look after Nicky when he went down with chickenpox. Then Brian decided to spend their savings on the garage rather than as a deposit on a home for them, and Gail, fearing she'd never escape Ivy's house, took Nicky and moved into a bedsit. Brian refused to run after her and decided to behave as if he was single. The result was that Ivy made him leave No.5. Brian threw himself on Gail's mercy and they were reconciled when he promised to find them a house. After Alf Roberts had pulled a few strings at the council, they took possession of a three-bedroomed council house at 33 Hammond Road.

10 Alf's Empire

Alf Roberts decided to enlarge his empire by turning the corner shop into a self-service mini-market. He had plans drawn up to turn the back living room into part of the shop which would also extend into No.13. Hilda Ogden turned down Alf's offer to buy her home, then panicked when Alf's builder, Les Pringle, warned her that her roof was collapsing. He advised her to sell to Alf for the fourteen thousand pounds he was offering. Hilda couldn't bring herself to sell Alf an unsafe house but worried that she would never be able to afford the repairs herself.

Alf realized that something was bothering her and was furious when she eventually broke down and told him about the roof. He accused Les of underhand dealing and refused to give him any more work. The plans were changed to include just the living quarters in the shop, and Hilda's home was saved.

Bet Lynch performed the official opening of the new shop as Miss Weatherfield 1955. Alf drank far too much during the party afterwards and proposed to a startled Rita Fairclough, who told him she could never look upon him as anything but a good friend.

However, athough Rita turned him down, by the end of the year Alf was a married man. The blushing bride was Audrey Potter, who had returned to the area and announced to daughter Gail that the time had come for her to settle down. She decided that Alf was the best catch and set about winning his heart after crashing his car then allowing him to comfort her. After marrying at the register office they spent Christmas Day honeymooning in Paris. During his stag night Alf sat on a Christmas pudding made by Percy Sugden and won, in a raffle, by Sam Tindall. After Alf had finished with it it was inedible.

CAST

Henry Wakefield	Finetime Fontayne
Gloria Todd	Sue Jenkins
Christine Millward	Julie Shipley
Martin Platt	Sean Wilson
Connie Clayton	Susan Brown
Harry Clayton	Johnny Leeze
Andrea Clayton	Caroline O'Neill
Sue Clayton	Jane Hazelgrove
Wilf Starkey	Jim Bywaters
Shirley Armitage	Lisa Lewis
George Wardle	Ron Davies
Stella Rigby	Vivienne Ross
Michelle Robinson	Stephanie Tague
Malcolm Nuttall	Michael Ball
Don Ashton	David Landberg
Frank Mills	Nigel Gregory
Tracy Langton	Holly Chamarette
Les Pringle	Sean Scanlan
Sam Tindall	Tom Mennard
Susan Barlow	Wendy Jane Walker
Pauline Walsh	Patricia Ford

1986

Behind the Scenes

The exodus of Street favourites over the past three years came to an end and it seemed to those working on the programme that the current characters would see the show well into the 1990s. Bet Lynch moved from being the nation's favourite barmaid to becoming landlady of the Rovers Return, Alf turned the Corner Shop into a self-service mini-market, Ken and Mike finally came to blows when Mike dared to court Susan Barlow, and Sally Whittaker's Sally Seddon became an instant pin-up.

However, the Street was trailing in the ratings, due to the success of its first real rival in twenty-five years. The saga of Den and Angie in *EastEnders* captured the public's imagination and Gail Tilsley's affair with Australian Ian Latimer couldn't compete.

In September Pat Phoenix lost her fight against lung cancer and died just days after marrying her boyfriend, the actor Tony Booth. Her funeral, at Manchester Cathedral, was an extravaganza with a brass band and some of the most elaborately colourful outfits ever worn at a funeral. Tony followed Pat's coffin into the cathedral along with his daughter Cherie and her husband Tony Blair. *The Times'* obituary dwelt on Pat's appeal as Elsie Tanner, the first great British soap star: 'Only when Miss Phoenix left the series did the BBC dare launch its rival series *EastEnders*.'

Top Twenty

Pos	Character	No of eps	Total	Pos Prev Year
1	Terry Duckworth	77	225	5
2	Bet Lynch	76	1227	3
3	Jack Duckworth	74	297	6
4	Rita Fairclough	72	1005	19
5	Mike Baldwin	71	616	11
6	Hilda Ogden	68	1576	6
7	Alf Roberts	68	1026	12
8	Ivy Tilsley	68	616	1
9	Kevin Webster	68	201	15
10	Mavis Riley	67	832	9
11	Vera Duckworth	67	464	2
12	Susan Baldwin	67	132	-
13	Betty Turpin	66	1229	10
14	Gail Tilsley	69	713	12
15	Gloria Todd	65	102	24
16	Audrey Roberts	64	147	30
17	Ken Barlow	62	1744	8
18	Curly Watts	60	185	17
19	Percy Sugden	60	202	17
20	Alan Bradley	60	60	60

"My life's all about struggling through, settling for what I've got."

Gail Tilsley

Key Dates

1986

January 27	Sally Whittaker's first appearance as Sally Seddon
May 14	Mike Baldwin marries Susan Barlow
September 26	Patricia Phoenix dies of cancer, aged sixty-two, two years after last appearing as Elsie Tanner
October 8	Kevin Webster marries Sally Seddon

STORIES

1 Rita's New Family

The year started badly for Kabin paper-girl Jenny Bradley when her mother, Pat, was knocked down and killed by a car on Rosamund Street. After she kept running away from a children's home, Donald Worthington asked Rita Fairclough to foster the girl until she could be reunited with her father, Alan, who had left the family when Jenny was eight. Jenny enjoyed living with Rita and was hostile to the idea of living in Leeds with Alan, whom she viewed as a stranger.

Rita worked hard to reconcile the pair and found herself falling for Alan, who transferred his work and moved to Manchester, renting a flat at 41 Ashdale Road, where Gloria Todd lived. Rita feared that Alan might shut her out of his life so she invited him to accompany her to the newsagents' ball, although she refused to let him stay the night afterwards. He grew frustrated and turned to Gloria for comfort but when she finished with him he told Rita he had decided she was the only woman for him. She melted and allowed him to stay the night.

Jenny longed for a career as a pop singer and auditioned for Alec Gilroy, who was keen to manage her, but Rita warned Alan that Alec was a dodgy character. Jenny was furious when Alan refused to let her sing and blamed Rita for influencing him.

After a family holiday in Jersey, Alan was suddenly made redundant and told Rita he couldn't commit to her long-term while he was out of work. He took a contract in Dubai and moved Jenny back in with her while he went abroad. Jenny threw herself at Martin Platt and refused to accept his protests that she was too young for him. Eventually she wore him down and they started going out together. When she entered a talent show in Rochdale she persuaded Rita to lend Martin her car to drive her there, then won first prize. On the way home she talked Martin into letting her have a go at driving. She lost control of the car, which rolled over in a field. Jenny walked away from the wreck but Martin was knocked unconscious.

2 Popular Gloria

Bet Lynch's romance with Frank Mills came to an abrupt end when she discovered he had made a pass at Gloria Todd. She threw him out and gave the pub her full attention. Gloria was just as unlucky in love: she started to receive red roses sent by an admirer who turned out to be Jack Duckworth, and then her ex-fiancé Steve Holt turned up on her doorstep fresh from prison and anxious to start again with her. Gloria was no longer interested in him but Steve wouldn't take no for an answer, until Bet stepped in and threatened to report him to the police for harassment.

No sooner had Steve gone than Terry Duckworth chanced his luck with Gloria. Again she wasn't interested and was troubled by his persistence. Eventually her neighbour Alan Bradley got rid of Terry, savagely beating him up in the Rovers. Although troubled by Alan's temper, Gloria was grateful to him and admitted she found him attractive. They started to see each other and she let him spend the night with her before discovering he was also seeing Rita Fairclough. She finished with him and tried to forget all about men. She was nearly over Alan when Canadian Richard Armstrong turned up and identified himself as her half-brother, explaining that the mother who had abandoned her aged four was now dying of cancer in Canada and wanted to see her. At first Gloria refused, feeling she didn't owe her mother anything, but her curiosity got the better of her and she left Weatherfield, not certain when, or if, she'd return.

3 Kevin Finds His Sal

Kevin Webster met the girl of his dreams after driving a van through a puddle and soaking Sally Seddon as she travelled to a job interview. He took her back to No.13 to dry out her tights and love blossomed, much to the disapproval of Hilda Ogden who knew of the rough Seddons' reputation. Terry Duckworth employed

Sally to answer the phone at the yard and made a pass at her. She was happy to respond, but when Kevin caught them kissing he gave Terry a black eye.

With Hilda away overnight, Sally stayed at No.13 and took Kevin's virginity. When her father threw her out, Hilda mellowed towards her and allowed her to move into No.13, but insisted Kevin slept on the sofa. She rigged up a trap on the stairs to alert her to any nocturnal activities but forgot it was there, tripped over it and fell down the stairs. Sally took over Hilda's cleaning jobs for a couple of weeks and Hilda had an insight into Sally's home life when her mother, Elsie, called round for Sally's dole money to give to her father.

After spending his twenty-first birthday with his family in Southampton and learning that they were going to live in Germany, Kevin felt he no longer had a family and proposed to Sally. She was happy to accept, even though her parents refused to get involved. Sally took a job as barmaid at the Rovers but resigned when Bet Lynch tried to cut her hours, and she went back to drawing the dole. The couple had a cheap register-office wedding and continued to rent Hilda's back room.

Although he missed the wedding, Sally's uncle, Tom Hopwood, gave the couple a financial wedding present and took an interest in Hilda, whom he wooed with fruit and vegetables from his greengrocers shop.

4 Ken and Mike Finally Come to Blows

Upset that his daughter Susan was seeing his arch-rival Mike Baldwin, Ken Barlow decided to tell her about Mike's affair with Deirdre. Deirdre sobbed when Ken broke the news, but Susan told Deirdre she despised her and left home to live with Mike, taking his side against Ken. Out of control, Ken burst into Mike's office and punched him, much to the delight of the workforce. Mike retaliated by proposing to Susan, who accepted and sought Ken's blessing, but he told her the marriage would be a travesty. Deirdre tried to talk Ken round, warning him that if he continued to oppose the match he might lose Susan for ever. Ken agreed to give her away, but on condition that she moved back to No.1. She complied and was thrilled when Ken threw a lavish party for her and Peter, her twin, on their twenty-first birthday. Then Mike tried to outdo Ken by giving Susan a car as a birthday present. Ken told Susan he had spent so much on her party that he wouldn't be able to pay for her wedding for another year, but his plan to stall the event backfired when Mike announced that he would fund the ceremony.

Three weeks later the couple were married. Ken refused to attend until the last minute when he rushed to give Susan away after Peter lectured him about how bad a father he had been all their lives.

Shortly after giving one daughter away, Ken gained another when Tracy's adoption went through and she changed her name to Barlow.

5 An Ideal Husband

Vera Duckworth took possession of a brand new Vauxhall Nova after Jack entered a competition in her name in *Woman's Choice* magazine. His winning slogan as to why he was the perfect husband ran: 'My husband is husband of the year because right from the day we were married he has made my life one long honeymoon.' Vera

went along with the pretence that she had written the slogan but told Jack he wouldn't be getting his hands on the car keys. She took driving lessons and amazed Jack by passing first time. In celebration, she took Ivy Tilsley out on the town where they ended up at a strip club. The next day Jack, having borrowed the car to entertain his mistress Dulcie Froggatt, found a pair of men's briefs stuffed down the back seat. He confronted Vera with the evidence and an embarrassed Ivy was forced to confess that she had ripped them off a male stripper.

6 The New Mrs Wilton

Mavis Riley had the shock of her life when Derek Wilton turned up and confessed to having married his boss's daughter, Angela Hawthorne. He told Mavis he had made a dreadful mistake and begged her to help him through the agony of his marriage. Mavis felt like a scarlet woman

as she met Derek in secret and was horrified when Angela's son Neville found them eating together in a restaurant. To appease him, Derek told him that Mavis was a client and followed this through by making Mavis order a huge number of diaries. Rita Fairclough was not pleased when they arrived and returned them, which prompted Neville to call at the Kabin and apologize for Derek's over-zealous behaviour.

7 A Facelift for the Rovers

Jack Duckworth attempted to change a fuse at the Rovers but started a fire in the fuse-box, which flared up one night. Sally and Kevin Webster, returning from a pop concert at five a.m. saw smoke billowing out of the pub doors and raised the alarm. Kevin attempted to rescue Bet Lynch from her bedroom but the smoke was too much for him. Luckily both Kevin and Bet were rescued by the fire brigade, but the pub was gutted. While the brewery refurbished the

premises, the regulars drank at the Graffiti club, now managed by Alec Gilroy. Betty Turpin decided that the Rovers had seen the last of her and retired.

During the refurbishment the pub's three bars were knocked into one, and Bet called upon the longest-serving staff member, Hilda Ogden, to perform the opening ceremony.

Bet was thrilled with the pub until Alec poached her barmaid, Alison Dougherty, but she had the last laugh when Alison ran off with Alec's takings. Bet replaced her with Gloria Todd, now back from Canada, and a few weeks later Betty came out of retirement to take over the pub's kitchen. Alec resented the opening of the new Rovers but introduced Bet to his talent agency, persuading her to book acts to bring in more custom. When the Graffiti was closed down Alec was sacked by the brewery but continued to hang around Bet. She began to wonder if he was interested in her or the pub.

8 Gail Goes Off the Rails

Shop work and Audrey Roberts did not get on together. She did as little as she could in the Corner Shop and threw her energies into persuading Alf to buy her a large detached house on Bolton Road. He flinched at the price and instead stunned her by buying No.11 for considerably less. He had a further surprise up his sleeve: he announced that she would be running a

hair-salon from the front parlour.

Meanwhile, Audrey's daughter Gail Tilsley found herself in a tizz after falling for Brian's Australian cousin, Ian Latimer. With Brian away on business, Gail moved Ian into her bed. Audrey realized what was going on and urged Gail to end her fling, but Gail replied that for the first time in years she felt alive.

When Brian returned he was full of the idea of emigrating to Perth, which upset Ivy who feared she'd never see her family again. After telling Brian she would never settle abroad, Gail was distraught when Ian suddenly returned to Australia. While distracted with anxiety over Gail's affair, Audrey left dye too long on Hilda Ogden's hair, which turned bright orange. Alf was forced to pay her twenty pounds compensation and insisted the salon was closed down.

When Gail discovered she was pregnant she confessed her affair to Brian and told him she wasn't certain who the father was. Brian walked out and returned to No.5 to start divorce proceedings. He told Gail he would only return if she had an abortion, which she refused point-blank. Brian decided he was single again and took up with businesswoman Liz Turnbull, which upset both Gail and Ivy.

9 Phyllis Gold-digs

After discovering that Sam Tindall had won the pools in the 1950s, Phyllis Pearce threw herself at him. She invited him to her sixty-fifth birthday party but her seduction plans were ruined by the arrival of Percy Sugden, who ate his way through her cake. When Sam confessed to Phyllis that he was penniless as he had invested in property,

which was now falling down, her passion for him left her but she let him down gently, telling him she was still in love with Percy.

10 Factory Capers

Ken Barlow's work life became confusing when he ran a bingo game in the *Recorder* and ended up with forty-three winners after the printers made a terrible mistake. He had only just got over that hassle when he started to clash with his daughter-reporter Susan Baldwin. She found it impossible to work with him because he kept making disparaging remarks about Mike and resigned.

Mike came down hard on his workers: sacking George Wardle for clocking Pauline

Walsh in then firing Vera Duckworth after discovering she had skived off work to go shopping. Vera accused Susan of snooping on her for Mike, but Susan felt sorry for her and persuaded Mike to reinstate her. After Susan threatened to seek employment with a rival firm, Mike took her on as head of sales at the factory, and humoured her when she told him she wanted to start up a company to make children's clothes. Then he confessed he had rather she got pregnant but agreed to give her funding so she formed Hopscotch and worked on a few designs. To show Mike how good they looked she borrowed a little boy from a playgroup to model them. Mike was stunned when the boy turned out to be his son Mark Redman. His mother, Maggie, was furious, flew at Mike, and wouldn't believe he had not known what was going on.

11 Burglars in the Street

Terry Duckworth got drunk when he discovered he had become a father with the birth of Paul Clayton. He threw his energies into work, and when Curly Watts resigned from the bins Cheap and Cheerful became the partners' main concern.

When Emily Bishop was taken in by bogus water-board men her house was ransacked and the men made off with her jewellery and Curly's telescope. Her home insurance refused to pay up as Curly was only a lodger so, feeling the robbery to be her own fault, she gave him the amount he still owed on the telescope. As the Cheap and Cheerful van needed repairs, Terry demanded that Curly use the money to pay for them. Curly agreed, but on condition that the firm had proper accounts, with Emily as their bookkeeper.

As well as house clearances, Terry and Curly attempted to dabble in antiques. When Hilda Ogden's friend Ada died, Hilda inherited her cat, Rommel, and an old oak bureau. Terry bought it from her for forty pounds, and then discovered a bill of sale inside dated 1889. An expert told him the bill did not belong with the bureau but bought the piece from the lads for a hundred and ten pounds. Curly insisted that the money was given to Hilda.

The legacy of the water-board men continued when Percy Sugden caught an official nosing around Hilda's backyard. He locked him in the outside toilet and called the police, who identified the man as genuine and cautioned Percy as a public nuisance.

CAST

Jenny Bradley	Sally Ann Matthews
Alan Bradley	Mark Eden
Sally Seddon Webster	Sally Whittaker
Ian Latimer	Michael Looney
Peter Barlow	David Lonsdale
Elsie Seddon	Brenda Elder
Alison Dougherty	Elizabeth Ritson
Neville Hawthorne	Mark Chatterton
Liz Turnbull	Catriona A Elliott
Richard Armstrong	Michael Thomas
Steve Holt	Ray Ashcroft
Tom Hopwood	Len Marten

1987

Behind the Scenes

One of the Street's strengths was its comic characters and storylines, carrying on the tradition of great northern comic turns. This year saw Roy Barraclough signing a long-term contract that moved shifty Alec Gilroy to centre-stage as the new landlord of the Rovers. Roy was another actor from Oldham Repertory Theatre and a well-known face on television as a feed for Les Dawson.

Just as he settled into the role, the programme was rocked by Jean Alexander's decision to hang up her rollers and retire as Hilda Ogden. Newspapers started their own 'Save Hilda' campaigns and Granada's switchboard was jammed by concerned callers. Hilda Ogden had become an institution and the Street was unthinkable without her. However, Jean knew that the departure of Pat Phoenix, Doris Speed and Violet Carson hadn't dented the show and neither would hers: 'It's the Street itself that's the star … we're just the players.' Her last appearance was aired on Christmas Day, and as the credits rolled over Hilda's farewell party at the Rovers the rating figures staggered executives at both ITV and the BBC: the Street had broken its own records with an incredible 26.6 million viewers.

> "My mother-in-law! If she lived in India, she'd be sacred. She's like Boris Karloff after a busy night at the graveyard."
>
> **Jack Duckworth**

Top Twenty

Pos	Character	No of eps	Total	Pos Prev Year
1	Alf Roberts	81	1107	6
2	Mavis Riley	76	908	10
3	Ivy Tilsley	76	692	6
4	Rita Fairclough	74	1079	4
5	Mike Baldwin	74	690	5
6	Ken Barlow	72	1816	17
7	Bet Lynch Gilroy	72	1299	2
8	Emily Bishop	71	1564	24
9	Hilda Ogden	71	1647	6
10	Alec Gilroy	70	99	32
11	Sally Webster	69	129	21
12	Gloria Todd	68	170	15
13	Deirdre Barlow	67	943	25
14	Vera Duckworth	66	530	10
15	Curly Watts	65	250	18
16	Kevin Webster	64	265	6
17	Audrey Roberts	63	210	16
18	Alan Bradley	62	122	18
19	Jack Duckworth	60	357	3
20	Susan Baldwin	60	162	10

Key Dates 1987

February 3	Sarah Louise Tilsley is born
August 16	Don Brennan's first appearance
September 9	Bet Lynch marries Alec Gilroy
November 23	Joan Lowther dies
December 25	Jean Alexander's last appearance as Hilda Ogden

STORIES

1 Rita's Arranged Marriage

Martin Platt recovered in hospital after being knocked unconscious inside Rita Fairclough's car. His girlfriend Jenny Bradley waited by his bedside, and when he came round she begged him not to tell the police she had been driving the car. He agreed, and took the blame for the accident, whereupon Alan Bradley, who was home on leave from working abroad, attacked him and accused him of nearly killing Jenny. Jenny broke down and confessed that she had been driving the car, so Alan marched the pair to the police station and made them tell the truth, for which they received a dressing down. Alan paid for the damage to Rita's car and decided that he did not want to return overseas. He proposed to Rita but she turned him down and instead invited him to move into No.7 as her common-law husband.

Alan settled into the house, raising a few of the neighbours' eyebrows, and talked Rita into closing down the record shop in the Kabin in favour of allowing him to run a video library. Rita was happy with the arrangement, but her assistant Mavis Riley took offence and resigned after Alan started bossing her about and insulted her friend Derek Wilton, whom she had called in to defend her. Rita secured Mavis's job by reminding Alan that the Kabin was her shop.

Bored with his lot, Alan attempted to improve his relationship with Rita by plotting to marry her in secret. Jenny and Mavis both thought the plan romantic but after being lured to the register office Rita refused to go through with the wedding and accused Alan of treating her like a fool.

2 The End of Cheap and Cheerful

After breaking into the Corner Shop and stealing alcohol, Terry Duckworth tried to lie low but Alf Roberts discovered that his stolen booze had been drunk at a party held at No.13. To prevent suspicion falling on Hilda Ogden, Terry confessed. Alf wanted to bring in the police but Vera pleaded with him to spare her son and paid him for the drinks. Then Terry bought a job lot of household goods and started to sell them door-to-door. He roped in Curly Watts to help him, but Emily Bishop disapproved of Terry's selling techniques; to evoke sympathy he lied about being unemployed.

While on the knocker down Cromwell Street, Terry befriended Dulcie Froggatt and spent several days in her bed. Her husband assumed she was seeing Jack and punched him. Both Terry and Jack were horrified to discover they had been sleeping with the same woman, and Jack insisted that Terry took the rap to get Vera off his back. Vera confronted Dulcie about seducing her son and was told that Jack had been worse so Vera threw him out. However, he managed to worm his way back by convincing her that Dulcie had lied because she was jealous of their strong marriage.

Down another street, Terry was amazed to find his old army pal Pete Jackson. As Pete was unemployed, Terry insisted he joined Cheap and Cheerful, without consulting Curly. Pete's wife Linda wasn't impressed by his friends and Terry tried to show her he was really a great guy. He wore her down and the pair became lovers. Pete found them together and went for Terry. Linda begged forgiveness but when Terry announced he was through with Weatherfield she packed and headed off into the sunset with him.

Left alone to fold the business, Curly splashed out his savings on a van that turned out to be a wreck. He tried to return it but the previous owner threatened him with a piece of lead piping. Emily threatened him with the police then retrieved Curly's money. She decided that Curly should take a job in insurance, but he had different ideas and enrolled on a business-studies course at Granston Tech.

3 Unhappy Families

Upset at the prospect of her daughter Gail Tilsley bringing up her children alone, Audrey Roberts wrote to Ian Latimer in Australia, informing him that Gail was pregnant with his child. He rushed to England and proposed to Gail but she turned him down. When estranged husband Brian found the pair together, he launched an attack on Ian, causing Gail to go into premature labour at five months. She was rushed to hospital where she gave birth to a daughter, Sarah Louise. While at the hospital waiting for news, Ian took a blood test that proved he couldn't be the baby's father. Unaware that Sarah was his daughter, Brian refused to visit the baby and instead moved in with girlfriend Liz Turnbull. When Gail got home with her baby, she grew disturbed at the idea of Nicky spending too much time with Liz and threatened to restrict Brian's access to him, while Audrey made it public knowledge that Sarah was Brian's child. However, he still refused to acknowledge her.

While Gail took up with plumber Jeff Singleton, Brian decided to make a fresh start away from Manchester with Liz. Alan Bradley agreed to buy the garage from him but Liz backed out of the relationship, realizing that Nicky would always mean more to Brian than she would. Brian was upset to see Nicky with Jeff and, on the spur of the moment, kidnapped his son. The police set up a nationwide search and Brian contacted Alan, telling him the garage was his if he could raise two

thousand pounds as an immediate down-payment. He arranged to meet Alan at a motorway service station to pick up the money but ran off when he saw that Alan had brought Gail along. She pleaded with him to give Nicky back but he refused. Eventually it became obvious to Brian that Nicky needed his mother and, rather than going to Ireland to live, he returned to Weatherfield. Gail was delighted to have her son back, and when Brian begged forgiveness she finished with Jeff and took him back.

4 Alf Loses His Seat

Ken Barlow used the *Recorder* newspaper to attack the local council, accusing the councillors of not being interested in the people. Alf Roberts objected to the slur but the Labour Party were impressed and asked Ken to stand as a candidate in the local elections. He eagerly agreed but his political career was ruined when Alf complained to Bob Statham that Ken was using the newspaper to promote his party's policies. When shopkeepers threatened to pull their advertising Statham told Ken to choose between the paper and politics. Ken chose the paper and backed out of the elections.

Outraged, Deirdre resigned from the Corner Shop and decided to stand against Alf herself as an Independent. She was backed by Ken but she soon realized that he only wanted to split the Independent vote so that Labour would win.

When a child was knocked down on Rosamund Street, Deirdre took up the fight for a public crossing. Her campaign picked up supporters and in the election she beat Alf by seven votes and was elected councillor. While her supporters celebrated Alf suffered a heart-attack and was rushed to hospital, where Audrey, beside herself with anxiety, accused Deirdre of killing him. Alf recovered slowly and was told to take things quietly.

Deirdre used her new position to help Emily Bishop launch an appeal for funds to fly a local boy to America for an operation. Emily held a fête in the Street and raised five hundred pounds. Then Deirdre upset Ken by volunteering to go to an environmental health conference in Bournemouth. He accused her of being a bad mother, especially when Tracy was rushed to hospital to have her appendix removed and she was too tied up at the Town Hall to visit her. Deirdre fumed when Ken wrote an article in the *Recorder* criticizing her for going to Bournemouth on the tax-payers' money.

5 Bet Secures a Wedding Ring

Annoyed by having the brewery continuously on her back, Bet Lynch decided to buy the tenancy from them. She only had three thousand pounds saved and tried to raise a loan on the fifteen-thousand-pound asking price but failed. She was on the verge of forgetting the idea but the brewery decided to sell the tenancy no matter what and gave her four weeks to raise the funds. Alec Gilroy came to the rescue, and Bet took his money, despite the warnings of Betty Turpin and Gloria Todd, just back from burying her mother in Canada. They felt Alec wanted to take over the pub and they were soon proved right. Then Bet disappeared, leaving a note saying that the repayments on Alec's loan

were too much for her. He was quick to tell brewery boss Cecil Newton that it was his money Bet had paid them, and Cecil agreed to let him take over the tenancy. After Alec insinuated he did not trust her near the till Betty walked out. In her place he employed busty Margo Richardson.

When Bet was located in Spain, Alec flew out to her to ensure that the five thousand pounds of his money that she still had was safe. She assured him it was and said she knew she had blown her chances with the brewery. Alec asked her to return to run the Rovers with him, as his wife, and was thrilled when she agreed. On her return Bet's first act was to sack Margo. When the couple married at All Saints' Church, no one in the congregation gave the marriage longer than six months.

Bet tried hard to be a good housewife but her cooking skills were minimal and Alec asked her to stick to lipstick and barwork. When he went down with flu, Bet brought Betty back to work the lunchtime shift and Alec was horrified when Bet became his personal nursemaid. After he had recovered he left Bet to the pub and took on the job of an entertainments officer, carting a troupe to Germany to entertain the British Army.

6 Scarlet Woman Mavis

Derek Wilton decided it was time for the worm to turn and announced to a delighted Mavis Riley that he intended to leave his wife, Angela. Mavis allowed him to spend the night on her sofa but in the morning Derek had had second thoughts and returned home before Angela could note his absence. Soon afterwards he discovered that Angela was seeing another man and roped in Mavis to spy on her for him. Mavis worked herself into a state following Angela and the man, who turned out to be a private detective trailing Derek. Derek was outraged when Angela started divorce proceedings and cited Mavis as co-respondent. He decided to fight for his rights and agreed to a quick divorce in return for a handsome pay-off. He moved into a bedsit and used the money to buy a stationery firm in Cornwall. Unfortunately he didn't tell Mavis of his plans and when she couldn't find him she feared he had killed himself. When he told her happily about his holiday in Cornwall she threw a glass of sherry in his face.

7 The Course of Young Love...

Sally Webster celebrated when she was taken on at the mini-market as sales assistant and was given the flat above it for herself and Kevin. The couple threw a flat-warming, which ended in Alf spilling red wine all over their new chair, which hadn't even been paid for.

Meanwhile, down the street, Jenny Bradley celebrated good O Level results – four As, three Bs and a C – but decided not to sit A Levels. Instead she ran off to France with Martin Platt to pick grapes. After the summer, Martin returned and signed on the dole, refusing to follow his father into the local print works. Jenny, however, returned with the news that she was going to marry French student Patric Podevin. Alan refused to let the marriage take place and was glad when Patric told Jenny they must wait two years; she had to content herself with an engagement. However, at Christmas, with Patric still in France, she grew bored and removed the ring to go to a party where she set out to steal her friend Lisa Wood's boyfriend, Gary Grimshaw. Gary liked Jenny so much that he finished with Lisa, who swore vengeance.

8 And Mother Makes Three

When Vera Duckworth complained about the state of No.9, Jack decided to install a living-flame gas fire as a treat. He did the

job himself, which bothered Ivy Tilsley, who reported him to the gas board. Surprisingly the job was approved, but then Jack decided to sweep the chimney. He borrowed brushes and ended up covering the lounge, himself and Vera in soot. To cheer Vera up, Ivy took her for a girls' night out and was pleased when their taxi driver, Don Brennan, called the next day to ask her out on a date.

When Vera's mother Amy Burton fell ill Vera decided she wanted her close by and horrified Jack by moving her into No.9's back bedroom. Amy had never liked Jack and filled the house with her friends, warning them to guard their handbags. Jack hit back: when he discovered Amy was frightened of birds he brought his pigeons into the house. He was in despair when she joined the staff at the Rovers as cleaner, feeling there was no escape from her.

9 The End of the Road for Mike and Susan

Ken Barlow worried about his daughter Susan's morals when she exaggerated the story of a local fire to create a free advertising feature for her range of children's clothes. Mike Baldwin was impressed but not enough to bail Susan out when Hopscotch suffered financial problems. He closed the company and ordered Susan to run his new factory shop, opened in the loading bay. When she refused he sacked her from the factory. The shop caused problems for Mike as he had not applied for permission from the council to erect a neon sign. He relied on Councillor Deirdre Barlow to sort the matter out but she refused and he had to remove the sign.

Mike told Susan he wasn't prepared to wait any longer for her to become pregnant and insisted she had a baby before he was too old to enjoy fatherhood. She walked out on him and returned to No.1, but Ken sent her back to her husband. Mike celebrated when Susan admitted she was pregnant but his plans to keep her stuck in a Glossop mansion as a housewife appalled her and she had an abortion. Mike called her a murderer and threw her out, then filed for divorce. She returned to Newcastle.

10 Hilda Sings Her Last Song

Percy Sugden organized the local troops and started his own over-sixties tea-dance. Hilda Ogden was annoyed when Phyllis Pearce decided that Tom Hopwood was the best dancer and made a play for him. When Hilda saw her off, Phyllis attached herself to Sam Tindall. Percy decided that the group was good enough to enter a competition but was furious when the members decided that Sam was the best teacher and voted him their leader. Percy took offence, cancelled the entry and banned the group from using the community centre.

Tom shocked Hilda by deciding to sell his shop and retire to Formby. He proposed to her and asked her to join him, but she decided she couldn't leave the Street: No.13 held all her memories. Tom bade her a sad farewell and she suffered another loss when Dr and Mrs Lowther decided to retire to Derbyshire. Hilda helped them pack and disturbed burglars on the look-out for valuables. She struggled with them and was knocked unconscious. She was placed on a life-support system and recovered to be told that Mrs Lowther had died of heart failure during the attack. Eddie Yeats visited and attempted to raise her spirits but on leaving hospital Hilda became frightened of the outside world and locked herself away in No.13. She gave up her cleaning jobs and contemplated a bleak future until Dr Lowther offered her the job of housekeeper to him in the country. She accepted and said a sad farewell to No.13 and the Rovers, where the residents gave her a rousing send-off.

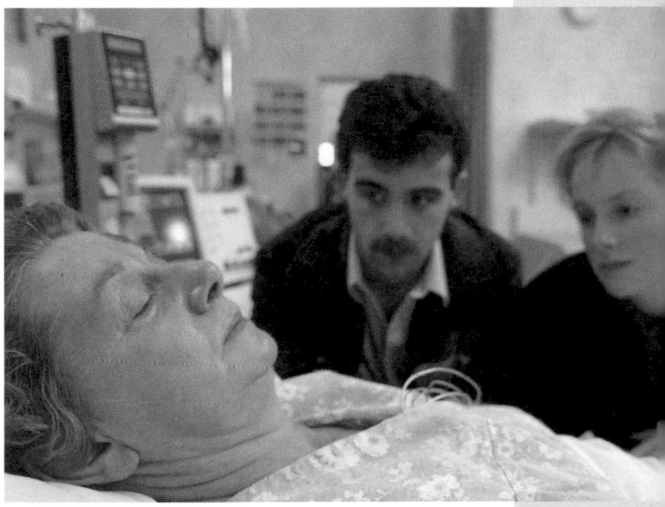

CAST

Sarah Louise Tilsley	Lindsay King
Linda Jackson	Kazia Pelker
Pete Jackson	Ian Mercer
Cecil Newton	Kenneth Alan Taylor
Jeff Singleton	Jonathan Barlow
Margo Richardson	Vicky Ogden
Don Brennan	Geoff Hinsliff
Patric Podevin	Frank du Posc
Amy Burton	Fanny Carby
Dr Lowther	David Scase
Gary Grimshaw	Colin Kerrigan
Lisa Woods	Ruth Whitehead

1988

Behind the Scenes

"Mike Baldwin might be a smooth lecherous Cockney. But there aren't many of the boss class left like him. Dedicated to grinding the faces of the working classes and laughing all the way to the bank. Now that's what I call job satisfaction."

Alec Gilroy

Top Twenty

Pos	Character	No of eps	Total	Pos Prev Year
1	Vera Duckworth	90	620	14
2	Betty Turpin	83	1361	24
3	Emily Bishop	82	1646	8
4	Jack Duckworth	80	437	19
5	Ivy Tilsley Brennan	77	769	2
6	Alec Gilroy	77	176	10
7	Bet Gilroy	75	1374	6
8	Mike Baldwin	73	763	4
9	Sally Webster	72	201	11
10	Alf Roberts	68	1175	1
11	Percy Sugden	68	328	22
12	Gloria Todd	68	238	12
13	Ken Barlow	67	1883	6
14	Alan Bradley	64	186	18
15	Kevin Webster	63	328	16
16	Mavis Riley Wilton	62	970	2
17	Deirdre Barlow	61	1004	13
18	Rita Fairclough	60	1139	4
19	Gail Tilsley	60	831	21
20	Curly Watts	54	304	15

It was all change in the producer's chair this year: John Temple left to join Scottish Television while Bill Podmore, the Street's longest-serving producer, retired and Mervyn Watson was brought back to take over, under the guidance of executive producer David Liddiment.

On screen the cementing of relationships seemed central. The divorced Tilsleys remarried while Ivy was united with down-to-earth, straightforward Don Brennan, and Peter Baldwin, after fifteen years of occasional appearances, was given a long-term contract and his character Derek was finally married to Mavis. Chris Quinten left the country to marry American television presenter Leeza Gibbons. He planned to carry on portraying Brian Tilsley but the writers couldn't agree to have the use of him for just part of the year while he pursued a Hollywood career and the decision was made to kill off Brian in the New Year.

Key Dates

1988

January 1	Margot Bryant dies, aged ninety, twelve years after her last appearance as Minnie Caldwell
February 24	Brian and Gail Tilsley remarry
June 13	Don Brennan marries Ivy Tilsley
November 9	Derek Wilton marries Mavis Riley

STORIES

1 Sally's Kid Sister

Delighted by Hilda Ogden's generosity in selling them No.13 at a knock-down price, Kevin and Sally Webster began making

alterations to the house before they moved in. They were stunned when their mortgage application was turned down as Sally had a court judgement against her on an unpaid debt. Kevin paid off the debt then applied again for a mortgage and came clean about the situation. His honesty was applauded and the mortgage was granted.

Shortly after moving into the house the couple gained a lodger in the shape of Sally's sister, Gina Seddon, whose boyfriend, Billy Wyett, was on probation, and who talked Brian Tilsley into employing him at the garage. While Billy worked under cars, a bored Gina entertained Martin Platt at No.13. After taking a car for a test drive while banned from driving Billy lost his job. He caught Martin with Gina and beat him up before he left. Kevin threw Gina out but two months later she was back, with a charge of accessory to car theft hanging over her. In court she was fined a hundred pounds and Sally was obliged to take her in permanently at No.13, much to Kevin's annoyance. To prove her worth Gina took a job at Jim's Café.

2 A Spinster No More

Mavis Riley faced rebellion in the ranks of the paper-boys and -girls when she agreed to employ pensioner Harry Ashton to deliver newspapers. The rest of the paper crew, led by Wayne Pickles, demanded his dismissal on the grounds that he was depriving a teenager of the job. Mavis stood firm and threatened to sack the others in favour of Harry, so they backed down. To

show his gratitude, Harry took Mavis for a meal but his sister, fearing romance, accused her of being after Harry's considerable fortune.

Dealing with paper-boy disputes and making up papers got to Mavis, and she decided to apply for a different job, as head of distribution at a stationery firm called Barker's. She was stunned on attending the interview to find Derek Wilton on the other side of the desk, and insulted when he refused to employ her. Instead of a job, though, Derek offered Mavis marriage, proposing through the Kabin letterbox because she refused to open the door to him. To her friends' amazement, Mavis agreed to marry him, but not before telling him how much he had hurt and humiliated her in the past. The couple were married at the register office and honeymooned in Paris before Derek moved into the Kabin flat.

3 A Double Wedding for the Tilsleys

As the family gathered to celebrate Sarah Louise Tilsley's first birthday, Brian surprised Gail by proposing to her. Although she didn't love him any longer, Gail agreed for the sake of the children, who she felt needed Brian around. The

wedding was a quick register-office affair, after which Brian presented Gail with an eternity ring. Audrey Roberts missed the wedding as just days before she had jetted off to Canada, leaving a shocked Alf and Gail to digest the news that her son had been involved in a car crash. They had no idea that Audrey had a son. Also, Alf was upset because the neighbours assumed Audrey had left him, but three months later she returned and explained to Gail that she had given birth to Stephen when she was sixteen and had been forced to give him up. Alf was further dismayed when his credit card was cut up as Audrey had spent so much in Canada, but his problems really started when Stephen's adoptive father, Malcolm Reid, arrived on a visit. He stayed at No.11 and wasted no time in urging Audrey to leave Alf and live with him and Stephen in Canada. The matter came to a head during the street's outing to Blackpool when Malcolm took Audrey boating and made a pass at her. She spelled out that she had no intention of leaving Alf. Unaware of this, however, Alf created a scene on the coach, and punched his love rival. As Malcolm fled to Canada, Audrey broke down when Gail told her she didn't respect her any more.

Meanwhile, at No.5, Ivy Tilsley was thrilled when Don Brennan proposed to her. They were married at St Luke's Catholic Church and honeymooned in Corfu. On their return he moved into No.5 and immediately fell out with Brian, whom he expected to service his taxi on the cheap.

Gail also had business troubles: she started a sandwich delivery round from the café but Alma Sedgewick disapproved, thinking it took custom away from the café itself. Gail threatened to resign so Alma backed down, not wanting the burden of running the café herself.

4 A Tale of Two Cleaners

Amy Burton started to annoy more people than just her son-in-law Jack Duckworth when Alf Roberts discovered she was shop-lifting at his mini-market. He tackled her, which led Vera to threaten to withdraw her custom. However, when Jack spied Amy stealing from the Rovers, Vera had to accept that her mother was no good. She packed her bags and sent her off, then discovered that Amy had taken with her everything of value at No.9. Jack was over the moon to see the back of her.

The cleaner's job at the Rovers was taken over by Sandra Stubbs, who alarmed Alec Gilroy by coming to the interview with a black eye. Bet felt sorry for her and gave her the job, and Mike Baldwin also took her on to clean his flat. Sandra's fourteen-year-old son, Jason, was employed at the Kabin as a paper-boy when Wayne Pickles was sacked. Hostile Wayne took to following Jason around and beating him up, which enraged Sandra who confronted his mother and ended up hitting her. Sandra was upset that she had resorted to violence and the residents soon discovered why: her estranged husband Ronnie turned up and talked Bet into giving him Sandra's address. He asked Sandra to return to him, and when she refused he attacked her. Jason ran to the Rovers for help but Ronnie escaped. Sandra had to go into hospital, and a court injunction was granted to keep Ronnie away from the family. Sandra attempted to rebuild her life again and she started going out with Pete Shaw but he broke her heart by two-timing her with her friend Gloria Todd. Sandra threw a pint of beer over Gloria who, promptly resigned from the Rovers and left the area.

5 Bet's Baby

As Alec kept refusing to take her on honeymoon, Bet Gilroy hit back by booking a Moroccan holiday with Stella Rigby, leaving Alec guessing as to what she and nymphomaniac Stella would be getting up to. On her return Bet was startled to discover that at forty-eight she was

pregnant. Alec and Bet both convinced themselves they wanted the baby but shortly afterwards she miscarried and they were united in grief.

As a child replacement, Bet took in an Alsatian as a guard dog, calling him Rover. Alec and the dog took an instant dislike to each other and Alec succeeded in getting rid of it by paying a little boy ten pounds to identify Rover as his lost pet and claim him.

When he was mugged on his way to the bank, Alec told the police he had been carrying two thousand pounds but neither Bet nor Cecil Newton believed him: they knew that the pub never took so much money and both assumed he was on the fiddle. The police found Alec's discarded briefcase, which still contained his paying-in books and he was able to prove he had been going to take both the Rovers' takings and some money from his theatrical agency. The agency grew slightly bigger when Alec put a rival out of business by lending him his 'star singer' Jack Duckworth to open a new club. Jack was dreadful and the rival agent was run out of town.

6 Devious Alan

Jenny Bradley's engagement to Patric Podevin ended when he learnt from Lisa Woods that she had removed his ring and kissed her boyfriend.

While Jenny wept into her pillow, her father Alan was on the up: he was employed by Dave Craig to work at his burglar alarm installation company and quickly decided he wanted a future in the profession. When Dave refused him a partnership Alan borrowed six thousand pounds from Rita Fairclough to set up in competition. Rita was amazed when he spent all the money on a car and threw Dave bodily out of the Rovers when he accused Alan of stealing his customers.

Alan talked Rita into letting him have the old building yard as his premises and she gave him another thousand pounds for stock. He employed Martin Platt as an assistant but decided he was too friendly with Jenny and sacked him. However,

Martin pointed out that he knew Alan was seeing a lot of client Carole Burns and threatened to tell Rita. Alan let him keep his job, but Jenny discovered the affair and told Rita. When confronted by Rita, Alan admitted seeing Carole, and accused Rita of driving him away with her coldness. He packed and left No.9, and was furious when Rita demanded the yard and her money back. Alone, Rita was terrified of the future and regretted sending Alan away. She pleaded with him to return to her but he turned her down. However, when he was refused a bank loan for new premises, he decided to return to her. He told Carole he would carry on seeing her as he was only returning for Jenny's sake, and once he was alone at No.7 he stole the deeds of the house and used them to secure a bank loan for fifteen thousand pounds.

7 Citizen Barlow

Bob Statham decided to retire to Spain and offered his partner Ken Barlow his 60 per cent share of the *Recorder* for thirty thousand pounds. While Ken weighed up his options the Clarion Group stepped in and bought Bob out. The group's leader, Nick Cavanagh, offered to buy Ken's share of the company too but Ken forced himself to adjust to being part of a large media group. Nick's daughter, Fiona, moved into Ken's office as his assistant, but wary Ken viewed her as a spy. He was promised a

company car but when it arrived the company logo was sprayed all over it.

Before long the Clarion Group hit financial difficulties and Nick disappeared with what assets he could grab. Bob flew in and revealed, in a panic, that he had never been paid for his shares. Delighted, Ken realized that all was not lost and promptly remortgaged No.1 to raise enough to buy Bob out of the paper. Fiona proved her worth in sticking by Ken and helping him break into the Clarion's offices to free the paste-ups and thus ensure the *Recorder* was printed.

Deirdre relaxed into being a councillor but felt inadequate when approached by Brian Roscoe, who complained that his family were starving because he couldn't find work. She irritated Ken by getting personally involved in the case but her kind-hearted gesture of buying the children Christmas presents backfired. When she delivered them she discovered that Roscoe's family had left him. He imprisoned Deirdrie in his flat and it was only by threatening to throw the television out of the window that she managed to escape.

8 Racism in the Street

Alf Roberts's bigotry became known when both Shirley Armitage and Curly Watts approached him independently about renting the shop flat. Alf favoured Curly because he was white and turned Shirley down, even though he had already agreed that she could have it. Shirley was used to racism but Curly was appalled and refused to take the flat until Shirley came up with a solution – that they move in together, as lovers. Initially Emily Bishop found the plan offensive – they were living together without being married – but ended up supporting the couple when Alf refused to have Shirley living on his premises. Emily blackmailed him into agreeing by

threatening to tell everyone just what a bigot he was. Even after the couple had moved in they faced problems, this time from both their families, who disapproved of their liaison.

As part of his business-studies course, Curly chose to examine Mike Baldwin's factory. His report criticized Mike for running it with Victorian conditions and Mike ripped it up. Ken Barlow was interested in the story and interviewed Mike's workers. He ran an article in the *Recorder* that accused him of running a sweat-shop. Mike threatened to sue, and Deirdre called on him in secret to beg him not to. Mike agreed, and enjoyed seeing Ken's anguish when he told him of Deirdre's visit.

9 Emily's New Lodger

Percy Sugden was horrified when his bosses at the Town Hall insisted he retired from his post as community centre caretaker because he was over sixty-five. He turned down the offer of a tower-block flat and barricaded himself inside the centre until Deirdre Barlow had talked him into coming out. He agreed to take a flat in Parliament Street, but as it wasn't ready for him he moved in with Emily Bishop at No.3, telling her it would be only for a couple of months. Two months later she was relieved when he finally left but her good nature got the better of her, and after seeing how

miserable he was away from all his friends, she invited him to move back in with his budgie, Randy. Phyllis Pearce wasn't happy with the arrangement and accused Emily in the Street of being after Percy's body. Percy tried to calm her down by pairing her off with an old pal, Arnold Swift, and was amazed when the couple started dating. Seeing Phyllis with another man disturbed Percy and she realized, to her great joy, that he was jealous.

10 The Return of the Bad Penny

Vera Duckworth attempted to seduce husband Jack on a romantic picnic but ended up losing out when she crashed her car into a lamp-post. Jack's nose was broken in the accident and to Vera's horror he sued her insurance company for compensation. While waiting for his windfall he blew the housekeeping money at a casino. Vera blamed Don Brennan for leading him astray. She felt awful when, just weeks later,

Terry returned and ran away from Don's taxi without paying the fare. Vera paid it and was pleased when Terry seemed to settle down, taking a job at the factory as Mike Baldwin's driver. Terry was sickened to see how happily married the Websters were and decided to rock them by getting factory girl Mandy Taylor to pretend to be Kevin's girlfriend. Sally was distraught at the thought of Kevin being unfaithful and broke down, prompting guilty Mandy to confess all.

Jack's insurance cheque came through but was of no use to him since he didn't have a bank account. Vera agreed to cash it for him but after she had splashed out on a new bed, a microwave and a washing machine he was left with just fifteen pounds. Terry, meanwhile, had a great time using Mike's Jaguar behind his back. He took his girlfriend out in it – and was dumbstruck when her husband sprayed 'Stay Away From My Wife' on the side. Terry tried to convince Mike that the message was meant for him but Mike realized what had been going on and fired Terry, who left town, heading for Bournemouth.

11 Mike Runs Out of Luck

Mike Baldwin started the year by wooing Gloria Todd, and changing production at the factory from denim to curtains, cutting the basic rate of his workers by 20 per cent. Outraged, Ida Clough accused Mike of exploiting the girls and was sacked. Gloria was puzzled by the way Mike blew hot and cold but it all fell into place when she discovered he was merely using her as a cover for his affair with Linda Farrell, the wife of one of his business associates. Linda left her husband for Mike but he didn't want her and sent her home, receiving a beating from the husband when Linda confessed all. After this Gloria was amazed when Mike sent her roses. She threw them at him and told him she disliked being taken for granted.

When he was breathalysed one night after leaving the Rovers, Mike realized the police had been tipped off. After hearing Vera Duckworth laughing about the incident he sacked her, accusing her of being responsible. When Ida told him it had been she who had informed the police, Mike reinstated Vera, but only after she had agreed to testify that Ida was a malicious troublemaker, thus ruining her plans to take him to a tribunal for unfair dismissal. Mike was banned from driving for twelve months and fined two hundred pounds. He was forced to employ a driver and, ironically, won Don Brennan's taxi in a poker game against a thousand-pound stake.

CAST

Harry Ashton	Keith Marsh
Wayne Pickles	Julian Walsh
Linda Farrell	Rosie Kerslake
Nick Cavanagh	George Irving
Fiona Cavanagh	Sharon Muircroft
Gina Seddon	Julie Foy
Billy Wyatt	Fabian Cartwright
Dave Craig	Alan Hulse
Lucy Armitage	Charmayne Golaub
Sandra Stubbs	Sally Watts
Jason Stubbs	Paul Simpson
Ronnie Stubbs	Eamon Boland
Carole Burns	Irene Skillington
Malcolm Reid	Shane Rimmer
Arnold Swift	Harry Littlewood
Mandy Turner	Daryl Fishwick
Peter Shaw	Alan Hunter
Tracy Barlow	Dawn Acton
Brian Roscoe	Rob Dickson

1989

Behind the Scenes

Chris Quinten was none too happy when he read in his scripts that Brian was to be stabbed to death and neither was Mark Eden when he was told that Alan Bradley was to be mown down by a Blackpool tram. These dramatic departures were part of a new breed of stories driven by David Liddiment and Mervyn Watson who saw the need to drag the Street up to date. The way the show was made was turned upside down: more location work meant weekend filming, which upset the cast who were used to having their weekends free. The old factory and community centre were demolished to make way for new houses, shops and units. More characters would be needed to occupy these, and then the biggest news was announced: the Street would be going out three times a week, instead of twice.

David Liddiment was fiercely proud of the ground-breaking move: 'A lot of technical changes had been made in the television industry, but the way *Coronation Street* was made had not changed at all. The schedule was substantially the same as it had been from when the Street stopped being broadcast live. It was a five-days-a-week routine and the show's producer was entirely constrained by that routine.' Suddenly characters were taken out of the studio and the world of Weatherfield opened up. Curly started at Bettabuy, under Reg Holdsworth, the warring McDonald clan moved into No.11, Rita had a breakdown and was filmed in Blackpool, No.9 was stone-clad, and Gail Tilsley took a toy boy. The audience greeted the new-look Street with enthusiasm and it regained its No.1 spot in the ratings, as *EastEnders* dropped down the chart.

> "When Alma Sedgewick's not chasing men she's chasing money, and Mike Baldwin is a combined operation."
>
> **Ivy Brennan**

Top Twenty

Pos	Character	No of eps	Total	Pos Prev Year
1	Audrey Roberts	91	346	27
2	Jack Duckworth	91	528	4
3	Vera Duckworth	88	708	1
4	Sally Webster	87	288	9
5	Alf Roberts	86	1261	10
6	Rita Fairclough	83	1222	18
7	Tina Fowler	83	83	–
8	Bet Gilroy	78	1452	7
9	Betty Turpin	77	1438	2
10	Ivy Brennan	77	846	4
11	Martin Platt	77	235	23
12	Gail Tilsley	76	907	18
13	Kevin Webster	75	403	15
14	Mavis Wilton	73	1043	16
15	Curly Watts	73	377	20
16	Emily Bishop	72	1718	3
17	Jenny Bradley	72	216	26
18	Mike Baldwin	71	834	8
19	Percy Sugden	70	398	11
20	Deirdre Barlow	69	1073	17

Key Dates

1989

February 15	Brian Tilsley stabbed to death.
October 20	First third-weekly episode transmitted.
October 25	Reg Holdsworth's first appearance.
October 27	Liz and Jim McDonald's first appearances.
December 4	3000th episode transmitted.
December 6	Steve McDonald's first episode.
December 8	Alan Bradley is killed.

STORIES

1 Baldwin's Empire Crumbles

Ivy Brennan had to dig deep into her savings to pay Mike Baldwin the thousand pounds he demanded in return for Don's taxi, which he had won in a poker game. Out in his taxi once again, Don was given a greyhound, Harry's Luck, in exchange for a forty-pound fare. He was delighted with the dog and planned to race her, but she turned out to be pregnant. Ivy cooed over her and her five pups but Don sold them all for eight hundred pounds and repaid Ivy the rest of what he owed her.

Mike was bemused when property developer Maurice Jones told him to name his price for the factory. Maurice had already bought the community centre and the land behind the factory so Mike was able to sell it at a huge profit as a going concern to Maurice, but then the workers found the gates firmly locked on them. Furious, Emily Bishop led the fight for redundancy pay and watched in horror as the bulldozers moved in to flatten the buildings. Emily and Deirdre Barlow organized a picket on the building site and pressured Maurice until he agreed to pay redundancies. Upset, Ivy wondered if she'd ever work again.

2 The End of the Road for the Tilsleys

Less than a year after remarrying, Brian and Gail Tilsley acknowledged that they were leading separate lives and that whatever love they'd shared was well and truly dead. Even so, when Gail asked for a divorce and refused to let Brian take Nicky from her he called her a selfish bitch and threatened her with a fight. That night he

went to a disco, met a girl and was stabbed to death by a gang of youths who pestered her. Ivy Brennan was devastated and tore into Gail when she refused to give him a Catholic funeral.

Nicky missed his father and became a handful for Gail. She was grateful when Martin Platt stepped in to mentor him and she turned to him for comfort when she was depressed. They spent the night together and she feared he would see her as just a sexual conquest but he declared his love, adamant that the ten-year age difference didn't mean anything. Gail was forced to break the news of her romance to Ivy, who promptly smacked Martin across the face. When Nicky went down with mumps, Martin caught it and was forced to remain a patient in Gail's house. Slowly he moved his belongings in and persuaded her not to hide their love.

3 Banger Rows

Gina Seddon left Weatherfield after her father, Eddie, died in a road accident and her mother gave both Sally and her a thousand pounds from his insurance. Following Brian Tilsley's death, Kevin considered buying the garage from Gail but couldn't raise the funds so it was sold to Tom Casey for eighteen thousand pounds. Tom made Kevin head mechanic but installed his own son, Mark, as his trainee. Kevin flexed his muscles by firing Mark for being inefficient but ended up taking him back because he missed his cheek.

Mark rekindled Kevin's interest in banger-racing, and Sally spent some of her inheritance on helping them buy a suitable car. Then she decided she wanted to race, but Kevin didn't think it a suitable pastime for a woman. She took driving lessons and passed her test, even though the police stopped her half-way through as she was driving Alf Roberts's car, lent to her by Audrey, which he'd reported stolen. Sally defied Kevin and took part in a race, which put her in hospital with a broken ankle after the car spun out of control and turned over.

4 Broken-hearted Curly

To celebrate their first anniversary of living together, Shirley Armitage threw a surprise party for Curly Watts, who threw all the guests out of the flat, saying he had to revise for an exam. This made Shirley feel she could never match him intellectually, and she decided to leave him, despite his marriage proposal. She returned to live with her family. As Curly owed eighty pounds in back rent, he was soon evicted by Alf Roberts but was taken in by the Duckworths at No.9. In the summer he passed his HND in business studies and was taken on as trainee assistant manager at Bettabuy supermarket by manager Reg Holdsworth. Vera used her position as

Curly's landlady to land a job at the supermarket but was sacked after Curly had to write an assessment on her.

After stumbling on Reg in a delicate position with the female store detective, Curly blackmailed him into keeping Vera on, but by then she had found out about the assessment and felt betrayed by her own lodger.

5 What An Eyesore!

To the horror of her neighbours, Vera Duckworth had the outside of No.9 stone-clad. She loved the effect and couldn't understand why everyone else thought it lowered the tone of the neighbourhood. Jack had trouble focusing on the house when his eyesight started to go, and was forced to wear glasses after Bet Gilroy caught him short-changing customers. He chose black-rimmed ones but almost immediately broke the frame and had to rely on a plaster to keep them together.

Worrying about his age, Jack tried to prove his desirability to women by making a play for the new barmaid, Tina Fowler. She was happy to let him spend his money on her but refused his offer of a quick fumble in the back seat of the car. To prove to Vera he was still attractive to women, Jack told her about his evening with Tina, who infuriated Vera by saying that no woman in her right mind would be attracted to Jack. Vera cut up all of Jack's trousers in an attempt to stop him roaming again.

Tina had better luck in the romance stakes when she fell for builder Eddie Ramsden. They had trouble getting their romance off the ground, though, as he was banned from the Rovers after the builders brawled with the local men. They sorted out their differences eventually by playing football, with Jack coaching the Rovers team. Tina was stunned to discover that Eddie had a little boy, Jamie, and was confused about her feelings towards him when he admitted to being estranged from Jamie's mother.

6 Rita's Nightmare

With fifteen thousand pounds in his pocket from remortgaging No.7, Alan Bradley opened premises in Curzon Street selling and installing alarm systems. He employed Dawn Prescott as receptionist and threw a grand opening party, which was ruined by the arrival of Carole Burns who warned Rita Fairclough that Alan was just after her money. Alan finished with Carole, turned his attention to Dawn and attempted to rape her. She fought him off and ran to Rita, telling her that Alan received mail addressed to Len Fairclough.

Rita did her own investigating and found out that Alan had sold her house to the building society. She confronted him, telling him she was bringing in the police, with the result that he went berserk and tried to kill her. It was only the return of Jenny, from her eighteenth birthday party, that saved Rita from suffocation. Alan went on the run from the police but was captured when Jenny tried to meet him with his passport. He was sent to Risley prison on remand and Rita slowly recovered in hospital, assuring Jenny that she wouldn't turn her back on her.

After passing her A Levels, Jenny decided to stay in Manchester and enrolled to read environmental studies at the Poly.

Rita became nervous as Alan's court case came closer. At the last minute he agreed to plead guilty to deception and actual bodily harm. He was given a two-year jail sentence but was released immediately as he had already served time in prison. Rita was horrified when he took a job on the building site opposite her house and started to terrorize her. When someone broke into the Kabin she accused Alan, who spent a night in the cells until the real culprit was caught.

Jenny started to think Rita was vindictive and decided to move out into halls of residence. Alone at No.7, Rita suffered a breakdown and disappeared. The police dug up the building site, thinking Alan had killed her and buried her there, while Mavis Wilton went through the ordeal of identifying a woman's body. Eventually Rita turned up safe in Blackpool but confused as to who she was and what year it was. Bet Gilroy tried to bring her home but Alan found out where she was, drove to Blackpool, and tried to force her into his car. She panicked and ran off, but he gave chase and was knocked down by a tram and killed instantly.

7 Performing Budgies and an Old Vent Act

When Alec Gilroy announced that the Rovers would be getting a new barman, Bet anticipated a fit young man in tight trousers. What she got was a retired ventriloquist called Charlie Bracewell, who outraged Betty Turpin by groping her backside. Bet found Charlie odious, too, and quickly hatched a plot to get rid of him, which involved allowing Stella Rigby to 'poach' him.

Alec was horrified when the tax man caught up with him for not declaring all his earnings from his artists agency, and was forced to write out a cheque for eight thousand pounds. To recoup, he took a job running a Middle Eastern tour and alarmed Bet by introducing her to Megan Morgan, an exotic dancer with a troupe of performing budgies.

As soon as Alec had gone away, Stella's husband, Paul, called on Bet and told her he'd promised to keep her company in Alec's absence. Bet enjoyed Paul's company and spent evenings with him at clubs and eating out. However, Alec returned home earlier than expected, and was furious to find Bet and Paul drunk together. He immediately leapt to the wrong conclusion and accused Bet of infidelity. Outraged, she refused to beg forgiveness for something that hadn't happened, and was saddened when Alec demanded a divorce. The customers were caught in the cross-fire as, first, Stella called Bet a bitch, and then Alec fired her from the pub. The final straw for Bet was when Alec moved Megan in as his housekeeper. She moved out and into the vacant Corner Shop flat.

Jack Duckworth, sensing his chance in a million to become landlord of the Rovers, reported the matter to the brewery, who sent an executive round to grill Alec. The brewery's disapproval made Alec see how foolish he was being and he apologized to Bet. The pair were reconciled and Jack's plan was thwarted.

8 Alma Makes Her Move

Alma Sedgewick divorced husband Jim and took the café as her settlement. She moved into the flat above the premises and immediately clashed with Gail Tilsley over the way things were run. She sacked Phyllis Pearce, which made Phyllis feel old and useless, and upset Gail so much that she walked out. Then Alma decided she needed Gail's help so sold her a 40 per cent partnership in the business. Gail took advice from Mike Baldwin in the matter, and Alma was immediately smitten by him. After discovering he was friendly with Alf and Audrey Roberts, Alma befriended Audrey and begged her to matchmake between them. Mike proved just as keen, so Alma slipped into a little black number and attempted to seduce him with oysters. The evening was spoilt when the food made her ill and she had to keep rushing to the bathroom. She had more success a week later when, after beating him at golf, she took her prize as a night with him in her bed.

When Mike decided to move to a new flat in the dockland development, Alma went along with him. The estate agent turned out to be Dawn Prescott and he decided she was a more interesting proposition than Alma. After dumping Alma, he bought the flat and asked Dawn to move in with him. Her brother, Robert, took an instant dislike to Mike and taunted him with details of a land deal in which he was interested in Alcazar in Spain. To prove he was the better businessman, Mike flew out to Spain and spent a hundred thousand pounds in buying the land for himself. On returning to England he smugly offered to sell the land to Robert for a hundred and fifty thousand pounds only for Robert to reveal that the land had been his in the first place and that it was worthless. Mortified, Mike threw Dawn out and reached for the bottle. When Alma saw him coming out of a club drunk, she took his car keys from him and sent him home in a taxi. Her gesture made Mike realize just what he'd thrown away.

9 Derek's Injured Pride

Eager to move away from the squalor of Weatherfield, Mavis and Derek Wilton decided to buy a bungalow called the Willows. Mavis boasted about her new home before discovering they had lost it as Derek had offered considerably less than the asking price. Derek decided that by working in a shop Mavis demeaned his social and professional standing and insisted she resigned.

He threw a dinner party to impress his boss but the boss didn't turn up and sent accountant Arthur Dabner in his place. Arthur enjoyed his evening chatting to Emily Bishop and started to pay court to her, upsetting her lodger Percy Sugden, who discovered Arthur was still seeing his estranged wife. Not wanting to be accused of interfering, Percy kept quiet but was pleased when Arthur told Emily they would have to stop seeing each other as he and his wife were going to be reconciled.

Soon afterwards Derek failed a company medical and was told that he couldn't handle stress. He was moved from Sales to Despatch, and when he threatened to resign he was told that would be an acceptable move for him to make. For a while he pretended that he was still working but when he was found out he felt a failure and suffered a breakdown. Mavis was forced to carry on working to support them both while Derek took a job selling novelties to toy shops. During Chuckles Novelties' Christmas party he was dressed as Father Christmas and accidentally locked into the warehouse. He managed to escape by climbing on to the roof, where he was spotted by a drunken Jack Duckworth, who convinced himself he'd seen the real Father Christmas. It wasn't until Christmas morning that Derek found a letter stuffed in his pocket telling him that he had been sacked.

10 The McDonalds Arrive

Audrey Roberts had set her heart on living in an expensive dockland flat so to prove that they could never sell No.11 Alf put it on the market. By the end of the first week an offer had been made by Jim McDonald, an ex-army sergeant. Audrey insisted on the sale going ahead but compromised with Alf and agreed that their new home should be a modest semi-detached on leafy Hillside Crescent. Moving day was a nightmare as the Robertses arrived at their new house to find the chain had broken and the vendors were staying put. As the McDonald family had already moved into No.11 Alf and Audrey were forced to move into the flat over their shop.

Liz McDonald was thrilled with the new house, having lived in army quarters all her married life. Her twin sons, Andy and Steve, were not so impressed by the neighbourhood and wound Alf up by kicking a football through the shop window.

11 Ken Loses His Footing

Ken Barlow found himself accused of informing to the police after finding Jason Stubbs drunk on lager. His mother Sandra was forced to give up cleaning the Rovers and flew at Ken when the authorities told her Jason needed constant supervision. The Stubbses left the area, and Ken busied himself with annoying Deirdre by quizzing her over council policy then printing articles in the *Recorder*. When he alerted readers to the council's plan to open a hostel for homeless youths in a community centre Deirdre was ticked off by her bosses, who assumed that he had learnt the details from her. She assured them she hadn't said anything, but they didn't believe her until Ken started to print details of meetings she had not attended. Ken admitted to Deirdre that the chief executive's secretary, Wendy Crozier, was the mole so Deirdre took the news to her boss and Wendy was sacked. Ken was furious with Deirdre and hit back by taking Wendy on to work at the *Recorder* as his secretary. The pair grew closer as Ken and Deirdre drifted apart and on his fiftieth birthday became lovers. For three months they managed to keep the affair a secret, although Wendy grew tired of just being his mistress. On Christmas Eve Deirdre confronted Ken with her suspicions and he broke down, admitting the affair and saying he didn't know what to do. On New Year's Eve Deirdre took action, and as the decade ended she threw Ken out into the street.

CAST

Charlie Bracewell	Peter Bayliss
Megan Morgan	Sue Roderick
Dawn Prescott	Louise Harrison
Arthur Dabner	Michael Sheard
Tom Casey	Edward Clayton
Mark Casey	Stuart Wolfenden
Tina Fowler	Michelle Holmes
Paul Rigby	James Tomlinson
Wendy Crozier	Roberta Kerr
Maurice Jones	Alan Moore
Reg Holdsworth	Ken Morley
Eddie Ramsden	William Ivory
Jamie Ramsden	Alexander Graham
Robert Prescott	James Gaddas
Liz McDonald	Beverley Callard
Jim McDonald	Charles Lawson
Steve McDonald	Simon Gregson
Andy McDonald	Nicholas Cochrane

1990

Behind the Scenes

Yuppies came to the Street in the shape of Des and Steph Barnes, played by Philip Middlemiss and Amelia Bullmore. They had a nerve-racking first week: their arrival scene in the Street was recorded in front of Prime Minister Margaret Thatcher, who was visiting the set. She was particularly taken with the Corner Shop which had the name 'Alf Roberts' emblazoned over it – that had been her father's name. To mark the move to three episodes a week, *Coronation Street* was presented with its own permanent home: a sound stage adjoining Granada's studios called Stage One. For the first time the actors were given their own dressing rooms, laid out on three floors, No.1 was Bill Roache's, and No.30 was Philip Middlemiss's. The interior sets were moved into the studio, with the Rovers, café and shops erected permanently and the houses put up as and when required. For thirty years the cast had rehearsed in large rooms with tape on the floors marking out their homes, now they could rehearse in their sets with the real props. Makeup and costume areas were set up, along with a relaxing Green Room. To mark the thirtieth anniversary a spectacular light entertainment show was produced, presented by Cilla Black, floor managed by David Hanson and produced by Jane Macnaught. Little did David and Jane know that before the decade was out they would both produce *Coronation Street*.

Top Twenty

Pos	Character	No of eps	Total	Pos Prev Year
1	Alec Gilroy	126	364	22
2	Deirdre Barlow	119	1189	20
3	Bet Gilroy	119	1572	8
4	Sally Webster	116	404	4
5	Ivy Brennan	109	955	9
6	Alma Sedgewick	108	180	24
7	Mike Baldwin	106	940	18
8	Audrey Roberts	104	450	1
9	Mavis Wilton	104	1144	14
10	Kevin Webster	103	506	13
11	Rita Fairclough	102	1322	6
12	Betty Turpin	101	1539	9
13	Jack Duckworth	101	629	1
14	Ken Barlow	99	2047	21
15	Liz McDonald	99	107	40
16	Don Brennan	96	203	25
17	Alf Roberts	95	1356	5
18	Percy Sugden	94	492	19
19	Martin Platt	88	323	9
20	Emily Bishop	86	1804	16

> "Alma's sort don't like work, they like to find a man who'll do it all for her."
>
> **Audrey Roberts**

STORIES

1 Deirdre's Second Divorce

Deirdre Barlow started the year by filing for divorce, while Ken moved in with his mistress, Wendy Crozier, and was forced to sell the *Recorder* to the *Weatherfield Gazette* in order to give Deirdre No.1 as settlement. Tracy was devastated by the break-up of her family and upset Deirdre by enjoying Wendy's company.

Ken and Wendy's relationship was shaken when he resigned from the *Gazette*. He left because his ideas were being blocked but she was given his job.

While Tracy was cooking chips, she started a fire in the pan and had to be rescued from the house by passing electrician Dave Barton. The kitchen was gutted, and while Ken shouted at Deirdre for leaving Tracy at home alone, Dave offered to fit a new kitchen. Soon Dave and Deirdre were lovers and Ken felt his world was falling apart. He sold his car to Curly Watts knowing that it had serious problems. When it broke down and Curly realized the truth, the residents came down heavily on his side and a frustrated Ken ended up fighting in the Rovers with Mike Baldwin.

Ken left Wendy and begged Deirdre to take him back but she refused. He started to stalk her, taking a teaching job at the comprehensive to be near Tracy and moving into the Corner Shop flat. Deirdre became obsessed with Ken's presence and ended up driving Dave away.

Then Tracy started to play truant from school and was caught hanging around amusement arcades. Deirdre decided to use her council weight to close the arcades down but owner Phil Jennings kept her sweet by promising to ban all under-sixteens. Deirdre fell for Phil and they embarked on an affair, upsetting Ken yet again. He discovered that Phil's real name was Smith and tried to expose him as a crook, but Deirdre thought it admirable that after a stint in prison Phil had changed his name to start afresh. After Ken burst into the house hoping to find Phil in her bed, Deirdre took out a court injunction against him. However, Phil took matters into his own hands and threatened to break Ken's legs if he didn't stop pestering her. While Deirdre and Phil spent New Year in Paris, distraught Ken turned to alcohol and pills in a suicide attempt.

y Dates 1990

ebruary 14	Des Barnes's first appearance
August 14	Peter Ingram dies
ecember 24	Rosie Webster is born
ecember 25	David Platt is born

2 The Gilroys' Stand

Alec Gilroy grew nostalgic for the past and sought out his estranged daughter, Sandra Arden. She was living in affluent Cheshire and had married a wealthy solicitor. She was horrified at his attempted reconciliation, seeing him as a grasping, vulgar man, and it took Bet to convince her that his heart was in the right place. Sandra's daughter, Vicky, liked her grandfather, who upset Bet by altering his will to leave her two thousand pounds.

The Gilroys, however, were united in battle when brewery executive Nigel Ridley announced plans to transform the Rovers into a theme pub called Yankees and replace them with a manager. Deirdre Barlow agreed to sell No.1 to the brewery for an inflated price and found herself ostracized when the residents joined the Gilroys in their battle to save the pub. The Gilroys barricaded themselves in the Rovers, so Nigel called in the bailiffs but at the eleventh hour Cecil Newton turned up to declare that the Rovers had to remain a working-man's pub.

3 Full House at No.7

After reconciling with Jenny Bradley, Rita Fairclough vacated No.7 in her favour. She closed the Kabin on Rosamund Street, opened new premises in one of the new units, at No.10, then moved into the flat above. Jenny turned the house into student digs along with her friend Flick Khan. For a few nights they were joined by homeless Rod Whitworth until Mark Casey, hoping to impress Flick, forcibly evicted him. Flick tried to dodge Mark's attention but he presented her with a gold chain. This turned out to have been left by a customer in a car, and Mark was ordered to return it. He had to buy it back for thirty-five pounds from the charity shop to which Flick had donated it.

Flick's younger sister Joanne caused a stir when both Andy and Steve McDonald fell for her. The twins fought for her affection and finally Steve won. When his parents tried to put a stop to them seeing each other Steve stole his father's motorbike and the youngsters ran away to the Lakes together. The romance was short-lived, and after she was forced to take a badly paid job in a hotel, Joanne returned home. Liz McDonald fetched Steve home and threatened to leave Jim if he laid a finger on him.

When Flick gave up her course to live in France, her place was taken by fashion student Angie Freeman. Jenny was expelled from her course for not working, and turned into a gold-digger. She threw herself at Mark after he was given the garage for his twenty-first birthday.

4 A Modern Marriage

Newlyweds Des and Steph Barnes moved into No.6, having bought the house at cost from her father, Maurice Jones. They enjoyed pranks, and Steph decided to have fun with Kevin Webster. At their

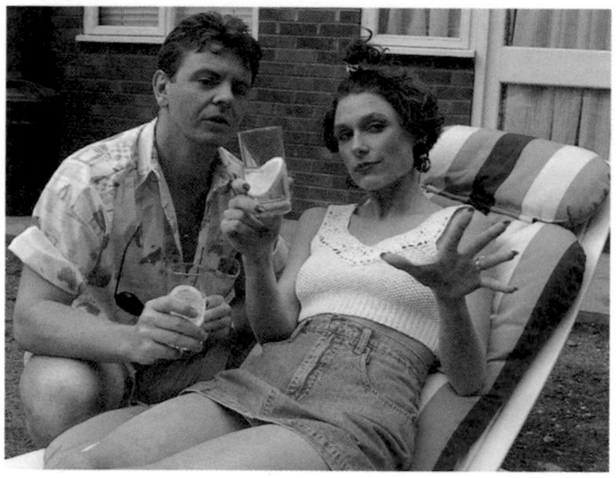

housewarming she got him drunk and shaved off his moustache, winning a bet she had made with Des so that he was forced to drink in the Rovers without his trousers.

Sally Webster was upset at how her husband had been taken in by Steph and, in revenge, pretended that Des had been chatting her up. This led to Steph throwing Des out.

The Websters weren't the only neighbours to fall out with the Barneses. Jack Duckworth grew convinced that bookie's clerk Des was giving him tips on horses. When he lost money he blamed Des and Vera threw a piece of stone-cladding at his window. Her aim was bad and instead she smashed one of the Wiltons' windows. In revenge Steph hired a policeman strip-o-gram to confront Vera at her own wedding anniversary party. Then she joined forces with Jenny Bradley and took an evening job advertising Pomme de Lite, non-alcoholic cider, in a skimpy costume. Des was not amused.

5 Middle-management Frolics

After he had been thrown out by his wife, Reg Holdsworth took to sleeping in the stock-room at Bettabuy. In an attempt to put his house in order, he transferred his store-detective lover to Bolton and moved into the flat over the Corner Shop. His landlord, Alf Roberts, became incensed when Reg put on a free bus to drive shoppers to the supermarket as it was scheduled to stop on Coronation Street outside Alf's shop. In revenge, Alf evicted Reg, who returned home to his wife.

Reg's assistant, Curly Watts, became frustrated when his girlfriend Kimberley Taylor refused to sleep with him until she was married. Her mother Brenda took an instant dislike to Curly but was pleased to announce their engagement when Curly assured her that his intentions were honourable. Stuck in an engagement he didn't want, Curly became anxious to free himself from Kimberley's clutches.

6 Mike Goes On the Prowl

Alma Sedgewick's friends thought she was mad to move in with Mike Baldwin, who was now keen to start up again in business. He took a job for Peter Ingram making up travel bags for one of his customers. With no premises or workers, Mike began sewing the bags himself in his flat, then employed outworkers from his former staff. Ivy Brennan refused to work for him and

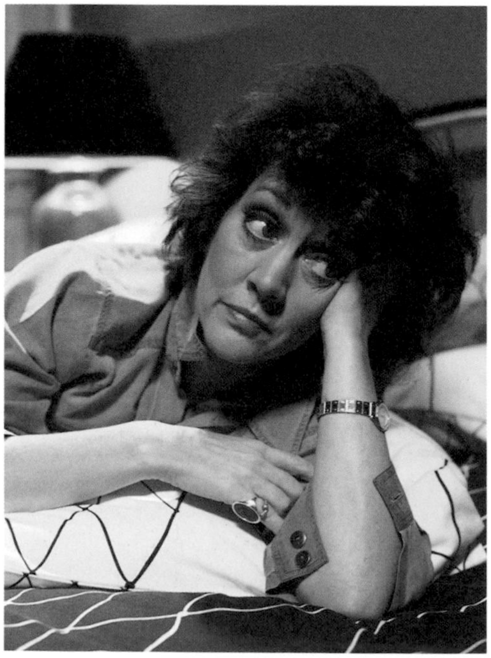

formed a co-operative to undercut him and steal the order. Mike hit back by going direct to the customers and undercutting Peter. He employed machinists and installed them in Alma's old flat above the café.

The noise and dust bothered Gail Tilsley, who had the sweatshop closed down by reporting Mike to Environmental Health. Mike was forced to admit defeat and was employed by Peter as a sales representative. He couldn't cope with the lowly post and, ignoring his contract by which he had promised not to poach customers, formed Phoenix Fabrics in opposition. Peter found out about this and demoted Mike to the shop floor. However, while he was ranting at Mike, Peter suffered a heart-attack and died.

At his funeral, Mike moved swiftly to convince his widow Jackie not to sell the factory. Then he got a friend to pose as a potential buyer and put in a ridiculously low offer for the business. The bid convinced Jackie that Mike was right in telling her not to sell and she made him general manager. Determined to secure his power base, Mike moved Jackie into his bed and split with Alma who, brokenhearted, returned to her flat.

7 The Return of the Saddleworth Sage

Unemployed Derek Wilton was mortified when Mavis begged her old beau Victor Pendlebury to employ him. However, he was desperate enough to take the job and joined Victor at his recycling plant, Pendlebury's Paper Products. He soon realized that Victor saw employing him as a way of getting close to Mavis, and he was furious at being sent on wild-goose chases while Victor wined and dined Mavis. One day, when he returned home unexpectedly, Derek caught Mavis flat on her back with Victor massaging her feet. He called her a Jezebel and demanded a divorce, until he grasped that she wasn't aware of her own

sexuality. Victor admitted he was obsessed with Mavis but retired defeated.

The Wiltons splashed out on a new house, buying No.4, but celebrations were cut short when their budgie Harriet died of shock after the move. She was buried in the back garden and a rosebush was planted over her. Shortly afterwards another budgie flew into the house and Mavis decided it was the spirit of Harriet. She loved it so much that Derek tracked down its owner and gave them a replacement bird.

Derek was delighted when Victor announced that he had married and showed off his new wife, Yvonne, who he said was identical to Mavis. Mavis found Yvonne timid and annoying and decided she was nothing like herself.

When Alec Gilroy was stuck with a holiday he couldn't take, Derek bought it from him. At the airport the Wiltons discovered that the tour operator had gone bust and they were stranded for two nights. On returning home they found that their house had been burgled. Distraught, Mavis refused to stay there and fled to Rita Fairclough's flat. Then Derek caught a burglar in the act of robbing No.6 and eventually talked Mavis into returning home.

Alec claimed on his credit-card insurance and was forced to repay the Wiltons.

8 Baby Boom

Sally Webster and Gail Tilsley both discovered they were pregnant, but while Sally celebrated, Gail wept. She didn't want the baby and feared heaping too much responsibility on to Martin Platt's young shoulders. She planned a secret abortion but Kevin Webster told Martin, who followed her to the clinic to plead with her not to kill his child. Gail returned home

with the pregnancy intact.

After Gail had a fall at work, Martin gave up his job as a hospital porter to help run Jim's Café. Kevin also resigned his job when his assistant Mark Casey was given the garage where they both worked. He resented having to work under Mark but Sally convinced him to swallow his pride as they needed the money.

When Sally went into labour on Christmas Eve Kevin was out at a breakdown so Don Brennan had to drive her to hospital in his taxi. The baby arrived before the taxi reached the hospital and was named Rosie because she was born on

Rosamund Street. The next day, during Christmas dinner, Gail went into labour and ended up in the bed next to Sally nursing her son, David.

9 The Wild Ones

Jim McDonald yearned to return to the Army and applied for a job as a recruitment officer but then turned the post down, fearing Liz would leave him because she hated the army so much. Instead he took a job as a television-repair man but lost it after dropping Alf Roberts's set when he grew annoyed with Audrey's flirting.

When Andy announced his intention to join the army Liz was horrified, but Jim readily agreed to sign the consent papers. It was only after Liz pleaded with her son that Andy agreed to drop the idea. She took a job behind the bar of the Rovers and Jim used his army pension to rent premises under the viaduct where he opened a motorbike repair shop. Jack Duckworth sold him a 1957 bike but mourned it so much that Jim allowed him to take Vera for a spin on it. When the police stopped them, doing 40 m.p.h. the wrong way down a one-way street with no tax or insurance, Jack and Jim feared prosecution but the matter was dropped when the policeman agreed to buy the bike.

To rejuvenate their marriage, Vera dragged Jack on a second honeymoon to Pwlhelli but the couple returned home separately after a row about her dalliance with entertainer Lester Fontayne. Jack was jealous that she'd spent so much time with him but Vera promised that nothing untoward had happened. As a Christmas present, Jack bought her an Alsatian called Boomer which ate the turkey and kept them prisoner in their bedroom all day. He discovered that the dog was called Boomer because, like a boomerang, it was always being returned to its shady previous owner.

10 Percy's Slip-up

When Phyllis Pearce won a trip for two to Holland she rushed to tell Percy during his school-crossing job. Her shopping bag split and he slipped on some apples, breaking his ankle. He was stuck in a wheelchair for a few weeks and raged against shops that weren't wheelchair-friendly. Then he complained at the Rovers, only to be barred by Alec Gilroy until public support came down in his favour. When it came to light that he'd lied about his age to become a lollipop man the council sacked him.

11 A Taxi-driver, a Brickie and a Barmaid

While he was in a betting shop, Don Brennan's taxi was stolen by joy-riders and involved in a hit-and-run. The police questioned Don, suspecting he was involved with the accident, but when Don saw one of the thieves he grew incensed and gave chase. When he caught up with the lad he was hitting him when the police arrived. They charged him with assault. In court he was fined fifty pounds.

His wife Ivy was taken on as supervisor at Ingram's and suffered a personality crisis after becoming involved with the Spiritualist church and believing herself to have a 'gift'. Don was relieved when she gave it up and confessed all to her priest.

Meanwhile, Rovers barmaid Tina Fowler went on a football trip to France with boyfriend Eddie Ramsden. She returned alone after he had been arrested for hooliganism. Marie Lancaster, the mother of his son Jamie, decided she wanted her baby back, saying she was over her post-natal depression, but Eddie refused to hand the child over and proposed to Tina in a bid to provide a secure home for him. Tina looked forward to her wedding but was jilted during her hen party when Eddie admitted to having secretly married Marie. Tina went on to be made the brewery's barmaid of the month and had an affair with Nigel Ridley. When she caught him with another woman and threw wine over him he had her sacked from the Rovers.

Don was sad to find Marie and Jamie

CAST

Vicky Arden	Helen Warburton
Sandra Arden	Kathy Jamieson
Peter Ingram	Tony Osoba
Des Barnes	Philip Middlemiss
Steph Barnes	Amelia Bullmore
Flick Khan	Rita Wolf
Marie L Ramsden	Joy Blakeman
Nigel Ridley	John Basham
Dave Barton	David Beckett
Rodney Whitworth	Peter Temple
Kimberley Taylor	Suzanne Hall
Brenda Taylor	Marlene Sidaway
Joanne Khan	Tania Rodregies
Jackie Ingram	Shirin Taylor
Angie Freeman	Deborah McAndrew
Phil Jennings	Tommy Boyle
Yvonne Pendlebury	Mary Healy
Rosie Webster	Emma Collinge
David Platt	Thomas Ormson

1991

Behind the Scenes

Mervyn Watson left Granada to work in the BBC's drama department and was replaced by the first female producer in twenty years, Carolyn Reynolds, who had produced an Anglo-Australian soap, *Families*, for Granada. Stories this year dealt with issues with which the Street was familiar – Liz McDonald's late pregnancy, Steve and Vicky's teenage romance, Mike Baldwin caught between two women and Ivy Brennan's objection to the adoption of her grandchildren.

Newcomer Sarah Lancashire arrived to play Raquel Wolstenhulme for a month and was so popular with the writers and viewers that she was brought back at the end of the year and given a long-term contract. Sarah's father Geoffrey had been a writer on the show in the 1960s and she had grown up surrounded by the Street and understood the importance of the actor–writer relationship.

Key Dates 1991

January 25	Raquel Wolstenhulme's first appearance
February 18	Amy Burton dies
July 19	Sandra and Tim Arden die
September 27	Gail and Martin Platt marry

> "If my wife put her mind to it, she could find reasons why Mary and Joseph were unfit parents."
>
> **Don Brennan**

Top Twenty

Pos	Character	No of eps	Total	Pos Prev Year
1	Audrey Roberts	108	558	8
2	Bet Gilroy	103	1675	2
3	Liz McDonald	102	209	14
4	Gail Tilsley Platt	100	1090	23
5	Vera Duckworth	99	877	28
6	Don Brennan	98	301	16
7	Mavis Wilton	96	1240	8
8	Ivy Brennan	96	1051	5
9	Des Barnes	96	159	29
10	Deirdre Barlow	95	1284	2
11	Jack Duckworth	93	722	12
12	Curly Watts	91	539	27
13	Jim McDonald	91	178	24
14	Rita Fairclough	89	1411	11
15	Ken Barlow	86	2133	14
16	Percy Sugden	86	578	18
17	Martin Platt	86	409	19
18	Alec Gilroy	82	446	1
19	Alma Sedgewick	79	259	6
20	Reg Holdsworth	76	111	40

STORIES

1 Another Bad Year for Deirdre

Ken Barlow continued to swallow tablets as the residents saw in New Year but was eventually stopped from killing himself by the timely arrival of Bet Gilroy. He was forced to admit to himself that he had lost Deirdre for good, and agreed to stop hounding her.

Meanwhile, Deirdre's boyfriend Phil Jennings made himself at home in the Street. He opened an arcade machine repair shop in one of the new units and considered opening a nightclub in the old Graffiti with the Gilroys, before announcing Alec was too 'small-fry' to interest him.

Furious, Alec decided to sell the Rovers to raise the capital needed to buy into the club venture, but Bet refused to let him. To get back at Phil, Alec persuaded Alf Roberts to stand in the local elections against Deirdre. She looked forward to a good clean fight, but Phil embarked on a smear campaign against Alf, spreading rumours that he was having an affair with one of his supporters, Vivian Barford. When Alf tore down a 'Vote Deirdre' poster Ken had stuck in his flat window, the two men had a scrap in the Rovers and a photograph of the clash appeared on the front page of the *Gazette*. In the election

Deirdre lost her seat to Alf, and Audrey Roberts ended up attacking Vivian with her handbag during his acceptance speech.

After trying telesales Deirdre took a job fronting PJ Leisure for Phil and soon discovered he had cash flow problems. To raise money Phil started card schools but refused to pay his debts, and was beaten up by a heavy. Deirdre was devastated when she learnt that he and his wife were fleeing the country – she had had no idea that she had been just one of his mistresses. Dejected, she took back her old job, serving at the Corner Shop.

2 Des Takes to the High Seas

Des Barnes bought an old boat for five hundred pounds and irritated Steph and the neighbours by renovating it in the back garden. Steph was also annoyed to be treated as a housewife: she felt that as they both worked they should split the housework. When Des refused she smashed every plate in the house. In a bid to make peace, Des took on Phyllis Pearce as cleaner, and was angry when Steph went on a skiing holiday without him, even though she had fallen off the boat and broken her leg. On her return Des discovered lines written in Italian on her plaster cast that translated as 'Rome was not built in a day but Steph was laid flat in two nights. None shall sleep.' Steph swore she had not been unfaithful, but Des wouldn't believe her and spent more and more time on the boat. Feeling neglected, Steph was flattered when architect Simon Beatty pestered her, and she embarked on an affair with him. While Des was putting in the engine, his boat rocked and crashed into the Wiltons' back garden. Derek took possession of it until Des agreed to pay for a new fence. Soon afterwards the boat was

launched, and during its maiden voyage Steph confessed her affair and packed her bags. Des frightened her by pouring petrol over the boat and blowing it up, allowing her to think that he was in it. She moved in with Simon anyway, and Des was charged with polluting the waterways. His solicitor Lynette Campion got him off with a conditional discharge then took him to bed before presenting him with a huge bill for her services.

Another woman leaving the Street for a professional man was Jenny Bradley, who dumped Mark Casey to become the kept woman of a married dentist, Robert Weston.

3 Sexploitation at Bettabuy

Rita Fairclough started to go tea dancing and found herself teamed with Reg Holdsworth. He showed a romantic interest in her but she was at pains to make him understand that sex wasn't on offer. Nevertheless he rigged a trolley dash contest so that Rita won. She was embarrassed and gave all the food she collected to the hospital, but Vera Duckworth spread rumours of a liaison between the pair.

Brendan Scott, from head office, was sent to investigate, keen to see his old rival Reg dragged through the mud.

He suspected a massive fraud when he discovered that Vera was Curly Watts's landlady and was frustrated when Vera, as a favour to Curly, withdrew her allegation about Reg. When the talk reached Veronica Holdsworth's ears, she started divorce proceedings and accused Rita of being Reg's lover. Reg moved himself and his water-bed into No.12, next door to Rita's flat, and was on hand to help her out when the shop was burgled.

Meanwhile, Kimberley Taylor had come to resent Curly's dislike of her mother Brenda and broke off their engagement. Once he was a free man again, Curly decided he wanted Kimberley after all, but she would have nothing to do with him and started dating her cousin Adrian Gosthorpe. Sales assistant Raquel Wolstenhulme decided to pursue Curly, thinking he might further her career, but he was obsessed with Kimberley and Adrian, especially after Adrian told him that he and Kimberley had had sex. Curly attacked him at the building society where he worked and was arrested and thrown into a cell. Kimberley was transferred to Bolton, and Curly moved into No.7, sharing with Angie Freeman. He turned his attentions to Raquel and supported her in her bid for the Miss Bettabuy North West title. However, Brendan was on the judging panel and voted against her. Nevertheless Raquel achieved a life-time ambition by modelling Angie's designs at her end-of-year degree show, and she was spotted by a photographer, who lured her away from Bettabuy for a career in 'artistic' poses.

Upset, Curly got drunk with Angie and the pair spent the night together. Afterwards Angie was ashamed of herself and told him it could never happen again. However, she agreed to design the Bettabuy float for the Weatherfield carnival, based on the Horn of Plenty, with Reg as Bacchus. Reg refused to pay Angie's bill so Curly stole from petty cash to refund her, and sparked off another Brendan investigation which resulted in him being denied promotion to his own store.

Curly was stunned to discover that the blind date Angie arranged for him was with none other than Raquel, back from a disastrous modelling career and homeless.

4 A Strange Inheritance

Vera Duckworth was distressed when her mother Amy died. At the funeral she met Joss Shackleton, who Amy had asked her to look after. Joss explained that he was Vera's real father. Jack thought he was just a chancer but Vera willed herself to believe he was her father and moved him into the back bedroom at No.9. Joss, a retired barber, was quick to let Vera into the family secret – that he was an illegitimate grandson of King Edward VII, making Vera a cousin to the Queen. Jack thought this hysterical, and as an April Fool joke, sent Vera a card from the Queen, which she took as the proof she needed.

After Joss had been reminiscing about his time in service, Jack decided to better himself and applied for a chauffeuring job, which was advertised with a housekeeper's job for Vera. The Duckworths went along for an interview with references forged by Joss and were offered the jobs. However,

when the stately home was burgled suspicion fell on them and they had to come clean.

Jack tried another scam in the summer: when the house was flooded after a water cut-off in the Street, he stripped the hall wallpaper and tried to claim on the insurance for that as well as for the lounge, but the assessor saw through him and refused to pay out any money. During the flood Joss returned to his own flat.

5 Orphaned Vicky

Alec Gilroy was stunned when, first, his ex-wife Joyce died, and then his daughter Sandra Arden was killed in a car crash with her husband on the way to the funeral. It was left to Alec and Bet to break the news

to orphaned Vicky on her return from boarding school. Vicky couldn't contemplate the idea of living at the Rovers and fought hard to stay with friends until Alec pointed out that nobody wanted her. He carried on paying for her exclusive schooling and, to raise funds, took a job MCing on a cruise. Annoyed at being abandoned again, Bet hired old flame Des Foster to decorate her bedroom. He thought she desired him and made a pass, then hit her when she rejected him.

6 Ivy Goes Too Far

When Gail Tilsley returned to working at the café, her boyfriend Martin Platt took over the care of their son David and Rosie Webster. After Nicky Tilsley hit David over the head with a cricket bat, the hospital viewed Martin with suspicion as David didn't have his surname. He asked Gail to marry him but she refused, thinking he was too young to be tied down. However, when she saw he was upset, she went down on one knee herself, and the couple were married with Kevin Webster and Alma Sedgewick as witnesses.

Ivy Brennan was enraged by the wedding and vowed to oppose Martin's plan to adopt Nicky and Sarah Louise. She altered her will to leave her house to Nicky on condition that his surname was Tilsley and she installed him as an altar-boy at St Luke's – the condition she imposed after getting him a place on the football team. Martin turned on Ivy and dragged Nicky off the football pitch. Ivy told Social Services that Gail was an unfit mother, but the adoption went through.

Don was appalled by Ivy's behaviour and forced her to apologize to Gail. Then, he befriended Julie Dewhurst, a barmaid at the Kit Kat Klub, and after a day at the races the pair became lovers. He told Ivy she had become old and hard and that he had decided to leave her, but she begged him to give her a second chance: they could move away to make a new start. Don dropped Julie and the Platts decided that, with Ivy leaving, they should buy No.8 from Maurice Jones, the builder, whose price had been reduced to £38,000 for a quick sale. After they had moved in Ivy dropped a bombshell: she was staying at No.5 after all.

7 The Shortest Street Marriage

In an act of revenge, Alma Sedgewick looked around Jackie Ingram's house, which was for sale, and slashed up her duvet. Undeterred, Jackie proposed to Mike and, after persuading her not to draw up a premarital agreement, he accepted. Meanwhile Alma suffered hardship when the landlord raised the rent on the café. She feared having to close down so Gail Tilsley begged Mike to help. He used some of Jackie's money to form Alcazar Holdings and bought the lease, thereby becoming Alma's landlord without her knowledge.

Mike and Jackie married but the day was ruined by Mike's horrified reaction to the news that Jackie intended to sell the business so that they could retire and spend time together. Best man Phil Jennings, annoyed that Mike had refused to loan him money, told Jackie all about Mike's past marriages and that he'd tricked her into keeping the factory. Jackie flew into a rage and threatened Mike with a loaded shotgun before walking out of their week-long marriage. Her lawyers were quick to pay him off with a hundred thousand pounds and the divorce papers were drawn up.

Alma, meanwhile, started a relationship with Ken Barlow after his friendship had restored some of her self-respect. Mike was furious to see them together and tried to annoy Ken by taking Deirdre out, but she saw what he was up to and refused to be manipulated. Instead, Mike took a flat in Weatherfield Quays and started hanging around the café, eventually revealing himself as Alma's landlord. He manipulated Tracy Barlow into getting Ken to spend Christmas at No.1, and manoeuvred lonely Alma into bed. Afterwards she confessed all to Ken, who promptly dumped her.

8 Parsnips

Mavis Wilton was delighted to find a fox in her garden and immediately christened him Freddie. Jack Duckworth wasn't so delighted when it killed two of his pigeons and set out on a fox hunt around the Street. Mavis sent Derek off to draw the scent of the hounds and assaulted Jack with her frying pan when he attempted to enter her garden.

A few months later, worried that the passion was ebbing out of her marriage, Mavis tried an aphrodisiac on Derek in the form of parsnips. She was pleased with the results but was alarmed when Derek, on impulse, slapped the office cleaner Mrs Shaw's backside. When Victor decided to

make Mrs Shaw redundant because of cutbacks she accused the company of sexual harassment and threatened Derek with a tribunal. She agreed to drop the case when Mavis explained about the parsnips.

9 The Roberts' Marriage Under Strain

After being sacked from Ingram's for spreading gossip, Ivy Brennan was taken on by Alf Roberts to work at the Corner Shop. Audrey Roberts disliked having her there and allowed her to take the blame for a turned-off freezer even though she knew her stepdaughter Sarah Louise was the real culprit. When Alf refused to sack Ivy, Audrey walked out and moved into a five-star hotel. Alf refused to put up with her nonsense and cancelled her credit cards, which forced Audrey to move in with Alma Sedgewick.

After she spotted Alf chatting in his dressing-gown to Vivian Barford, Audrey decided to move to Canada to live with Malcolm Reid, only to find out that he was about to be married. She felt no one wanted her and had a breakdown. Ivy was tired of the situation and resigned to take a job at Bettabuy, but was on hand luckily when Alf collapsed of nervous exhaustion on the shop floor. Audrey rushed to his side and the pair were reconciled.

10 Dirty Tricks at No.3

Emily Bishop busied herself by opening a charity shop in the unit at No.2 to raise money for the Friends of Weatherfield Hospital. After holidaying at Rhos-on-Sea

she decided she had had enough of living in a city and would retire to the coast. Her lodger, Percy Sugden, was shattered by the news and did all he could to put buyers off the house. When someone finally made an offer he moved into lodgings with Winnie Dyson, but Emily was startled to realize that now Percy was gone she no longer wanted to move. Then Percy was rushed to hospital: he had had an allergic reaction to her cat Fluffy. Emily was plunged into guilt, especially when Phyllis Pearce blamed her for Percy's illness. She insisted that Percy move back into No.3.

In December he put on a white beard to be Bettabuy's Father Christmas, but was sacked when he told the children not to be so greedy in what they wanted for Christmas. The end of the year also saw Emily unemployed as the charity shop lease was not renewed.

11 Money Problems for the Websters

Needing extra cash, Kevin Webster started taking on private jobs in work-time but came unstuck when he crashed an unofficial customer's car. Mark Casey refused to claim on the garage's insurance and sacked Kevin. The customer demanded compensation and his solicitor wrote threatening legal action. Sally grew terrified that Kevin would go to prison and was relieved when her mother came to the family's rescue and gave them the money

they needed to pay the compensation claim. Sally returned to working at the Corner Shop in the evenings and Kevin worked for a while at an exhaust centre before being sacked once more. Then he set up on his own outside his house but Derek Wilton thought he lowered the tone and reported him to the police.

Sally's nerves suffered as she struggled to make ends meet and the last straw came when Kevin's dole was stopped. Mike Baldwin came to the rescue this time by opening his own garage in the Street and employing Kevin as mechanic. Kevin tasted the sweetness of revenge when Mike bought all Casey's equipment after Mark went bust.

12 Parental Headaches at No.11

Jim McDonald was proud of his son Andy when he discovered he was running a book on the FA Cup. Unfortunately headmistress Sue Jeffers didn't share his feelings and had the book closed and all monies returned. After terrible exam results, Steve left school but the McDonalds pressed Andy to stay on as he was bright. Andy rebelled and took a job selling unofficial posters outside concerts until he was seen off by the official sellers. He returned to school while Steve left home and moved into No.6 where he helped Des reconstruct his boat and had developed a crush on Steph, which embarrassed her and forced her to belittle him as a play to make him forget about her.

The twins built a transmitter and started their own radio station, broadcasting Just Can't Wait from the bikeshop. Their school chums thrilled to the adventures of Captain Kenny the Android Warrior of Weatherfield until Liz forced the boys to stop broadcasting as they were offending the neighbours.

When Liz discovered she was pregnant she decided to have an abortion but allowed Jim to talk her out of it, realizing it was her last chance to have a baby. Jim started to build an extension in the backyard to accommodate the new member of the family, but the Duckworths objected to the noise and reported Jim for not having planning permission. Jim applied for permission and had to be restrained from hitting Jack when Vera started a petition against the extension.

Steve, meanwhile, became involved with a local gang and sold car stereos they stole. Unfortunately he sold Derek Wilton Alf Roberts's stereo and the police were brought in. Steve refused to shop his mates but, seeing Liz's distress, Andy gave their names to the police and was beaten up for his trouble. Steve feared that he'd be next and disappeared on New Year's Eve, running off to Cheshire with Vicky Arden.

CAST

Raquel Wolstenhulme	Sarah Lancashire
Adrian Gosthorpe	Philip Brook
Brendan Scott	Milton Johns
Julie Dewhurst	Su Elliott
Veronica Holdsworth	Patricia Maynard
Joss Shackleton	Harold Goodwin
Robert Weston	Philip Bretherton
Vivian Barford	Paula Tillbrook
Sue Jeffers	Romy Baskerville
Mrs Shaw	Jane Cox
Simon Beatty	Peter Gowen
Vicky Arden	Chloe Newsome
Winnie Dyson	June Ellis
Lynette Campion	Colette Stevenson

1992

Behind the Scenes

Carolyn Reynolds settled into her role as producer and decided to liven up the programme with a vamp. Denise Black burst on to the screen as hairdresser Denise Osbourne and was immediately called 'the new Elsie Tanner' by the press - a hard act for her to follow.

While the on-screen antics involved three weddings in a month, off-screen the major event was a comment made by Lord Rees-Mogg, chairman of the Broadcasting Standards Council, that the Street was old-fashioned. He also criticized the low representation of ethnic minorities. His remarks drew an outraged backlash from the public and the press. *The Times* said, 'Lord Rees-Mogg has said something very silly,' while the *Daily Express* said, 'The Street is a timeless place which is unconnected with the outside world. It has a style, mood and format that is unique.' Councillors were quick to quote the 1991 census, which stated that Salford, the region closest to Weatherfield, was 97.8 white. Writing in *The Times*, Patrick Stoddart summed up the general mood: '*EastEnders* does, for sure, feature blacks and Asians, but it is difficult to believe that the producers are not working from a checklist of ethnic types and issues which have to be shoehorned into the plot at regular intervals in order to keep the soap opera socially credible. That it is, but at the cost of the pace and humour of which *Coronation Street* has always been properly proud. The millions who watch *Coronation Street* - and who will continue to do so despite Lord Rees-Mogg - know real life when they see it even if it is heightened and sometimes lightened in the most confident and accomplished soap opera television has ever seen.'

> "Mike Baldwin is like a vampire, draining the life out of people, destroying lives."
>
> **Ken Barlow**

Key Dates 1992

January 1	Katie McDonald is born
January 2	Katie McDonald dies
May 25	Terry Duckworth marries Lisa Horton
June 5	Ted Sullivan marries Rita Fairclough
June 19	Mike Baldwin marries Alma Sedgewick
September 9	Tommy Duckworth is born and Ted Sullivan dies

Top Twenty

Pos	Character	No of eps	Total	Pos Prev Year
1	Gail Platt	130	1220	4
2	Raquel Wolstenhulme	127	152	37
3	Mavis Wilton	123	1363	7
4	Jack Duckworth	121	843	11
5	Vera Duckworth	115	992	5
6	Rita Fairclough Sullivan	110	1521	14
7	Derek Wilton	108	415	23
8	Curly Watts	107	646	12
9	Liz McDonald	101	310	3
10	Bet Gilroy	99	1774	2
11	Martin Platt	99	508	15
12	Alma S Baldwin	94	353	19
13	Audrey Roberts	93	651	1
14	Jim McDonald	89	267	12
15	Percy Sugden	88	666	15
16	Ken Barlow	86	2219	15
17	Steve McDonald	86	194	31
18	Angie Freeman	85	177	21
19	Ivy Brennan	81	1132	7
20	Deirdre Barlow	79	1363	10

STORIES

1 Tragedy for the McDonalds

The worry of believing that Steve had been killed by the gang brought on labour for Liz McDonald. She was rushed to hospital but her daughter Katie was born prematurely and died after just a few hours. A remorseful Steve couldn't bring himself to attend the funeral and instead turned himself in to the police, telling them all they needed to know to arrest the radio thieves. Andy embarked on his first love affair when he fell for fellow sixth-form student Paula Maxwell. Steve attempted to steal Paula from Andy but she only had eyes for his brother. Then, Steve fell out with Andy: he thought it unfair that he had to pay twenty pounds a week in rent, because he was employed at Jim's bike shop, while Andy lived free. Fed up with his complaints, Andy took a part-time job at Bettabuy.

Liz and Jim were put out to find that Andy had had sex with Paula under their roof, but he assured them that they had taken precautions. However, Paula's relationship with Andy was affecting her studies and, after a talk with Sue Jeffers, she stopped seeing him so much but was upset when he took it the wrong way and finished with her. Reconciled, they took their exams and went Interrailing together.

Business was bad for Jim and he was forced to close the bike shop. Liz sold her grandmother's ring to give the twins two hundred pounds each for their eighteenth birthday. Steve took a job at Jim's Café, Jim became a security guard, and Andy went off to university in Sheffield, to read combined studies. He was upset when Paula, thinking them too young to settle down, changed her course so that she could stay in Manchester. He was lonely without her and decided to quit his course but Jim made him change his mind by telling him that the family were proud of him and that he wasn't a failure.

2 Food Battles at the Rovers

Angie Freeman lost her job at the Rovers when she threw a pint over cheating boyfriend Des Barnes. Alec Gilroy replaced her with Des's new love, Raquel Wolstenhulme, at whom Angie flung her shoes across the bar. Bet thought Raquel was useless and tried to sack her, but Alec found her decorative and refused to employ Bet's choice, Liz McDonald, instead. When Alec said Liz was too old Jim went for him in the pub. Alec barred Jim and, in retaliation, Jim told him that he'd reported him for serving food with inadequate facilities. It was a lie that rebounded on Jim, for Alec panicked and sacked Betty Turpin. Percy Sugden felt Betty had been treated badly and complained to the Environmental Health people, who investigated the Rovers and told Alec he needed a brand new kitchen if he was going to serve food.

Custom dipped with the lack of food so Alec displayed a mouse-eating spider as an attraction, but the pub emptied of staff and customers when the spider escaped. It resurfaced during the Environmental Health inspection of the new kitchen and Alec had to squash it with his bare hands.

Betty returned to the pub but refused to serve food in the evenings, so Liz gave up her job at the Legion to become evening chef and barmaid.

3 No Escaping Scheming Mike

In desperation, Alma Sedgewick put up the café for sale, hoping to run away and escape Mike Baldwin's attentions. He responded by giving her the lease of the café and proposing marriage. She accepted the lease and decided to stay in Weatherfield, but told Mike she could never marry him as she didn't trust him. Then she received notice that Jackie Ingram was citing her as co-respondent in her divorce from Mike.

She did not know that Mike had told Jackie to name her. She was frantic, and Mike's plan worked: after telling Alma it had cost him thousands to leave her out of the divorce, she agreed happily to marry him. A day before the wedding, however, Alma learnt the truth from Jackie and told Mike that she might not marry him. Her friends were astounded when she went through with the ceremony, maintaining that Mike would never be able to lie to her again.

4 Cupid's Arrow

Curly Watts was given the task of showing management trainee Vanessa Morgan the ropes at Bettabuy. After discovering she was the chairman's daughter he gave her an easy ride. Then he found out that Reg Holdsworth had blocked his promotion and in revenge did not tell him who she was. Reg made her life hell for several weeks and then was discomfitted to discover the truth.

Now that he was a salaried employee and doing well, Curly bought No.7 and decided to chance love by joining a computer dating agency. Calling himself Gerald Murphy he arranged a meeting with Janet Shaw, who turned out to be his ex-fiancée Kimberley Taylor. Both decided that fate had brought them together again and revived their engagement. Kimberley's mother Brenda was won round to the match with the knowledge that Curly had his own house, but was appalled to find Angie Freeman's bra on the sofa when she called round. Curly refused to wait until the wedding to bed Kimberley so she gave in to his advances. Afterwards he cooled towards her and feared she'd grow into her mother. Then he splashed out on having the loft converted into an observatory and bought a telescope for two thousand pounds, which so horrified Kimberley that she broke off their engagement.

5 Mike and the Mechanics

Kevin Webster soon found out what it was like to work for Mike Baldwin when a customer offered his firm's contract in return for a thousand-pound backhander. Mike instructed Kevin to pay the money then add fifty pounds to each of the firm's jobs. Kevin felt his principles were compromised but he went ahead. When he complained about the amount of work Mike expected of him he hoped for a pay-rise, but instead Mike took on Steve McDonald to help him. However, Steve was useless and Kevin sacked him, so Mike employed Steve to run his new printing business and at last gave Kevin his rise. Kevin took on Doug Murray as a mechanic, but Doug was trailed by men searching for 'Dave Matthews'. He had to confess that he was a bankrupt on the run from his creditors.

Steve failed his driving test for speeding, but pretended he had passed it as he feared losing his job. Out in Mike's Jaguar a speeding car smashed into him. Policemen witnessed the crash and Steve had to give his name. He said he was Kevin Webster, which rattled Kevin, who had to show up at a police station with his licence to get Steve out of a hole.

6 Confused of Coronation Street

Percy Sugden grew concerned when his landlady, Emily Bishop, started to behave oddly. She became obsessed with details and seemed confused, forgetting engagements and letting herself go. Percy tried to alert her friends but they felt he was the problem and interfered too much in Emily's life. He burst into tears when she went missing in her slippers, and the neighbours were forced to accept that he had been right. Emily was found at the railway station and was admitted to hospital, having suffered a nervous breakdown. After treatment she was allowed home and thanked Percy for being a true friend.

During her illness Emily had lent Mike Baldwin ten thousand pounds for a business deal and Percy felt Mike had taken advantage of her. Ken Barlow was quick to accuse Mike of swindling Emily so Mike decided to sue him for slander, calling Emily as his key witness. She told Ken she was appalled that he would use her to get back at Mike, and he was shamefaced when Mike decided to drop the action and pay back the money.

Later in the year Percy was forced to alter his opinion of Germans when Klaus Muller tracked him down and explained that having been a POW in Percy's care during the war he had a lot to thank him for. The pair got drunk together and were so hung-over that they missed a march to celebrate the anniversary of El Alamein.

7 Rita Finds Love

Rita Fairclough became nervous after the Kabin was twice raided in the middle of the night. Reg Holdsworth attempted to use

the break-ins as an excuse to push himself into her affections but she wasn't interested. Instead she started to date retired toffee salesman Ted Sullivan. When Reg investigated Ted he discovered he'd inherited a large sum following the death of his first wife in mysterious circumstances. Rita refused to let Reg put her off, though, and went on holiday with Ted to Florida. He told her of his plans to retire there and proposed to her. She accepted, but was stunned when he told her he had a brain cancer and only months to live. Rita felt cheated of long-term happiness but insisted on going ahead with the wedding.

Afterwards Ted declined rapidly, suffering head pains, and at one point was picked up by the police who assumed he was drunk. He died just a few months after the wedding, in Rita's arms during a bowls match. At the reading of his will, Ted's sister Sarah Brookes accused Rita of marrying him for his money and threatened to contest the will by saying that Ted wasn't of sound mind when he wrote it. Rita offered to split with her the proceeds of the sale of his house but Sarah demanded everything, and instructed her solicitor accordingly.

8 Derek's Search for Employment

After drawing up a cost-cutting exercise at Pendlebury Paper Products Derek Wilton found he'd made himself redundant. Mavis begged Victor Pendlebury not to let Derek go and was dumbstruck when he announced that he was no longer infatuated with her and just wanted them out of his life. Derek felt he was washed up and useless, and feared he would never be employed again. Rita Fairclough, planning a new life in Florida, agreed to sell the Kabin and her flat to the Wiltons and Derek eagerly arranged a loan from the bank. He turned down a well-paid job selling office furniture to own the newsagent's but Rita pulled out of the deal, having decided to stay in Weatherfield after all. Furious, Mavis accused Rita of playing around with her life so Rita compensated by making her manageress and Derek her assistant while she went into semi-retirement.

Derek caused a mass walk-out by the paper-boys and -girls, who picketed the shop after he docked them money for lateness. Mavis sorted it out, and Derek decided he wasn't suited to working behind a counter. To prove his worth he took a job as assistant caretaker at Weatherfield Comprehensive but was victimized by his boss, Harold Potts. He decided to resign, but Sue Jeffers begged him to stay and compile a dossier on Potts: she knew he was a bully and wanted him sacked.

9 Des's Loves

Angie Freeman started the year as Des Barnes's girlfriend but soon lost that post to Raquel Wolstenhulme, who moved into No.6 as his lodger but never occupied the spare bed. Raquel's romantic dreams were shattered when Des's estranged wife Steph returned, having finished with her boyfriend Simon. Des made no attempt to stop Raquel leaving in a huff and she moved into the Rovers. He hoped that Steph had returned for good but she confessed to having another man and moved out again.

Raquel befriended Gordon Blinkhorn, the publicist at Weatherfield County Football Club. Through him she met star striker Wayne Farrell and became his girlfriend. Meanwhile Angie fell for builder Neil Mitchell and started going out with him. After getting a 2:2 degree she was taken on by Hanif Ruparell at Onyx Fashions. Her relationship with Neil faltered when his estranged wife, Denise Osbourne, bought No.2 and he helped her fit out her new hair-salon there.

10 Alec Calls Time

Alec Gilroy had a lot of explaining to do when Cherie Watkins, a wealthy admirer, turned up at the Rovers: he had told her he was a widower and that Bet was his mother. Bet attacked him with her handbag then saw off Cherie. Vicky was also angry with Alec: she discovered he had claimed against her estate for rent and her Christmas present. She took up the cudgels against him when he attempted to stop her friendship with Steve McDonald, which ground to a halt anyway when she refused sex.

Sunliners Cruises offered Alec a job in Southampton, as their director of entertainment, and he startled Bet by accepting the job and selling the Rovers back to the brewery. She realized that the pub meant more to her than he did and refused to leave. Brewery boss Richard Willmore agreed to let her stay on as manager, but put her on six months' probation, and she bade a sad farewell to Alec, who told her to remember that she was the one ending their marriage.

Willmore pressed Bet for higher takings so she entered the Rovers in a superquiz, with Reg Holdsworth as organizer. The event was a disaster as the teams bickered between themselves.

11 Nurse Platt

Martin Platt returned to Weatherfield General as a porter, leaving Sally Webster to look after David. After saving the life of an elderly woman with whom he was stuck in a lift, Martin was encouraged to train as a

nurse. Gail assumed he was too thick to qualify but Martin proved her wrong when he was taken on as a student.

David fell downstairs while in Sally's care and the authorities came down on her for not being a registered child-minder. To get round the law, Sally was forced to mind the children in the Platts' house and became resentful when Gail started to treat her as a servant.

Martin befriended student nurse Carmel Finnan, who started to babysit for the family and eventually moved in. Sally grew suspicious when Carmel passed off David as her own son but when she voiced concern to Gail she was told to mind her own business. Martin was stunned when, after a drunken night, he awoke to find Carmel in his bed. She confessed to being madly in love with him and told him she knew he loved her too.

12 Don's Suicide Bid

Don Brennan decided he'd had enough of being married to Ivy and tracked down ex-girlfriend Julie Dewhurst. He begged her to take him back but she wasn't interested. When Ivy asked him to renew their wedding vows, Don planned to leave home but after Julie refused to take him in, he decided to kill himself. He drove at 70 m.p.h. down a country lane and crashed his car but survived.

Ivy and Julie clashed over his hospital bed and Ivy was beside herself when Don told her he wanted nothing more to do with her. He had to have his lower right leg amputated and moved into a B&B, refusing to be nursed by Ivy. She turned to drink, which upset Gail Platt who refused to let Ivy see her grandchildren. Ivy stayed away from work and continued to drink. Eventually Don came to the rescue: he agreed to return to No.5 if she gave up drinking, although he insisted on leading his own life and moved into the back bedroom.

13 A Little Duckworth

Jack Duckworth took a moonlighting job as a pall-bearer. Vera knew nothing of this, so when she saw him driving a hearse she took it as a premonition of his death. However, he was forced to give up the job when Alec Gilroy attended a funeral and saw Jack carrying in the coffin.

When Vera hired a private detective to track down their grandchild Paul, son of Andrea Clayton, Jack had to admit that he had known for some time that the boy had been adopted. Terry heard of Vera's search and begged her to drop it, then introduced her to his pregnant girlfriend, Lisa Horton. Jack and Terry came to blows in the Rovers when Jack advised his son to get rid of Lisa while he could.

After being charged with grievous bodily harm, Terry was put on remand at Strangeways and proposed to Lisa. She accepted and moved into No.9 to be with him, then talked round her father Jeff, who was horrified at the thought of her marrying Terry. Terry married Lisa in handcuffs, which were taken off for the official photographs. Seizing his chance, Terry ran away from the guards, leaving Lisa questioning whether he had ever loved her. Later Jack incurred Vera's wrath by selling the wedding pictures to the papers for a hundred pounds.

On the run, Terry contacted Vera and arranged to meet her at Bettabuy so she could give him her savings but he was spotted by Reg Holdsworth, who called the police. Terry was sent to prison for three years.

When Lisa gave birth Vera was with her and the little boy was named Tommy. As she wanted the baby to have fresh air, Lisa took to calling on Des Barnes because he had a garden. Vera worried that their friendship was more than platonic and warned Terry, with the result that Des got a nasty beating. Appalled, Lisa refused to stay married to a thug and returned to her parents in Blackpool. Once she had gone Des realized he loved her. He tracked her down and asked her to return to live with him.

14 Baldwin's Son and Heir

Ken and Deirdre Barlow celebrated their divorce together: he was lying flat on his back in her house with a slipped disc. Tracy had hoped that if Deirdre nursed him back to health romance would follow, but nothing was further from Deirdre's mind.

Nicky Tilsley started at Weatherfield Comprehensive and befriended Mark Redman. When Ken noticed that the pair were being bullied he acted quickly to help them. Mark's mother Maggie thanked him and the couple started seeing each other. Deirdre recognized Maggie as Mike Baldwin's old flame and told Tracy that Mark was Mike's son. Then Tracy told Ken, who had to think long and hard before deciding to continue seeing Maggie.

Mike was amazed to see Mark playing with Nicky, and admitted to Alma that he had a son. She felt insecure because she thought he was bound to want to get back together with Maggie. When Mike decided to call on the Redmans, Ken opened the door and he was shocked to realize that Maggie and Ken were an item.

15 Alf's Christmas Blues

When Percy Sugden accused him of selling out-of-date Christmas puddings, Alf Roberts settled down in the Rovers and ate a whole one himself. Then he went out with Audrey to an official dinner and collapsed into his dessert. Audrey feared a heart-attack but the doctors at the hospital diagnosed an ulcer. She decided he needed to diet and bought him an exercise bike for Christmas.

CAST

Lisa Horton Duckworth	Caroline Milmoe
Paula Maxwell	Judy Brooke
Cherie Watkins	Christina Greatrex
Ted Sullivan	William Russell
Vanessa Morgan	Imogen Boorman
Sarah Brookes	Zulema Dene
Hanif Ruparell	Ayub Kan-Din
Neil Mitchell	John Lloyd Fillingham
Gordon Blinkhorn	Mark Chatterton
Wayne Farrell	Roy Polhill
Carmel Finnan	Catherine Cusack
Mark Redman	Chris Cook
Richard Willmore	Oliver Beamish
Tommy Duckworth	Darryl Edwards
Doug Murray	Brian Hibbard
Harold Potts	Russell Dixon
Denise Osbourne	Denise Black
Jeff Horton	Dicken Ashworth
Klaus Muller	Carl Duering

1993

Behind the Scenes

Carmel Finnan and Terry Duckworth battled for the year's title as Most Hated TV Character while audiences delighted in their antics. The story of crazy Carmel was followed closely by the press and television chat shows, who marvelled at the idea of an erotomaniac, while the fact that Terry could sell his own child dragged his character deeper into the pits of soap hell.

Comedy actress Sherrie Hewson joined the cast as Maureen Naylor, and award-winning West End actress Elizabeth Bradley was cast as her wheel-chair-bound mother Maud Grimes.

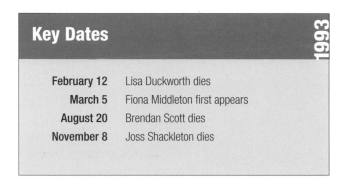

Key Dates

1993

February 12	Lisa Duckworth dies
March 5	Fiona Middleton first appears
August 20	Brendan Scott dies
November 8	Joss Shackleton dies

"This place is like the village of the damned. No one seems remotely normal."

Brendan Scott

Top Twenty

Pos	Character	No of eps	Total	Pos Prev Year
1	Jack Duckworth	103	946	4
2	Raquel Wolstenhulme	102	254	2
3	Deirdre Barlow	101	1464	20
4	Liz McDonald	101	411	9
5	Curly Watts	100	746	8
6	Mavis Wilton	99	1462	3
7	Gail Platt	97	1317	1
8	Alma Baldwin	93	446	12
9	Alf Roberts	93	1583	27
10	Steve McDonald	92	286	17
11	Rita Sullivan	92	1613	6
12	Jim McDonald	92	359	14
13	Audrey Roberts	91	742	13
14	Kevin Webster	741	87	23
15	Emily Bishop	85	2025	26
16	Vera Duckworth	85	1077	5
17	Sally Webster	84	614	34
18	Des Barnes	83	317	24
19	Denise Osbourne	80	91	44
20	Ken Barlow	78	2297	16

STORIES

1 Martin's Nightmare

Gail Platt was stunned when Martin threw Carmel Finnan out of the house and told her he did not love her. Carmel told Gail she was too old for Martin and assured him she'd wait for him, however long it took. Gail believed Martin when he said nothing had happened between him and Carmel, and she laughed in the girl's face when she claimed the child she was carrying was his. However, after discovering that Martin had spent the night in the same bed as Carmel, Gail freaked and started to doubt his word. Then Carmel warned Gail calmly that she intended to steal Martin from her and tried to snatch David, but Sally Webster refused to let her have him. Gail confronted Carmel and pushed her down a flight of stairs. Carmel broke her leg, and Gail feared she had harmed the baby but to the Platts' relief the doctors reported that Carmel wasn't pregnant. Carmel's grandfather collected her and apologized to the Platts, explaining that she had been obsessed with a man before. Everyone was relieved when she returned to Ireland.

2 A Tangled Web

When Tracy Barlow broke the news to Mark Redman that Mike Baldwin was his father, Maggie hit back and told her of Deirdre's affair with Mike. While Ken stood by smugly, Tracy called Deirdre a tart and rebelled, drinking and throwing herself at Deirdre's new boyfriend, Doug Murray. When Doug needed a two-thousand-pound cheque cashing, Tracy banked it but used it to make him take her out. Deirdre found out and made Tracy give the money back, then finished with Doug for getting Tracy to break the law.

Alma grew depressed and fearful when Mike insisted on being part of Mark's life. Ken warned Maggie that Mike would attempt to control Mark's life, and Mark had had enough of having boring Ken around the place. Maggie hated being caught in the middle of all the sniping and, to Mike's delight, finished with Ken. Mike decided that his son deserved the best education he could buy but Maggie refused to have him sent to a boarding-school. She compromised by letting Mike pay for Mark to attend the local Oakhill private school, but Alma was shocked at the amount of money Mike had started to spend on his son.

Tracy left school with four GCSEs and was taken on full-time at Maggie's florist's. She fell for twenty-two-year-old delivery lad Craig Lee and stunned her parents by moving into his flat. Deirdre felt she was a failure as a mother but agreed to the pair staying at No.1 when they were evicted. However, the situation soon got to her and, tired of being treated as a servant, she ordered them both to leave. At the end of the year Deirdre had to rush to the Midlands when her mother Blanche had a stroke.

3 Jealousy Surrounding Denise

Curly Watts stood by, green with jealousy, as Neil Mitchell continued to romance Angie Freeman. Eventually he declared his love for her and said he couldn't cope with having just her friendship. Angie left No.7 and moved into the flat over Jim's Café with Neil, but after he began to pick a fight with any man who showed an interest in his estranged wife Denise Osbourne, she realized he still loved her. She threw him out then dumped all his belongings in his cement mixer, and made him crawl before eventually taking him back. Angie's boss, Hanif Ruparell, was attracted to Denise and became her lover. Angie lost her job when Neil tried to break the couple up by telling Denise that Hanif slept with his workforce. Angie was humiliated when Neil attempted to fight Hanif in the Rovers and blurted out his love for Denise. Realizing that Denise would never take him back, Neil left for Australia, but not before forcing her to pay him back the three thousand pounds he had lent her to start her own business. Angie was left alone and,

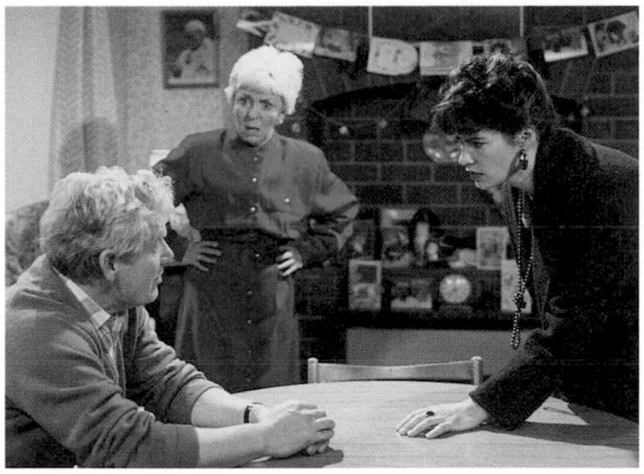

with a miserable future to look forward to, surprised everyone by packing her bags and going to study native designs in Mexico.

Denise accepted a loan from Don Brennan to cover the money she had been forced to pay Neil, and became confused about her feelings for Hanif when she learnt he had told his mother he loved her only to get out of an arranged marriage. When she decided she did love him he told her bluntly that he didn't love her and ended their relationship.

When Don made it clear that he wanted more from Denise than friendship she insisted she was only interested in friendship. However, she started to be plagued by mystery phonecalls at all hours and leant on Don for support. She accused Hanif of making the calls, only to discover he had been out of the country on his honeymoon when most had been made. Through his contacts Denise discovered that the calls had been made principally from No.5 and confronted Ivy, only to have Don confess to making them himself, saying he liked having her asking for his help and that he loved her. Denise and Ivy were both disgusted with him and after Ivy attacked him, Don agreed to start afresh with her.

4 The Duckworths' Heartache

Lisa Horton upset her parents by leaving Blackpool and taking Tommy to live with Des Barnes. Vera Duckworth was staggered to see her living across the Street and told her she was a bad mother for deserting Terry. However, Des put the house on the market and the couple looked forward to a new start away from the Street. Then while she was out buying a bottle of wine to celebrate finding a new house, Lisa was knocked down in the Street. She was rushed unconscious to hospital, where Des and Terry came to blows over her bed. When she

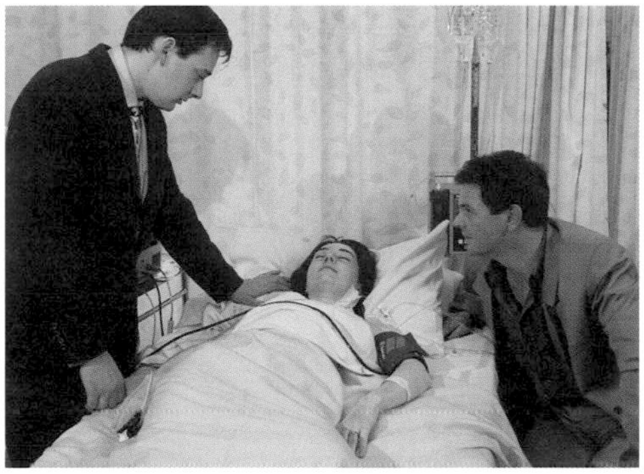

died, Vera snatched Tommy before the Hortons could, and a devastated Des found that everyone blamed him for bringing Lisa back to die. Vera resigned her job to look after Tommy, and soon the Duckworths were exhausted from stress. When Des gave a statement saying the driver wasn't to blame, the courts settled on minimum compensation, which led Jack to accuse Des of robbing Tommy of money he needed.

Vera believed her luck had turned with wins on the horses and at bingo, but was shattered when her father, Joss Shackleton, died. Jack was outraged when Vera spent all her winnings on the funeral. Terry was released from prison on parole, and Vera looked forward to having him at No.9. She was shattered when he told her that Tommy was to be brought up in Blackpool by the Hortons. Jack guessed correctly that Jeff had paid Terry for his grandson and disowned his son. Vera was heartbroken when Tommy was taken from her.

5 Rita's Cash

Rita Sullivan lived through a traumatic week as the courts sat in judgement on Ted's will. Derek Wilton was called as a witness for Sarah Brookes and was forced to admit to having thought that Ted was mad. The judge laid aside the will and gave the entire estate to Rita. She refused to celebrate, upset that Ted's memory had been sullied.

A few months later she suffered another disappointment when Jenny Bradley returned, having left Robert Weston. She brought with her Robert's valuable Japanese Akita, Mitzi, but Robert followed her and snatched the dog back. Jenny took a job behind the bar at the Rovers and, on hearing of Rita's inheritance, asked her for a thirty-thousand-pound loan to start her own beauty salon. Rita realized that she was only interested in her money and wrote her a cheque for a thousand pounds, saying that was all Jenny was ever going to get from her. Disgruntled Jenny left town.

6 First Love

Reg Holdsworth was stunned when his first love, Maureen Naylor, was taken on to work at Bettabuy, twenty-four years after her mother had broken them up. He was over the moon and, on discovering that Maureen's mother Maud Grimes was still alive and living with Maureen, swore she wouldn't stand in the path of true love again.

Maud tried hard to stop Maureen seeing him, but Reg lured her into his water bed. Unfortunately the seduction didn't go to plan: Derek Wilton, working in the room beneath the flat, drilled a hole into the bed and burst it. When Maureen agreed to marry him, Reg warned Maud that he would take her daughter away from her if she tried to stop the wedding. Maud admitted defeat but was horrified to learn that Reg was planning to put her in a home.

Reg decided to leave Bettabuy and agreed to buy Alf Roberts's shop for sixty-eight thousand pounds but was advised by Brendan Scott that he was paying too much. Alf was outraged when Reg knocked five thousand off his offer, and instead sold to Brendan for the asking price. Reg was stunned by Brendan's nerve although pleased when Bettabuy promoted him to area manager.

Brendan's time at the shop was short. He called it Best Buys, and went for an olde-worlde look, wearing a boater and sending delivery-boy Nicky Tilsley out on a cast-iron bike. He worked too hard and ended up dying of a heart-attack on the shop floor. His widow, Debi, offered the shop to Reg but when he tried to buy it cheap she put it up for auction. When Maureen found Reg wining and dining Debi and grovelling to her, she broke off their engagement; then she ripped up her wedding dress. Then she got drunk and spent the night with Curly Watts. After being reconciled with Reg she confessed but urged him not to harm innocent Curly.

7 Audrey's Dream Comes True

A one-way system caused havoc for the local residents when traffic down the Street increased. However, although his wife Audrey was run over and fractured her wrist, Alf Roberts refused to cause trouble at the Town Hall over the traffic. Enraged, Sally Webster took matters into her own hands and blocked the Street with Alf's car, then posted his keys in the pillar-box. The police were called, and when Alf tried to stop them smashing his car window he was arrested. Audrey decided she had had enough of being tied to a counter and Alf sold the shop to Brendan Scott. He had an emotional last day before heading off into retirement, taking with him the bacon-slicer as a memento.

Audrey celebrated when Alf agreed to buy a luxury bungalow in Lytham but hated his idea of retirement: putting his feet up and lazing about with other retired grocers. She went off the idea of leaving Weatherfield and to prove she was serious took a job in a dress shop. Alf decided to sell their house by auction but got carried away on the day and ended up buying back the Corner Shop instead. Audrey was appalled. During his grand reopening Alf got drunk and told Rita Sullivan he would leave Audrey for her at the drop of a hat. Then when he refused to honour OAP Christmas vouchers sold by Brendan he found himself labelled Scrooge in the local press.

8 Chalk and Cheese Twins

Steve McDonald successfully passed his driving test and allowed the besotted Vicky Arden to pay for the insurance on his new Ford Escort. In return he drove her to Birmingham for the night and took her virginity.

Back from university for Easter, Andy returned to Bettabuy and fell for check-out girl Amy Nelson. He took her out but dropped her after discovering she had a five-year-old son. However, he soon realized he had deep feelings for her and took up with her again. Then he decided to give up his studies, proposed to her and arranged to rent the flat over Jim's Cafe.

Amy feared he was too young to settle down and went off to Trinidad to visit relatives. There, she was reconciled with her old boyfriend and decided to stay. She sent her friend, nurse Alison Rathbone, to break the news to Andy. While Andy licked his wounds, Steve turned his attentions away from hairdresser Fiona Middleton and pursued Alison. They started going out together but Vicky, not knowing who Alison was, introduced herself to her as Steve's girlfriend. Both girls realized he had been two-timing them and finished with him.

9 Jim's Temper

While collecting the takings at Bettabuy, security guard Jim McDonald found himself caught up in an armed robbery. He was horrified when Andy heroically tackled one of the robbers and was hit over the head with a shotgun butt. The incident made him feel a coward for not aiding his son and he felt everyone was sneering at him. The next time he came across a thief he laid in with his fists, only to find that the culprit was only fifteen. He resigned, feeling he couldn't control himself.

Meanwhile, Liz's career was flying high. After acting as manager at the Rovers for three weeks, she applied for her own pub and was taken on by Richard Willmore as a trainee. There were celebrations when she was given a flagship pub, the Queens, and Jim joined her behind the bar. Unfortunately Jim couldn't accept that Liz had won the pub on merit and he accused her of sleeping with Richard. He convinced himself this was so and thumped Richard, expecting Liz to be sacked. Instead she stayed at the pub and told Jim their marriage was over.

The twins found themselves caught in the middle as Jim called Liz a whore and she took on Des Barnes's brother Colin as her barman and lover. Jim saw the error of his ways and pursued Liz into bed, which upset Colin who returned to Hartlepool. Not knowing where he stood with Liz, Jim filed for divorce and she cross-petitioned, each accusing the other of unreasonable behaviour. However they were still drawn to each other and New Year's Eve found them kissing and reconciled.

10 Bar Wars

Bet Gilroy and Stella Rigby joined forces against Councillor Harold Potts when they discovered he was playing them both for mugs, extracting free beer from them on the understanding that he would block road-widening schemes that would demolish their pubs. Potts was terrified when they loomed up on him and demanded he bought drinks all round at the Rovers.

When Liz McDonald left the Rovers, Bet was jealous of her success and stole her barmaid, Tanya Pooley. Depressed and feeling her age, Bet was vulnerable enough to spend the night with Don Brennan, but regretted the mistake later. Just when she thought she wouldn't find another man she was given a lift in a lorry by Charlie Whelan, a country-and-western addict, who made it clear he was interested.

Gordon Blinkhorn opened Raquel Wolstenhulme's eyes to the fact that footballer Wayne Farrell was cheating on her, and after catching him in bed with another woman she pushed him into a canal. Gordon moved in on her and she discarded football for his sport, which was cricket, and took French lessons from Ken Barlow to impress his friends on holiday. She soon realized her relationship with Gordon wasn't going anywhere so dumped him and went on a modelling course in Croydon. On her return a few weeks later, she was saddened when the job offers didn't flood in and had to return behind the bar, where she clashed with Tanya. Out of jealousy Tanya sent Raquel on a bogus photo shoot for Armani, but the joke backfired when Des Barnes found out, rescued humiliated Raquel and spent the night comforting her.

11 Romance for Emily and Percy

After buying Vera Duckworth's Nova, Emily Bishop headed out on the road for the first time in nearly thirty years and after being wheel-clamped waged a campaign against the company that had so inconvenience her.

Phyllis Pearce was delighted to win a competition in a women's magazine concerning the man in her life. To help her claim her prize, Percy Sugden went out with her and a photographer for the day. The article was seen by Olive Clarke, the

widow of his wartime pal Nobby and, to Phyllis's fury, she started calling on Percy. He proposed to her and was puzzled when she found the idea comical. A few months later, he was stunned to be invited to Olive's wedding. He went along with Emily to St Saviour's and had a terrible time. Emily, however, enjoyed flirting with the vicar, Bernard Morten. They became friends and she helped him when he started to question his faith. Seeing Emily so happy put Percy in an even worse mood than normal and after he snapped at the Platt children they burned an effigy of him on their bonfire.

12 Derek's War Against Des

Doug Murray lodged at No.9 until Jack Duckworth evicted him for not paying the rent. He moved into a derelict Dormobile parked in the Street, but Derek Wilton reported him to the police, wanting the eyesore moved. Des Barnes took in Doug, and paid to have the Dormobile craned and dumped in Derek's back garden. Derek retaliated by cutting it up and throwing pieces of it into Des's garden when a prospective buyer was looking around.

After he heard Derek telling Sarah Louise Platt about the magic tree growing in his garden, Des had some fun replanting the tree with a larger one each night, forcing Derek to question if it really was magic. After spotting his neighbour at work on the tree, Derek hit back by making a crop circle in his back garden. Des played along, pretending to believe that aliens had done it. When Derek put the tennis racquets back on his feet to make another circle, Des took a photograph of him, which he framed and hung up in the Rovers.

At work Derek had a rough time after Harold Potts was promoted to a better job and Derek was left to do the work of two people. He turned his hand to poetry, entering a competition at the Rovers, but Mavis objected to his work 'Mavis, My Marilyn', which referred to her breasts, so he withdrew. Phyllis Pearce won the twenty-five-pound prize with her 'Ode to Percy'.

13 Sally's Temptation

Doug Murray grew tired of staying in the Street and stole Mike Baldwin's Jaguar, exchanged it for a Mercedes and fled to Germany. Mike called in the police, who recognized the Jaguar from Steve McDonald's accident the previous year. An investigation took place, which resulted in Kevin Webster and Steve being charged with conspiracy to pervert the course of justice.

While this was going on Sally started to mind Jonathan Broughton, whose parents had split up and who had behavioural problems. His father Joe paid for the Websters to go on holiday to the Lake District on condition they took Jonathan with them. Glad of a chance to forget the court case, the family holidayed and had fun, until Joe arrived and declared his love to Sally. He begged her to leave Kevin but she refused and tried to avoid him.

Jonathan's mother, Hazel, realized something was going on and told Kevin she suspected Sally was having an affair with Joe. Kevin refused to believe her and was occupied in his court case. He was stunned when the judge accused him of corrupting Steve and fined him eight hundred pounds while Steve was sentenced to just 200 hours' community service.

14 Another Love Interest for Mr Watts

Curly Watts was finally made manager of Bettabuy when Reg Holdsworth was promoted. His new assistant manager was ambitious Elaine Fenwick, who was eager to prove her worth. She caught Vera Duckworth shoplifting on the security camera and was furious when Curly spoilt her conviction by tackling Vera at the check-out. Elaine complained to head office and an investigation was started, but Curly was cleared as Maud Grimes had videoed over the security tape. After Maud read his palm and told Curly that he had already met his future wife at work, Curly made more of an effort to get on with Elaine. They started to enjoy each other's company, and when Reg decided to transfer her to Goole, Curly blocked the move, infuriating Elaine. She told Curly she'd have sex with every manager until she was promoted.

CAST

Fiona Middleton	Angela Griffin
Maureen Naylor	Sherrie Hewson
Amy Nelson	Louise Duprey
Maud Grimes	Elizabeth Bradley
Tanya Pooley	Eva Pope
Joe Broughton	John Wheatley
Jonathan Broughton	Tom Lewis
Olive Clarke	Joan Scott
Elaine Fenwick	Pippa Hinchley
Colin Barnes	Ian Embleton
Debi Scott	Lesley Clare O'Neil
Bernard Morten	Roland MacLeod
Craig Lee	Kieran O'Brien
Hazel Broughton	Fiona McArthur
Alison Rathbone	Rachel Smith
Charlie Whelan	John St Ryan

1994

Behind the Scenes

The year started with a new producer because Carolyn Reynolds became executive producer. Sue Pritchard was brought in to take charge of the day-to-day running of the show. Since 1985 the press had spoken of a ratings war between the Street and *EastEnders* but it was only in 1994 that this actually happened. In the spring the BBC launched the third weekly episode of its popular soap opera, scheduling it to go out at eight p.m. on Mondays, directly after the Street on ITV.

Pundits eagerly watched for the ratings the next morning, which declared *EastEnders* had been viewed by 11.1 million, and the Street by 16.7 million. ITV claimed a victory but needed to be certain so the following week two episodes of the Street were edited together, creating an hour-long show, which was put out directly against *EastEnders*. Ladbrokes entered into the spirit of the contest by offering odds of 1–4 for a Street victory and 5–2 for an *EastEnders* win. The double episode featured the break-up of Emily Bishop's engagement and was viewed by 14.9 million, with 8.1 million tuning in to BBC. ITV executives sat back with contented smiles, the battle won. Writing in *The Times*, Alexandra Frean commented, 'the results defy critics who claimed that the Street's audiences were too old and downmarket for the new-look, youth-oriented, profit-driven, action-packed and upwardly mobile ITV.' William Roache brought some commonsense into the debate by pointing out that there was plenty of room for both the Street and *EastEnders* as they appealed to different audiences: 'You feel that if you got knocked over by a car in *EastEnders* someone would probably nick your wallet. On the Street they would invite you in for a cup of tea.'

> “I'm the bitchy type, the manipulating type, the homebreaking type. I'm surprised you haven't heard about me.”
>
> **Tanya Pooley**

Key Dates 1994

January 26	Reg Holdsworth marries Maureen Naylor
March 28	Lynne Perrie makes her last appearance as Ivy Brennan after 1205 episodes
August 29	Fred Elliott's first appearance
November 4	Sophie Webster is born
November 16	Doris Speed dies, aged 95, eleven years after last appearing as Annie Walker
November 25	Deirdre Barlow marries Samir Rachid
December 14	Tony Warren collects his M.B.E. from Buckingham Palace

Top Twenty

Pos	Character	No of eps	Total	Pos Prev Year
1	Gail Platt	117	1435	7
2	Raquel Wolstenhulme	112	366	2
3	Curly Watts	109	855	5
4	Rita Sullivan	109	1722	10
5	Mavis Wilton	105	1567	6
6	Alma Baldwin	105	551	8
7	Alf Roberts	102	1686	8
8	Maureen Holdsworth	97	162	28
9	Steve McDonald	95	381	10
10	Bet Gilroy	93	1946	20
11	Des Barnes	93	411	18
12	Ken Barlow	92	2389	20
13	Reg Holdsworth	91	342	22
14	Denise Osbourne	89	181	19
15	Liz McDonald	89	501	4
16	Mike Baldwin	87	1245	23
17	Betty Turpin	86	1829	24
18	Emily Bishop	83	2105	15
19	Vera Duckworth	83	1161	16
20	Audrey Roberts	82	825	13

STORIES

1 The Websters' Fairy Godmother

Kevin Webster was surprised to learn that his fine had been paid for him. Sally suspected Joe Broughton had stepped in, and told Kevin how Joe kept pestering her, declaring his love. Kevin laid into Joe, beating him up and telling him to stay away in future. Then Sally discovered that Alma Baldwin had paid the fine – she had been annoyed that Mike wouldn't help him.

When Sally told Kevin she was pregnant he was so furious that he walked out of the house. He felt they couldn't afford another child. However, Rita Sullivan admired the way the family struggled against the odds and gave them five thousand pounds. She became part of the family, joining them when they holidayed in Blackpool and when the baby was born she opened a building-society account for her, putting a thousand pounds in it. The Websters originally called their daughter Lauren but when Rosie kept calling her Sophie they changed her name.

2 Spoilt for Mayoresses

Alf Roberts sold the Corner Shop to devote himself to his new duties when he was elected Mayor of Weatherfield. As Audrey thought the idea was hysterical, Alf asked Rita Sullivan to be his mayoress but Audrey made him drop her by threatening to spread rumours that they were lovers.

Audrey enjoyed dressing up and being gracious, but refused to meet many members of the community. A black pudding contest in France found her being pestered by butcher Fred Elliott, who made it clear that he found her attractive. After Fred attempted to bribe an official, Alf came down on his side and rashly cancelled the twinning of Weatherfield with Charleville, then learnt that Fred had a reputation for dishonesty. Audrey was outraged when Alf decided to stop using the official limousine because he didn't like her flirting with the chauffeur. She resigned as mayoress and was annoyed when Alf replaced her easily with Betty Turpin.

3 Reg Empire-builds

When Maureen Naylor was threatened with redundancy at Bettabuy Reg Holdsworth fought to save her by threatening to resign – only to have his resignation accepted. Reg used his redundancy money to buy the Corner Shop from Alf Roberts, installing a ramp behind the till for Maud's wheelchair. Reg and Maureen married at St Christopher's and immediately fell out when Reg rowed with his new brother-in-law as to who should have the burden of living with Maud.

Alarmed by Reg's plans to buy a house and convert its garage into a flat for her, Maud sold her house to a finance company, which outraged Maureen, who had been paying the mortgage for years. The Holdsworths moved into Reg's flat at No.12 but Maureen worried about her mother

and returned to her after Maud let her believe she had had a break-in. Percy Sugden felt sorry for Maud, too, and found himself proposing to her.

Maud cancelled her arrangement with the finance company, then went to Normandy with Percy and Maureen on the anniversary of D-Day. While Percy saluted his dead comrades, Maud showed Maureen the grave of an American serviceman, Danny Kennedy, and told her he was her real father. While Maureen came to terms with the revelation, Percy broke off the engagement: Maud had been unfaithful with Danny while her husband was serving overseas.

Reg left the shop to run his best man Eric Firman's freezer firm, and Maureen took over the running of the business. However, she found the stress too much and had a breakdown, then employed Sally Webster to work in the evenings.

4 Steve Dabbles on the Horses

When she reconciled with Jim, Liz McDonald was forced to give up the Queens and took a job behind the bar of the British Legion. They found themselves alone at No.11 when Steve moved out after a brawl with Jim over his addiction to gambling.

When Mike Baldwin found out that Steve was using the print shop to create and sell his own T-shirts he sacked him, but Steve turned the situation round by renting the unit from Mike and, on money he had won on the horses, took the dockland flat next to him. Mike admired his cheek when Steve asked him to invest twenty thousand pounds in a printing venture and the pair became partners. Keen to show Steve who was top dog, Mike swindled him into doing all the work then pocketed the profits, citing a clause in their contract. When his probation officer refused to believe he'd come by his new possessions legally, Steve begged Mike to falsify the company accounts so that it looked as if he had made all the profits. In return Steve found himself agreeing to work for Mike.

Hair stylist Fiona Middleton was pleased when Steve invited her to move in with him, which upset Vicky Arden who still remained besotted with him.

Andy was reunited with ex-girlfriend Paula Maxwell when she took a holiday job at Bettabuy where he was training to be a manager. However, her arrival made him question his future and he resigned to return to university and moved back into No.11.

Meanwhile, Mike employed Jim as a driver at his new executive taxi firm. He was also missing his son Mark Redman, who had moved south to Felixstowe when Maggie became engaged to a man with a yacht. The only good news Mike had was that his Spanish land had been sold and he received seventy thousand pounds.

5 Teenage Tantrums at No.8

The Platts were sent into turmoil when Sarah Louise collapsed and was rushed to hospital with a ruptured appendix. She recovered, but Gail was shocked when the girl in the next bed died of an asthma attack. The child's mother, Janice Baker, decided to sue the hospital as the ward was understaffed and asked Gail to appear as a witness at the tribunal. Martin worried that he would lose his job as he had admitted this to Gail and was relieved when she sided with him and told Janice she couldn't support her.

Nicky started as a paper-boy at the Kabin and alarmed Gail by developing a romanticized picture of his father Brian. He saw him as a tough biker and came to despise Martin for being a soft nurse. He started to smoke and told Martin he couldn't push him around as he wasn't his real father. Sarah Louise grew anxious over the rows and fretful when Nicky left home to move into No.5.

Ivy Brennan had left the Street for a religious retreat and Don was glad of the boy's company. Under his influence Nicky stopped smoking but Gail was furious when Don allowed the boy to drink lager. Nicky refused to return home so Martin washed his hands of him. The Platts rowed

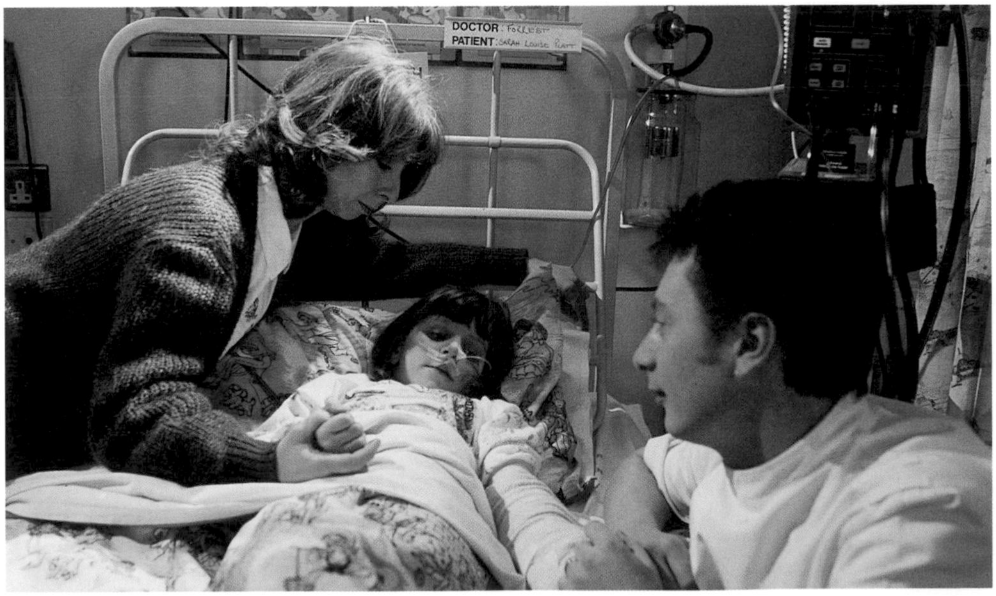

constantly and, on the Christmas Day shift, Martin got drunk and had sex with nurse Cathy Power. Unknown to him, Alf Roberts saw them kissing.

Gail was relieved when Nicky eventually missed his home comforts and returned to No.8.

6 Raquel's Heart Is Broken

When Tanya Pooley's father threw her out after discovering she was having an affair with a married man she moved into the flat over the Café. Her lover was Alex Christie, owner of the betting shop where Des Barnes worked. At the same time Des attempted to show commitment to Raquel Wolstenhulme by moving her into No.6. However, he remained attracted to Tanya and when Raquel had an overnight modelling assignment he ended up in bed with Tanya. Tanya was pleased to have another man on the go as she was tired of being Alex's bit on the side. However, Des felt guilty as Raquel waited happily for him to propose to her. He tried to fight his attraction to Tanya but became obsessed with her. Tanya was delighted when Alex decided to leave his wife and moved into the flat but Des decided he wanted her for himself and confronted the pair in bed, witnessed by a horrified Raquel. Alex fought Des and sacked him, before calling Tanya a whore and walking out of her life. Raquel ran to Bet Gilroy for comfort and, aware that she needed to do something drastic, Tanya punched her own face and told them Des had forced her into his bed. Bet fell for her lies, and Raquel left for a modelling course in Croydon. Sean Skinner opened a betting shop in Rosamund Street and employed Des as manager, impressed by him thumping Alex. Des threatened to take Alex to a tribunal for unfair dismissal and called Tanya as a witness, which forced Alex to offer him an out-of-court settlement.

7 Something for the Weekend?

After cutting Ken Barlow's hair, Denise Osbourne became intrigued as to his age. Her questioning amused him and he started to take her out. She was surprised to find his company enjoyable and he was surprised when she told him she was pregnant. Ken grew confused over his feelings: he wanted to be part of his child's life but not to be tied to Denise.

When Deirdre returned from nursing her mother, she hoped to reunite with Ken, and she was flabbergasted to hear that Ken had made the hairdresser pregnant. Sue Jeffers received complaints from parents about Ken's morals, and he accused Denise of ruining his reputation. She refused to involve him in her pregnancy then collapsed in agony and was rushed to hospital where she lost a baby. However, she found she was still pregnant with the twin. Ken moved into No.12 and refused to get out of her life so Denise tried to sell the salon to stylist Jon Welch, who wasn't interested.

8 The Bird Man of Weatherfield

Vera Duckworth discovered that a china dog she had inherited from her father was worth forty-five pounds but that a pair would be worth considerably more. Jack sold the dog for twenty-five pounds to an antique shop where Vera saw it and bought it for forty-eight. When she discovered it was the same dog she threw it at Jack, smashing it.

Vera took a break in Blackpool to see Tommy and was astonished to find herself sharing digs with Lester Fontayne, her old flame. He thought fate had brought them together and offered her a bungalow in Filey if she would leave Jack. She was tempted but in the end returned home.

When Jack's pigeon Fergie flew into Curly Watts's observatory Jack climbed on to the roof to try to reach it. Curly removed the ladder and Jack spent the night on the roof before being rescued by the fire brigade. The national newspapers picked up on the story, calling Jack 'the Birdman of Weatherfield'. He enjoyed the fame until

Dulcie Froggatt was interviewed by the press and embarrassed Vera by talking about their 'five-times-a-night' sexual exploits.

It was Vera's turn to be coy when Jack's brother Cliff dumped himself at No.9 and openly flirted with her. Jack had never liked him but discovered a fondness for him when Cliff said he was dying and wanted to leave Jack everything in his will. Jack rushed around trying to sort out the will while Cliff turned his hand to decorating, and painted some of the stone cladding blue.

9 Tanya Leaves

Bet Gilroy's romance with Charlie Whelan intensified and he became a regular sight at the Rovers. She was amused by his fascination with country-and-western until he entered her in a Dolly Parton lookalike contest. She wasn't impressed when he started to smuggle lager into the country either and when his lorry was hijacked she admitted to wondering if it was an insurance job. After being caught speeding, Charlie decided to give up driving and delighted Bet by saying he would like to work behind the bar, although she was concerned about giving up her independence. Then Bet went to Croydon to search for Raquel and found her working in a pub after being thrown off her modelling course. She persuaded her to return to Weatherfield and Raquel put on a brave face at meeting Des and Tanya again. Tanya was furious to see her and publicly humiliated her, telling all the regulars that she had been thrown off the course. Bet sacked Tanya on the spot, telling her she was poison.

Charlie felt sorry for Tanya and disliked the way Bet had treated her. He comforted her and they found themselves in bed together. She persuaded him to take her to Hamburg on a job with him, humiliating Bet, who refused to take him back when he returned and begged for a second chance. Bet and Raquel ended up getting drunk together and decided that men were worthless.

10 Jealousy and Passion Chez Wilton

Derek Wilton organized a culture trip to London to see *Miss Saigon* and was put out when Mavis spent the entire journey belittling him. At a service station he nipped off to the toilets then discovered that the coach had left without him. A salesman called Norris Cole gave him an overnight lift home. The next day Derek fell asleep at work and the school was broken into. Mavis wrote to Sue Jeffers, explaining about the coach, but when the governors found the incident amusing Derek resigned his job.

Norris came to visit Derek, saying he'd left his wife after being inspired by dominant Derek. He moved into No.4 and introduced Derek, or Dirk, as he called him, to the world of pyramid selling. Derek paid out two thousand pounds on stock from EnviroSphere and set about making his fortune, only to find that Norris was the superior salesman. While Derek struggled to sell anything Norris had soon made enough money to move into a luxury flat, and sold Derek his car, which promptly fell to pieces. Derek managed to offload his products on to his exwife Angela Hawthorne, who took him on at her stationery firm as a salesman.

Mavis was upset at the thought of Derek spending every day with Angela, but he found her jealousy erotic. She joined art classes and met librarian Roger Crompton, who felt that she needed saving from insensitive Derek. He painted her portrait and had it exhibited in the library, which upset Derek.

When Derek was cited in Angela's divorce case Mavis threw him out of the house, with the result that Angela rounded on her and accused her of playing into her husband's hands. Following the death of their budgie the Wiltons were reconciled and threw a dinner party to prove to their friends that they loved each other. Derek bought Mavis a new budgie, Beauty. Mavis was content until she discovered Roger had become friendly with Rita Sullivan and had offered now to paint her portrait. Jealous, she warned Roger off, saying that Rita was a man-eater.

11 Jilted Emily

After a crisis of faith Bernard Morten resigned from the Church of England and took Emily Bishop on a walking holiday in the Dales. He felt they should end their friendship when he developed strong

feelings for her but was delighted when she said she shared his feelings and they became engaged. However, when he learnt of her nervous breakdown Bernard told Emily he could never marry her because his mother had been mentally unbalanced and he couldn't live with it again. Emily broke down in despair at being old and lonely – then surprised Percy Sugden by admitting that she had replaced his budgie, Randy, in 1988, without him knowing it.

12 Raquel Becomes a Star

Curly Watts was horrified when Elaine Fenwick was made area manager over him, while she was unnerved by the way he kept declaring his love for her.

After he had caught ten-year-old Jamie Armstrong shoplifting, Curly was talked into dropping charges by his mother Tricia who offered herself to him. He took her out, leaving Jack Duckworth babysitting. Tricia's estranged husband mistook Jack for her new boyfriend, thumped him and Curly dropped Tricia.

When Elaine submitted a sexual harassment complaint against him, Curly was sacked from Bettabuy and, after a disastrous week working at the betting shop, took a job as manager of SoopaScoopa. To impress his new bosses he pretended to be engaged and managed to talk Raquel Wolstenhulme into posing as his fiancée. However, he faced up to the fact that he really loved her and proposed. Even though she didn't love him she accepted. At Christmas he delighted her by having a star named after her.

13 Young Love for Deirdre

After holidaying in Morocco, Deirdre Barlow took a job at Bettabuy and pined for the twenty-one-year-old waiter she'd fallen for out there. She borrowed money from Emily Bishop and amazed her friends by sending it to him, inviting him over for a holiday. Samir Rachid arrived, frightened by the western world but hopelessly in love with Deirdre. After his holiday he refused to leave, much to her delight, and let the plane fly away without him. He took a job in a local Moroccan restaurant and moved into No.1, much to the scorn of visiting Tracy Barlow.

Tracy was horrified when Ken told her of Denise's pregnancy and she told him he'd be a lousy father to the baby as he'd been a terrible one to her.

When immigration officers showed an interest in Samir, Deirdre proposed to him to keep him in the country. They married at the register office, upsetting both Ken and Tracy, who rushed from the service in tears. Immigration refused to believe the Rachids loved each other and both were interrogated. Samir felt like a prisoner, and Deirdre was isolated when her friends refused to believe he loved her. Samir feared deportation so Deirdre sold No.1 to Mike Baldwin and the couple emigrated to Morocco on the proceeds.

CAST

Eric Firman	Malcolm Terris
Alex Christie	Gavin Richards
Jamie Armstrong	Joseph Gilgun
Tricia Armstrong	Tracy Brabin
Norris Cole	Malcolm Hebden
Lester Fontayne	David Ross
Jon Welch	David Michaels
Sean Skinner	Terence Hillyer
Roger Crompton	Donald Gee
Samir Rachid	Al Nedjari
Fred Elliott	John Savident
Angela Hawthorne	Diane Fletcher
Cliff Duckworth	Dave King
Cathy Power	Theresa Brindley
Janice Baker	Jane Hollowood

1995

Behind the Scenes

Key Dates

1995

January 4	Daniel Osbourne born
May 3	Maxine Heavey first appears
June 2	Samir Rachid dies
July 19	Roy Cropper first appears
August 9	Vicky Arden marries Steve McDonald
August 23	Ivy Brennan dies
October 2	Gary and Judy Mallet first appear
October 16	Bet Gilroy leaves the Street
October 20	Betty Turpin marries Billy Williams
December 8	Raquel Wolstenhulme marries Curly Watts in the programme's first hour-long special

> "The worst thing about my life is waking up and seeing what's on the pillow next to me."
>
> **Des Barnes**

Julie Goodyear's decision to leave the programme after twenty-five years alarmed the viewers but not the writers, who effortlessly moved the Duckworths into the Rovers. Julie's departure was amicable. She was looking forward to tackling new ventures, and said, 'When you have played another character for twenty-five years it's almost like schizophrenia.' The same applied to Ken Morley, who had become popular as the outrageous supermarket boss Reg Holdsworth. The first ever specially written hour-long episode was aired on the show's thirty-fifth anniversary and featured the wedding of Raquel and Curly. It was followed up with a video, which went on sale the day after the wedding was broadcast and showed the events of the couple's honeymoon. It was snapped up by a million viewers, eager to see the goings-on.

Top Twenty

Pos	Character	No of eps	Total	Pos Prev Year
1	Fiona Middleton	111	189	30
2	Vera Duckworth	107	1268	19
3	Jim McDonald	106	547	22
	Gail Platt	106	1541	1
5	Steve McDonald	103	484	9
6	Des Barnes	102	513	11
	Liz McDonald	102	603	15
7	Betty Turpin Williams	101	1930	17
8	Jack Duckworth	100	1124	27
	Raquel Wolstenhulme	100	460	2
10	Alma Baldwin	93	642	6
11	Ken Barlow	92	2481	12
12	Mavis Wilton	89	1656	5
13	Don Brennan	88	604	32
	Andy McDonald	88	424	25
	Rita Sullivan	88	1810	4
16	Vicky McDonald	87	197	37
17	Curly Watts	82	937	3
18	Maureen Holdsworth	81	243	8
	Maud Grimes	81	179	21
20	Mike Baldwin	80	1325	16

STORIES

1 A Dad at Fifty-five

Denise Osbourne's resolve to cut Ken Barlow out of her life weakened in the delivery room, and he rushed to her side in time to see his son born. The boy was named Daniel Albert, and Ken was determined to see at least one of his children grow up. He broke into No.1 to clear the house of Albert Tatlock's furniture, which annoyed Mike Baldwin who set the police on him. He was disappointed when Denise wasn't allowed to put his name on Daniel's birth certificate because they weren't married, and upset Tracy by being so obsessed with his son that he forgot her eighteenth birthday.

When Denise used him as a babysitter while she went out with Jon Welch, Ken sought legal assistance in claiming paternal rights, only to discover he had none. Jon fell for Denise and when she rejected a pass he accused her of leading men on. He resigned from the salon, telling Denise she had a serious problem. She believed he was right and, exhausted by constant badgering over access, left Weatherfield with Daniel. They stayed with her sister Alison Dunkley and husband Brian, determined never to return to the Street. However, a month later she decided she needed stability and made her way back to Coronation Street to tell Ken she was willing to give their relationship a go. Delighted, Ken bought No.1 from Mike and settled into family life. Within weeks Denise was suffocated with boredom and resumed an affair with brother-in-law Brian Dunkley, using her old flat as a love-nest.

2 Love or Greed?

On her eighteenth birthday, Vicky Arden inherited £240,000 from her parents' estate and dropped out of school. She persuaded Bet Gilroy that even though she had a posh accent she was not bright enough to go to university. Her old flame Steve McDonald had financial troubles and admitted to Fiona Middleton that he was six thousand pounds in debt. He was amazed when she didn't wash her hands of him but instead scaled down his spending, renting the flat over Jim's Café for them to live in which was cheaper. At a hair-styling contest Steve modelled for Fiona and proposed to her but she refused to think of marriage until he was out of the red.

Vicky stepped in to invest in Steve's business, forcing him into a partnership with her and opening Dun 2 A T print shop. Fiona was upset to discover that Vicky had lent Steve money and was devastated when he showed no concern after she was threatened by a thug as a warning to him. After the same thug beat up Steve with a baseball bat Vicky took control of his finances and Fiona threw him out of the flat. He slept rough in the print shop and celebrated his twenty-first birthday there. Vicky came to him that night and undressed. The next day he proposed to her.

Alarmed at this news, Bet sent for Alec, who managed to stop the couple getting married straight away at a register office by urging Vicky to plan a white wedding. After learning of Steve's debts he tried to get the creditors to lean on him, and when that failed he offered Steve five thousand pounds to dump Vicky. Vicky grew frustrated at Alec's stalling tactics and the couple eloped to St Lucia where they married and honeymooned for a month. Alec returned to Southampton after Bet had made it clear that there was nothing for him to stay for.

On their return the couple moved into a Quayside flat and opened a joint bank account. Steve was annoyed when Vicky tried to limit his gambling and tried to earn his own cash by receiving stolen whisky. When the police raided the unit and the flat, Steve was arrested.

3 Tracy's Bad Trip

Ken Barlow was terrified when Tracy was rushed into Intensive Care after collapsing at a nightclub having taken Ecstasy. Deirdre and Samir Rachid rushed back from Morocco and were thrilled when Tracy came to, only to discover she had kidney damage. Tracy felt she would rather die than spend her life on dialysis, but when Deirdre decided to give up one of her kidneys, Samir grew distressed. He knew that if she did she wouldn't be able to have any more children. However, neither Deirdre nor Ken could donate a kidney as their tissue types weren't compatible with Tracy's. Samir insisted on taking the test and everyone was amazed to find that he was a perfect match. The Rachids lodged at No.11 while Ken looked after Tracy at No.12. Samir was apprehensive about the operation but wanted to please Deirdre. However, on his way to hospital he was stopped by a group of youths and later found unconscious on a towpath. He was rushed to hospital but died just after arriving. Deirdre had to decide whether or not to allow the operation to go ahead. She eventually agreed that it should, and Tracy recovered, but Deirdre refused to see her, wishing she had died instead of Samir. Afterwards Tracy went to live in Blackpool while Deirdre was distraught at not knowing exactly why Samir had died.

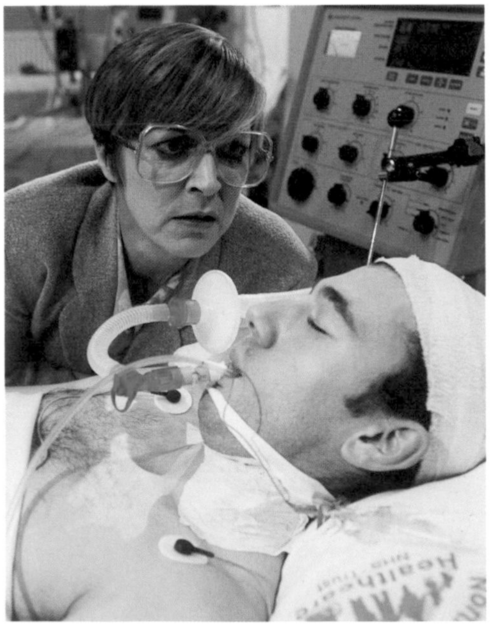

4 Ivy Causes Havoc From the Grave

Don Brennan started a relationship with doctor's receptionist Josie Clarke after giving her a ride in his cab. She was attracted to him, and hurt when he refused to spend the night with her. He admitted he wasn't a nice person and told her all about his phone calls to Denise. However, after he saved her from a thug who held her captive at the doctor's surgery, Josie moved in with Don at No.5. The Street was stunned by Ivy's sudden death from a stroke and Josie found herself being verbally attacked by Vera Duckworth, who accused her of jumping into Ivy's grave.

Ivy's will caused a stir as she had left No.5 to Nicky Platt on the condition he changed his name to Tilsley. Don was determined to contest the will but Gail was equally determined that Nick should have the house and, with Martin's approval, he legally changed his name back to Tilsley. At that point Don changed the locks and refused to let any of the Platts over the threshold.

Fighting for Nicky's inheritance brought the Platts together after months of bickering. Martin had confessed that he had sex with a nurse and Gail had suffered terrible depression, bursting into tears for weeks. When Nicky found out about Martin's infidelity he went for him, and Martin blamed his lapse on Nicky having driven a wedge between him and Gail. Gail was put on anti-depressants and was finally reconciled with Martin during a family holiday in Wales.

5 Mike's New Enterprise

Tricia Armstrong and her son Jamie became Mike Baldwin's tenants when they moved into No.1. Tricia took a job cleaning at the Rovers and resumed her relationship with Curly Watts, then turned to wealthier Sean Skinner. She was enraged when Mike put the house on the market and barricaded

the doors, refusing to let anyone view it. When Mike tried to break a window, Jamie tipped a bowl of water on his head. Eventually Mike talked the pair into moving to one of his new flats: he had bought a Victorian house with seven flats in it in Crimea Street. Tricia lost her job at the Rovers over her time-keeping and went back on the dole. She moved into the flat opposite Deirdre Rachid's. Deirdre lived there rent-free for acting as caretaker. Both women were disturbed by long-standing resident Roy Cropper, whom Jamie named 'Creepy Cropper'.

Alma was stunned to discover that Mike had bought the flats and feared he was having an affair with Deirdre. When her first husband, Jim Sedgewick, died she inherited two thousand pounds and splashed out on a sports car. Mike had it checked to make sure it wasn't stolen, then Alma hit back by checking his Mercedes which indeed had been stolen. Mike tried to sell it to retired policeman Rodney Bostock, who called in the police as he had discovered it was stolen and Mike lost his wheels when the car was returned to its rightful owner. As Mike had business deals she didn't know about, Alma started her own catering business.

6 Bet Leaves the Street

When Bet Gilroy set sail on a cruise with her leopardskin luggage, the Rovers was run by temporary manager Rodney Bostock, a trombone-playing retired policeman. He ran a karaoke evening at the pub that coincided with Bet's return. When she joined in, singing 'Dancing In The Street', Rodney fell for her. He started to hang around and Bet found him amusing. Her world was shattered when the brewery put the Rovers up for sale for sixty-eight thousand pounds. When the bank refused her a loan Bet asked Rita Sullivan and Vicky McDonald for help but both refused. She left the Rovers and the Street, feeling she had no friends.

Rita was upset to have let Bet down but knew that she was a bad risk. When her life insurance matured she decided to take a break, and paid for Mavis Wilton to join her on a trip on the *QE2*.

7 Alf Gets His Gong

When she learnt that Royalty was going to visit the area, Audrey Roberts told Alf that she would be his mayoress that night, not Betty Turpin. However, Betty refused to

step down and insisted that, as the official mayoress, she would meet the Princess. Audrey convinced herself that she had been a popular mayoress and set off on her own, with Fred Elliott as her escort. She threatened to embarrass Alf unless he allowed her to attend the royal occasion so he sent both women in his place. Later Audrey was forced to act as hostess when the Mayor of Charleville came to stay. Alf asked Raquel Wolstenhulme to act as the Frenchman's escort and she was outraged when he assumed that she was a prostitute. Alf and Audrey were thrilled when he had a letter from Downing Street offering him the OBE. However, the honour was put in jeopardy when the Town Hall started an investigation over seven thousand pounds that was missing from the mayoral fund, for which Alf, who signed the cheque, was responsible. The *Gazette* branded him a thief and Alf became a recluse until he found out that Harold Potts had embezzled the money with Alf's secretary. Potts was arrested and was imprisoned for nine months and Alf kept his date with the Queen at Buckingham Palace. Audrey was enraged when she arrived too late to watch the investiture and Betty took her place.

8 Trouble at the Bookies

After getting drunk to celebrate his divorce, Sean Skinner offered Liz McDonald a job at the betting shop. This bothered Des Barnes, who didn't like working with neighbours. Liz was appalled to see how much Steve spent on betting but was ordered to view him only as a customer. However, Sean, too, grew annoyed when Steve's debts rose to two thousand pounds. He had Steve blacklisted by other local bookies and took eight hundred pounds off him after seeing him winning at the dogs. Steve accused him of mugging him and reported him to the police but was accused of wasting police time when no witnesses could be found to back his claim.

When Liz had a pregnancy scare, Jim had a vasectomy and the couple decided to buy the Rovers. Unfortunately they were too late: Jim couldn't get away from work as

he was driving Mike Baldwin around. After dumping Mike to rush to Liz, Jim was sacked and blamed Liz. She accused him of continuously dragging her down, and on his fortieth birthday he admitted he hated her. Afterwards Liz was comforted by Des and they kissed. She was tempted to have an affair but held back and asked Des to lay her off work. He did so, which infuriated Jim who accused him of unfair dismissal.

9 Curly Gets His Girl

Curly Watts threw an engagement party to show the world how much he loved Raquel Wolstenhulme and was devastated when, after Des Barnes begged her to marry him instead, she told Curly she couldn't go on with him. Curly fought Des, telling him he ruined every woman he came into contact with, and lost his job at SoopaScoopa after going berserk in the store. Reg Holdsworth took pity on him and employed him as his assistant at Firman's Freezers, having told the staff he was gay so they would leave him alone. He panicked when he heard an American company was interested in buying the firm and, fearing the sack, bought a wig to make himself look younger. The American buy-out fell through and instead Eric Firman's nephew Leo was made boss.

While Curly took shop-worker Anne Malone out, Leo made a play for Raquel and tried to rape her in the storeroom. She ran to Curly and, enraged, he hit Leo and backed Anne when she accused Leo of sexual harassment. Eric hushed the matter up and moved Leo to another branch.

After taking part in an identity parade, Reg was picked out as being the Red Rec Flasher and word spread that he was a pervert. Reg burned his wig in frustration, as the police thought it was part of his disguise, and was relieved when Phyllis Pearce cornered the real flasher when he exposed himself to her. Reg took promotion at a different branch and left for Lowestoft, swearing to Maureen that their marriage would survive the distance.

After spending a night with Des, Raquel was disgusted with herself and told Curly she would marry him immediately if he told no one. He agreed and they were married in a register office with strangers as witnesses. After honeymooning on the *QE2* they returned to the Street, where Des told her she was a fool.

10 The Duckworths' Good Fortune

When his wife caught up with him Cliff Duckworth left No. 9. She took him home, after telling Jack and Vera that he wasn't dying, just crafty and sponging off them. Then Vera was sacked by Bettabuy for deliberately denting tins to buy them cheap. She went to church and prayed for money. An answer came in the news that Cliff had been killed while on holiday and Jack had inherited thirty thousand pounds from his holiday insurance plus his camel coat. Awash with money for the first time in their lives, the Duckworths toyed with the idea of buying the Corner Shop before putting in an offer on No.6 as they fancied the garden. Des Barnes agreed to sell to them and affectionate Jack bought Vera an engagement ring as she had never had one before. Gary and Judy Mallet agreed to buy No.9 but the Duckworths stalled when Des changed his mind about moving and cancelled the sale.

When the Rovers came up for grabs, the Duckworths put in an offer and were stunned when the brewery sold it to them. They vacated No.9 and moved the pigeon loft up the Street to their new home. At first they struggled with being bosses and running a business. Vera upset Betty Williams by asking her to clean the pub as well as cook. Betty resigned. She only returned after Vera begged her to and swore she would have complete control over the food. The Rovers became a freehouse and Jack enjoyed being courted by the local breweries.

Meanwhile, back at No.9, the Mallets annoyed the neighbours with Gary's drum kit, while Judy erected a Christmas neon sign that read 'Santa's Nookie Nest'.

11 A Tale of Two Gnomes

Derek Wilton set off on a fitness spree and was talked into buying a Mile Muncher

from salesman Norris Cole. Mavis had a go on it while wearing court shoes and was thrown off and rushed to hospital. Derek decided to sue Mile Muncher and forced Mavis to stay off work when there was nothing wrong with her. Eventually Norris's new girlfriend, Angela Hawthorne, ordered Derek to drop the claim. Derek was alarmed at the thought of his ex-wife and Norris becoming an item and plunged into consternation when Norris was made chairman of Hawthorne's.

Then Derek took in two gnomes, Arthur and Guinevere, but was puzzled when Arthur kept disappearing and sending him postcards from around the world. When he was sent a severed gnome's ear along with a ransom note for fifty chocolate doubloons, Derek lay in wait for his tormentor and was arrested by the police on suspicion of being a peeping Tom.

On the eve of his marriage to Angela, drunken Norris confessed to his best man Derek that he had stolen the gnome. In revenge Derek took him to the wrong church, making him late for the wedding and incurring Angela's wrath.

12 Old But Not Past It

When Emily Bishop found Percy Sugden's bedroom was damp, she farmed him out to Curly Watts while she had it decorated. Percy felt certain she would use the patch as an excuse to evict him.

Meanwhile, Phyllis Pearce was distressed to discover that Des Barnes cleaned his house before she did. He admitted that he thought the work was getting too much for her and they compromised: she would do the ironing instead.

Across the Street at the Rovers, Betty Turpin was reunited with an old flame, Billy Williams, with whom she had shared a passionate moment on VE-Day in 1945. He was keen to take up where they had left off and proposed to her, but she wasn't

interested. He persisted, and after helping her over a burglary he proposed again, while he was drunk in the Rovers. This time Betty accepted him and they were married in style. Betty was given away by her son Gordon Clegg, who couldn't help wondering if Billy was his real father.

13 A Rover Returns

Following the break-up of his marriage in Germany, Bill Webster returned to Coronation Street after an absence of ten years. Kevin was delighted to see him but Sally wasn't so keen when he set fire to her kitchen while cooking. He undertook to build a new kitchen at No.13 then moved into the Rovers, where he took a job as cellarman.

After he had started up a building partnership with Jim McDonald, he received a hefty tax demand and was pleased when the Websters loaned him the money to pay it. Rita was far from happy, though, and scolded Sally, saying she had given her money to the family, not to Bill. Sally hit back, saying that her family wasn't for sale.

14 Stylists and Soccer

Fiona Middleton was joined in the café flat by schoolfriend and fellow stylist Maxine Heavey, who fell for Des Barnes and threw herself at him. She became his latest plaything whenever he needed a bed partner. However, he dropped her after bumping into his ex-wife Steph, who was heavily pregnant and down on her luck. Des gave her some money to move into a decent flat but refused to take her back, saying he could never love her child.

Then Des joined a gym with Curly Watts in an attempt to get fit. They started a five-a-side football team but Curly was dropped as he was useless. Instead they poached Tony Horrocks from a rival team, using Fiona as bait to get him on to the Rovers' team. Tony fell for Fiona, and became a mechanic at MVB Motors.

CAST

Daniel Osbourne	Lewis Harney
Josie Clarke	Ellie Haddington
Rodney Bostock	Colin Prockter
Maxine Heavey	Tracy Shaw
Billy Williams	Frank Mills
Roy Cropper	David Neilson
Leo Firman	John Elmes
Anne Malone	Eve Steele
Gary Mallet	Ian Mercer
Judy Mallet	Gaynor Faye
Brian Dunkley	Benny Young
Alison Dunkley	Maggie Saunders
Tony Horrocks	Lee Warburton

1996

Behind the Scenes

> "Steve wasn't even innocent in the womb."
>
> **Andy McDonald**

The decision to start making four episodes a week horrified both cast and writers, who were already struggling with a three-episode schedule. However, the structure of the show was altered, with rehearsal days being dropped in favour of actors rehearsing in front of cameras then recording scenes straight away while the moves were fresh in their minds. Most warmed to this new approach as it meant that, although they were making more episodes, they had more spare time. However, Sarah Lancashire decided that it was too much for her as she had been carrying lengthy storylines for months without breaks. She announced her decision to quit and left a week before the first fourth episode was transmitted in November. Sue Pritchard also bowed out as producer and was replaced by Brian Park, who promised great changes.

Key Dates 1996

January 1	Julie Goodyear is awarded the MBE in the New Years Honour's List
April 15	Episode 4,000 is transmitted
November 13	Tracy Barlow marries Robert Preston

Top Twenty

Pos	Character	No of eps	Total	Pos Prev Year
1	Vera Duckworth	113	1381	2
2	Liz McDonald	105	708	7
3	Andy McDonald	101	525	15
4	Jack Duckworth	100	1224	9
5	Rita Sullivan	98	1908	16
6	Ken Barlow	97	2578	12
7	Deirdre Rachid	97	1684	32
8	Bill Webster	93	219	31
9	Don Brennan	91	695	14
10	Jim McDonald	89	636	3
11	Mike Baldwin	89	1414	21
12	Mavis Wilton	88	1744	13
13	Alma Baldwin	87	727	11
14	Audrey Roberts	86	990	23
15	Kevin Webster	85	981	24
16	Des Barnes	85	598	6
17	Fiona Middleton	85	274	1
18	Curly Watts	83	1019	18
19	Judy Mallett 82	96	45	
20	Maureen Holdsworth	82	325	19

STORIES

1 The Hairdresser, Her Lovers and the Nanny

Denise Osbourne realized that her affair with Brian Dunkley was getting out of hand when he told her he loved her and begged

to spend more time with her. To show him she wasn't interested she proposed to Ken Barlow, who was delighted until he overheard Brian pestering Denise at Daniel's birthday party and realized what had been going on. Ken threw Denise out, telling her she was an unfit mother. Denise agreed with him and left town with Brian.

Determined to keep Daniel with him, Ken employed an ex-pupil, Kelly Thomson, as nanny. She took to Daniel immediately and proved her worth, despite letting her boyfriend Ashley Peacock stay in the house overnight in Ken's absence. Afterwards Kelly moved into No.1 to be of more help to Ken while Ashley became Don Brennan's lodger at No.5. Under Don's influence, Ashley attempted to be more macho with Kelly but she soon put a stop to that nonsense.

Ken's love-life looked rosy when Sue Jeffers's husband left her and she leant on him for comfort. They went to a conference together, but during the night she slipped in his bathroom and was knocked unconscious. They were both embarrassed when the gossips got to hear about it.

Ken and Deirdre were brought together when Tracy announced her intention to marry Robert Preston, a twenty-five-year-old carpet-fitter. Blanche Hunt arrived for the wedding and was shocked when Tracy was married in a dress that had cost fourteen pounds from a charity shop. Ken and Deirdre had to work together on the day of the wedding to find Robert, who had been locked in a freight-container on his stag night. At that point they realized they were still attracted to each other and fell into bed, but the moment was ruined by the return of Denise who told Ken that legally he had no right to Daniel. She took him to Scotland to live and hired Kelly to look after him. Ashley and Kelly parted, and Ken told Deirdre he didn't have time for her: his only concern was Daniel.

2 Liz Enters Steve's Shady World

Both McDonald marriages crumbled this year. Steve's shady contact Malcolm Fox told the police that Steve had supplied him with stolen whisky. To get him to change his statement, Steve persuaded Vicky to pay Fox six thousand pounds and in court Fox said he'd incriminated Steve because of a vendetta against him. Months later Fox's wife told the police about the bribe and Vicky was arrested and charged with conspiring to pervert the course of justice. Steve tried to talk her into taking the blame for the whole incident, but she left him and cleared out their joint account. Facing the same charges, Steve continued to hound Vicky, begging her not to testify against him. In court he lied and said that the bribe had been Vicky's idea but the judge saw through him and sentenced him to two years in prison. Vicky was released. Wanting to put as much distance between them as possible, she signed up for a hotel-management course in Switzerland as Steve started his sentence at Strangeways.

Jim and Liz also had their problems when he grew jealous and suspicious of her movements. When she admitted to having had an affair with his best friend Jim hit her and abandoned her in the middle of the night. Then Liz announced that she wanted a divorce and took possession of the house, changing the locks. Jim attempted to smash his way into No.11 but was arrested and charged with assault. When he failed to meet bail conditions and continued to pester Liz he was sent to Strangeways for three weeks.

Liz took a job managing a wine bar, the Hourglass, and was hurt when the twins turned on her for thinking that Jim might be capable of killing her.

When his mother died Jim decided to buy Liz out of the house but she demanded a share of his four-thousand-pound legacy. She followed that up by demanding half his earnings so Jim gave up work and hit the bottle. Eventually he sorted out the mess by paying her a one-off thousand pounds.

Liz started going out with Sean Skinner but while she was visiting Steve in Strangeways, she caught the eye of the prison Mr Big, Frazer Henderson. When he heard she needed cash he sent her a thousand pounds and saw off Sean by having him beaten up. Liz was terrified, until Steve talked her into visiting Frazer in prison, and she was charmed by him.

3 The Malletts Settle In

The year started badly for the Malletts when their central heating broke down and Gary was electrocuted while using a faulty socket. The whole house needed rewiring so Judy demanded that the Duckworths paid for it to be done but they refused and barred the couple from the Rovers. Eventually the dispute was sorted out and Judy was taken on to work in the evenings behind the bar. Her mother, Joyce Smedley, was also employed at the Rovers, as cleaner.

Along with Jack and the other menfolk, Gary formed a formed a syndicate and bought a racehorse, Betty's Hot Shot. Judy was furious that he'd spent money they couldn't afford so he sold his share to Jack. Joyce encouraged Judy to buy goods from her catalogue as she was on commission and the Malletts ended up winning a

conservatory, which they sold to the Wiltons. Gary became flustered when Rovers' barmaid Samantha Failsworth showed an interest in his motorbike. She talked him into taking her for a ride but when Judy became jealous she stepped in to say she was buying the bike. Poor Gary was forced to go along with this and handed over his beloved bike. It was now that Judy decided to try for a baby: she knew that Gary wanted children and feared he might leave her if she didn't have one.

Meanwhile, Joyce fell behind with her rent and into financial difficulties after becoming addicted to scratchcards.

4 Alec Returns

Alec Gilroy returned to Weatherfield to take over the Rosamund Street branch of Sunliners travel agent, employing Deirdre Rachid as his assistant and Joyce Smedley as his cleaner. He bought No.12 from Reg Holdsworth and tried to resurrect his theatrical agency. As he enjoyed Joyce's company, he took her away for the weekend to the Lakes but she was insulted when he didn't make a pass at her. He explained that marriage to Bet had scarred him and that he was only after companionship. When he caught Joyce stealing from his flat Alec sacked her.

When Jack Duckworth fell off Betty's Hot Shot and was hospitalized for six weeks, Alec stepped in to help Vera behind the bar, but was aghast when she started flirting with him. The he attempted to make a star of Roy Cropper when he discovered his fantastic memory, but Roy refused to be exploited and frightened Alec off by offering to introduce him to his dead aunt. Fiona Middleton was more willing and, when he found she could sing, Alec launched her on the club circuit.

Fiona's life was always changing. She borrowed funds from her brother, bought the lease of the salon, started her own business and moved into the flat above.

Tony Horrocks finished with her when she visited Steve McDonald in prison and she smarted when he started taking Maxine Heavey out almost straight away. While singing at a club, Fiona was admired by Detective Constable Alan McKenna, who started to court her. Meanwhile Tony grew tired of clingy Maxine and dumped her.

5 The Ruining of Don Brennan

The matter of ownership of No.5 was established when Don Brennan bought the house from Nicky and felt that Ivy was finally dead. He couldn't believe it when Vera Duckworth reported seeing her ghost and had to get a pal to perform a fake exorcism to please her. Then Vera felt that Ivy's spirit had moved to the Rovers and was furious when Jack tried to cash in by calling in the press to the haunted pub.

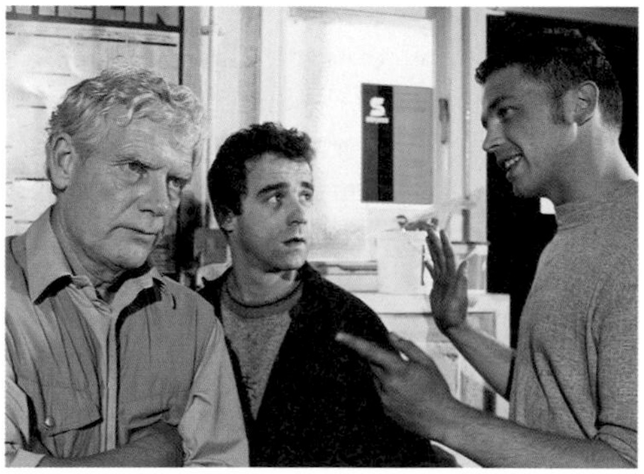

Josie Clarke, Don's girlfriend, gave up her job at the surgery to run Baldwin's Sportwear for Mike. After reading a valuation on his desk, she suggested to Don that they should buy Mike's garage business. Don was delighted when Mike accepted his offer but soon discovered he'd bought a turkey as the equipment kept failing.

After a row over business practices, Josie resigned from Baldwin's after Mike told her the valuation had been false and the garage was worth considerably less than Don had paid. Don felt he'd been swindled and blamed Josie, who left him, demanding back her investment in the garage. Don attempted to find a new business partner so that he could pay her off. When Kevin Webster and Tony Horrocks refused to get involved, he tried to talk Nicky Tilsley into buying into the garage, which infuriated Gail. Eventually the receivers took it over and Don went for Mike in the Rovers, only to be thumped to the floor.

Desperate for money, Josie talked Kevin and Tony into buying the garage from the bank. They were delighted to own the business but Don sank into despair. He lost his licence after being breathalysed and tried to kill himself by locking himself in the garage with his car exhaust turned on, only to be rescued by Kevin and Martin.

Meanwhile, Nicky grew tired of living at home and ran away, causing Gail to think she was a bad mother. Gail issued 'missing' posters and had to identify a boy's body before Nicky returned, having had a boring time wandering around in Torquay. The family all went on holiday to Canada where it was decided that Nicky would remain, using his inheritance to pay for a private education.

6 Fertile Terry Strikes Again

Hard-up Tricia Armstrong was so desperate for cash that she offered sex to Mike Baldwin for money. He merely warned her against using her flat for immoral purposes. When she failed to pay a fine issued for non-payment of a TV licence she was sent to prison for a week and Jamie was taken into care. He soon ran home and Deirdre Rachid took him in. Then he started a scam: he punctured bicycle tyres then charged to repair them.

When Tricia was released she earned a little money for Mike, but her benefits were stopped. In order to secure his rent Mike took her on as a machinist.

Terry Duckworth surprised his parents

when he turned up with Tommy, having taken him from the Hortens when Jeff attempted to stop paying the annual two thousand pounds he had agreed to give Terry in order to keep the child. Terry was interested to see his parents now owned a pub and paid a thug to go for Jack so that Terry could see him off and win Jack's approval. After discovering that the Rovers wasn't a gold mine, Terry made another deal with Jeff: he sold Tommy to him for ten thousand pounds and signed a residency order so that he wouldn't be able to remove him again. Terry left the area but not before spending a night with Tricia and leaving her pregnant.

Horrified, Jack offered Tricia money to have an abortion but she refused and visited her husband Carl in Strangeways to break the news to him. He thumped her and upset Jamie by saying he didn't think he was his son, while Vera took Tricia under her wing.

The Duckworths had a shock when they went on holiday and left Betty and Billy Williams in charge of the Rovers. On their return they discovered the takings were up as they hadn't been borrowing from the till all the time as Jack and Vera were wont to do.

7 Raquel Leaves the Street

Curly and Raquel Watts had fun matchmaking between his new assistant manager Anne Malone and Andy McDonald. When Anne bought a house, 16 Orchard Close, she asked Andy to move in with her but startled him by giving him a rent book.

Raquel took up aromatherapy and hired the back room at the salon to work on clients. She was sacked from the Rovers after Terry Duckworth caused trouble for her when she rejected his pass. Then she decided to take a course in Maidenhead and unnerved Curly when she returned more confident. She went after a job with a big international firm, removing her wedding ring before the interview to show she had no commitments.

Curly was aghast when she admitted she had been offered a job in Kuala Lumpur and was going to take it. It was the end of the marriage after just one year. Wanting more from his own life, Curly decided to go travelling and let No.7 to Samantha Failsworth. However, he spent a night of passion with Maxine Heavey and Anne declared her love for him. Curly changed his mind and returned home.

8 Norris Cole - Murderer?

The Wiltons took on their own allotment and started growing vegetables to enter shows. They grew alarmed when Norris Cole planted himself on them and told them he wanted to kill his wife. When Norris spent time alone at the allotment Derek feared he had buried Angela's body there and started to dig around. He was relieved to uncover only her golf clubs.

Mavis upset Derek when she forgot his sixtieth birthday, thinking him only fifty-nine, and the couple upset Emily Bishop when they gave permission for their house to be visited on a historical tour. Emily overheard the guide pointing out the site of Ernest's murder and accused the Wiltons of cheapening his memory.

9 Daddy Des

Phyllis Pearce got herself into a pickle when Maud Grimes read her tea leaves and advised her to propose to the man she loved. Afterwards Maud realized she had read her own cup and when both women proposed to Percy Sugden he thought they were having a joke at his expense.

Phyllis was delighted when Des Barnes fell for market trader Claire Palmer, but he was frustrated because Claire insisted on taking their relationship slowly as her teenage daughter Becky was still grieving after her father Jeff's death. Becky was hostile to Des and accused Claire of forgetting about Jeff, but Des worked hard to show her he wasn't trying to replace her father. The Palmers moved into No.6, which alarmed Des when he discovered that Claire had had to give up her widow's pension for him. When Claire insisted Des got rid of his cannabis plant, Des gave it to the Wiltons, but the joke backfired when they ruined Becky's birthday party by accusing him of pushing drugs.

Claire tried to hang on to her pension by pretending to rent the flat over the betting shop but her ploy was exposed to the RAF by her father-in-law.

10 Alf's Honour

Audrey Roberts was sent into a spin by the arrival of her son, Stephen Reid, from

Canada. Gail Platt was intrigued to meet her brother for the first time, and even Alf had to admit he was a nice man.

While Mike Baldwin secured a business deal to supply K-bec, Stephen's firm, with sportswear, Alma fell head over heels for Stephen and made a clumsy pass at him. When he rejected her she felt foolish, and worse when Audrey went for her.

Mike opened a new factory unit, employing old lag Ida Clough and making bored housewife Sally Webster his factory manager. Alma confessed her feelings for Stephen to Mike, and was aghast when he shrugged them off. She realized he cared more for the business contract than for her.

Another visitor from Canada was Angie Freeman, who turned out also to be working for K-bec. Mike was aggrieved when he found that she had the power to approve or reject his garments.

Alf was thrilled when the council decided to rename the old folks' home Mayfield Court in his honour. The OAPs weren't so thrilled and, led by militant Lily Dempsey, protested. They gatecrashed an official occasion and Lily threw an egg at Audrey, ruining her outfit. Alf backed out of the proposal and instead was told that Coronation Street would be renamed Alfred Roberts Place. Audrey loved the idea but the residents protested, and the idea was dropped. Instead Alf was put in charge of the Millennium plans. After he had celebrated his seventieth birthday, Alf's driving licence was taken from him because he backed his car into the doctor's.

11 Love Blossoms

Maureen Holdsworth struggled to cope with running the shop and driving up and down the motorway to see Reg. When he resigned from his job she searched Lowestoft for him before she discovered he had disappeared with heiress Yvonne Bannister. Maureen was shattered when Maud Grimes urged her to face the world, and after receiving a visit from pregnant Yvonne, she agreed to a quick divorce, taking the shop as settlement. She placed an ad in a lonely hearts column but was nervous of meeting strange men so Bill Webster tagged along for support. To Maud's delight Maureen and Bill started a relationship but there was a blip when he decided to spend Christmas with his son, Carl, and cancelled a trip to Spain with Maureen. In anger Maureen turned to Curly Watts and ended up in his bed on Christmas Day. When Bill returned she confessed to him.

Bill's old friend Rita Sullivan started to spend time with Fred Elliott and was startled when he proposed to her. After realizing she was going to turn him down he backtracked to save face, saying he was a womanizer and proposed to several different women.

CAST

Malcolm Fox	Glyn Pritchard
Stephen Reid	Todd Boyce
Joyce Smedley	Anita Carey
Kelly Thomson	Sarah Moffett
Ashley Peacock	Steven Arnold
Claire Palmer	Maggie Norris
Becky Palmer	Emily Ashton
Yvonne Bannister	Clare Cathcart
Robert Preston	Julian Kay
Lily Dempsey	Thelma Ruby
Carl Armstrong	Jim Millea
Alan McKenna	Glenn Hugill
Frazer Henderson	Glyn Grain

1997

Behind the Scenes

Actors held their breath and viewers tried to come to terms with the events off- and on-screen this year as producer Brian Park grasped the Street by the scruff of the neck, shook it hard, and said, 'Decisions have to be taken to create space and give the show some oxygen. Some characters have run their course.' On his first day at work Brian sacked Peter Baldwin, causing an outcry across the globe, but he'd only just started: out went Don Brennan, Percy Sugden, Andy McDonald, Anne Malone, Bill Webster, Billy Williams, Scamper the dog and Maureen Holdsworth. Thelma Barlow, outraged by the sacking of her screen partner, quit after twenty-five years, and the writing team lost Barry Hill, Adele Rose and Julian Roach. Writing in the *Daily Mirror*, Victor Lewis-Smith voiced an opinion matched by many viewers: 'The Street is currently being terrorized by a smiling axeman. Apparently it doesn't matter that this is a first-class soap, superbly scripted and flawlessly performed by a seasoned repertory company.' However, the departures were part of a plan to revitalize the programme and new blood was introduced in the shape of single mother Zoe Tattersall, neighbours from hell the Battersbys, and a new look Nick Tilsley, played by heart-throb Adam Rickitt. Alison Graham, writing in the *Radio Times*, was caught up in the general hatred of the Battersbys when she wrote, 'They have become mere cartoons, vastly exaggerated and awful. *Coronation Street* may have its faults, but cartoon characters have never been a problem that I can recall. They have the feel of an ill-fitting proboscis grafted on to the Street, itching and demanding to be scratched. Or, better still, removed altogether.' However, by the end of the year most viewers had to admit that the family had grown on them and that Brian Park had succeeded where many of his predecessors had failed in creating a brand new family who could help lead the show into the next century.

> "When women leave this street, they don't do it by halves!"
>
> **Audrey Roberts**

Key Dates 1997

January 11	Jill Summers dies after appearing in 528 episodes as Phyllis Pearce
February 14	Brad Armstrong is born
February 21	Joyce Smedley dies
April 7	Derek Wilton dies
August 27	Shannon Tattersall is born
September 22	Fred Elliott marries Maureen Holdsworth
October 8	Don Brennan dies
October 10	Mavis Wilton leaves the Street to live in Cartmel
October 20	Percy Sugden's last appearance
November 3	Billy Williams dies
December 24	Ivan Beavis dies, thirty years after his screen character, Harry Hewitt, was killed off

Top Twenty

Pos	Character	No of eps	Total	Pos Prev Year
1	Kevin Webster	140	1121	15
2	Judy Mallet	122	218	19
3	Sally Webster	121	935	22
4	Jim McDonald	120	756	10
5	Vera Duckworth	119	1500	1
6	Gary Mallet	117	205	23
7	Alec Gilroy	117	722	31
8	Rita Sullivan	115	2023	5
9	Chris Collins	115	115	–
10	Fiona Middleton	114	383	15
11	Deirdre Rachid	113	1797	6
12	Ken Barlow	109	2387	6
13	Gail Platt	108	1731	25
14	Natalie Horrocks	102	102	–
15	Mike Baldwin	102	1516	10
16	Jack Duckworth	101	1325	4
17	Angie Freeman	100	335	41
18	Samantha Failsworth	99	152	30
19	Ashley Peacock	98	139	32
20	Maxine Heavey	96	208	29

STORIES

1 Unloved Curly

Samantha Failsworth refused to give up No.7 for Curly Watts so he ended up sleeping on Anne Malone's sofa. Furious that he hadn't left the country and thus she was robbed of her promotion to manager, Anne turned on him. Andy McDonald decided he'd had enough of her obsessive behaviour and moved out. This alarmed Curly as Anne changed tack and started to refer to herself and Curly as a couple. Curly fled back to No.7, and persuaded Samantha to let him move in by reducing her rent.

Annoyed, Anne complained to Eric Firman that Curly had been sexually harassing her and refused to be left alone in the store with him. Curly was bemused by Anne's behaviour and tried to talk sense into her but ended up shouting at her. When Eric found him shaking her he was sacked and Anne given his job. Then Anne convinced herself that Samantha had lured Curly from her, planted goods in her bag and accused her of shoplifting. An assistant told Eric what had really happened and Anne was sacked while Curly was reinstated.

Curly's ex, Angie Freeman, returned and lodged at No.6 in Des Barnes's absence. She fell for mechanic Chris Collins but their affair was short-lived as she felt they were going nowhere. When Samantha started seeing Des, a drunken Angie proposed a swap: she would move back to No.7, and Samantha into her room at No.6. In the morning, Angie was appalled to realize she was back living with Curly.

2 Don's Reign of Terror

Stephen Reid paid a flying visit to Weatherfield and, after hearing of Don Brennan's hate campaign against Mike Baldwin, cancelled the contract between K-bec and Underworld. Alma Baldwin accused him of using Don as an excuse to break with Mike because of the pass she had made at him, and felt humiliated when he accused her of still fancying him. She ended up in a row with Gail Platt over Stephen and walked out of the café when Gail slapped her. She sold her share in the café to Roy Cropper for thirty thousand pounds and slapped Stephen's face when he attempted to stop the sale on Gail's behalf.

Then she encouraged Mike to play dirty with K-bec: he sold the Crimea Street flats and started to copy K-bec's clothing illegally. He pushed Sally Webster into selling the counterfeit goods on the market but she felt like a criminal and resigned.

Sacked from K-bec herself, Angie Freeman warned Mike that the company were on to him. He fired his workers and closed down the factory, planning to move the stock. Don Brennan took umbrage at Mike having sacked his workers and set fire to the factory unit, then phoned the police to tell them Mike had done it for the insurance money. He delighted in telling

Mike that he'd started the fire, knowing that Mike couldn't prove he had. However, to Don's chagrin, the insurance company paid out in full and Mike thanked him in public for burning all the evidence of his K-bec scam.

In revenge, Don picked up Alma in his taxi and took her on a terrifying ride, saying he wanted to hurt Mike. She believed he was going to rape her and tried to fight him off but when he drove the car into the Irwell she ended up saving him from drowning. Don was arrested for attempted murder and tried to frame his lodger Ashley Peacock for the factory arson. Mike and Fred Elliott joined forces to prove Ashley's innocence. Meanwhile Alma nervously started work as an assistant at Firman's Freezers, and was promptly voted the Face of Firman's for their ad campaigns.

Shortly after his arrest Don was admitted to hospital suffering from cancer. He made his peace with Gail and Alma but then escaped custody and went after Mike, intent on killing him. Angie, who had recently entered into a partnership with Mike to produce lingerie, disturbed Don, and Mike watched in horror as the lunatic drove Alma's car into the viaduct and died in a fireball.

3 Old Neighbours, New Neighbours

Derek Wilton died of a heart-attack during a road-rage incident, leaving Mavis a devastated widow. At the funeral Norris Cole gave an impromptu speech and upset her even more by referring to Derek as 'Dirk'. After the funeral tea, Mavis turned on the residents, accusing them of only ever seeing Derek as a joke. She couldn't cope alone and decided to move to the country. Rita Sullivan was taken with the idea and the pair attempted to run a B&B together in Cartmel, but after a week Rita decided she couldn't live in the country and cancelled her plans. Mavis wouldn't be put off so took on the venture herself and left the Street.

No.5 was bought by the council, and the problem Battersby family were housed in it. They drove the neighbours mad with their loud music but when Curly Watts broke in and smashed the CD player he was punched by father Les. Toyah took a part-time job at the café while Leanne joined mother Janice at Underworld, only to be sacked for smoking and setting off the fire alarm. Les had fun using the interconnecting loft spaces to roam aroundhis neighbours' houses, upsetting Percy Sugden so much that he left Emily Bishop's and moved into Mayfield Court. Leanne fell for Nick Tilsley, who returned from Canada to study PE at the Tech. After she took his virginity they started a relationship. Toyah fell for Emily Bishop's nephew, Geoffrey 'Spider' Nugent, an eco-warrior who had moved into Emily's spare room. With Toyah he liberated the live turkey, Terry, that Les was planning to eat on Christmas Day but the bird wandered into the Street and Les ran over it.

4 A New Duckworth

Tricia and Jamie Armstrong moved into the Rovers Return and it was in the back room, on Valentine's Day, that Betty Williams delivered baby Brad, five weeks' premature. Tricia wasted little time in bouncing back at life and was soon dating Ray Thorpe after meeting him at a club. When Terry Duckworth returned to the pub she was quick to drop Ray and threw herself at him. He struggled to remember who she was and pretended to be interested in his new son, but his mind was on the pub takings. When he offered to bank them Jack saw through him and gave him cut up newspaper instead of money, infuriating Terry who told Tricia he wasn't interested in her or her kid. When he shoved her, Ray thumped him and Jack kicked him out. Shortly afterwards the Armstrongs moved in with Ray on the other side of town.

When Alec Gilroy was made redundant from Sunliners, he salvaged a holiday to Las Vegas and entered into a scam with Jack to raffle it in the Rovers. The holiday was won by an old man who dropped dead from shock and was then revived by Jack. As a reward the man insisted Jack and Vera took the holiday. What none of the regulars knew was that the man was also known as Lazarus the Living Corpse and had made a living out of 'dying' on cue.

The Duckworths went to Las Vegas before discovering they owed seventeen thousand pounds in tax. Jack tried to interest Rita Sullivan in a 50 per cent partnership in the Rovers but Alec talked her out of the idea then snapped it up himself. Vera accused Jack of selling their dreams but he insisted that Alec's partnership wouldn't affect them. He had to reassess the situation when Alec charged them to use the pub for their fortieth wedding anniversary party. Alec talked Vera into sacking Betty, but when Billy dropped dead of a heart attack Vera found herself assuring Betty she had a job for life.

Alec started a sideline in the form of a dating agency called Golden Years. He paid Ken Barlow to escort lonely ladies to dinner but Jack got the impression that sex was involved and posed as Ken to meet Renee Turnbull at her hotel. She was also interested in sex but proved too much for Jack!

5 Des and Samantha Jump Together

Samantha Failsworth started dating Sean Skinner and told him she didn't like sex and was running away from her past. He kept pursuing her so she challenged him to take part in a parachute jump. When he sprained his ankle in practice, Des Barnes took over and made the jump. Afterwards he made a pass at Samantha but she tricked him into taking off his trousers before throwing them – and him – into the Street. Claire Palmer witnessed the spectacle and walked out on him, taking her daughter Becky and leaving the Street. Des was annoyed with himself for ruining another relationship and took off on his boat for a holiday.

In his absence Samantha tried to give herself to Sean but ended up fighting him off. After three months Des returned and started to court Samantha who, after rescuing Leanne Battersby from an attempted rape, told him how she had been raped at sixteen. He helped her to face her parents and she was appalled when her husband, Richie Fitzgerald, tracked her down and begged for a reconciliation. She refused him and instead gave herself to Des. After she moved into No.6 Richie attacked the house and beat up Des but was seen off by Les Battersby.

6 An Armed Siege at No.11

On release from prison, Frazer Henderson promptly bought the Hourglass and installed Liz McDonald in a flat as his lover. Fiona Middleton was upset when her boyfriend Alan McKenna offered to protect Steve in prison in return for Liz spying on Frazer. Liz enjoyed the gifts Frazer gave her and slapped Andy's face when he called her a whore. Alan tried hard to get something on Frazer and, after talking to his estranged wife, led a swoop on a job Frazer was doing raiding a warehouse. When Frazer was arrested his henchman Gerry Turner blamed Liz when he found Alan's business card in her bag. He tried to run her over and then, when she sought refuge at No.11, he held her, Jim and Andy hostage with his shotgun, annoyed as he'd just wanted to kill Liz. When he was distracted, the family jumped him and he was arrested but Andy was traumatized by the siege and started drinking heavily.

Frazer believed Liz hadn't spied on him and offered her a new life in Spain. When she learnt he really had been behind the warehouse job he left her, threatening to smash in her teeth if she called the police. Fiona was upset by the way Alan hadn't offered Liz any protection and was appalled by Andy's breakdown. Jim worked hard to help Andy recover and was relieved when he graduated from university with a 2:2 in combined studies.

Alan and Fiona's engagement party coincided with Steve's release from prison. Jealous Alan threatened to have him arrested if he pestered Fiona, but the strain of having him around the Street was too much and Alan broke the engagement. Fiona reached out for comfort and ended up spending a night with Jim, who couldn't believe his luck. Reconciled with Alan, Fiona tried to rush the wedding along and was frustrated when he wanted a big, traditional one.

Steve received fifteen thousand pounds from Vicky for an uncontested divorce and set up a building business.

Fiona was horrified to discover she was pregnant but Jim underwent tests which proved that the baby was Alan's. Liz ended up back in Jim's bed, depressed over her fortieth birthday, but Jim was obsessed with his love for Fiona. He turned up at Alan and Fiona's wedding and begged Fiona not to marry Alan. Fiona had to confess their night together, and Alan jilted her at the altar. Steve, too, was sickened by his father's behaviour and moved out of No.11 while Andy decided that he'd had enough and left the country.

7 Judy Loses a Mother and a Baby

Tony Horrocks took possession of a flash new car and promptly ran over Joyce Smedley while she was out walking her dog,

Scamper. Joyce's neck was broken and she was killed instantly. Tony had a breakdown and left the area to live in Leeds.

Judy Mallett was devastated by her mother's death and became cold towards Gary. She had trouble at the arcade where she worked with teenagers Liam Shepherd and Zoe Tattersall. Gary stopped them when they tried to steal money from Judy and in return they threatened to tell the police that Gary had broken Liam's arm. Judy gave them money to keep quiet but was horrified when Zoe admitted that it would buy her an abortion. Judy slapped Zoe and refused to hand over any more. She had tests to find out why she couldn't conceive and was forced to tell Gary that an abortion at sixteen had left her infertile.

After finding Zoe begging in the streets, Judy took her in and stunned Gary by suggesting they bought her baby from her. Zoe agreed and Judy allowed people to believe that Gary was the baby's father. Gary was present at the birth, an emergency Caesarean, and Zoe was paid after Gary was registered as the little girl's father. Judy was thrilled and named her Katie Joyce then had a big christening party with Curly Watts and Samantha Failsworth as godparents. After Zoe ran away the

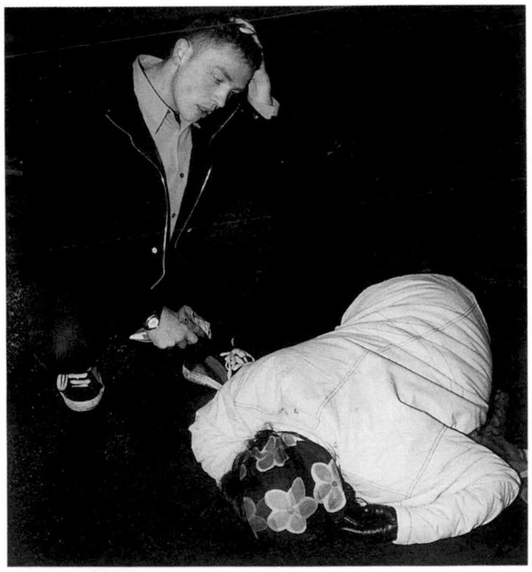

authorities allowed Katie to live at No.9 with her 'father' Gary and everyone agreed Judy was a saint to take on the baby as her own. However, Leanne Battersby thought her a hypocrite and encouraged Zoe to return as the money had run out. Judy panicked and told Gary they should run away to his family in Newcastle but Zoe managed to snatch Katie from them. Thinking Zoe wanted more money, Judy had sex with her boss, Paul Fisher, in return for a two-thousand-pound sub on her wages. Liam was keen to take the money but Zoe decided she wanted her baby instead and broken Judy returned the money. Zoe announced that her baby was now to be known as Shannon.

8 Maureen Marries Mr Wrong

Bill Webster became obsessed with the thought that Maureen Holdsworth had had sex with Curly Watts. He moved into the flat over the Corner Shop and surprised Maureen by taking her away overnight. So as to avoid Bill, Curly ended up locked in the storeroom all night but in the morning Bill found him and thumped him, then finished with Maureen. She started to see butcher Fred Elliott and grew fond of him after he had spent a night stranded on a golf course with a broken leg. She leant on him for support at the shop after two youths raided it and threw Maud Grimes out of her wheelchair. When Fred proposed marriage, she agreed, although she didn't love him. Fred bought No.4 and carried Maureen into the house after their wedding in a country hotel. Maud annoyed Maureen by selling her house and moving into the old folks' home, Mayfield Court.

Maureen soon felt trapped and realized she hated Fred. Just days after marrying him she ran off to Germany with Bill Webster. Devastated, Fred hit back by putting buyers off the Corner Shop so that he could buy it cheap for sixty-two thousand pounds. When she found out about his dirty tricks Maud dropped a fish into one of the counters and left it to rot, which successfully saw off the customers.

Fred's nephew Ashley Peacock moved into No.4 with his girlfriend Maxine

Heavey, who had originally shunned him, thinking him dull, before discovering his great virility. He proposed to her but she turned him down, then moved out when he took in homeless Zoe Tattersall. Zoe, grateful, took Ashley to bed.

9 Kevin Strays

Tony Horrocks's mother Natalie took over his share of the garage and became Kevin Webster's business partner. She made it clear she found him attractive and after leaving her husband made a pass at him. Sally was away in Scarborough nursing her mother through the aftermath of a stroke and lonely Kevin ended up in bed with Natalie. Rita Sullivan suspected something was going on and warned her off but Kevin swore innocence. When her mother had recovered, Sally returned home and soon realized all was not well. She tracked Kevin down to Natalie's house and caught them in bed together. Kevin raced after her to Scarborough and the couple were united

briefly when Rosie went missing for a day.

Back in Weatherfield Sally gave Kevin five minutes to pack before throwing him out and Natalie took him in. Then she realized she needed money so took a job as a machinist at Underworld. She decided to forgive Kevin, but he upset her by admitting he loved Natalie. When the couple went on holiday together Sally got mechanic Chris Collins to let her into Natalie's house and turned on the taps, starting a flood. Furious, Natalie threatened Sally with legal action and the women ended up brawling in the Street, rolling around on the cobbles.

Sally fell for Chris and started an affair with him but stopped seeing him as she didn't want her daughters confused. Kevin missed his family and left Natalie to return home, then found out about Sally's affair. He called her a slut and thumped Chris, but by Christmas the Websters were reconciled.

10 Deirdre's Bogus Boyfriend

Ken Barlow agreed to let his son Daniel live in Scotland with Denise Osbourne. He was faced with redundancy but his job was saved by Sue Jeffers, who told him she found him attractive. As a thank-you he took her to bed but was caught in the act by Deirdre Rachid, with whom he had been thinking of reuniting. Deirdre refused to have anything more to do with him, while Sue was insulted when Ken admitted he did not find her attractive. When the school governors investigated why Ken hadn't been made redundant Sue admitted to blocking the move and resigned. Ken was forced to accept early retirement and stared into a lonely, bleak future. To top it all he couldn't cope with looking after homesick Daniel at weekends and decided to forgo his rights to see him.

Meanwhile, Deirdre was made manageress at Sunliners, moved into the flat over Skinner's bookie's and fell for airline pilot Jon Lindsay. Jon house-sat for a friend and passed off the detached property as his own, explaining that Deirdre couldn't live there with him as his ex-wife had taken possession of it. Ken discovered that Jon wasn't a pilot and in fact managed a shop at the airport. Deirdre confronted him and he admitted to lying, but promised he loved her. She forgave him and told her friends that he'd had to give up being a pilot after failing a medical. She gave him five thousand pounds to use as a deposit on a home for them and was delighted when he proposed. They bought a four-bedroomed house in Didsbury, but Deirdre's joy turned sour when she found out that Jon still lived with his wife Linda and their children.

CAST

Brad Armstrong	Caleb Flanagan
Natalie Horrocks	Denise Welch
Chris Collins	Matthew Marsden
Ray Thorpe	Chris Walker
Gerry Turner	Keith Woodason
Zoe Tattersall	Joanne Froggatt
Liam Shepherd	Andrew Knott
Jon Lindsay	Owen Aaronvitch
Linda Lindsay	Margot Gunn
Sophie Webster	Emma Woodwood
Janice Battersby	Vicky Entwistle
Les Battersby	Bruce Jones
Leanne Battersby	Jane Danson
Toyah Battersby	Georgia Taylor
Shannon Tattersall	Lucy Whipday
Nick Tilsley	Adam Rickitt
Renee Turnbull	Lynda Baron
Ritchie Fitzgerald	Sean Dooley
Paul Fisher	Niven Boyd
Spider Nugent	Martin Hancock

1998

Behind the Scenes

For years the Street had clung proudly to the fact that it wasn't awash with 'issues' but now the traditional stories made way for eco-warriors, a transsexual, drug-dealers and religious cults. Satisfied that his job was done, Brian Park left to set up his own production company and was replaced by David Hanson. However, before he went Brian created the most talked-about Street story of all time when he sent innocent Deirdre Rachid to prison for three weeks. Nineteen million viewers tuned in to see Deirdre sent down and straight away everyone was caught up in 'Free Deirdre' mania, sporting T-shirts and stickers in their cars. The *Daily Mail* summed up people's reaction, saying, 'Now the dividing line between *Coronation Street* fiction and real-life fact has not so much blurred as completely disappeared up the nation's aerials.' The situation became ridiculous when Prime Minister Tony Blair took up the matter in Parliament, calling for the Home Secretary to intervene in Deirdre's case, while the *Evening Standard* wondered if the world had gone mad: 'As the "Justice for Deirdre" campaign gathers pace and "Free the Weatherfield One" becomes a catchphrase uniting politicians on both sides of the fence – even newspapers as diverse as the *Sun* and the *Guardian* – it gets even harder. There is a serious risk of incurring the hatred of the public at large. However, one should not shirk one's duty: "SHE ISN'T REAL, YOU KNOW!"' Granada had always intended Deirdre to spend just three weeks in her cell before being released, but when freedom came four different newspapers claimed the victory for themselves and their readers, saying public opinion had swayed the writers to be lenient. Brian Park was delighted.

> "I'm not pulled as easy as a pint of Newton and Ridley's."
>
> **Natalie Horrocks**

Key Dates 1998

January 30	Nick Tilsley marries Leanne Battersby
February 18	Morgan Middleton born
April 14	Shannon Tattersall dies
October 9	Anne Malone dies
October 23	Des Barnes marries Natalie Horrocks
November 18	Des Barnes dies
December 25	The Mallett twins born
December 30	Alec Gilroy leaves the Street to live in Brighton

Top Twenty

Pos	Character	No of eps	Total	Pos Prev Year
1	Leanne Tilsley	133	190	40
2	Janice Battersby	129	204	3
3	Alec Gilroy	123	846	6
4	Les Battersby	121	181	39
5	Gail Platt	120	1851	13
6	Sally Webster	117	1052	3
7	Natalie H Barnes	117	219	14
8	Jim McDonald	114	869	4
9	Rita Sullivan	113	2136	8
10	Toyah Battersby	113	164	43
11	Vera Duckworth	112	1612	5
12	Greg Kelly	112	112	–
13	Kevin Webster	111	1232	1
14	Nick Tilsley	110	701	50
15	Roy Cropper	107	221	37
16	Mike Baldwin	102	1618	14
17	Maxine Heavey	99	307	20
18	Ashley Peacock	98	237	19
19	Des Barnes	98	780	26
20	Audrey Roberts	97	1182	21

STORIES

1 Deirdre the Convict

After confronting Jon Lindsay over the fact that he was married, Deirdre Rachid refused to believe he loved her and moved out of their house. She used a bank card Jon had given her to withdraw the five thousand pounds she had lent him from their joint account, only to be arrested as the account was in the name of a Captain Jenkins. Numb with horror, Deirdre was charged with obtaining money and property by deception and was sacked from Sunliners. She told the police about Jon, but as he had disappeared they refused to believe her. Ken Barlow was amazed that Deirdre had believed Jon had really bought the house himself, rather than assuming Captain Jenkins's identity, and refused to believe in her innocence, but Mike Baldwin stood by her and let her stay in his flat. He acquired a false passport for her and bought a plane ticket to Spain but at the airport Ken made her see that there was no point in running away.

When Jon turned up on the doorstep, Deirdre called the police but he told them she had masterminded the whole thing. Deirdre's friends supported her during the court case but Jon's counsel called Ken as a witness against her and he was forced to admit that she had lied to cover for Jon not being a pilot. Eventually the judge ruled that Deirdre was a manipulative woman who had pushed Jon into lying to secure a house for herself. She was sentenced to eighteen months' imprisonment while Jon walked free.

Emily Bishop and Mike threw themselves into the campaign to clear Deirdre's name while Deirdre was locked up with violent Jackie Dobbs. Jackie tried to show her the ropes of prison life but Deirdre's constant assertions that she was innocent annoyed the inmates and warders and she was sedated.

After three weeks she was released when another woman tricked by Jon came forward and gave evidence against him. As she left prison, Deirdre watched Jon being taken into custody. Ken was delighted that Deirdre was free and offered her a home at No.1 but instead she returned to the flat above the bookie's, sharing with Liz McDonald.

The fight to free Deirdre left Mike Baldwin with a vast solicitor's bill. He covered it with Underworld money, infuriating his partner Angie Freeman, who decided he was never going to treat her equally and took a job in London. When Alma found out about the money, she accused Mike of still being in love with Deirdre and shocked the residents by making public the knowledge of the pair's affair. Deirdre was quick to reassure Alma she was not Mike's lover, and her misery at all the residents knowing her business was overshadowed by the arrival of Jackie, who dumped herself and her sixteen-year-old son Tyrone on her. Deirdre felt she owed Jackie for having looked after her in prison but hated the way she took over her flat.

Jackie took a job at Underworld, but was soon sacked for stealing knickers. When she heard that Curly Watts had disappeared, she broke into No.7 and claimed squatter's rights. Deirdre heaved a sigh of relief at having got rid of her.

2 Nick's Revenge

Nick Tilsley enjoyed seeing Leanne Battersby in secret, knowing that his mother Gail would never approve of her as his girlfriend. After spending a weekend together in Scotland they eloped to Gretna Green. He was seventeen, she sixteen. When they returned and broke the news to Gail that they were married, Gail was appalled, but Leanne set about proving her worth and took a job as Rita Sullivan's assistant at the Kabin. After lodging at No.5 for a while the newlyweds rented a room from Ashley Peacock at No.4.

While at college, Nick's class received a visit from convicted murderer Darren Whately and Nick realized that he was the man who had killed his father. He became obsessed with avenging Brian's death and, learning that Darren's parole was coming up, started to write to him in Leanne's name asking to meet him. Darren was flattered and, free from prison, called on Leanne, looking for her to fulfil some promises. Leanne was terrified and couldn't believe that Nick would put her in so much danger. She struggled to fight Darren off. When Nick revealed his identity, Darren threatened to stab him just as he had stabbed Brian, but then made Nick see he was just a kid who didn't know what he was talking about. Nick hit back by telling the police that Darren had hunted him down and attacked Leanne. As a result Darren was sentenced to another five years.

The couple struggled to survive on Leanne's wages so Nick secretly took a job as a model at the college art classes run by Miranda Peters. Leanne grew suspicious of his movements and ended up confronting him while he posed naked for Miranda. She accused him of infidelity and walked out on him, refusing to attend his eighteenth birthday party on New Year's Eve.

3 Des's Complicated Life

Des Barnes started the year by proposing to Samantha Failsworth. She accepted, then panicked when he started to plan the wedding. She feared that marriage would

trap her and make her run away again. She visited Richie Fitzgerald and begged him not to agree to give her a divorce, therefore delaying her marriage to Des. He delighted in telling Des her plans and Samantha was forced to move out of No.6 into lodgings at Natalie Horrocks's house. Natalie worked to reconcile Des and Sam and Sam returned to him. However, she also started an affair with Chris Collins. The Websters found out about this and, aware that Sally was jealous of Samantha, Kevin told Des what was going on behind his back.

Des broke down the door of Chris's flat over the Corner Shop and caught the couple in bed together. Samantha moved back in with Curly Watts at No.7 and, sacked by Kevin, Chris left for his native Coventry, upset when Sally refused to leave with him. Samantha was horrified when Des started to take Natalie out and became determined to split them up. She played practical jokes on Natalie, and told Des that she, Sam, was pregnant with his child. Des was stunned when Samantha told him she would be aborting the baby but grew confused when she admitted she wasn't pregnant after all. She also caused trouble for the Websters, telling Sally that Kevin had resumed his affair with Natalie. Eventually the residents turned on her. She left the Street, telling Des that he would never know if she was pregnant or not.

After attending his brother Colin's wedding, Des proposed to Natalie and after a whirlwind courtship they were married at the register office. Natalie was delighted when her son Tony arrived to stay but Des discovered he was a drug-dealer on the run from creditors. Tony begged Natalie to give him the money he needed to pay off the thugs but she refused. When Des found Tony being beaten up in No.6, he was knocked unconscious when he attempted to stop it. In hospital he came round long enough to tell Natalie he loved her then died of a heart-attack. Natalie blamed Tony for Des's death, as did Colin who shouted at her at the funeral. Natalie paid Tony off and told him she never wanted to hear from him again.

4 Alec Heads South

Rita Sullivan caused alarm in the Street when she was found collapsed in her flat. A leaking gas fire, fitted by Steve McDonald, was the culprit and Rita was told she might well have died. Seeing her so vulnerable made Alec Gilroy realize just how much she meant to him. He set the police on to Steve but Rita refused to lodge a complaint, putting the matter down to experience. She was touched by Alec's concern and slowly allowed him to court her. He proposed marriage, but she couldn't see that working and instead gave consent for a door to be built between his flat and hers. All was well until Rita put up Betty Williams for the night and Alec sneaked into the bed thinking he was cuddling up to Rita.

Meanwhile, at the Rovers, the Duckworths employed Jim McDonald to replace their rotten staircase. Alec refused to pay half of the bill, stating that the stairs were the Duckworths' property. Jim lost patience with the squabbling between them, and removed the stairs, trapping Vera upstairs and causing her to call the fire brigade to rescue her from her bedroom window. He returned the stairs when Jack settled the bill.

When Jack suffered leg pains the doctor demanded he change his diet and give up smoking. Vera worried about Jack's health and sent him to a hypnotist to help him stop smoking. Jack had fun pretending to have been sent back to a former life, as Lusty Jack, a seventeenth-century squire. The barmaids complained when he started fondling them and he used his new-found social status to stop working in the pub. When Vera found out it was all a pretence, she hit back by pretending to cook his pigeons and taking on hunky Sandy Hunter as barman. Sandy didn't stay long as Alec poached him for his escort agency. As the Duckworths were in financial trouble again, Alec bought them out of the Rovers and, while they holidayed in Blackpool, had the locks changed. Barmaid Natalie Barnes warned the Duckworths, who rushed back and took possession of their bedroom. Alec turned off the heating and tried to starve them out but the residents rallied round and fed them. Alec became frustrated with the situation and decided to move to Brighton where his granddaughter Vicky McDonald was starting up her own wine bar. He sold the pub to Natalie, told her the Duckworths were now her problem, and left.

5 Emily the Eco-warrior

When the council decided to build on the Red Rec, ecologist Spider Nugent rallied the local troops and led a protest against consumerism. While Roy Cropper organized protest meetings Spider and a besotted Toyah Battersby practised chaining themselves up and set up home in a tent in Alf Roberts's back garden. When the council took no notice the protestors took to the trees in the park to save them from being cut down. The press covered the story when Emily Bishop spent the night in a tree. Les Battersby, employed as a security-man on the site, refused to allow Toyah to take part and was delighted when the bulldozers arrived. However, when Roy fell through a tunnel a Roman bath house was discovered and Alf was forced to declare the Red Rec a site of historical interest.

Spider celebrated his victory by launching a new attack on Firman's Freezers for selling Norwegian prawns. Curly Watts sympathized with the cause but was forced to stand against the protest. Toyah went so far as to pour anti-freeze into the freezers but went off the boil when Spider moved his girlfriend, Log Thwaite, into No.3. Toyah vowed to separate the pair and succeeded by trapping 'vegan' Log into

eating a bacon sandwich, which caused an enraged Spider to finish with her. However Toyah's hopes for romance were dashed when he started dating Lorraine Brownlow, the new barmaid at the Rovers. When Alf retired from the council, Spider stood for his seat but lost out to Audrey Roberts.

Curly decided to change his life by adopting a new image and was alarmed when Firmans was taken over by Freshco's Freezers. He worried for his job when his new boss turned out to be Anne Malone. She launched an attack on him, setting him up so that the police thought he was blackmailing the company by threatening to poison its products. Curly panicked and disappeared, leaving Spider and Alma Baldwin to join forces and clear his name. Spider flattered Anne into confessing she had masterminded the plan and, accidentally, she was trapped inside one of the freezers overnight and was found frozen to death. Curly's name was cleared but no one knew his whereabouts to tell him.

6 Jim's World Crumbles

Fiona Middleton and Steve McDonald moved back into a relationship following the birth of her son Morgan. Alan McKenna wasn't interested in his son and Steve surprised himself by taking to the baby. Fiona realized she still loved him and he moved in with her above the salon. He continued to hate Jim for having slept with Fiona and refused to employ him in his building firm.

When Jim, drunk, visited Steve's site to boast about being taken on at Kevin Webster's garage, the pair ended up arguing. Steve pushed Jim then watched in horror as he fell off scaffolding and was rushed to hospital, where he was in a coma for over a week. Liz kept a bedside vigil with guilty Steve and they both supported Jim when he came round, only to be told he wouldn't be able to use his legs again. Steve was relieved that Jim had no memory of the accident. Gradually Jim became bitter about his disability and tried to kill himself, buy Maud Grimes made him see that being in a wheelchair didn't mean his life was over. Liz moved back into No.11 to nurse Jim while his physiotherapist, Michael Wall, taught him how to cope.

After falling out with Fiona, Steve made a pass at Maxine Heavey and talked her into bed. Distraught Maxine told Fiona about the incident and Fiona decided she had had enough. She told the McDonalds that Steve had caused Jim's accident, left the Street with Morgan to live with her parents and sold the salon to Audrey Roberts.

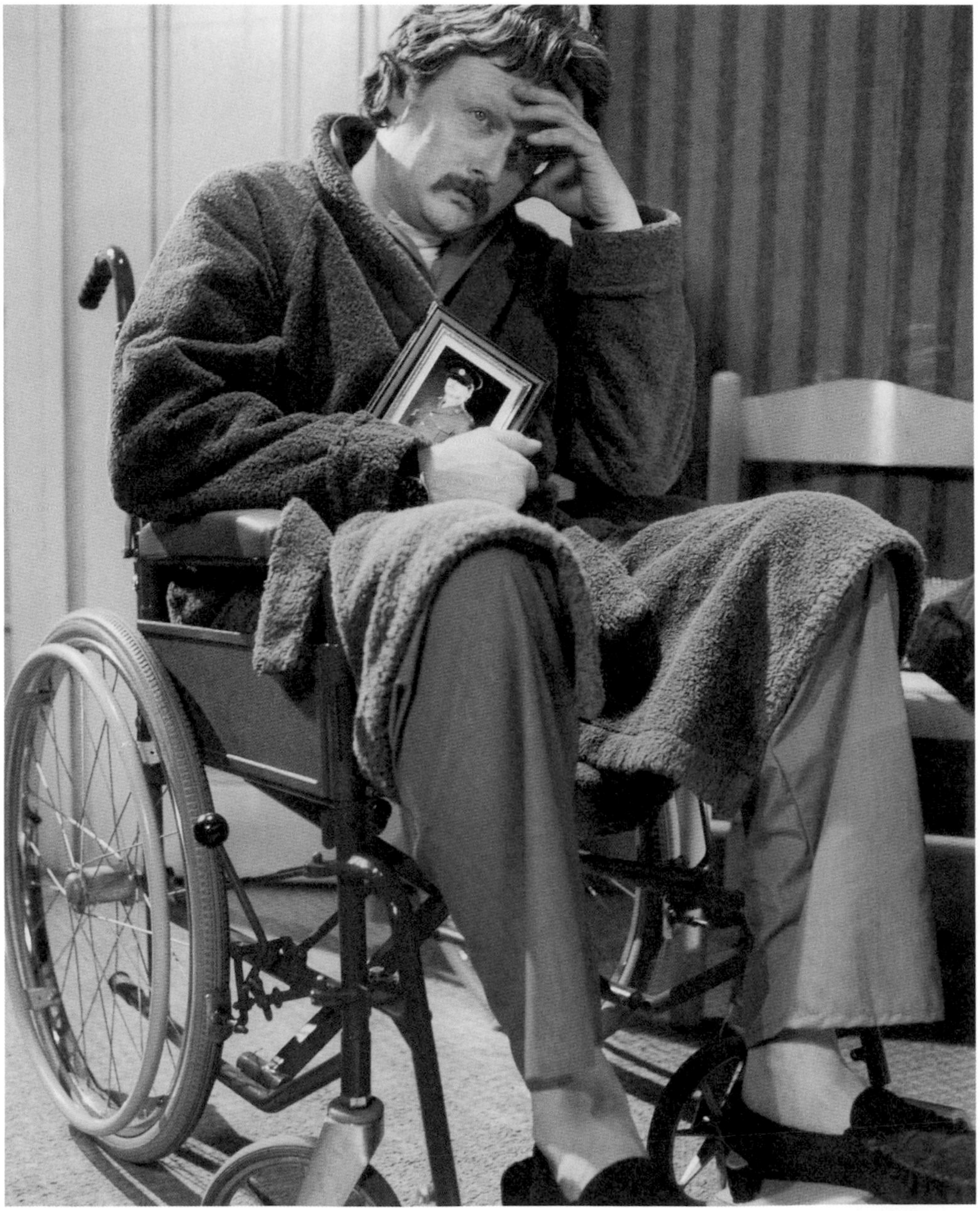

While Jim dreamed of remarrying Liz, she found herself attracted to Michael and the pair embarked on a passionate affair. Jim was delighted to regain the use of his legs but his joy turned sour when he found Liz and Michael in bed together. Michael urged Liz to put her feelings before Jim's and the pair ran off to live in Milton Keynes where he found work.

7 Roy Finds Romance

At work Alma Baldwin befriended timid loner Hayley Patterson. She supported her over the death of her father and did some matchmaking between her and Roy Cropper. Roy and Hayley were attracted to each other but their courtship ended suddenly when Hayley broke the news that she was a transsexual whose real name was Harold. Confused, Roy refused to have anything more to do with her but Alma made him understand that if he really cared for Hayley nothing else mattered.

Hayley went to Amsterdam to have the final operation to make her a woman and was delighted when Roy tracked her down and asked her to return with him. She moved into his flat over the café and took a job as a machinist at Underworld. However, Mike Baldwin found out about her past life when her tax details were in Harold's name. He made his distaste clear, which caused Roy to throw a pint of beer over him. The news spread around the Street and Hayley suffered jibes from machinist Linda Sykes, who told her she was a freak.

8 Les's Son and Heir

Les Battersby had a shock when twenty-eight-year-old Greg Kelly turned up on his doorstep and introduced himself to him as his son. Greg was the result of a fling between Les and Moira Kelly and Janice panicked, fearing Les would leave her for wealthy Moira. Greg decided to stay around the Street and was taken on at Underworld as a manager. He started dating Maxine Heavey, who threw herself at him, and rented the flat over the Corner Shop.

Les tried to rekindle his affair with Moira but she refused his advances and, returning home drunk, Les smashed into a police car. He was fined two hundred pounds and banned from driving for eighteen months. When Janice found out that he had been with Moira, she threw him out of the house and he was forced to rough it in a camper-van parked in the Street until he succeeded in romancing Janice into taking him back.

Having heard that someone was offering cash for cobbles, Les attempted to dig them up in the Street but ended up in hospital when one landed on his toe. There, he drove Martin Platt mad with his complaints and demands, and helped himself to the unlocked drugs trolley behind Martin's back. He overdosed and had to have his stomach pumped, but swore Martin had given him the extra dose on purpose. Martin was suspended and told the matter would be investigated.

In an attempt to better herself, Toyah took English lessons from Ken Barlow and started writing articles for *Just 16* magazine. When Les continuously belittled her efforts and head-butted Ken, thinking he was a dirty old man, Toyah ran away to London to find her real father. She was trapped by Neil Flynn, whom she mistakenly thought was her father, and was terrified when he tied her up and imprisoned her in his flat. Worried about her disappearance, Janice and Les followed her trail and were reunited with her after she ran away from Flynn. To help her over the ordeal, Toyah was allowed to go on holiday to Spain, where she fell for Dobber Dobson, a Manchester lad, who when they got home talked her into having sex with him and stealing from the café. She was besotted with him but before long realized what he was up to and dumped him.

9 The Cult of Nirab

Ashley Peacock found himself turning into a babysitter as Zoe Tattersall left Shannon with him every night as she partied. She refused to listen to his criticism but was shattered when Shannon died of meningitis. While Ashley and the Malletts tried to comfort her, Zoe had a breakdown. She was appalled by the news that Judy was finally pregnant and set fire to Shannon's pram outside No.9. Then she cut off her hair and kidnapped Fiona Middleton's baby Morgan from the salon before throwing herself into the canal in a suicide bid. Gary dived in after her and dragged her to safety, after which she was committed to hospital. There, she met Paul Fisher who was undergoing treatment for the guilt he felt at having blackmailed Judy into having sex with him for money.

When she returned to the Street Zoe assured Judy her secret was safe but Judy panicked and told Gary of how she had had sex with Fisher. He was devastated and

walked out on her, but three weeks later he returned and the pair were reconciled.

Zoe fell under the spell of a religious cult, the Etheric Foundation and, to Ashley's horror, moved out of No.4 to join them. The leader Ben Andrews selected her to be his sexual partner, so Ashley and Gary kidnapped her and dragged her back to the Street. However, they couldn't hold her against her will and she decided to live in America with Ben at the cult's headquarters. Meanwhile, back in Weatherfield, Gary was present when Judy gave birth to twins on Christmas Day.

10 Sally's Big Mistake

Sally Webster inherited fifty thousand pounds following the death of her mother. Kevin hoped she would use the money to buy Natalie Horrocks out of the garage but Sally refused, saying the money was hers and not his. She agreed to a family holiday in Florida but by the time they returned she had had enough of Kevin. She embarked on an affair with Greg Kelly, who finished with Maxine Heavey. Kevin found out about the affair and threw Sally out. She moved into Greg's flat over the Corner Shop and fought Kevin for custody of the children.

When Greg involved Sally in his scheme to steal Mike Baldwin's contacts and set up in competition Kevin found out and tipped Mike off. Then Greg talked Sally into using her inheritance to set up their own business and she did so happily, until he hit her because Mike had snapped up deals before he could. Frightened by his violence, Sally allowed Kevin to take back the girls and moved in with Rita Sullivan. With most of her inheritance gone, Sally took as much stock as she could from Greg and was left with thousands of pairs of knickers. Greg swore vengeance and broke into Rita's flat on New Year's Eve, intent on harming Sally.

CAST

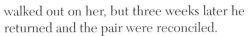

Morgan Middleton	Connor Chatburn
Log Thwaite	Zoe Henry
Hayley Patterson	Julie Hesmondhalgh
Jackie Dobbs	Margi Clarke
Greg Kelly	Stephen Billington
Darren Whateley	Andy Robb
Moira Kelly	Carolyn Pickles
Sandy Hunter	James Murray
Michael Wall	Dominic Rickards
Neil Flynn	Tim Dantay
Lorraine Brownlow	Holly Newman
Dobber Dobson	John Donnelly
Linda Sykes	Jacqueline Pirie
Ben Andrews	Burn Gorman
Miranda Peters	Francesca Ryan
Tyrone Dobbs	Alan Halsall

1999

Behind the Scenes

The death of much-loved Bryan Mosley shocked cast and viewers alike, and photographs of Alf's trilby lying on his coffin flooded the newspapers.

Under David Hanson, the programme calmed down after an eighteen-month rollercoaster ride. Adam Rickitt left Nick behind to pursue a pop career, Sharon Gaskell returned after a sixteen-year absence to jilt her fiancé in church, and Judy Mallett's death, in her own backyard, brought tears to viewers' eyes. Jane Macnaught became the twenty-ninth producer of the programme. She had worked on the Street as a production assistant during the Ken-Deirdre-Mike love triangle and had been a life-long fan of the show. Her love for the characters, story and history calmed anxious fans and cast, who feared another spate of sackings.

November saw the broadcast of six spin-off programmes, shot on location in Brighton, which brought Bet Gilroy and Reg Holdsworth back to the screen. It seemed that the public's hunger for the Street was reaching epic proportions and the first ever Saturday episode, an hour long, was broadcast on Christmas Day, viewed by 15.5 million, making it the most watched programme that day.

Top Twenty

Pos	Character	No of eps	Total	Pos Prev Year
1	Steve McDonald	159	861	23
2	Gail Platt	150	2001	5
3	Leanne Battersby	149	339	1
4	Janice Battersby	143	347	2
5	Toyah Battersby	140	304	9
6	Natalie Barnes	139	358	6
7	Sally Webster	138	1190	6
8	Mike Baldwin	137	1755	16
9	Audrey Roberts	135	1317	20
10	Linda Sykes	134	136	42
11	Rita Sullivan	131	2267	9
12	Maxine Heavey	123	430	17
13	Martin Platt	116	1074	25
14	Fred Elliott	116	331	30
15	Alma Baldwin	115	1026	21
16	Kevin Webster	113	1345	13
17	Les Battersby	113	294	4
18	Spider Nugent	112	207	27
19	Vera Duckworth	111	1723	11
20	Jack Duckworth	110	1520	29

Key Dates

1999

January 1	Alf Roberts dies
February 9	Bryan Mosley dies, just six weeks after Alf Roberts' screen death
April 21	Roy Cropper marries Hayley Patterson
June 25	Fred Feast dies fifteen years after his last appearance as Fred Gee
September 24	Ashley Peacock marries Maxine Heavey
	Judy Mallett dies
November 1	Ian Bentley marries Sharon Gaskell
December 25	First Saturday episode transmitted, a one-hour special for Christmas Day

"Natalie Barnes is that hard faced, if she fell on the pavement she'd crack a flag."

Vera Duckworth

STORIES

1 Sally and Kevin's New Lives

Greg Kelly's vicious assault on Sally Webster ended when Nick Tilsley chased him off. Greg stole what money he could find at No.5 and disappeared into the night. Sally called the police and set them on his trail.

Meanwhile, Kevin started a relationship with machinist Alison Wakefield and fought Sally through the courts for custody of the girls. He lost, and she moved them into her rented home at No.6 briefly, before taking over No.13 when distraught Kevin disappeared for six weeks. On his return he admitted he had had a breakdown and attempted to sort his life out, employing Jim McDonald and Tyrone Dobbs at the garage.

Sally fell for market trader Danny Hargreaves but felt she couldn't start a relationship with him as Rosie was behaving badly and had been suspended from school for bullying. She was jealous when he started dating Sharon Gaskell but thrilled when he told her eventually that she was the only woman he loved. She agreed to go out with him and was pleased when the girls gave their approval.

Kevin and Alison became engaged and moved into the flat over Skinner's bookie's.

Alison revealed her dark secret: that as a child her younger sister Cheryl had died while in her care. Her parents blamed Alison for her death. Then Kevin showed he didn't trust her with the girls when she was late home from taking them out. She was deeply hurt, packed and left him. He was miserable without her and eventually tracked her down to Morecambe where she was working. She told him she was pregnant with his child, but refused to return to Weatherfield with him.

2 Les Breezes Through Life

As Les Battersby looked forward to receiving compensation from the hospital, Martin Platt resigned his job, disgusted that his bosses believed Les over him.

When Janice learnt that Les was planning to take Jackie Dobbs on holiday to Las Vegas with the money, she told the hospital board that Les had taken the overdose himself.

Martin took a job at the Rovers before starting as an assistant at Weatherfield Vale, an old folks' home. Soon after his arrival he fell out with the owner over the way the place was run and was sacked after inspectors swooped to investigate. Councillor Audrey Roberts leant on the hospital to give Martin his nursing job back.

Janice grew worried about Les's infatuation and was relieved when Jackie finally left the Street, giving up the house to Curly Watts, its rightful owner, who had returned from travelling in Australia. Jackie was reunited with her husband but was soon back in prison, leaving Tyrone homeless on the streets.

Janice broke down when the electricity was cut off as Les had drunk the money she had saved to pay the bill. She grew frustrated that she was the only breadwinner while he just played at life. During a rare holiday in Wales, where they found themselves at the same caravan site as the Platts, Janice was flustered by the attention of young Owen Williams, who made a pass at her.

Martin was on hand to save Les's life when he electrocuted himself on the site and Janice decided she couldn't be unfaithful to Les. Owen followed the family back to Weatherfield and Les beat him up when he urged Janice to leave him for a new life in Wales.

3 Secrets and Lies

Audrey Roberts was grief-stricken when Alf died of a heart-attack during Nick Tilsley's eighteenth-birthday party. While mourning him she was alarmed to discover that his life hadn't been insured and, after legacies to the grandchildren, she was left with only fourteen hundred pounds plus the house and the salon. While she attended her son Stephen's wedding in Canada, Maxine Heavey took on Tom Ferguson at the salon. On her return Audrey was impressed with his work and sacked Maxine in his favour.

She was forced to back down when Tom and Maxine set up in opposition in the flat over the salon, calling themselves A Cut Above.

Fred Elliott was quick to pursue the widowed Audrey but she told him she was only interested in him as a friend. He confided in her that he had a son, so she told Maxine, who told Ashley Peacock.

Fearful of his inheritance, Ashley confronted Fred and was stunned to be told that he was the son in question. Ashley's mother Beryl admitted that Fred was right and that she had adopted him as a baby. Fred tracked down Ashley's real mother, Kathleen Gutteridge, and reunited the pair. In response, Ashley suffered an identity crisis, unsure of who he was. He started going out with Maxine again and she moved into No.4 with him. They became engaged and when Maxine's friend Melanie Tindell cancelled her wedding she grabbed her slot at the church. All the Street turned out for the wedding and afterwards Ashley conquered his fear of flying to honeymoon in the Caribbean. However, he couldn't face the return trip and came home the long way round by trawler.

The newlyweds got off to a rocky start when Maxine's mother, Doreen, left her husband Derek and moved into No.4. After Ashley begged Derek to take her back he parked his lorry across the Street and refused to move it until she returned to him.

Tom took over Maxine's flat above the salon and started an affair with Melanie but he finished it when she became too serious. He was angry when his father Duggie tracked him down and bought into a local development to be close to him. Tom blamed him for his mother's death and didn't want him around.

When Ashley returned from overseas, his shipmate Sergei Kasparov followed and made a play for Audrey, proposing marriage and begging her to marry him. She was tempted, but before she could answer, the immigration officials, tipped off by jealous Fred, arrested him for jumping ship.

4 A New Family

Fred Elliott opened a new butcher's counter at Freshco's and moved Ashley Peacock out of the Corner Shop, employing Nita Desai to take over. She turned out to be the daughter of Ravi, who owned six such shops, and in possession of information gleaned by her he put in a low bid for the shop. Fred found out that Nita was a spy and forced Ravi to increase his offer.

Nita took over the running of the shop, assisted by her younger brother Vikram. She moved into the flat above the shop and offended Rita Sullivan by selling newspapers and prompting a price war with the Kabin. Ravi didn't approve of her tactics and settled the situation with Rita.

When his brother died, Ravi went to Bombay to sort out his affairs and was forced to sell all seven of his shops to his cousin Dev Alahan. Vikram was furious at the loss of his inheritance, but Nita focused on her new career as a manager at Freshco's and she excelled at a 'bonding weekend', Forward with Freshco's, where she caught the eye of executive James Kitching. He encouraged her to apply for a head office job and talked his way into her bed. When she didn't get the job, she felt cheap.

5 Losers in Love

After falling into financial problems, Steve McDonald closed down his building firm and moved back into No.11. He alarmed Jim by smuggling tobacco into the country then moved on to alcohol. Lorraine Brownlow threw herself at him but he discarded her for Linda Sykes, who lost interest when she found out he wasn't wealthy. Lorraine made a scene by brawling with Linda over him and was sacked from the Rovers by her aunt, Natalie Barnes, when her work suffered as a result. Steve moved on to Nita Desai, upsetting Spider Nugent who was besotted with her.

Jim was upset when Liz wrote saying she was getting married and he made a pass at Natalie, which she rejected. Then he started to date Gwen Loveday, a machinist at Underworld whose husband had been in his old regiment.

Natalie also had a troubled year in the romance stakes. After attending the court

hearing of the men who had murdered Des, she ended up spending the night with his brother, Colin, when they reached out to each other in grief.

Drayman Vinny Sorrell became cellarman at the Rovers, brewing his own stout, Vinny's Velvet, in the cellar. At Christmas he and Natalie acknowledged their attraction to each other and ended up in bed together.

6 Total Eclipse of the Heart

Spider Nugent pitched his tent on the Red Rec to watch the eclipse with Toyah Battersby, but they missed the magic moment as they were overcome with lust for each other. Spider was startled by the strength of Toyah's love for him and they started a secret relationship.

Les was appalled by the thought of the pair of them together and attacked Spider, whereupon Toyah left home. She moved into No.3 to lodge with Spider, then accidentally set fire to the living room with candles while Emily Bishop was away. They moved into a small bedsit, and Spider was forced to show his love for Toyah by taking a job as a claims officer at the DSS.

Once there, he discovered that Les was signing on while working on the canal. He told Les that if he didn't leave Toyah and him alone, he would tell Janice what he was up to. Les was forced to agree but was then called in for a real dressing-down when the DSS photographed him at work. Spider tried to destroy the evidence but was caught red-handed. Les was told that the matter would go to court and that he might receive a prison sentence.

7 Rita's Bitter Lesson

Rita Sullivan was delighted when her foster-daughter Sharon Gaskell turned up with news of her impending marriage to a sales representative called Ian Bentley. Sharon prepared for the wedding, blissfully unaware that Ian was two-timing her with Natalie Barnes. Natalie knew that Ian had a fiancée but had no idea it was Sharon, until Betty Williams spied Natalie and Ian together and told Rita, who confronted her. Natalie finished with Ian, then Sharon jilted him at the altar.

Eager to keep Sharon around, Rita had her move into No.12 and gave her the Kabin as a birthday present, ignoring all her friends who thought the gesture foolish. Sharon started going out with Danny Hargreaves and was inconsolable when he left her for Sally Webster. Let down by yet another man, Sharon took an overdose but ended up vomiting the pills. Just before her suicide bid, she had phoned Ian and now he rushed to her side. The couple realized they still loved each other and were married behind Rita's back. When she found out Rita was furious with Sharon and felt betrayed when Ian forced Sharon to put the Kabin up for sale so that they could buy a house in Bolton. However, she swallowed her pride and bought the shop back from them. Blanche Hunt assisted behind the counter for a week but she drove Rita up the wall and was replaced by Norris Cole, who had returned to the area down on his luck.

8 A Marriage of Minds

Hayley Patterson took on the role of social secretary at Underworld and organized a Valentine's disco at the Flying Horse. She was upset when Roy Cropper started behaving mysteriously and feared he had another woman, only to discover that he was having dancing lessons as he didn't want to embarrass her. The pair became engaged at the disco and Hayley bought Gail Platt out of the café, which enabled Roy to move premises from Rosamund Street to Victoria Street. The opening was delayed when the café was flooded, and Roy had to serve food from an outside cart.

The couple were delighted when the female curate at St Paul's agreed to marry them in church, but the occasion was ruined by the arrival of the press, who had been tipped off by Les Battersby that two men were getting wed. Instead, their friends gathered in the new flat and the service was performed there, after which

Hayley changed her name by deed poll to Cropper. Eager to take up pastimes together, they became active members of the Weatherfield first-aiders and led their group to safety on Bonfire Night when the first-aid tent burned down.

9 The Rise of Linda Sykes

Mike Baldwin was flattered when attractive sales representative Julia Stone seduced him. He had no idea she was an ex-prostitute and that photographs of them were being taken. These arrived in the post, along with a demand for ten thousand pounds at the same time as Alma discovered a lump in her breast. She feared she was going to die and suffered a week of agony before being given the all-clear. Meanwhile, to save Alma more unhappiness, Mike paid the blackmail demand and was horrified when Julia asked for more money. Eventually, she grew uncomfortable with fleecing Mike, and told him that Greg Kelly was behind the scheme. Finally Greg demanded another ten thousand and laid siege at No.13, holding the Websters prisoner until Mike paid up. The plan backfired when Kevin found out what was going on and called the police. Fearing that her girls might be hurt, Sally attacked Greg with a chair and he was arrested.

When Mike confessed to Alma what had been going on she moved out to live with Audrey Roberts, infuriated that he could see himself as the injured party. Mike was surprised when machinist Linda Sykes offered him comfort, and the pair became lovers. She hardened him against Alma's financial claims by letting him know that Alma had been seen out in the company of Ravi Desai. In return Alma made it public knowledge that Mike and Linda were an item. Then Deirdre Rachid resigned from Underworld, refusing to tolerate mouthy Linda as the boss's girlfriend. However, Linda talked her into returning so that she and Mike could take a three-week holiday in the Far East. On their return she moved into his Quayside flat but their cosiness was disturbed by the arrival of his eighteen-year-old son Mark Redman.

Mark started work at the factory and outraged Mike by dating Leanne Battersby. He took on a new role, as chauffeur, when Mike lost his licence for drink-driving, and disliked the way Linda poked fun at him. Linda, meanwhile, walked out on Mike after he embarrassed her by throwing out all her friends during an impromptu party in the flat.

10 Retired but not Redundant

In June the residents celebrated Betty Williams's thirtieth anniversary behind the bar of the Rovers, while Maud Grimes shocked her friends by announcing her engagement to Sidney Templeton. Fred Elliott and Audrey Roberts took it upon themselves to quiz Sidney to ensure that he wasn't a gold-digger but during their questioning he died of a heart-attack. He left Maud ten thousand pounds in his will so she paid Emily Bishop to accompany her to the East to shower his ashes over the bridge he had helped build as a prisoner-of-war.

Blanche Hunt dumped herself on daughter Deirdre Rachid and promptly set about matchmaking between her and Ken Barlow. She didn't succeed but their daughter Tracy Preston did: after leaving husband Robert she fled to her parents, who worked together to reconcile the couple. After this, they acknowledged they worked well together and Deirdre moved back into No.1, closely followed by Blanche.

Ken took a job pushing trolleys at Freshco's and celebrated his sixtieth birthday with a party organized by Blanche. When Mike Baldwin heard that Ken had come into money, he demanded repayment of the ten thousand pounds he had paid out for Deirdre's defence. Ken gave it to him gladly and celebrated when Deirdre's name was finally cleared at the court of appeal.

11 Terry Wrecks More Lives

Judy and Gary Mallett had their twins christened William and Rebecca, with the Duckworths as godparents. There was embarrassment at the church when Jack realized he hadn't been christened, so as he was baptized Vera and Ken Barlow stood in as his godparents.

Shortly afterwards Gary was laid off work and became a window-cleaner, and Judy returned to the Rovers, under Natalie

Barnes, who moved into the pub and promptly demoted the Duckworths to cellarman and cleaner.

Jack and Vera moved into Eunice Gee's B&B on Park Road. Jack found himself an object of desire. Eunice made a pass at him behind Vera's back and was horrified when he suffered a heart-attack. Diagnosed with angina and ordered to rest, Jack was forced to retire from the Rovers. When Eunice moved to Spain, Vera took over the running of the B&B, with the help of Tyrone Dobbs who rented a box room.

After suffering a massive heart-attack Jack underwent a successful triple by-pass operation, which annoyed his son Terry, who had turned up hoping to come into his inheritance. While in town, Terry took Sharon Gaskell out and sold Vera a second-hand car. The car was involved in an accident when Vera was giving Judy a lift. Judy's leg was injured in the crash and she experienced pains that didn't go away.

One day, while at home with the twins, she collapsed in the backyard and died of an embolism caused by the crash.

Gary discovered the car was a cut-and-shut job and broke the news to the Duckworths that Terry had sold Vera a death trap. Jack accused Terry of murder, and while the residents attended Judy's funeral Terry stole back the car and had it crushed in a breaker's yard.

When Terry returned to the B&B on Christmas Day, Gary punched him and Vera smacked him round the face, telling him he was no longer her son. Instead Vera became maternal towards Tyrone and allowed him to adopt stray greyhound

Monica. Jack encouraged the lad to race her under the name Tyrone's Torpedo, but she only managed one race before being knocked over in the Street and having to have her leg pinned.

Tyrone was embarrassed when he had to admit he couldn't read or write and agreed to be tutored by Ken.

12 Pregnancy Scares for Leanne and Gail

Leanne Tilsley shocked husband Nick with the news that she was pregnant. He was appalled at the thought of being a teenage parent and, urged on by Miranda Peters, demanded that Leanne had an abortion. She went along with the operation but afterwards was shocked that he had told everyone she had miscarried. She realized she didn't love him and turned down his plans to emigrate to Canada, so he went alone.

Leanne bounced back by dating Vikram Desai and playing the casinos. After being suspected of theft she left the Kabin and took a job behind the Rovers bar, moving into the pub and owing Ashley Peacock back rent. When Nick pressed for a divorce she demanded cash and eager Gail Platt wrote her a cheque for two thousand pounds. When Martin found out what she had done, he emptied their bank account but was forced to release the money when Leanne threatened to set the police on Gail for buying her off. Everyone was appalled when she blew all the money on one visit to the casino. Then she dropped Vikram, and Steve McDonald introduced her to Jez Quigley, who started supplying her with cocaine. She quickly became addicted and stole money to pay for the drugs. She fell into debt to Jez, and found herself agreeing to help him rob the Rovers on New Year's Day.

Meanwhile, Gail had a pregnancy scare and demanded that Martin had a vasectomy but he refused. She put a ban on sex, then panicked that he was having an affair when he befriended fellow nurse Rebecca Hopkins. With Sarah Louise out at all hours and rebelling, Gail felt her family was falling apart. Rebecca turned to Martin for support following the break-up of her marriage and, fed up with hysterical Gail, Martin made love to her.

CAST

Alison Wakefield	Naomi Radcliffe
Nita Desai	Rebecca Sarker
Ravi Desai	Saeed Jaffrey
Vikram Desai	Chris Bisson
Ian Bentley	Jonathan Guy Lewis
Tom Ferguson	Tom Wisdom
Julia Stone	Fiona Allen
Danny Hargreaves	Richard Standing
Beryl Peacock	Anny Tobin
Owen Williams	Richard Harrington
Doreen Heavey	Prunella Gee
Derek Heavey	Richard Albrecht
Melanie Tindell	Nicola Wheeler
Kathleen Gutteridge	Elizabeth Rider
Sidney Templeton	Randal Herley
Vinny Sorrell	James Gaddas
Mark Redman	Paul Fox
Dev Alahan	Jimmi Harkishin
Jez Quigley	Lee Boardman
Gwen Loveday	Annie Hulley
Sarah Louise Platt	Tina O'Brien
Duggie Ferguson	John Bowe
James Kitching	Nicholas Irons
Sergei Kasparov	George Jackos
Rebecca Hopkins	Jill Halfpenny

2000

Behind the Scenes

As *Coronation Street* approached it's fortieth anniversary in December 2000, producer Jane Macnaught created storylines that shocked and delighted the viewers. The year started with a forty-five-minute two-hander, which saw the much-awaited return of Raquel Watts. Her visit was only fleeting but it left Curly with a young daughter. Next, the nastiest villain ever to walk the Street, Jez Quigley, was charged with a brutal murder that rocked the Street while Linda Sykes became the most oversexed woman in the programme's history as she balanced relationships with father and son Mike and Mark Baldwin. Sarah Louise's pregnancy, at the age of thirteen, started a national debate on underage sex, and the three key actors in the story were presented with awards at the British Soap Awards for Best Storyline. The press commented on axings and an exodus when news was leaked that the characters Leanne, Spider, Mark, Gary and Jim were all to leave, but in their place viewers warmed to newcomers Eileen, Geena and Emma.

Betty Driver went to Buckingham Palace to collect her MBE and was joined by Elizabeth Dawn, who received her honour later in the year in the Queen's birthday list. The BBC devoted hours of screen time to celebrating *EastEnders* fifteenth birthday but they lost out in the ratings battle when *Coronation Street* took the top four places that week as 15 million viewers tuned in to see Gail being told her daughter was pregnant.

Key Dates 2000

January 1	Betty Driver awarded the MBE
January 23	Kevin and Alison Webster marry
June 4	Bethany Platt born
June 5	Jake Webster is born and dies
June 7	Alison Webster dies
June 12	Elizabeth Dawn awarded the MBE
September 10	Mike and Linda Baldwin marry
September 15	Jez Quigley dies

STORIES

1 The Evil Jez

As the residents saw in the new Millennium with a fancy-dress street party, Leanne Battersby tried to stop Jez Quigley's planned raid on the Rovers by having sex with him. She was horrified when, afterwards, he went ahead with his plans and sent two thugs round for the takings. Leanne tried to fight them and was knocked unconscious and hospitalised. She confessed all to Natalie Barnes, who stood by her through drug counselling. Natalie's sister, Debs Brownlow, arrived in town and moved into No. 6 taking a job at Audrey's hair salon. She started dating Duggie Ferguson and helped him overcome his emotional block concerning women following his wife's death. However, when he refused to sleep with her she humiliated herself by spending the night with Dev Alahan, who saw her as an easy lay. Debs eventually got Duggie into bed and the pair started a relationship. Natalie's relationship with Vinny Sorrel took a different turn when he resigned from the Rovers saying she saw him as a lackey and not a lover. Duggie had employed Steve McDonald to develop his Victoria Street complex and Vinny was taken on as a labourer. While on the site he fell through a hole and uncovered the body of a dead man. The body was identified as that of Tony Horrocks who had been murdered. Confused by her feelings Natalie suffered a breakdown: she had hated Tony for being involved in Des's death. Colin Barnes turned up at Tony's funeral and caused a scene, which led the police to question him. To avoid arrest he was forced to tell them that on the night of Tony's murder he had been in bed with Natalie.

Steve borrowed £8,000 from Jez to open a taxi-cab firm with Vik Desai. He grew alarmed when Jez refused repayment of the money, saying that he was a sleeping partner and wanted to use the cabs to deliver drugs. When Steve tried to stand up to him, Jez threatened him with the same fate that had befallen Tony. Natalie put up a £10,000 reward for information on Tony's murder and Steve told her he knew Jez was involved. Jez was arrested but was found not guilty in court after Steve's motives as a witness were questioned. A free man, Jez told Steve that he had, in fact, killed Tony. Leanne grew alarmed when Jez told her he wanted her as a girlfriend and in an attempt to escape his clutches she left the country to work in Amsterdam. In an act of revenge, Jez had Steve brutally beaten up, causing Jim to attack him. In hospital, Jez dropped dead from a ruptured spleen caused by Jim's attack. Horrified, Jim gave himself up to the police as a murderer.

2 Curly's New Life

Curly Watts was stunned when his estranged wife, Raquel, turned up on his doorstep to tell him he had a three-year-old daughter, Alice. Raquel explained that she was to marry a French count and wanted Curly to be part of his daughter's life. He joined a singles' club and befriended Colette Graham, but she had a spurned boyfriend, Simon Cavanagh, who read more into the situation and started to stalk Curly. When his car was moved around the Street at night Curly reported the matter to the police and it was dealt with by Cavanagh, a Detective Constable. Sergeant Emma Taylor grew interested in the case and encouraged Curly and Colette to confront Cavanagh. He was charged, and Curly was thrilled when Emma admitted she found him attractive. They embarked on a relationship and she moved into No. 7

but he grew worried when her job started to involve firearms.

3 A Desperate Woman

Jim McDonald's relationship with Gwen Loveday suffered a set-back when she revealed that her ex-husband had been violent. He confessed to her that he had hit Liz, and the couple had to work hard to prove they trusted each other. Gwen had debts, which got out of hand, and she took an evening job at Alahan's shop to pay them off. When debt collectors troubled her, she moved in with Jim and reverted to her maiden name, Davies. Gwen couldn't help herself where money was concerned and pushed Jim into buying new furniture on HP. The name change didn't work and Gwen was tracked down by the finance company. They demanded full payment so she stole £35,000 that Jim had earmarked to buy Webster's garage and planned to leave the country. Jim found out about the plan when Gwen's bag was stolen and recovered by the police. He saw red and threw Gwen out into the gutter. She left the area and he had a bonfire in the Street with all her furniture.

4 Linda's Tangled Love Life

Linda Sykes decided she couldn't fight her attraction to Mark Redman any longer and they had sex at Underworld, just minutes before Mike Baldwin told them both he wanted them to be his partners: Linda in life and Mark in the business. Mark was horrified when Linda agreed to marry his father. He moved into the flat at No. 12 and watched as Linda rose at the factory, persuading Mike to make her a salesperson. She threw her weight around too much, though, and the girls threatened to strike. Mike sorted out the mess by making Hayley Cropper supervisor and telling Linda to stick to sales. Mark tried hard to stay away from Linda but kept falling into her arms. She insisted she loved both father and son and didn't want to lose either. Mike bought her a flash sports car and forced Mark to give her driving lessons, unaware that they used the lessons as a cover for sex. Just when Linda had decided to choose Mark, Mike suffered a heart-attack. He recovered, but the attack shocked Mark, who decided to leave and live in Amsterdam. Before he went, he agreed to return to be best man at the wedding and he kept his word. However, as Linda and Mike exchanged vows he felt sick at his behaviour and during the reception confessed all to Mike. Furious, Mike believed that Linda had been forced into an affair against her will and told Mark he was no longer his son.

5 The Vegetarian Butcher with a Murderous Ancestor

Fred Elliott became the talk of the Rovers after visiting a masseur to seek relief from back pain. He stripped off but was disturbed by a police raid. He had only just recovered from the humiliation when Ken Barlow uncovered a dark Elliott family secret. While researching a book he was writing on local history, Ken discovered that Victoria Street had once been named Cartwright Street but the name had been changed following the execution of Bernard Cartwright for the murder of his wife. Cartwright was revealed to be Fred's grandfather. Fred attempted to halt the book but Ken went ahead and published it.

There was more embarrassment for Fred when his son Ashley Peacock followed his wife Maxine's lead and became a vegetarian. The couple were influenced by Toyah Battersby and Spider Nugent, who introduced them to an alternative lifestyle. However, Toyah and Spider's relationship developed cracks when he became engrossed in his work and contemplated a mortgage. When Toyah pointed out how much he had changed Spider resigned from the DSS and suggested a spiritual year-long journey to India. When Toyah felt she couldn't leave her friends and family Spider took off on his own.

6 Turmoil in the Platt Household

Martin Platt realized he was no longer in love with wife Gail and embarked on a passionate affair with nurse Rebecca Hopkins. Her estranged husband Jerry warned Gail about the pair but she trusted Martin and refused to listen. Martin became confused as to what to do and confessed all to Danny Hargreaves. Rebecca tried not to be jealous of Martin's family but threatened to end the affair when she discovered Martin still had sex with Gail. Martin decided he had to leave Gail but his confession was halted by the news that, at thirteen, their daughter Sarah Louise was five months pregnant. Martin was forced support his family while distraught Gail threatened to take them all to live in Canada. Audrey Roberts lashed out verbally when she found out, calling Sarah a slut, and Gail's plans to run away were spoilt when news leaked out about the pregnancy. Martin was promoted to charge nurse and refused to let Rebecca leave when she tried to resign from the hospital. When Jerry turned up at the nurses' home and attacked Rebecca, Martin moved her to a private flat, paying half the rent himself. Sarah's pregnancy prompted Audrey to tell Gail about her own father, who was called Ted Page.

Danny was forced to tell Sally Webster about Martin's affair and she attempted to warn Rebecca off but Martin told her it was nothing to do with her. He was in bed with Rebecca when Sarah went into labour but rushed to the hospital, just missing the birth of her daughter. Rebecca realized Martin would always put his family first and took a job in Dubai, telling him she'd never return, even though she loved him. Heartbroken, Martin told Gail all about the affair. She was stunned but refused to throw him out, saying the family needed him.

Sarah christened her daughter Bethany and the Platts had to cope with jealous David who became rebellious and turned to shop-lifting.

7 Kevin's Tragic Year

After persuading Alison Wakefield to return to Weatherfield with him, Kevin Webster proposed marriage. The couple married in a register office with Kevin full of guilt after having taken his ex-wife Sally to bed on the eve of the wedding. Sally urged Kevin to forget about their session, and promptly moved Danny Hargeaves into No. 13 as her live-in lover. Together, Sally and Danny gave up their market stalls and opened a shop, D & S Hardware, on Victoria Street. There were celebrations when Alison gave birth to a son, Jake, but the infant was infected with a virus and died just hours old. His death sent Alison over the edge and she left the hospital with Sarah Louise Platt's baby. The police were alerted and a search started. Kevin tracked Alison down outside a baby shop and persuaded her to hand over the baby. She broke down, insisting that she would have been a great mother, before running out into the path of a lorry. Kevin had his wife and son cremated together.

8 Tyrone Falls in Love

Les Battersby was sentenced to 150 hours' community service for defrauding the DSS, and was set to work scrubbing at graffiti on Coronation Street. After he teased Tyrone Dodds for being illiterate, Tyrone sought revenge by spraying on new graffiti each time Les cleaned a wall.

Later, when Les was helping out at the local park, Tyrone removed his rowing boat so that he was marooned on an island in the boating lake overnight.

Tyrone passed his driving test second time round when his instructor suffered a heart-attack the first time. He decided to breed Monica to raise funds to buy himself a car and fell for kennelmaid, Maria Sutherland.

Jack Duckworth took a job as lollipop warden on Rosamund Street, causing Vera to take a job at Roy's Rolls so she could spy on him and make sure he didn't spend all day in the bookie's. The couple holidayed in Blackpool, looking after grandson Tommy. While staying with them, Tyrone and Maria became engaged on top of the Tower, and Gary Mallett fell for local girl Paula Shipley after saving her son from drowning. Gary and Paula kept up their romance and eventually he decided to sell up and move with the twins to Blackpool.

9 Alma's New Start

On receiving her decree absolute, Alma reverted back to her maiden surname, Halliwell, and threw herself into being a single woman again. She was flattered when Bob Bradshaw from the Town Hall started to take her out. Her landlady Audrey Roberts was stunned when Bob made a pass at her. She told Alma, who accused her of being a jealous troublemaker. Alma was forced to apologize when Bob was arrested for defrauding the Council.

When Tom Ferguson left town to get away from his father Duggie, Audrey let the flat over her salon to barmaid Geena Gregory and machinist Bobbi Lewis, and was thrilled when Alma threw a birthday party for her and invited all her friends. Her joy turned sour, though, when it was revealed she was sixty and not fifty-eight.

10 Roving Dev and the Perfect PA

Shopkeeper Dev Alahan was horrified when his ex-girlfriend Amy Goskirk tracked him down from Birmingham. She announced she was pregnant but Dev refused to believe her, causing the residents to turn against him when Amy broke down. She disappeared for a week, allowing everyone to think she had killed herself and on her return announced she had miscarried. Her bandaged wrists backed up her story that she had attempted to take her own life. Dev refused to believe her and took a gamble, ripping off the bandages to show everyone her skin was flawless. In fury Amy told the residents they were gullible fools and left the area.

Nita Desai left the Street to take promotion in Scotland and her brother Vik opened a mini-cab firm, Streetcars. Dev wished him well and employed his aunt, Maya Desai, in the shop. Maya enjoyed using Vik's taxis for free, annoying cab controller Eileen Grimshaw, who hit back at her by starting a discount cab service to Freshco's supermarket.

Ken Barlow was employed by the Gazette to write a weekly column. After machinist Edna Miller complained of Mike Baldwin's working conditions at Underworld, Ken wrote a piece condemning him. Furious Mike suspected factory manager Deirdre Rachid of giving Ken information and made life hell for her. She resigned, and was angry with Ken for not helping her by revealing his source.

Blanche Hunt was horrified when Deirdre took a job at Alahan's shop but she proved her worth to Dev, becoming his PA and helping him sort out his life. When Mike discovered Edna was the real leak he dismissed her and she became cleaner at the Rovers.

11 A New Interest for Rita

Rita Sullivan underwent training and opened a sub post office in the Kabin. Becoming interested in her genealogy, she visited a local bookstore and met the owner, Anthony Stephens. He assisted her in her research and the two became friends. Rita realized she had feelings for Anthony but withdrew when she discovered he was married. He explained his wife had Alzheimer's and convinced Rita they could be friends. Rita's assistant, Norris Cole, moved into lodgings at No. 3 after Emily Bishop was burgled by two youths who ransacked her house. Emily insisted that he called her by her first name rather than Mrs B, which she said made her sound like an old char.

CAST

Amy Goskirk	Jayne Ashbourne
Debs Brownlow	Gabrielle Glaister
Bob Bradshaw	David Roper
Geena Gregory	Jennifer James
Bobbi Lewis	Naomi Russell
Colette Graham	Susanna Shelling
Simon Cavanagh	John Griffin
Emma Taylor	Angela Lonsdale
Maya Desai	Indira Joshi
Jerry Hopkins	Ken Christiansen
Eileen Grimshaw	Sue Cleaver
Maria Sutherland	Samia Ghadie
Antony Stevens	John Quayle
David Platt	Jack Shepherd
Edna Miller	Joan Kempson
Paula Shipley	Joanne Rowden
Tommy Duckworth	Joseph Aston

INDEX OF STORYLINES

This is an index of storylines. Follow the year and paragraph number for each character to read their stories, from beginning to end.

SPECIALS & SPIN-OFFS

PARDON THE EXPRESSION (1965–6)
Thirty-six half-hour comedy programmes, which followed Leonard Swindley after he left Gamma Garments and took a job running Dobson and Hawks department store.

THE QE2 VIDEO (1995)
Curly and Raquel Watts honeymoon on the QE2 at the same time as Rita Sullivan and Mavis Wilton holiday on the liner. During the cruise Raquel realizes she does love Curly, while Mavis is hunted by a gigolo who thinks she's wealthy, and Rita realizes she has strong feelings for Alec Gilroy, on board as Entertainment Manager.

VIVA LAS VEGAS (1996)
Jack and Vera Duckworth fly out to Vegas and discover they are staying in the same hotel as Fiona Middleton and Maxine Heavey. The Duckworths fall out when he reveals he lied about his age when they married and that they aren't legally wed. Fiona finds herself pairing up with a cop as they attempt to rescue Maxine when she's kidnapped by gangsters. Vera and Jack get married again in a chapel of love and fly home in first class where they meet Joan Collins. Ray Langton appears briefly, working as a waiter at the hotel.

THE WOMEN OF CORONATION STREET (1998)
Betty Williams visits Hilda Ogden at her house in Derbyshire and they reminisce about all the female residents over the years.

THE BRIGHTON BUBBLE (1999)
Steve McDonald and Vikram Desai venture south to drive a van full of alcohol from France into the UK to be sold on. En route Steve diverts to Brighton, where he finds his ex-wife Vicky about to remarry. He decides to stay and stop the wedding. Another visitor is Bet Gilroy, enjoying the good life after the death of a wealthy lover. Vikram goes on to France and falls for a local girl, but returns with the alcohol unaware that hypermarket boss Reg Holdsworth is in the back of his van. Delighted, Bet uses Reg to pose as her dead lover in order to sell his luxury yacht and pockets the profits. Steve tries hard to stop Vicky's wedding but fails.

DIARY OF ANNIVERSARIES

JANUARY

1	Katie McDonald born 1992
	Alf Roberts died 1999
2	Katie McDonald died 1992
4	Spider Nugent born 1972
	Daniel Osbourne born 1995
5	Jim McDonald married Liz Greenwood 1974
7	Les Clegg married Maggie Preston 1946
8	Linda Cheveski born 1940
	Vicky McDonald born 1977
9	Bill Webster married Elaine Prior 1985
11	Vera Lomax died 1967
	Ernest Bishop died 1978
13	Maureen Elliott born 1945
14	Samir Rachid born 1973
15	Concepta Regan born 1926
16	Bert Tilsley died 1984
18	Gordon Clegg married Caroline Wilson 1982
19	Alfred Sharples married Ena Schofield 1920
22	Blanche Hunt born 1936
23	Kevin Webster married Alison Wakefield 2000
24	Ashley Peacock born 1976
	Tracy Preston born 1977
26	Maureen Naylor married Reg Holdsworth 1994
27	Valerie Barlow died 1971
29	Lynne Johnson died 1975
30	Nick Tilsley married Leanne Battersby 1998

FEBRUARY

1	Doreen Lostock born 1941
2	Hilda Ogden born 1924
3	Sarah Louise Platt born 1987
4	Betty Williams born 1920
6	Stephen Reid born 1956
7	Phyllis Pearce born 1921
8	Ray Langton born 1947
12	Des Barnes married Steph Jones 1990
	Lisa Duckworth died 1993
14	Ivan Cheveski born 1936
	Brad Armstrong born 1997
15	Jenny Bradley born 1971
	Brian Tilsley died 1989
16	Mike Baldwin born 1942
	Morgan Middleton born 1998
18	Jamie Armstrong born 1984
20	Vikram Desai born 1979
21	Janet Barlow died 1977
	Joyce Smedley died 1997
22	Tricia Armstrong born 1960
24	Harry Hewitt born 1925
	Brian and Gail Tilsley remarried 1988
25	Rita Sullivan born 1932
	Cyril Turpin died 1974

MARCH

3	Renee Roberts born 1943
5	Elsie Tanner born 1923
	Norris Cole born 1940
	Tricia Hopkins born 1958
	Samantha Failsworth born 1976
6	Jed Stone born 1940
8	Gordon Davies married Joan Walker 1961
14	Reg Holdsworth born 1942
20	Alf Roberts married Renee Bradshaw 1978
22	Sharon Bentley born 1965

APRIL

1	Maud Grimes born 1922
	Dennis Tanner born 1942
	Ivan Cheveski married Linda Tanner 1958
3	Ernest Bishop married Emily Nugent 1972
7	Mavis Wilton born 1937
	Derek Wilton died 1997
8	Percy Sugden born 1922
	Ivy Brennan born 1936
	David Barlow died 1970
9	Darren Barlow died 1970
11	Shirley Armitage born 1965
15	Peter and Susan Barlow born 1965
16	Gail Platt born 1958
17	Shannon Tattersall died 1998
19	Christine Hardman born 1939
20	Gloria Todd born 1958
	Len Fairclough married Rita Littlewood 1977
21	Frank Barlow died 1975
	Roy Cropper married Hayley Patterson 1999
23	Alan Howard born 1924
	Sheila Birtles born 1940
24	Des Barnes born 1965
26	Jack Walker born 1900
27	Neil Mitchell married Denise Osbourne 1990
30	Nita Desai born 1975

MAY

1	Frank Barlow married Ida Leathers 1938
3	Suzie Birchall born 1958
4	Bet Gilroy born 1940
6	Janet Barlow born 1942
9	Mark Redman born 1981
10	Esther Hayes 1924
11	Sonia Peters died 1967
12	Gary Mallett married Judy Smedley 1993

Steph Jones	Des Barnes	12.2.90	reg. office	Maurice Jones
Jackie Ingram	Mike Baldwin	5.7.91	reg. office	Phil Jennings, Hazel Lightfoot
Gail Tilsley	Martin Platt	27.9.91	reg. office	Kevin Webster, Alma Sedgewick
Lisa Horton	Terry Duckworth	27.5.92	St Mary's	Curly Watts
Rita Fairclough	Ted Sullivan	5.6.92	reg. office	Derek and Mavis Wilton
Alma Sedgewick	Mike Baldwin	19.6.92	reg. office	Alec Gilroy, Audrey Roberts
Olive Clark	Edwin Turner	29.9.93	St Saviour's	
Maureen Naylor	Reg Holdsworth	26.1.94	St Christopher's	Eric Firman
Deirdre Barlow	Samir Rachid	25.11.94	reg. office	Omar Bemmani, Liz McDonald
Vicky Arden	Steve McDonald	9.8.95	St Lucia	witnesses from off the beach
Betty Turpin	Billy Williams	20.10.95	St Mary's	Archie Wardle, Raquel Wolstenhulme
Raquel Wolstenhulme	Curly Watts	8.12.95	reg. office	witnesses from off the street
Tracy Barlow	Robert Preston	13.11.96	reg. office	Paul Davies, Deirdre Rachid
Fiona Middleton	Alan McKenna	7.11.97	St Mary's	Dave O'Grady, Maxine Heavey
Maureen Holdsworth	Fred Elliott	22.9.97	reg. office	Ashley Peacock, Maud Grimes
Leanne Battersby	Nick Tilsley	30.1.98	Gretna Green	witnesses from off the street
Natalie Horrocks	Des Barnes	23.10.98	reg. office	Tony Horrocks, Lorraine Brownlow
Sharon Gaskell	Ian Bentley	7.3.99	St Mary's	Tim Woods, Sally, Rosie and Sophie Webster
Hayley Patterson	Roy Cropper	21.4.99	Roy's Rolls	Martin Platt, Toyah Battersby, Sarah Louise Platt
Maxine Heavey	Ashley Peacock	24.9.99	St Christopher's	Gary Mallett, Melanie Tindell
Sharon Gaskell	Ian Bentley	1.11.99	reg. office	Danny Hargreaves, Sally Webster
Alison Wakefield	Kevin Webster	23.1.00	reg. office	Jim McDonald, Linda Sykes
Linda Sykes	Mike Baldwin	10.9.2000	country house	Roy Cropper, Geena Gregory

Deaths

Victim	Date of Death	Circumstances	Buried or Cremated	Next of kin
May Hardman	31.12.60	Heart attack in the hallway of No.13	buried	Christine Hardman (daughter)
Ida Barlow	11.9.61	Run over by a bus	buried	Frank Barlow (husband)
Amy Carlton	4.7.91	Old age	buried	Minnie Caldwell (daughter)
Colin Appleby	12.10.62	Car crash	buried	Christine Appleby (wife)
Martha Longhurst	13.5.64	Heart attack in the Rovers Return	buried	Lily Haddon (daughter)
Nellie Bailey	18.10.64	Lung cancer	buried	Stanley Fairclough (son)
Alice Raynould	22.3.65	Heart-attack in Sheffield	buried	Ena Sharples (sister)
Robert Maxwell	15.9.65	Heart-attack while driving Elsie Tanner home	buried	Moira Maxwell (wife)
Vera Lomax	11.1.67	Brain tumour; in the Mission of Glad Tidings	buried	Ena Sharples (mother)
Harry Hewitt	4.9.67	Crushed to death beneath Len Fairclough's van	buried	Concepta Hewitt (wife)
Steve Tanner	28.9.68	Pushed downstairs by Joe Donnelli	buried	Elsie Tanner (wife)
David Barlow	8.4.70	Car crash in Australia	buried	Irma Barlow (wife)
Darren Barlow	9.4.70	Car crash in Australia	buried	Irma Barlow (mother)
Jack Walker	30.6.70	Heart attack while visiting family in Derby	buried	Annie Walker (wife)
Joe Donnelli	12.12.70	Shot himself during siege at No.5	buried	none
Valerie Barlow	27.1.71	Electrocuted in maisonette	buried	Ken Barlow (husband)
Phyllis Roberts	18.9.72	Cancer	cremated	Alf Roberts (husband)
Tom Schofield	7.5.73	Old age in America	buried	Ena Sharples (sister)
Cyril Turpin	25.2.74	Heart attack outside home	buried	Betty Turpin (wife)
Lynne Johnson	29.1.75	Murdered by husband inside No.9	cremated	Roy Johnson (husband)
Martin Downes	9.7.75	Car crash in Northern Ireland	buried	Bet Lynch (mother)
Frank Barlow	21.4.75	Old age in Bramhall, Cheshire	buried	Ken Barlow (son)
Edna Gee	1.10.75	Burnt to death in warehouse fire	cremated	Fred Gee (husband)
Jerry Booth	10.11.75	Heart attack	buried	none
Janet Barlow	21.2.77	Overdose in No.1	cremated	Ken Barlow (husband)
Edie Riley	17.8.77	Old age	buried	Mavis Riley (niece)
Ernest Bishop	11.1.78	Shot in wages snatch at Baldwin's Casuals	buried	Emily Bishop (wife)
Renee Roberts	30.7.80	Car crash, hit by a lorry	buried	Alf Roberts (husband)
Monty Shawcross	12.11.78	Old age	cremated	none
Arnold Swain	22.12.80	Mental illness	cremated	Emily Bishop (wife)
Frankie Baldwin	4.7.82	Heart attack in London	cremated	Mike Baldwin (son)
Archie Crabtree	18.5.83	Stroke	buried	Hilda Ogden (sister)
Len Fairclough	7.12.83	Car crash, falling asleep at the wheel	buried	Rita Fairclough (wife)
Bert Tilsley	16.1.84	Mental illness	buried	Ivy Tilsley (wife)
Albert Tatlock	14.5.84	Old age, while visiting daughter	buried	Beattie Pearson (daughter)
Stan Ogden	21.11.84	Stroke in hospital	buried	Hilda Ogden (wife)
Don Ashton	3.6.85	Drove into canal when drunk	buried	Sandra Ashton (wife)
Pat Bradley	6.1.86	Knocked down on Rosamund Street	cremated	Jenny Bradley (daughter)
Joan Lowther	23.11.87	Heart attack after being mugged	buried	Robert Lowther (husband)
Eddie Seddon	11.1.89	Lorry crash	cremated	Elsie Seddon (wife)

Brian Tilsley	15.2.89	Stabbed to death outside a night-club	buried	Gail Tilsley (wife)
Alan Bradley	8.12.89	Run over by a tram in Blackpool	buried	Jenny Bradley (daughter)
Peter Ingram	17.8.90	Heart attack while shouting at Mike Baldwin	buried	Jackie Ingram (wife)
Amy Burton	18.2.91	Heart attack while playing bingo	cremated	Vera Duckworth (daughter)
Sandra and Tim Arden	19.7.91	Car crash	cremated	Vicky Arden (daughter)
Katie McDonald	2.1.92	Premature baby, died just hours old	buried	Jim and Liz McDonald (parents)
Ted Sullivan	9.9.92	Brain tumour; while watching bowls match	cremated	Rita Sullivan (wife)
Lisa Duckworth	12.2.93	Knocked down in the Street	buried	Tommy Duckworth (son)
Brendan Scott	20.8.93	Heart-attack; on the Corner Shop floor	buried	Debi Scott (wife)
Joss Shackleton	8.11.93	Old age	cremated	Vera Duckworth (daughter)
Mandy Baker	25.3.94	Cardiac arrest while in hospital	cremated	Janice Baker (mother)
Samir Rachid	2.6.95	Fractured skull; under mysterious circumstances	buried	Deirdre Rachid (wife)
Cliff and Elsie Duckworth	21.6.95	Car crash while abroad	cremated	Jack Duckworth (brother)
Ivy Brennan	23.8.95	Stroke while at religious retreat	buried	Don Brennan (husband)
Joyce Smedley	21.2.97	Broken neck after being knocked down	cremated	Judy Mallett (daughter)
Derek Wilton	7.4.97	Heart-attack after road-rage incident	buried	Mavis Wilton (wife)
Don Brennan	8.10.97	Crashed car into viaduct	buried	Maggie Bell (daughter)
Billy Williams	3.11.97	Heart-attack at home	buried	Betty Williams (wife)
Babs Fanshawe	18.3.98	Heart-attack while being escorted by Ken Barlow	cremated	Colin Fanshawe (brother)
Shannon Tattersall	17.4.98	Meningitis	buried	Zoe Tattersall (mother)
Elsie Seddon	25.5.98	Stroke in Scarborough	buried	Sally Webster (daughter)
Anne Malone	9.10.98	Frozen to death, locked in freezer at Freshco	cremated	Ed and Sarah Malone (parents)
Des Barnes	18.11.98	Heart-attack after being beaten up	cremated	Natalie Barnes (wife)
Alf Roberts	1.1.99	Heart-attack at No.8	cremated	Audrey Roberts (wife)
Sidney Templeton	6.8.99	Heart-attack in Fred Elliott's car	buried	Sandra Hesketh (daughter)
Judy Mallett	24.9.99	Blood clot resulting from car crash	buried	Gary Mallett (husband)
Jake Webster	5.6.2000	Virus	cremated	Alison and Kevin Webster (parents)
Alison Webster	7.6.2000	Knocked down by a lorry	cremated	Kevin Webster (husband)
Jez Quigley	15.9.2000	Ruptured spleen	cremated	unknown

THE STREET IN PRINT

Over thirty books have been published about *Coronation Street* in the past forty years. Most are now out of print.

Autobiographies
Jean Alexander, *The Other Side of the Street,* Lennard Publishing, 1989
Johnny Briggs, *My Autobiography*, Blake, 1998
Elizabeth Dawn, *Vera Duckworth, My story*, Blake, 1993
Betty Driver, *Betty,* Andre Deutsch, 2000
Tony Warren, *I Was Ena Sharples' Father,* Gerald Duckworth and Co, 1969
Ken Morley, *Knowledge is Power,* Blake, 1995
Lynne Perrie, *Secrets of the Street – My Life as Ivy Tilsley,* Blake, 1994
Patricia Phoenix, *All My Burning Bridges,* Arlington Books, 1974
Patricia Phoenix, *Love, Curiosity, Freckles and Doubt,* Arlington Books, 1983
William Roache, *Ken and Me,* Simon and Schuster, 1993
Bill Waddington, *The Importance of Being Percy,* Boxtree, 1992
Bill Waddington, *Percy's War,* Wordstar, 1994

Biographies
Sally Beck, *Queen of the Street: The Amazing Life of Julie Goodyear,* Blake, 1995
Chris Gidney, *Street Life: A Biography of Brian Mosley,* HarperCollins, 1999

Historical
Graeme Kay, *Celebrating 30 Years,* Boxtree, 1990
Daran Little, *Life and Times at the Rovers Return,* Boxtree, 1993
Daran Little, *The Coronation Street Story*, Boxtree, 1995
Graham Nown, *Coronation Street 25 Years,* Ward Lock, 1985
Jack Tinker, *Coronation Street,* Octopus Books, 1985

Characters
Anthony Haywood, *Street Cred,* Boxtree, 1990
Daran Little, *The Life and Loves of Elsie Tanner,* Boxtree, 1992
Daran Little, *The Ogdens of No.13,* Boxtree, 1992
Daran Little, *Weatherfield Life,* Boxtree, 1992
Daran Little, *Around the Coronation Street Houses,* Boxtree, 1997
Daran Little, *The Women of Coronation Street,* Boxtree, 1998

Behind the Scenes
David Hanson, *Access all Areas,* Andre Deutsch, 1999
Ken Irwin, *The Real Coronation Street,* Corgi Books, 1970
H.V. Kershaw, *The Street Where I Live,* Granada Publishing, 1981
Bill Podmore, *Coronation Street: The Inside Story,* Macdonald, 1990

Quiz
The Coronation Street Quiz Book, Boxtree, 1994

Novels
H.V. Kershaw, *Early Days,* Mayflower, 1976
H.V. Kershaw, *Trouble at the Rovers,* Mayflower, 1976
H.V. Kershaw, *Elsie Tanner Fights Back,* Mayflower, 1976
Daran Little, *Coronation Street At War,* Andre Deutsch, 1999
Daran Little, *Victory on Coronation Street,* Andre Deutsch, 2000

Criticism
BFI Monograph No.13, 1981

Humorous
Street Talk: the Language of Coronation Street, Ward Lock, 1986
John Stevenson, *How to Live The Life of Riley by Jack Duckworth,* Virgin, 1996

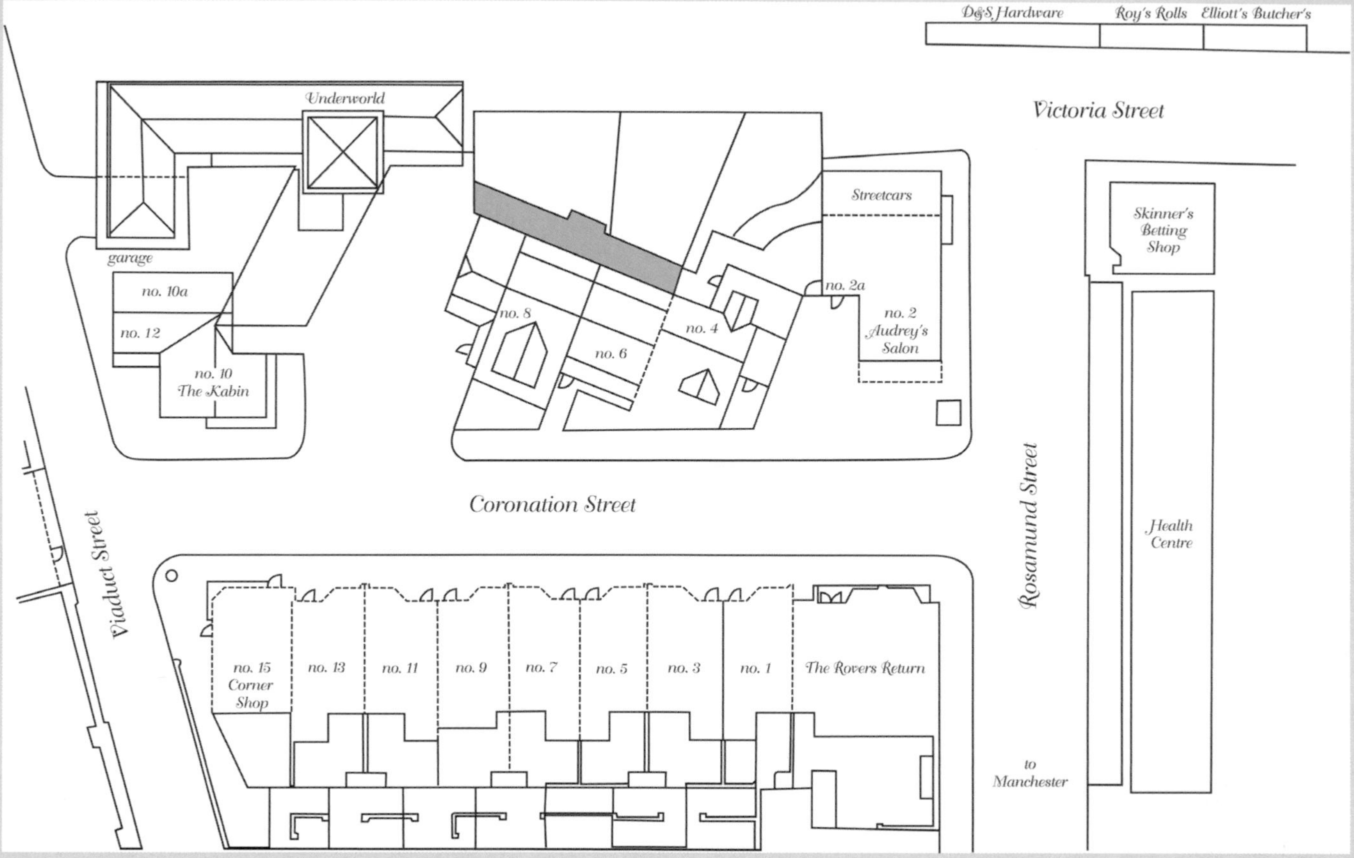

WHO'S LIVED WHERE?

Rovers Return

Jack, Annie and Billy Walker	1960–84
Lucille Hewitt	1964–74
Emily Nugent	1968–72
Fred Gee	1976–84
Bet and Alec Gilroy	1985–95
Raquel Wolstenhulme	1992–95
Jack and Vera Duckworth	1995–99
Natalie Barnes	1999–
Leanne Battersby	1999–2000

No.1

Albert Tatlock	1960–84
Ken, Deirdre and Tracy Barlow	1976–
Tricia and Jamie Armstrong	1995
Denise Osbourne	1995–6
Blanche Hunt	1999–

No.3

Frank, Ida, Ken and David Barlow	1960–64
Dickie and Audrey Flemming	1968–70
Ernest and Emily Bishop	1972–
Curly Watts	1983–8
Percy Sugden	1988–97
Spider Nugent	1998–9

No.5

Esther Hayes	1960–62
Minnie Caldwell	1962–76
Mike Baldwin and Bet Lynch	1976
Ray, Deirdre and Tracy Langton	1977–9
Bert, Ivy, Brian and Gail Tilsley	1979–88
Don and Ivy Brennan	1988–97
Les, Janice, Leanne and Toyah Battersby	1997–

No.7

Harry, Concepta and Lucille Hewitt	1960–64
The house fell down in 1965	
Len and Rita Fairclough	1982–90
Alan and Jenny Bradley	1986–91
Curly and Raquel Watts	1991–
Jackie and Tyrone Dodds	1999

No.9

Ivan and Linda Cheveski	1961
Ken and Val Barlow	1962–8
Len and Rita Fairclough	1968–82
Ray Langton and Jerry Booth	1970–75
Chalkie Whitely	1982–3
Jack, Vera and Terry Duckworth	1983–95
Gary and Judy Mallett	1995–2000

No.11

Elsie and Dennis Tanner	1960–84
Alan Howard	1970–73
Ken and Janet Barlow	1973–6
Gail Potter and Suzie Birchall	1977–9
Bill, Kevin and Debbie Webster	1984–5
Harry, Connie, Andrea and Sue Clayton	1985
Alf and Audrey Roberts	1986–9
Jim, Liz, Steve and Andy McDonald	1989–

No.13

May and Christine Hardman	1960–62
Jerry and Myra Booth	1963–4
Stan, Hilda and Irma Ogden	1964–87
Eddie Yeats	1980–83
Kevin, Sally, Rosie and Sophie Webster	1986–

THE CORNER SHOP

Florrie Lindley	1960–65
Lionel and Sandra Petty	1965–6
David and Irma Barlow	1966–8
Les, Maggie and Gordon Clegg	1968–74
Granny, Idris and Vera Hopkins	1974–5
Alf, Renee and Audrey Roberts	1976–94
Brendan Scott	1993
Reg and Maureen Holdsworth	1994–8
Fred Elliott	1998–9
Ravi, Vik and Nita Desai	1999–

No.15A

Doreen Lostock and Sheila Birtles	1962–3
Emily Nugent	1966–8
Betty and Cyril Turpin	1969–70
Irma Barlow and Bet Lynch	1970–72
Norma Ford	1972–3
Tricia Hopkins and Gail Potter	1974–6
Bet Lynch	1976–5
Deirdre Langton	1980–81
Kevin and Sally Webster	1987–8
Curly Watts and Shirley Armitage	1988–9
Ken Barlow	1990–95
Bill Webster	1996–7
Chris Collins	1997–8
Greg Kelly	1998–9
Nita Desai	1999–2000
Dev Alahan	2000

No. 12

Reg Holdsworth	1991–4
Alec Gilroy	1996–9
Sharon Gaskell	1999
Mark Redman	2000

No.10

Rita Sullivan	1990–

No.8

Martin, Gail, Nick, Sarah Louise and David Platt	1991–

No.6

Des and Steph Barnes	1990–98
Debs Brownlow	2000

No.4

Derek and Mavis Wilton	1990–98
Fred and Maureen Elliott	1998
Ashley and Maxine Peacock	1998–

No.2

Denise Osbourne	1992–5
Fiona Middleton	1995–8
Maxine Heavey	1998–9
Tom Ferguson	1999–2000
Geena Gregory and Bobbi Lewis	2000

WHO WAS WHO AND WHO IS WHO

CHRISTINE APPLEBY, née Hardman, was the original occupant of No.13. An independent woman in her early twenties, she worked at Elliston's raincoat factory and lived alone following the death of her mother, May, in 1960. Christine was the Cinderella of Coronation Street, a tragic, put-upon figure who appeared more confident than she was. Living alone with memories drove her to a nervous breakdown, and she climbed the factory roof where she contemplated suicide. Ken Barlow, the boy she had a crush on, talked her down, and she shocked the neighbours a month later by eloping to London with an old flame, Colin Appleby. Within three months she had returned, a widow, and became Elsie Tanner's lodger at No.11. Ken's father, Frank, started to court her and in 1963 she agreed to marry him, giving the gossips plenty to talk about. Three weeks before the wedding she admitted she didn't love him and the wedding was cancelled. She left the Street to live with Esther Hayes and then moved to work for Miami Modes' head office in Southampton.

SHIRLEY ARMITAGE worked as a machinist at Baldwin's Casuals from 1984 to 1989. For much of that time she gossiped and laughed with the rest of the factory floor, but after catching the eye of Curly Watts she moved into the Corner Shop flat with him. Their relationship amused the residents as he was intelligent and she had dropped out of school with no qualifications. They also faced criticism from both their parents for getting involved with someone of a different race but they ignored the prejudice. In the end it was the difference in their intellects which drove them apart and Shirley, turning down Curly's marriage proposal, returned home to her parents.

TRICIA AND JAMIE ARMSTRONG lived for a short time at No.1, renting the house from Mike Baldwin. Tricia first came to the Street in 1994 when she dated Curly Watts after talking him out of prosecuting Jamie for shoplifting at Freshco's. Curly was soon frightened off by her violent husband Carl, but shortly afterwards the couple split and Carl ended up in Strangeways. Tricia became one of Mike Baldwin's tenants at his flats in Crimea Street and for a short period worked as cleaner at the Rovers. Her short temper, quick tongue and roving hands landed her the sack, but she eventually ended up living at the pub after becoming pregnant by Terry Duckworth. Terry's parents, Jack and Vera, took her and Jamie into the pub when she threatened to abort the baby unless they supported her. Little Brad was born in the living room, delivered by Betty Williams. Terry wanted nothing to do with the baby or Tricia but luckily **RAY THORPE**, fell in love with the family and Tricia was happy to leave the Street to live with him on the other side of Weatherfield.

MIKE BALDWIN opened his denim factory on Coronation Street in 1976 and brought business with him from his London office. He employed plenty of the locals and bought No.5, installing Bet Lynch in it as his live-in lover. A Cockney with a bulging wallet and a taste for expensive cigars, he has a long-standing feud with Ken Barlow, following his affair with Ken's wife Deirdre. Plenty of women have passed through Mike's bed but he never married until 1986 when Ken's daughter **SUSAN** became the first Mrs Baldwin. The marriage lasted a year, ending in divorce when she aborted the child he longed for. Mike is a father, however: his son **MARK REDMAN** was the result of an affair with florist **MAGGIE DUNLOP** in the early 1980s. She refused to marry Mike because he wouldn't invest in her business and instead wed a much older man who brought up Mark as his own. Mark only found out the truth when his mother had an affair with Ken Barlow. In 1992 Mike married **ALMA SEDGEWICK.** Alma used to run Jim's Café on Rosamund Street, Jim being her first husband. She fell for Mike as soon as she saw him but had to wait in the wings until he had married and divorced heiress **JACKIE INGRAM** before agreeing to marry him. Never having had children of her own, Alma saw Mark as a threat to her stability but Mike worked hard to prove his love for her. She embarrassed herself by falling for Audrey Roberts's son, Stephen Reid, but he wasn't interested in her. Alma sold her business when Mike had financial problems but the marriage fell apart when he was blackmailed for spending a night of passion with scheming Julia Stone. Mike and Alma divorced in 2000 and he pressed ahead with his marriage to machinist **LINDA SYKES**, unaware that she was having an affair with his eighteen-year-old son Mark. Alma became Audrey Roberts' lodger.

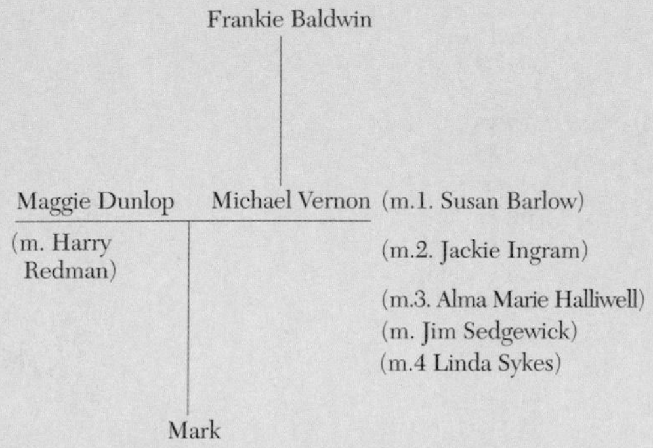

THE BARLOWS: **FRANK** was a postman who believed that his home at No.3 was his castle. He was set in his ways and proudly refused to believe in credit.

His wife, **IDA**, worked in the kitchens of a large hotel and was a domesticated woman, totally devoted to the care of husband and sons, **KENNETH** and **DAVID**. Kenneth had the brains while easy-going David was a practical lad. He gave up an engineering apprenticeship to move to London and a football career in a Second Division team. For a time his bedroom was occupied by Ida's mother **NANCY LEATHERS** but the old lady moved out following Ida's death under the wheels of a bus. Lonely Frank proposed to Christine Appleby, who had been at school with Kenneth, but just before the wedding she had cold feet. He bounced back by opening his own DIY shop on Victoria Street but after a year sold up following a five-thousand-pound win on the Premium Bonds. He moved to Bramhall.

Kenneth left university and became a teacher. He married **VALERIE TATLOCK** from No.1 and bought No.9 to live in.

She ran a hair salon from the front parlour until their children, twins Peter and Susan, were born in 1965. Kenneth was a man who always put his principles before his family, even to the point of going to prison for seven days for taking part in an anti-Vietnam demonstration. David, on the other hand, was a more caring husband to his wife Irma. They married in 1965, and the following year he left professional football and bought the Corner Shop. They ran the venture together before emigrating to Australia, where their son Darren was born. Tragically, Darren and David were killed in a car crash and Irma returned, a widow, to the Street for two years before eventually settling in Canada. Meanwhile, Valerie struggled through life looking after the children and earning pin money at the Corner Shop. She loved Ken although he patronized her and belittled her values. For all his dismissive ways, though, he was devastated in 1971 when she was electrocuted and died in their maisonette. As Ken was unable to cope with the twins, they were brought up in Scotland by Val's parents.

Ken took responsibility for Val's uncle, Albert Tatlock, and enjoyed the life of a bachelor before making the mistake of marrying Town Hall clerk Janet Reid who, as soon as she had the ring on her finger, announced that she had no intention of bringing up his children. The marriage ended soon afterwards.

Ken's working life has never remained constant: for the most part he has taught, but he has also been a factory boss, a social worker, a taxi driver, a male escort, and at one stage owned and ran his own newspaper, the *Weatherfield Recorder.* In 1981 he married **DEIRDRE LANGTON**, a divorced woman with a young daughter, **TRACY**. They moved into No.1 with Albert but Deirdre soon felt suffocated in the relationship and had an affair with Mike Baldwin. Ken fought Mike off but started a bitter feud with him, which still rages. This feud was deepened when Mike married twenty-one-year-old Susan, Ken's daughter. Ken himself had an affair, in 1989, with **WENDY CROZIER**. Deirdre filed for divorce, then Ken watched as his affair ended and his life crumbled. He ended up moving into the flat over the Corner Shop while Deirdre took a twenty-two-year-old Moroccan, **SAMIR RACHID**, as her third husband. Their marriage was frowned upon by the residents and the authorities, and ended in Samir's death after a mugging. He gave his kidney to Tracy, who had suffered renal failure after a drug overdose.

Ken's love life perked up when twice-married hair stylist **DENISE OSBOURNE** moved in with him and gave birth to their son, **DANIEL**. Denise ran the hair-salon at No.2 but had a troubled existence, pestered by obsessive Don Brennan and her estranged husband Neil Mitchell. Eventually it was her affair with her brother-in-law, Brian Dunkley, that ended her relationship with Ken and she fled to Scotland with Daniel.

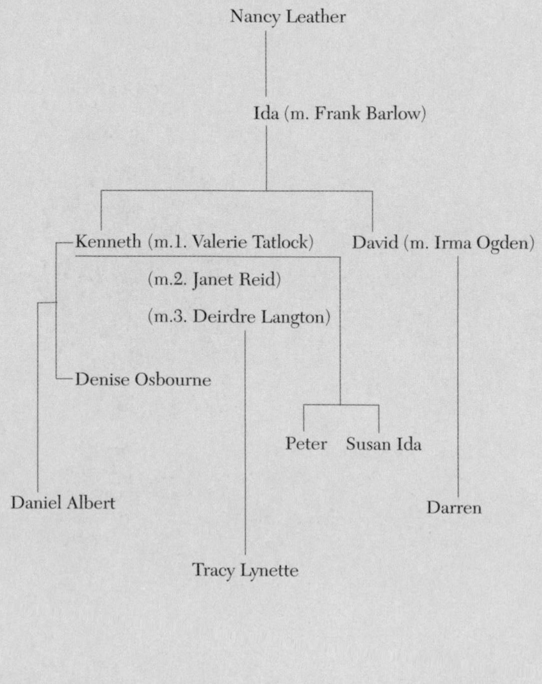

In 1997 Deirdre took up with pilot **JON LINDSAY** only to discover that he really sold ties and had dragged her into a tangled web of deceit, which left her being sent to prison. Mike and Ken joined forces to secure her release and afterwards she moved back in with Ken. She refuses to remarry him, despite the pleas of her mother **BLANCHE HUNT** who lives with the couple. Blanche, originally a resident of Victoria Street, moved to the Midlands in 1976 with her lover Dave Smith. Following a stroke she has nothing better to do now than meddle in Deirdre's life. Tracy lives in London now with her husband **ROBERT PRESTON.**

DES AND STEPH BARNES moved into No.6 on their wedding day in February 1990. He was a bookie's clerk and she worked as a perfume demonstrator in a department store. Her father, **MAURICE JONES,** had built the new houses on the Street and gave them No.6 at cost price. The Barnes marriage was turbulent; she was a tease and he was childish. Steph left Des in 1991 for another man, but returned a few years later, pregnant but not by Des. By that stage Des no longer loved her and they divorced.

Des remained at No.6, moving in a string of girlfriends, including Raquel Wolstenhulme and widow **CLAIRE PALMER**, who came complete with teenage daughter Becky. Des shied away from relationships though and always strayed when domesticity became too threatening. He had affairs with Tanya Pooley and Samantha Failsworth before falling for **NATALIE HORROCKS.** After wrecking the Websters' marriage she had a reputation as a man-eater but won the neighbours round by falling for Des.

They married in October 1998 but the honeymoon was short-lived: her son, **TONY,** moved into the house with them. Tony was no stranger to the Street: he had worked as a mechanic at the garage, dated Fiona Middleton but had left after knocking over Joyce Smedley and killing her. In his time away from the Street he had become a drug-dealer and moved his business into No.6. Des interrupted thugs beating him up and was knocked unconscious. Later he died in hospital in Natalie's arms. Natalie turned Tony over to the police and faced the hostility of Des's brother, **COLIN.** He had once lodged with Des at No.6 and had had a brief fling with Liz McDonald. After arguing about who was to blame, Colin and Natalie found comfort together in a one-night stand. Natalie took over the licence of the Rovers Return and moved in as landlady. In 2000 she started an affair with her cellarman, **VINNY SORRELL** and was rocked by the discovery that Tony had been murdered.

THE BATTERSBYS: LES, JANICE, LEANNE AND TOYAH moved into their new council house, No.5, in 1997. Janice worked at Mike Baldwin's Underworld factory but Les tried his best to avoid work. While Toyah studied at school, Leanne took a job at the Kabin and, almost immediately, fell for Nick Tilsley.

They ran away together to Gretna Green and married in secret, moving into No.4 to lodge with Ashley Peacock (see **TILSLEY/PLATT**). Toyah took English literature lessons from Ken Barlow and studied hard, becoming the first ever Battersby to enter college. After a row at home she ran away to London to find her real father, but instead ended up held hostage by a crazed man. She managed to escape and returned, physically unharmed, to the Street. In 1999 she fell for eco-warrior Spider Nugent and moved into a bedsit with him.

Les and Janice's marriage was rocked when Janice was tempted to leave him for Owen Williams, a young caravan site worker. Despite being tempted Janice stayed with Les but has had to put up with his roving eye and work-shy antics. After taking a dose of too many pain-killers in hospital he lost Martin Platt his job by accusing him of giving him the tablets on purpose. Les has a son, **GREG KELLY,** who sought him out and worked at Underworld before fleecing Sally Webster of thousands and holding her hostage at No.13. Desperate for money, he blackmailed Mike Baldwin after setting him up with a prostitute. He only got ten thousand pounds for his pains before the police caught up with him.

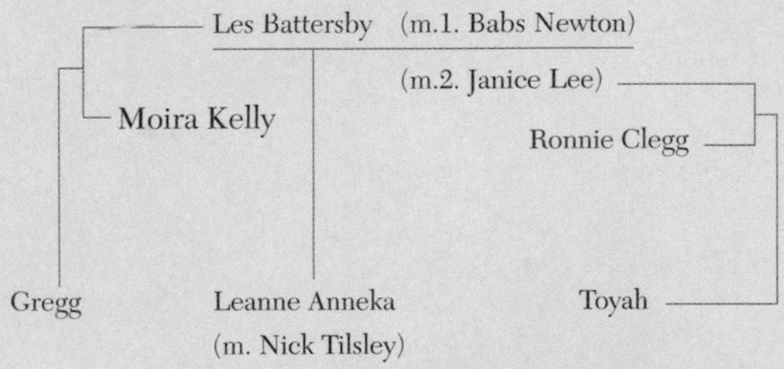

THE BENTLEYS: see **FAIRCLOUGHS**

SUZIE BIRCHALL came to the Street in 1977 to lodge with Gail Potter at No.11, with landlady Elsie Tanner. She worked at the Western Front boutique before becoming a machinist at Baldwin's Casuals and having an affair with the owner, Mike Baldwin. Keen to show she could win any man, she seduced Gail's boyfriend, Mike's right-hand man **STEVE FISHER.** Steve struggled to fit into management but let Mike down as he constantly sided with the workers. To harden him up Mike sent him to run operations at his London factory and Suzie followed him, tired of living in a back street. Three years later she returned, escaping from her violent husband, **TERRY GOODWIN,** who followed her and attempted to kill her when she finished with him. After Gail boasted of her happy marriage, Suzie attempted to seduce her husband, Brian, but the plan backfired and Elsie threw Suzie out. Her whereabouts are now unknown.

ERNIE BISHOP had his own photographic shop and studio on Rosamund Street. At his mother's funeral he met her friend **EMILY NUGENT** and fell in love.

Emily lived as a paying guest at the Rovers Return and for many years had been connected to the Mission circuit as secretary to the committee. In the early 1960s she had worked at Gamma Garments, first as assistant to Leonard Swindley, then as manageress. When Gamma folded in 1968 she continued to work behind shop counters and eventually became Ernie's partner in the camera shop. Emily had once been besotted with Leonard Swindley and had jilted him at the altar after realizing she was in love with the idea of being in love. Her courtship with Ernest lasted three years, and suffered a blow when he was arrested in Spain for photographing a scantily clad model.

After eventually marrying, the couple moved into No.3. The camera business folded and Ernest was declared bankrupt. To his shame, Emily was forced to take on menial work while he became wages clerk at Baldwin's Casuals. During a wage heist at the factory he was shot in the chest and died in hospital.

Emily remained at No.3, taking in Deirdre Langton as a lodger before falling in love with pet-shop owner **ARNOLD SWAIN.** They married in September 1980 but three months later the marriage ended when Emily discovered he was a bigamist. He was arrested and died shortly afterwards in hospital. Emily took a job as Mike Baldwin's assistant at his factory, and threw herself into good works, becoming a leading light at the Friends of Weatherfield Hospital. She took in lodgers, starting with Curly Watts, then was stuck with objectionable pensioner Percy Sugden. He interfered with her life and meddled in her relationships but proved his loyalty by helping her over a nervous breakdown in the early 1990s. She became engaged to local vicar, Bernard Morten, but when he found out about her breakdown he broke with her.

When Percy went into a retirement home, Emily swore she wouldn't have another lodger, but a few months later her nephew, **GEOFFREY 'SPIDER' NUGENT,** turned up on her doorstep. She got carried away with his ecological warfare and ended up sleeping in a tree to protect it from being cut down. Spider moved out of No.3 in 1999 to share a bedsit with his girlfriend Toyah Battersby. A year later the couple split when Spider went on a spiritual journey to India.

JERRY BOOTH, from Viaduct Street, became Len Fairclough's apprentice at his building firm in 1962. He was shy and spent most of his free time cycling with the Weatherfield Wheelers. After an abortive romance with Sheila Crossley, Jerry was pushed into marriage by domineering typist **MYRA DICKENSON.** They took out a mortgage on No.13 but quickly fell into debt. When Myra discovered she was pregnant the couple moved in with her father but separated after their daughter was stillborn. Jerry returned to work for Len and lodged with him. Sheila re-entered his life but the fact that she had an illegitimate son caused him to pull out of their relationship. In 1968 he left the area but three years later he was back, sleeping rough. Len took him on as a partner, along with Ray Langton, and the three lived at No.9. Jerry started to romance Mavis Riley but suddenly, in November 1975, he died of pneumonia.

THE BRADLEYS: ALAN and **JENNY** entered the Street in 1986 when Jenny's mother Pat was knocked down and killed on Rosamund Street. Jenny was a paper-girl at the Kabin and her boss, Rita Fairclough, took her in and attempted to reconcile her with her estranged father Alan. It was an uphill struggle but finally Alan persuaded Jenny to forgive him for walking out on her eight years before. They moved into a flat on Ashdale Road and Alan fell for neighbour Gloria Todd, but was forced to give her up when she discovered he was also romantically involved with Rita. Rita refused his offers of marriage but installed him at her home, No.7, as her common-law husband. Alan set up his own company, selling security systems, borrowing money from Rita then stealing the deeds of her house to raise fifteen thousand pounds. He tried to hold down an affair with Carole Burns but realized he needed the financial security Rita could offer him.

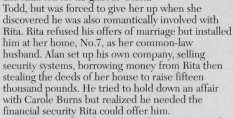

When Rita found out about the mortgage on her home she confronted Alan, who tried to kill her. He was arrested and spent months on remand before being allowed to walk free. He terrorized Rita, who suffered a breakdown and disappeared. She was traced to Blackpool, and while attempting to drag her home Alan was knocked down and killed by a tram.

Jenny's love life was just as unsuccessful: she was engaged to a French student, Patric Podevin, and had flings with Martin Platt and Mark Casey before running off with a married dentist. She came back to Rita when he grew tired of her but was only interested in Rita's money. Rita gave her a cheque for a thousand pounds and told her she never wanted to see her again.

DON BRENNAN was a mild-mannered taxi driver when he first rode into the Street in 1987. He fell for widowed **IVY TILSLEY** (see **TILSLEYS**) and married her in June 1988, before moving into her home at No.5. Shortly afterwards he discovered that Ivy was tormented by the souls of her dead husband and son, and as she became more obsessed with them she pushed him out of her life. He embarked on an affair with barmaid Julie Dewhurst but when she finished with him he decided to kill himself. He drove into a field hoping to crash, but ended up alive but lost a leg. When Ivy turned to drink he returned to her as he realized how much she needed him.

After losing her job at Baldwins, Ivy became a shop assistant at Bettabuys supermarket while Don become obsessed with hair-stylist Denise Osbourne and plagued her with obscene phone calls. This was the last straw for Ivy, who entered a religious retreat where she eventually died of a stroke.

Don remained at No.5, buying it from Ivy's heir, her grandson Nick, for fourteen thousand pounds. For a time **JOSIE CLARKE** lived with Don but he grew bitter after buying a garage in a bad business venture from Mike Baldwin. Josie left him and Don become obsessed with getting even with Mike. He kidnapped his wife Alma and attempted to kill himself and her by driving into the Irwell but Alma managed to free herself then dragged him to safety. The garage business collapsed and Don lost his job after being caught drinking and driving. He burnt down Mike's factory and tried to set up his lodger Ashley Peacock as the perpetrator, but the police caught up with him and he was arrested. Escaping from custody, he tried to kill Mike, then ended up driving a car into the viaduct and was killed in the ensuing explosion.

MINNIE CALDWELL lived at No.5 from 1962 to 1976. Prior to that she was at Jubilee Terrace with her mother but when the old lady died she moved to be nearer her friend Ena Sharples. Minnie acted as Ena's deputy in keeping the Street's morals in check. She had no children but was devoted to her cat, Bobby, and numerous lodgers, including **JED STONE,** a Scouser who called her Ma. She called him Sunny Jim, and turned a blind eye to the dodgy stock he stored in the house. When he went to prison for handling stolen goods in 1966 she was devastated. She nearly died during the Street's coach crash in 1969, and was in a coma for two weeks. In 1973 Albert Tatlock proposed marriage to her but she was relieved when the engagement ended six months later as she found some of his habits irritating. In 1976 she moved to Whaley Bridge after a long illness.

CHEVESKI – see **TANNER**

THE CLAYTONS: HARRY, CONNIE, ANDREA and **SUE** lived at No.11 for eight months in 1985. Harry was a milkman, Connie a dress-maker, hard-working ordinary people struggling to bring up a family. Andrea fell for Terry Duckworth and became pregnant. The family realized it would be impossible to cut the Duckworths out of their lives while staying in the Street so moved to the other side of town. Andrea's son, Paul, was born the following year and was adopted.

THE CLEGGS: LES, MAGGIE and **GORDON** took over the Corner Shop in 1968 and introduced the residents to herbal remedies. They were a family on the run from Les's history as a violent alcoholic. The move was meant to be their fresh start but within a month Les was drinking again. When he assaulted Maggie, Gordon knocked him unconscious. He recovered in hospital but Maggie refused to have him back and started divorce proceedings.

Gordon trained to be a solicitor and went to live in London after jilting fiancée Lucille Hewitt: he felt that at eighteen he was too young to marry. Maggie's sister, **BETTY TURPIN,** moved into the shop to help her out, along with policeman husband **CYRIL.** When Maggie found her too much to cope with at the shop bossy Betty took a job at the Rovers. Divorced from Les, Maggie had relationships with Len Fairclough and Alf Roberts before falling for reformed alcoholic **RON COOKE.**

The couple married in 1974 and went to live in Zaïre, leaving the shop in Gordon's hands. He let it to the Hopkins family who discovered his birth certificate, which revealed that he was really Betty's son. Betty had been widowed recently, following Cyril's fatal heart-attack. She was thrilled when Gordon accepted her as his mother, relieved that Les was not really his father.

Betty has worked at the Rovers for over thirty years and her hotpot has become legend in the area. She served six months as mayoress of Weatherfield and in 1995 married her wartime sweetheart, **BILLY WILLIAMS.** They had a couple of happy years together before he died of a heart attack. Betty lives in Hillside Crescent with her cat, Marmaduke. Gordon lives with his family in Wimbledon. He has never pressed Betty to reveal the identity of his father and has no idea that in 1982 Betty was reunited with the man, Ted Farrell, but never told him he had a son.

Harold Turpin (m. Margaret Preston)

Betty (m.1. Cyril Turpin) (m.2. Billy Williams) — Maggie (m.1. Les Clegg) (m.2. Ron Cooke)

Ted Farrell

Gordon (m. Caroline Wilson)

Peter

NORRIS COLE entered the Street as Derek Wilton's best friend. He ended up marrying Derek's ex-wife Angela and becoming his boss. When the marriage failed he became Rita Sullivan's assistant at the Kabin newsagents.

CHRIS COLLINS was employed as mechanic under Kevin Webster. He lived at the flat over the mini-market and had an affair with Kevin's estranged wife Sally, then slept with Des Barnes's girlfriend Samantha Failsworth. After being sacked by Kevin he left the area.

ROY CROPPER was something of an enigma when the residents first came to know him. He was a sitting tenant at the Crimea Street flats purchased by Mike Baldwin, and was seen by the other tenants as a strange recluse. He found employment at Jim's Café and became an important member of the community when he used his life savings to buy Alma Baldwin's share of the café and changed its name to Roy's Rolls. In 1998 he fell in love with **HAYLEY PATTERSON** only to have her confess she was really a transsexual christened Harold. Hayley went to Amsterdam for her final operation and was thrilled when Roy realized she was the only woman he could love. They set up home together and stood together against the hostility of the street's residents when the truth was revealed. Hayley works at Underworld but owns a share of the café. The couple live above the premises in Victoria Street, having been married in the café in 1999. Hayley changed her name by deed poll to Cropper.

SHEILA CROSSLEY née **BIRTLES** lived in the flat over the Corner Shop throughout 1962 and 1963, with her best friend Doreen Lostock. Sheila worked at Elliston's raincoat factory while Doreen served behind the counter at Gamma Garments. They double-dated and jived to their transistor radios but their idyllic existence changed when Doreen joined the Women's Royal Army Corps and Sheila attempted suicide after being rejected by her lover Neil Crossley. She went to live in Rawtenstall where her son, Danny, was born. Three years later she returned and took up with her old boyfriend Jerry Booth but he couldn't cope with the idea of her having an illegitimate child. When she met Neil again by chance, she told him about Danny and was thrilled when he proposed marriage. They went to live in Scarborough as a family. From time to time Sheila visited her friends on the Street until 1974.

THE DESAIS: RAVI, NITA and **VIKRAM** took over the Mini-market in 1999. It was Ravi's sixth shop and he divided his time between them all. Nita moved into the flat above the shop but refused to spend her life working in the family firm and set out on her own to work for Freshco's. Vikram was given the task of running the shop but was more interested in gambling and girls, such as Leanne Tilsley. Ravi returned to his native India to become head of the family clan, selling all his shops to his distant cousin, **DEV ALAHAN.** In 2000 Nita took promotion in Scotland and Vik opened a mini-cab firm.

THE DOBBS: JACKIE befriended **DEIRDRE RACHID** in prison, where she was serving six months for GBH after assaulting her husband Darren's girlfriend. On her release she tracked Deirdre down and moved in with her before squatting at No.7 with her troubled son, **TYRONE.** Jackie took a job at Underworld but was sacked for stealing more knickers than she actually sewed.

When Curly Watts returned from overseas he demanded his house back but Jackie held firm until Darren turned up and took her back. Tyrone refused to live with them and slept rough until the Duckworths took pity on him and gave him a home at their B&B. Tyrone is an apprentice mechanic at Kevin Webster's garage and is devoted to his pet greyhound Monica.

THE DUCKWORTHS: JACK, VERA and **TERRY** moved into No.9 in September 1983, much to the horror of the neighbours. The family were well known, having been regulars at the Rovers since the mid-1970s. Vera worked at Baldwin's Casuals and cabbie Jack had already had an affair with Bet Lynch. Terry worked in the meat market and was muscle-bound. He had inherited his dad's eye for the ladies and soon impregnated Andrea Clayton. He ran off with his friend's wife, Linda Jackson, before turning to a life of petty crime. In 1991, while in police custody on a charge of GBH, he married pregnant **LISA HORTEN** and slipped his police guard after the ceremony. He was captured and sent to prison so Lisa moved into No.9 to be near him. Their son **TOMMY** was born and left orphaned after Lisa was knocked down in the Street. At the time she had been living with lover Des Barnes, with whom Terry brawled at her funeral.

On his release from jail Terry sold Tommy to Lisa's parents for ten thousand pounds. Next he fathered a child, Brad, on Tricia Armstrong. Whenever Terry reappears it spells trouble, and in 1999 he sold Vera a cut-and-shut car, which was involved in an accident that led to Judy Mallett's death, for which his parents can never forgive him.

Jack and Vera have calmed down over the years and have stopped having affairs. For a time Jack was enamoured by **DULCIE FROGGATT** but she slept with Terry at the same time. In the mid-1980s Jack became barman at the Rovers Return and nearly burnt down the pub by putting too big a fuse in the fuse box. Vera lost her job at Baldwin's when the factory was demolished and took a job at Bettabuys. In 1995 the couple sold their house and used an inheritance from Jack's brother Cliff to buy the Rovers Return. However, they couldn't make the business work and were forced to sell out to Alec Gilroy, who eventually evicted them. They moved to Park Road to live in Eunice Gee's B&B. Vera works at Roy's Rolls but Jack was forced to give up his cellarwork after a triple heart bypass. In the late 1980s, Vera's shoplifting mother, **AMY BURTON**, lived with the couple, and when she died Vera inherited a father in the shape of Josh Shackleton, who claimed to be descended from King Edward VII, making Vera the Queen's cousin.

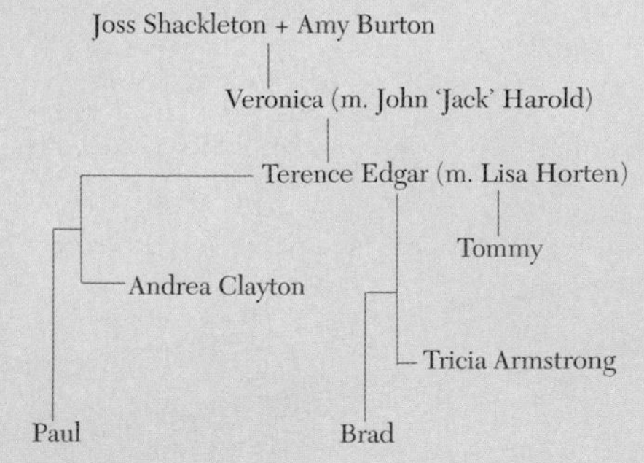

FRED ELLIOTT, master butcher, was a regular at the Rovers and a leading light of the Weatherfield branch of the Square Dealers. His nephew, **ASHLEY PEACOCK**, followed him into the trade as apprentice and lodged with Don Brennan at No.5. Fred married shopkeeper **MAUREEN HOLDSWORTH** after Rita Sullivan turned down his marriage proposal. He bought No.4 for Maureen but just days after the wedding she ran off to Germany with Bill Webster. Fred refused to stay in the house and let it to Ashley, who took in homeless **ZOE TATTERSALL** and the newlywed Tilsleys. Ashley fell for Zoe, but after the death of her baby, Shannon, Zoe came under the influence of a religious cult and went to live in America. The Tilsleys left, too, and Ashley was alone until he rekindled an old romance with hair-stylist **MAXINE HEAVEY.**

Maxine put her past as a man-eater behind her to settle down with Ashley. She was employed at the hair-salon at No.2 and had drifted from man to man, dating rats like Greg Kelly, Tony Horrocks and Des Barnes. Just before marrying Maxine, Ashley discovered that Fred was actually his father and was reunited with his birth mother, Kathleen. As a present, Fred gave the Peacocks No.4 and longs to be made a grandfather.

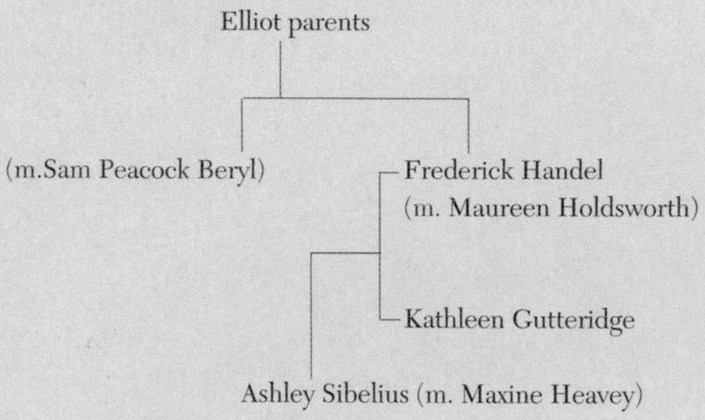

SAMANTHA FAILSWORTH rode into the Street on her motorbike and took a job behind the Rovers bar. She shied away from the ogling men and revealed to Des Barnes how she had been traumatized by being raped at sixteen. He worked her through the memory and she moved in with him but had an affair with Chris Collins. Des threw her out and she left the area, telling him she was pregnant with his child.

THE FAIRCLOUGHS: LEN was a builder by trade, hot-tempered and ready-fisted. When his wife Nellie ran off with the insurance man and took their son **STANLEY** to live in Nottingham, Len proposed to Elsie Tanner, but she felt that no good would come of marrying her best friend. Then Len drifted from woman to woman and filled his spare time with council work, after being elected to office in 1966. In 1968 he bought No.9 and moved out of his old house in Mawdsley Street to live next door to Elsie. He took in Ray Langton as a lodger and then Jerry Booth as well.

In 1973 he bought an old newsagent's on Rosamund Street, called it the Kabin and installed his girlfriend **RITA LITTLEWOOD** as manageress. Rita was a night-club singer who had once dated Ken Barlow and had a common-law son, **TERRY BATES,** whom she looked on as her own. Rita moved into the flat over the Kabin and became Len's lover. Their relationship was rocky, and during one break he dated Bet Lynch, who fell for Jimmy Graham. Finally, in 1977, Len and Rita married and she moved into No.9 and gave up singing.

The same year Stanley also married but made it clear to his father that he did not want him to attend the wedding as he hated him. Len lost his council seat after being arrested for being drunk and disorderly. Rita left him for six months when he refused to carry out home improvements, but they were reconciled and became foster-parents. Their long-term foster daughter, **SHARON GASKELL,** helped Len to build a house at No.7 and the family moved into it. A year later, however, Len was killed in a car crash. Sharon left for Sheffield after becoming besotted with Brian Tilsley, who was married, and Rita was on her own until the arrival of the Bradleys (see **BRADLEYS**).

In 1990 Rita moved the Kabin to new premises at No.10 Coronation Street and moved into the flat above. She was romanced by retired toffee salesman **TED SULLIVAN** and married him despite knowing he had a brain tumour. They had three months together before he died. Then Rita started to take an interest in the Webster family, giving them money and acting as a surrogate grandmother to the children. A badly installed gas fire nearly killed Rita, which led Alec Gilroy to declare his love for her.

In 1999 Rita was delighted when Sharon returned in preparation for her marriage to **IAN BENTLEY.** The ceremony ended in chaos when Sharon attacked Ian over his affair with Natalie Barnes. To keep Sharon in the area, Rita gave her the Kabin and became her assistant. The plan didn't work as, after an attempt at suicide, Sharon took up again with Ian and married him. He persuaded her to sell the Kabin and move to Bolton. Rita bought back her own shop for forty thousand pounds.

STEVE FISHER: see **BIRCHALL**

THE FLEMMINGS: DICKIE and **AUDREY** were eighteen and sixteen respectively when they eloped to Gretna Green then set up home at No.3. Audrey's devotion to apprentice engineer Dickie didn't last long and she threw herself into an affair with the lodger, Ray Langton. Dickie was devastated when Audrey said she could never love him as much as she loved Ray. The couple split and, rejected by Ray, Audrey sold the house to Ernie Bishop.

THE FORDS: JACKO and **NORMA** moved into the Street in 1972. She was Maggie Clegg's resident shop assistant and he was her jailbird father. Norma was ashamed of Jacko's past but Maggie persuaded her to stand by him. Jacko left the area after being framed for a break-in at bookie Benny Lewis's flat and Norma followed after being rejected by lover Ken Barlow.

TINA FOWLER worked as barmaid at the Rovers from 1989 to 1990. She fell for builder **EDDIE RAMSDEN** and hoped to marry him but he jilted her during her hen party to marry the mother of his son, Jamie. Tina bounced back by dating brewery boss Nigel Ridley but was sacked after giving herself airs at work.

ANGIE FREEMAN came to the Street as a fashion design student, sharing No.7 with Jenny Bradley. She remained at the house after Curly Watts bought it but was ashamed of herself for spending the night with him. She fell for Neil Mitchell but he was infatuated with his ex-wife Denise Osbourne. After failing to set herself up as a designer, she left to study native artefacts in Mexico. Later she returned and went into partnership with Mike Baldwin, setting up the underwear factory Underworld. She dated Chris Collins but decided she was getting nowhere in Weatherfield and moved to London.

THE GEES: FRED and **EDNA** lived in Inkerman Street up to Edna's death in the warehouse fire of 1975. Prior to this their marriage had been far from stable, with Edna gaining a reputation as the local good-time girl. Widowed Fred was taken on by Annie Walker as resident cellarman at the Rovers and doubled as her chauffeur. Always one with an eye for the ladies, he was besotted with Rita Fairclough and kept trying to lure Bet Lynch into his bed. In 1981 he married **EUNICE NUTTALL**, a gay divorcee, in the hope that, as a married man, he would be given his own pub. Unfortunately he picked the wrong bride: Eunice had been sacked from a pub on suspicion of shoplifting and the couple's request for a pub was turned down. Annie refused to let them stay in the Rovers so they took a job caretaking at the community centre, living in its flat. Fred was rude to the regulars and Councillor Ben Critchley ordered the couple out. Eunice decided to leave Fred and moved into Ben's hotel. Fred started divorce proceedings and returned to the Rovers. When Annie retired he hoped to take over the business but her son, Billy, sacked him. Mike Baldwin took him on as a van driver but sacked him when he discovered he was calling himself Mike Baldwin to clinch business deals. Fred left Weatherfield but Eunice remained. She started up a B&B in Park Road, and in 1999 let a room to the Duckworths. She fell for Jack but he had a heart-attack after she had made a pass at him. When her sister needed her in Spain, Eunice made the Duckworths managers of the B&B and flew out.

THE GILROYS: ALEC was a theatrical agent and manager of a working-men's club when he first appeared on the Street. A crafty, mean-minded man, he built up his agency and became entertainment manager for Newton & Ridley. While running the Graffiti Club on Rosamund Street, he fell for **BET LYNCH**, manageress of the Rovers Return, and pursued her.

Bet was a woman who had grown up in the school of hard knocks. Pregnant at sixteen, she'd been forced to have her son Martin adopted then heard, nineteen years later, that he had been killed in a car crash. She worked at Elliston's PVC factory before becoming the Rovers' barmaid in 1970. She went through a long string of unsuitable bed partners, including Len Fairclough, Mike Baldwin, Jack Duckworth and Des Foster, before taking over the Rovers in 1985. She borrowed money from Alec to buy the tenancy of the pub but then fell into debt and ran off to Spain. Alec tracked her down and proposed marriage. He was given the tenancy of the pub, and after their wedding, he gave her the bar as a present. A year after getting wed Bet discovered she was pregnant but miscarried. The incident prompted Alec to locate his estranged daughter **SANDRA ARDEN.**

He found her living in comfort and married to a successful lawyer, but tragedy struck and the pair were killed in a car crash, leaving their daughter **VICKY** to be brought up by the Gilroys. At first Vicky disliked the smoky pub but after falling for Steve McDonald she decided it was worth staying around.

The Gilroy marriage fell apart when Alec took a job on a cruise line and Bet refused to leave the Rovers. She took over the tenancy and was delighted when Vicky stayed with her. Trucker Charlie Whelan turned Bet's life upside down when she fell for him but he was lured away by barmaid Tanya Pooley. Vicky married Steve (see **MCDONALDS**) and when the brewery put the Rovers up for sale Bet, unable to raise the cash to buy it, packed her bags and left the Street.

MAUD GRIMES: see **HOLDSWORTH**

ESTHER HAYES lived alone at No.5, her family home, until moving into a modern flat in 1962. A quiet statistics clerk, she gave good advice and was a good neighbour. She continued to visit her old friends until the mid-1970s. She now lives in Scotland.

THE HEWITTS: Harry was a bus inspector who had lived at No.7 all his life. His daughter **LUCILLE** was brought up in an orphanage following her mother's death in 1959. She returned home after Harry married barmaid **CONCEPTA RILEY** in 1961. All went well until Concepta gave birth to a son, **CHRISTOPHER**, and Lucille became jealous. When Christopher was kidnapped from outside Gamma Garments, Lucille was suspected of killing him, but after two days he was recovered, unhurt, after being snatched by a deranged woman. When Concepta's father fell ill in Ireland, Harry gave up his job to emigrate and run the family business. Lucille refused to leave Weatherfield and was allowed to move into the Rovers as the Walkers' ward. After leaving school she took a series of jobs, being too lazy to hold on to one for more than a few months. While visiting in 1967 Harry was crushed to death in an attempt to repair Len Fairclough's van. Concepta returned to Ireland alone and married a young mechanic, **SEAN REGAN.** Lucille remained in the Street until 1974 when she went to live with Concepta. She never married, although came close to doing so in 1969 until her fiancée Gordon Clegg jilted her as she tried on her wedding dress.

REG HOLDSWORTH was manager of Bettabuy supermarket from 1989 to 1994. He was a ladies' man with a roving eye whose strident wife, Veronica, left him to live in New Zealand. His hopes for romance were always dashed as no woman was really interested in him, until an old flame, **MAUREEN NAYLOR,** re-entered his life. Reg felt that meeting her again was fate but had to contend with her disapproving mother **MAUD GRIMES.**

Despite Maud's attempts to separate them, Reg and Maureen were married in 1994 and took over the ownership of the Mini-market. Reg soon grew tired of the small shop and took a job at Firman's Freezers, leaving Maureen and Maud to run the shop.

Maureen split her time between Reg's flat at No.12 and Maud's house on Nightingale Road. When Reg was transferred to Lowestoft the marriage collapsed and the couple divorced, with Maureen taking the shop as settlement. After a fling with Bill Webster, she agreed to marry butcher Fred Elliott (see **ELLIOTT**) but just days later realized she had made a mistake and ran off to Germany with Bill. Maud continued to work in the shop until Fred sold it to the Desais. She had a flutter of romance when she became engaged to Percy Sugden, but he called off the relationship after she confessed that Maureen was the result of a wartime romance with an American. Maud now lives in the retirement complex Mayfield Court.

THE HOPKINS: IDRIS, VERA, GRANNY and **TRICIA** took over the running of the Corner Shop in 1974, renting it from Gordon Clegg. Granny ruled the family and despised English-born Vera, but needed her money to help run the shop. Idris was caught in the women's bickering, while Tricia was besotted with Ray Langton. When Granny tried to use the knowledge that Gordon was Betty Turpin's son to blackmail him into reducing the rent, the family were evicted and left town. Tricia remained in the shop flat with friend Gail Potter. They looked for Mr Right together but never found him. When Renee Bradshaw bought the shop she evicted the girls and Tricia joined the rest of her clan.

ALAN HOWARD: see **TANNER**

GREG KELLY: see **BATTERSBYS**

RAY LANGTON came to the Street direct from Borstal in 1966 to work as a plumber with Len Fairclough. He stole from the residents and attempted to rape Lucille Hewitt before being seen off by Len. Two years later he returned, a reformed character, and moved into No.3 as the Flemmings' lodger. He attempted to seduce Audrey Flemming and spent nine months in a wheelchair after injuring himself during the Street outing to Windermere. He became engaged to Sandra Butler, but she finished with him after discovering he was still seeing Audrey.

After regaining the use of his legs he went into partnership with Len and employed **DEIRDRE HUNT** as his secretary. Deirdre lived in Victoria Street with her mother **BLANCHE** and became engaged to Billy Walker. When she expressed doubts about marrying him he called the whole thing off and instead, with just a day's notice, she married Ray, astounding the residents. The Langtons converted the top floor of Blanche's house into a flat, and their daughter **TRACY** was born in 1977.

After running the Corner Shop, Blanche left the area to live with old flame Dave Smith in the Midlands. She sold her house so the Langtons moved into No.5 Coronation Street. Deirdre suffered a breakdown after being molested under the viaduct and chilled towards Ray, who had an affair with waitress Janice Stubbs. Deirdre found out and the couple separated. He went to live in Holland and she married Ken Barlow (see **BARLOWS**).

FLORRIE LINDLEY bought the Corner Shop in 1960 and told the residents she was a widow, although she was only estranged from her husband. She was a lonely person who rarely socialized. When her husband **NORMAN** tracked her down she agreed to emigrate to Canada with him and give their marriage one last try.

MARTHA LONGHURST was the first cleaner at the Rovers, and drinking companion to Minnie Caldwell and Ena Sharples. She lived in Mawdsley Street and once harboured desires to marry wealthy Australian Ted Ashley, but he was not interested in her. She died in the Rovers' Snug of a heart-attack in 1964.

DOREEN LOSTOCK: see **CROSSLEY**

THE MALLETTS: GARY and **JUDY** moved into No.9 in 1995. He was a cable layer, she worked in a local amusement arcade. Both wanted children but an abortion at sixteen had left Judy unable to conceive. Her mother Joyce Smedley became cleaner at the Rovers and carried a torch for Alec Gilroy, but her life ended suddenly when she was knocked down and killed by Tony Horrocks. Judy befriended homeless pregnant teenager Zoe Tattersall and paid her two thousand pounds to hand over her baby when it was born. They called the child Katie, but Zoe missed her and snatched her back, renaming her Shannon.

The Malletts were devastated by Shannon's death from meningitis but at the same time Judy was stunned to discover she was pregnant with twins. Gary left Judy after she confessed to having had sex with her boss in exchange for the money she needed to buy Katie back, but he returned a few weeks later, having decided to stick by Judy. The twins, **WILLIAM AND REBECCA,** were born on Christmas Day 1998 but were orphaned less than a year later when Judy died from injuries resulting from a car crash. In 2000 Gary moved away to start a new life.

THE MCDONALDS: JIM, LIZ, STEVE and **ANDY** moved into No.11 in December 1989. The boys were educated at Weatherfield comprehensive, and Liz took a job at the Rovers while Jim set up a motorbike-repair shop under the old viaduct. Andy was the more studious twin but dropped out of university to train as assistant manager at Bettabuy supermarket. He romanced single mother Amy Nelson and hoped to marry her but she went to live in Trinidad.

Steve left school as quickly as he could and became an entrepreneur, starting up business after business and blowing most of his money on the horses. He dumped girlfriend Fiona Middleton for heiress **VICKY ARDEN** and eloped with her to marry in St Lucia. He bought an expensive flat and car and set up a printing business, making his way through Vicky's money. Having been arrested for receiving stolen whisky, Steve paid a local villain to take the blame and then, when the police found out, blamed Vicky. The marriage broke down as they both stood in the dock. Steve was given a two-year sentence and Vicky, walking free, sold up and went to study hotel management and catering in Switzerland. After serving a year in prison, Steve returned to the Street, started up his own building firm and moved in with Fiona. However, their relationship ended when he seduced Maxine Heavey.

Liz and Jim's relationship was stormy. They were devastated when their baby daughter Katie died when just hours old, but Liz fought back by taking on the tenancy of her own pub, the Queens. Jim didn't like her being the boss and accused her of sleeping with the brewery chief. Liz left Jim and filed for divorce, while having an affair with Colin Barnes at the same time. However, she was drawn back to Jim and they were reconciled, briefly, until she confessed to having slept with his best friend. He hit her and she had him arrested. This time the divorce went through.

Liz had an affair with local villain **FRAZER HENDERSON** and Jim slept with Fiona, driving Andy to wash his hands of them both and leave for Spain. Steve tried to kill Jim by pushing him off some scaffolding, and as a result Jim was wheelchair-bound for months, during which time Liz had an affair with his physiotherapist **MICHAEL WALL** and left to live with him in Milton Keynes.

Jim was taken in by conman **GWEN LOVEDAY** whilst Steve fell in with drug dealer Jez Quigley.

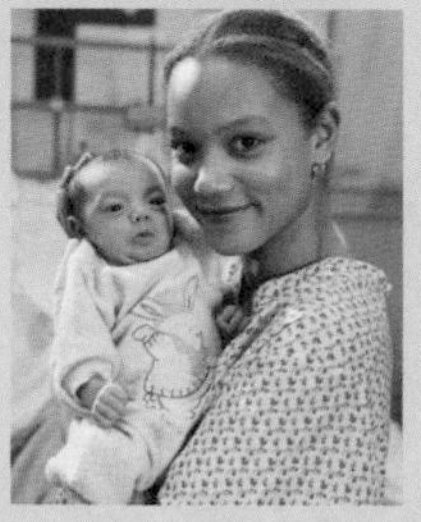

FIONA MIDDLETON came to the Street as a trainee hair-stylist, working for Denise Osbourne. She moved into the flat over Jim's Café with best friend Maxine Heavey and fell for bad boys Steve McDonald and Tony Horrocks. When Denise sold up Fiona borrowed money from her brother Lee to buy the business and moved into the flat over the salon. She tried her hand as a nightclub singer and fell for policeman **ALAN MCKENNA.** They became engaged but he jilted her in the church when she confessed to having had a one-night stand with Jim McDonald. She was pregnant and shortly afterwards gave birth to a son, **MORGAN.** She rekindled her relationship with Steve and agreed to marry him, then discovered he had slept with Maxine. She quickly put the salon on the market and left to live with her parents.

EMILY NUGENT: see **BISHOPS**

THE OGDENS: STAN, HILDA, IRMA and **TREVOR** moved into No.13 in June 1964. Stan was a long-distance lorry driver, keen on beer and handy with his fists. He undertook a variety of jobs, from scrap-art sculptor to milkman, before landing on his feet as window-cleaner. Hilda, however, was a char through and through, and during her working career cleaned at the Rovers, Baldwin's Casuals, the Capricorn Club, the bookie's, the Graffiti Club, Mike Baldwin's flat and a posh house belonging to Dr and Mrs Lowther. Irma worked behind the bar at the Rovers and served at the Corner Shop before marrying **DAVID BARLOW** (see **BARLOWS**). Trevor left the Street after only a couple of months, stealing from the neighbours and seeking his fortune in London. Nine years later the Ogdens found him living in Chesterfield, having told his wife he was an orphan. Stan had a permanently roving eye while Hilda only had one dalliance, with a park-keeper called George Greenwood. However, she felt too guilty about sharing cups of tea with him and broke off their friendship.

The Ogdens seemed to be followed by bad luck wherever they went, although Hilda once won five hundred pounds on the Premium Bonds. They fantasized about how to spend the money before realizing it would just about cover their debts. Hilda loved home improvements, and No.13 boasted a serving hatch, flying ducks and a scenic vista, or 'murial', as Hilda called it. Throughout the 1970s and early 1980s, Stan's business partner Eddie Yeats was a frequent visitor, and eventually he became a lodger at No.13.

In 1984 Stan died and Hilda took in Kevin

Webster as a lodger. She was romanced by **TOM HOPWOOD** but refused to marry him and, in 1987, after being mugged, she moved to Derbyshire to be housekeeper to the widowed Dr Lowther.

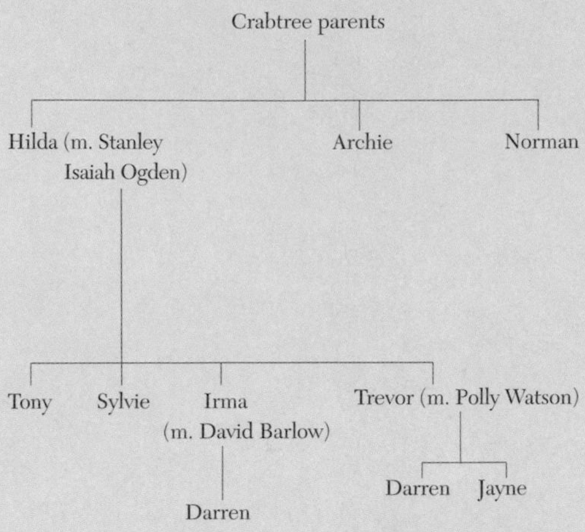

DENISE OSBOURNE: see **BARLOWS**

THE PEACOCKS: see **ELLIOTTS**

PHYLLIS PEARCE lived in Mayfield Court but was a regular in the Street, chasing boyfriends Chalkie Whitely and Percy Sugden. She was a lonely old woman, and delighted to be employed by Des Barnes as his char. She was constantly frustrated in her attempts to seduce the unwilling Percy.

THE PETTYS: LIONEL and **SANDRA** ran the Corner Shop in the mid-1960s. Lionel was an ex-sergeant major, who dominated his daughter Sandra. She was besotted with Dennis Tanner but he never returned her affection so she moved out. Lionel followed shortly afterwards.

MARTIN PLATT was employed in 1985 to wash dishes at Jim's Café. He had a brief relationship with Jenny Bradley before falling for recently bereaved **GAIL TILSLEY** (see **TILSLEY**). Despite being ten years her junior he moved in with her. She discovered she was pregnant and planned an abortion, but he found out and stopped her. Their son **DAVID** was born on Christmas Day 1990, joining Gail's other children, **NICK** and **SARAH LOUISE**.

Gail and Martin married and, despite opposition from her former mother-in-law Ivy Brennan, he adopted the children and bought No.8 for the family.

Gail worked at the café while Martin trained to be a nurse. He fell under the spell of **CARMEL FINNAN**, a fellow student who became infatuated with him and attempted to break up his marriage but failed. Instead, Martin got drunk one Christmas and had sex with another nurse, for which Gail eventually forgave him. When Roy Cropper took over the café Gail sold her share of the business to him and carried on working there as an employee.

Martin lost his job at the hospital when Les Battersby accused him of trying to kill him with an overdose; his name was eventually cleared.

Family rows have dominated the Platts' lives. Nick rebelled and changed his name back to Tilsley in compliance with Ivy's will and thus inherited No.5 from her. He sold it to Don Brennan. He then went off to live in Canada for two years. Sarah Louise became pregnant at the age of thirteen and gave birth to a daughter **BETHANY**. After the birth Martin confessed to Gail that he'd been having a six-month affair with nurse **REBECCA HOPKINS**.

TANYA POOLEY worked as barmaid at the Rovers in the mid-1990s and lived in the flat over Jim's Cafe. She stole Des Barnes from Raquel Wolstenhulme, and Charlie Whelan from her boss, Bet Gilroy, before disappearing into the night.

WALTER POTTS lodged at No.11 in 1963. Discovered by Dennis Tanner, he gave up his job as a window-cleaner to be launched as pop sensation Brett Falcon. His début single 'Not Too Little, Not Too Much' was a smash hit.

ALF ROBERTS worked for the Post Office until he married **RENEE BRADSHAW** and joined her behind the counter of the Corner Shop in 1978. His first wife, Phyllis, died of cancer in 1972, and for a while he had harboured hopes of marrying Maggie Clegg, but she kept turning him down. Alf was big in the council, twice serving as mayor of the borough. He also became a cornerstone of the retail organization WARTs.

Renee was an independent woman, who had bought the shop to provide a stable home for her brother **TERRY,** but he found her too much of a nag and left his job at Fairclough and Langton to rejoin the army. Shortly after marrying Alf, Renee thought she would be widowed when he was comatose for three weeks following a lorry crash in the Street. When recovered, the couple decided to sell up and move to the country but just before they were due to leave Renee was killed in a car crash. Alf continued alone at the shop, transforming it into a self-service mini-market. In 1985, he married flighty **AUDREY POTTER.**

Audrey was Gail Tilsley's mother and had finally decided to settle down, with Alf, after chasing men for years. She had aspirations to live in a huge house and live a life of lesiure but Alf bought No.11 and made her open a hair-salon in the front parlour. However, that folded after she dyed Hilda Ogden's hair orange by mistake. Alf was stunned to discover Audrey had a son, **STEPHEN REID,** in Canada. Stephen's father, Malcolm, tried to persuade Audrey to leave Alf for him and she was thrilled when Alf hit him and warned him off. Audrey finally had her way when Alf agreed to buy a house more fitting to his status and they moved to Grasmere Drive. After selling the shop Alf retired and was delighted to receive the OBE in 1995 from the Queen. He died of a heart-attack in 1999, leaving Audrey financially unstable. She had already bought the hair-salon at No.2 but her plans for retirement had to be shelved. Less than a year later she received a marriage proposal from Sergei Kasparov, but watched in horror as he was deported by the authorities.

BRENDAN SCOTT was area manager at Bettabuy before taking redundancy and buying the Corner Shop. He worked too hard and died of a heart-attack on the shop floor, leaving his fortune to his young wife Debi.

ENA SHARPLES acted as the upholder of Street morality for twenty years. She was a woman who spoke her mind and was either loathed or respected. She worked as caretaker at the Mission of Glad Tidings until it was demolished in 1968, and in later years ruled the roost at the community centre. She was passionately loyal to her friends and always ready to offer support to her neighbours, even if it was delivered with a sermon. Her lowest point came in 1966 when she was forced to shoplift after giving her daughter **VERA LOMAX** all her money. Her appearance in front of the magistrate devastated her. Vera died of a brain tumour the following year, and Ena was left with only the company of friends. Slowly, they too died, and Ena found that her moral standards no longer reflected those of her new neighbours. In 1980 she went to live in St Anne's.

DAVE SMITH was a Cockney bookie who had his fingers in plenty of pies. He divorced his wife Lilian and wooed Elsie Tanner for ten years, before eventually moving to the Midlands with Blanche Hunt.

JED STONE: see **CALDWELL**

PERCY SUGDEN moved into the Street in 1983, when he was appointed caretaker at the community centre. He offended the neighbours by watching their every move in his Home Watch scheme. He was forced into retirement and moved into lodgings at No.3 with Emily Bishop and his budgie, Randy. He romanced Olive Rowe and Maud Grimes, and was chased by Phyllis Pearce before he moved into Mayfield Court.

RITA SULLIVAN: see **FAIRCLOUGHS**

LEONARD SWINDLEY ran Gamma Garments on Rosamund Street and preached at the Mission of Glad Tidings. He stood for the council but came bottom of the polls and suffered a nervous breakdown when his principles were compromised. His assistant Emily Nugent proposed to him but jilted him in the Mission. In 1965 he left to work in Gamma's head office.

THE TANNERS: ELSIE and **DENNIS** lived at No.11. Elsie divorced her husband **ARNOLD** and struggled to cope with tearaway Dennis and his wilful sister **LINDA,** who was married to Pole **IVAN CHEVESKI.**

Elsie was the Street's siren, a woman who attracted the attention of an endless supply of men. She fell in love time and time again, and each new liaison left her hurt anew. She set herself rules – never go after another woman's man, and never, never date a married man – but often the men failed to mention their wedding rings. She had on-off relationships with **BILL GREGORY,** Len Fairclough and Dave Smith and married American **STEVE TANNER** then Geordie **ALAN HOWARD.** One boyfriend had a heart attack on her, another tried to shoot her, often she was slapped around and stolen from, but she continued to bounce back.

She had first met Steve during the war and their 1967 wedding was meant to be a fairy-tale for her, but he turned out to be a selfish drunk. After spending three months living in America with him, she came home. Steve was murdered by Joe Donnelli during a brawl over a debt, and two years later she married Alan. He wasn't the rich businessman she had thought, and Elsie became the main breadwinner when he turned to drink. They moved to Newcastle for three years but the marriage ended in failure. Back at No.11, Elsie took in lodgers to fill her life with young people, but her heart continued to lead her into trouble. She held down a variety of jobs – from sales assistant to croupier, model and factory supervisor. When she eventually left the Street it was to live in Portugal with Bill Gregory, helping him run his wine bar.

While Elsie was hard-working, her son Dennis drifted from one job to another. His passion in life was showbusiness but he had no real talent for it. With Jed Stone, he was often involved with schemes that sailed dangerously close to illegality and was once threatened with eviction after turning No.11 into a hippie commune. In 1968 he married **JENNY SUTTON** and moved to Bristol.

Elsie's daughter Linda emigrated to Canada with Ivan shortly after the birth of baby **PAUL.** Five years later they returned to live in Birmingham and in 1980 her son Martin moved into No.11 with Elsie and tried to court factory worker Karen Oldfield. After Elsie had left, Linda stayed in the house while divorcing Ivan. She hoped for a relationship with Bill Webster, but when he said he wasn't interested she returned to Birmingham.

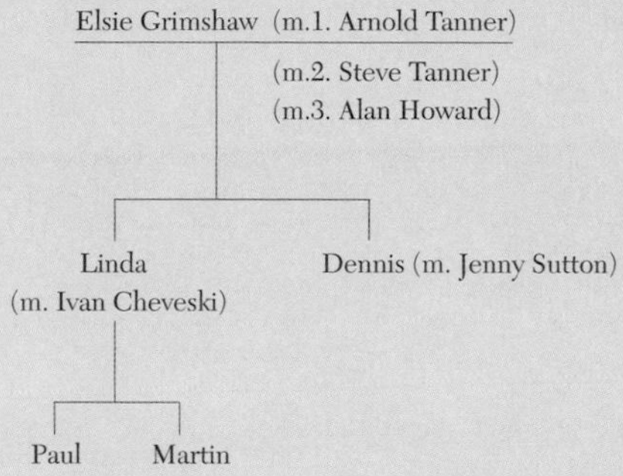

ALBERT TATLOCK lived at No.1 from 1960 to 1984. He was a retired Town Hall clerk who, as the years passed, became more and more dissatisfied with his lot. His daughter, Beattie Pearson, seldom visited so Albert looked to his favourite niece, Valerie Barlow, for companionship. Following her death, her husband Ken became his surrogate son and cared for him. Albert nearly married three times. In 1965 Clara Midgeley proposed, but he turned her down. Four years later he was all set to marry **ALICE PICKENS** but the vicar did not turn up, and in the mid-1970s he was engaged to Minnie Caldwell. In 1984 he died in his sleep, aged eighty-eight.

THE TILSLEYS: BERT, IVY and **BRIAN** moved into No.5 in 1979. Bert was a hard-working foundryman and Ivy served as supervisor and shop steward at Baldwin's Casuals. Brian was their only son and much doted on. He was the apple of Ivy's eye and when he married non-Catholic **GAIL POTTER** she was horrified.

Gail lived at No.11 with Elsie Tanner and had grown up on the Street. Brian was her second boyfriend; the first was an older, married man, Roy Thornley, who took her virginity. She moved into No.5 with the family but before her son **NICKY** was born in 1980 she and Brian had moved into a small house on Buxton Close. Gail worked at Jim's Café as manageress while Brian was a mechanic. They sold the house to set him up in business and moved back in with Ivy after Bert suffered a stroke and died after a nervous breakdown. Ivy went on to become engaged to van driver **GEORGE WARDLE** but the knowledge that he was divorced rather than widowed put her off.

The younger Tilsleys' marriage was stormy and they separated a couple of times. Gail had an affair with Brian's cousin **IAN LATIMER** and when her daughter **SARAH LOUISE** was born she had no idea who the father was. Brian divorced her, but after snatching Nick and attempting to leave the country with him was reconciled to his family and acknowledged Sarah as his daughter. Ivy was delighted when Gail and Brian remarried in 1988, and a few months later she married cabbie **DON BRENNAN** (see **BRENNANS**).

The Tilsleys' marriage did not flourish, and in 1989 Brian was stabbed to death outside a disco on the day Gail had told him she wanted another divorce. Just six months after being left a widow Gail stunned the family by moving her toyboy **MARTIN PLATT** into the house. She gave birth to his child, **DAVID,** then married him (see **PLATTS**).

When Ivy died she left No.5 to Nick on condition that he changed his name back from Platt to Tilsley. He did so, and sold the house to Don, using the money to be educated in Canada. He returned to study PE at college and horrified Gail by marrying **LEANNE BATTERSBY** (see **BATTERSBYS**) at eighteen. They lodged at No.4 together and he took a modelling job to earn money. He became obsessed with avenging his father's murder and used Leanne as bait to get to the killer, Darren Whately. The youngsters' marriage collapsed when he forced Leanne to have an abortion then emigrated to Canada. She moved into the Rovers and changed her name back to Battersby, before going to live in Amsterdam.

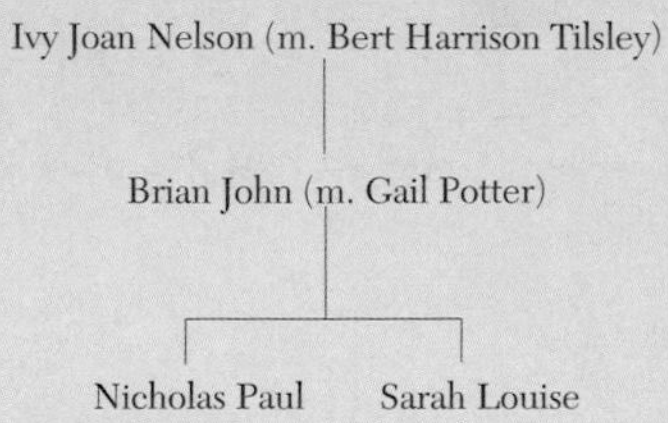

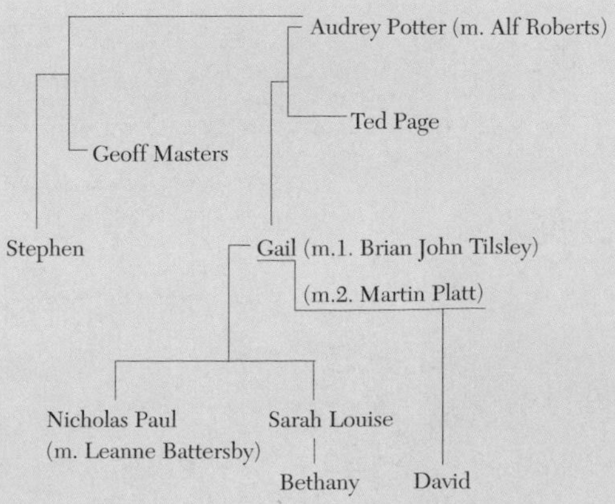

GLORIA TODD served behind the Rovers bar from 1985 to 1988. She lived in a flat on Ashdale Road and had an affair with neighbour Alan Bradley, before discovering he was two-timing her. She resigned from the pub after stealing Sandra Stubbs's boyfriend.

THE TURPINS: see **CLEGGS**

THE WALKERS: JACK, ANNIE, BILLY and **JOAN** ran the Rovers Return Inn from 1960 to 1984. Jack was a jovial landlord, beloved by his staff and customers. Annie was a snob who ruled with an iron fist, while Billy was lazy and always on the look-out for a dodgy deal. Joan married teacher **GORDON DAVIES** and fled to Derby, where she became an even worse snob than her mother.

When Jack died in 1970 Annie took over the licence and ran the pub with the help of Bet Lynch, Betty Turpin and Fred Gee. She was a leading light in the Licensed Victuallers Association and in 1973 served as mayoress of Weatherfield. When she retired and went to live in Derby, Billy took over the pub but his heart wasn't in it and he sold out to the brewery.

CURLY WATTS came to the Street in 1983 as a binman. He lodged at No.3 with Emily Bishop and started a rag-and-bone business with Terry Duckworth. Always unlucky in love, Curly, real name Norman, has had a string of disastrous relationships. Shirley Armitage lived with him above the Corner Shop until he became too serious for her; **KIMBERLEY TAYLOR** was engaged to him twice but would never have sex with him; Angie Freeman had sex with him and regretted it; and **ANNE MALONE** was obsessed with him and tried to frame him for extortion when he rejected her. After gaining a diploma in Business Studies, Curly entered the retail world of supermarkets and has managed stores for Bettabuy, Firman's and Freshcos. In 1995 he married **RAQUEL WOLSTENHULME,** with whom he had been in love for years. She worked as barmaid at the Rovers and had lived above the pub. She had been hurt countless times by men and had trained as a model but had failed to develop a successful career. Des Barnes had won her heart and she had been devastated when she discovered his affair with Tanya Pooley. She married Curly on the rebound after Des had seduced her once again and she tried hard to make the marriage work, but it only lasted eleven months. She took an aromatherapy job in Kuala Lumpur and left Curly. Curly now lives at No. 7 with girlfriend **EMMA TAYLOR**.

THE WEBSTERS: BILL, KEVIN and **DEBBIE** moved into No.11 in 1984. Builder Bill ran his own firm in Rita Fairclough's yard, Debbie worked as a waitress at Jim's Café and Kevin served under Brian Tilsley as a mechanic. Bill married hairdresser **ELAINE PRIOR** and went to live in Southampton, then Germany. He took Debbie with him but Kevin opted to stay in Weatherfield.

Kevin became Hilda Ogden's lodger and, after falling for posh Michelle Robinson, started a relationship with **SALLY SEDDON** who moved in with him. They married in October 1987 and lived in the Corner Shop flat before buying No.13. Sally was from the wrong side of the tracks but strove to create a secure family environment. Following the birth of **ROSIE** in 1990 she became a child-minder but gave it up when client Joe Broughton made a pass at her. **SOPHIE** was born in 1994. Kevin worked for various bosses before going into partnership with Tony Horrocks and buying the Coronation Street garage. When Sally was away nursing her sick mother, he had an affair with Tony's mother Natalie and Sally threw him out. The relationship with Natalie turned sour but love was around the corner in the shape of machinist **ALISON WAKEFIELD**. She moved into the flat over Skinner's bookie's with Kevin and married him after falling pregnant. Following the birth and death of their son **JAKE**, Alison became disturbed and was killed under the wheels of a lorry. Sally lived with Greg Kelly in the flat over the mini-market and went into business with him. He made his way through her savings then turned violent and was eventually arrested after holding her and the girls prisoner. She started up as a market trader, selling underwear, and had an affair with **DANNY HARGREAVES.** Bill returned from Germany in the late 1990s and found employment as cellarman in the Rovers before going into business with Jim McDonald. He found it hard to settle and eventually returned to Germany with Maureen Elliott.

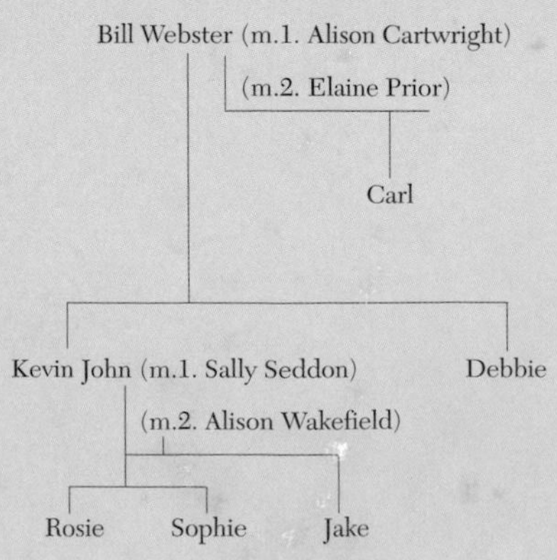

THE WHITELYS: CHALKIE, BOB and **CRAIG** were three generations of men who moved into No.9 in 1982. Bob worked on the oil rigs and stunned Chalkie by taking young Craig to live in Australia. Chalkie stayed on, pestered by Craig's maternal grandmother, Phyllis Pearce, until he won over three thousand pounds on the horses and set off to join his family.

DEREK WILTON was a salesman who first came to Weatherfield in 1976 and started to romance **MAVIS RILEY.** She was a lonely, romantic spinster who worked as a sales assistant at the Kabin newsagent's and sought romance from a variety of men, including Jerry Booth. Derek and Mavis had a twelve-year courtship during which time he married his boss Angela Hawthorne and she was proposed to by Victor Pendlebury. Mavis and Derek were engaged in 1984 but jilted each other at the church. Four years later they married in a register office and, after honeymooning in Paris, bought No.4. Mavis continued to work at the Kabin but Derek undertook a variety of jobs, including joke salesman and school caretaker. They married too late in life for children but owned budgies and a gnome named Arthur. Always the butt of everyone's jokes they were a strong couple until Derek died of a heart attack during a road-rage incident. Mavis felt unable to stay on without him and bought a B&B in Cartmel.

EDDIE YEATS came to the Street from prison and lodged with Minnie Caldwell and Len Fairclough before casting in his lot with the Ogdens. Always keeping two steps ahead of the law, he handled stolen goods and at one time used his job as a window cleaner to case joints for robberies. In 1980 he settled down, becoming a binman and moving into No.13. He was never lucky in love until he took up CB radio, called himself Slim Jim and met Stardust Lil, otherwise known as **MARION WILLIS.** She was a florist and fell helplessly in love with Eddie, moving into lodgings with Elsie Tanner at No.11. When she discovered she was pregnant the couple married and went to live in Bury to nurse her mother.